Praise for *Common Preservation* and Jeremy Brecher

"Jeremy Brecher's work is astonishing and
refreshing; and, God knows, necessary."
—Studs Terkel

"Chapter by chapter, I learn from it; and I admire its ambition. When
I sampled it, it engaged me so much that I set aside other work
until I finished it. Overall, a fine manuscript. Rich in content. Also
engaging. Is it not all or part of a philosophy or worldview?"
—Charles Lindblom, Sterling Professor Emeritus of Political Science
and Economics at Yale University; author of *The Market System*

"Ever since I read the draft of *Common Preservation* a year ago, I've been
compelled to urge a surprising variety of colleagues to read it, above
all else, to understand the history, the successes, the failures, and
the profound lessons to be learned from social justice movements:
professional and volunteer organizers and activists, engaged citizens
who yearn to be more effective. This history is systematically informed
by an extraordinarily broad, cross-disciplinary reach for scholarly works
that provide practical insight to the lessons to be learned. I know that
I am not alone in finding much scholarly work difficult to relate to
my experience as an advocate. By integrating the direct experience of
the author with such work, Brecher has enabled me to do just that."
—Mike Pertschuk, former chair, Federal Trade Commission

"It is an autobiography of intellectual exploration and of practical
experimentation with the problems of social injustice. It is
a project of the urgent transmission of the lessons learned
undertaken under the duress of historical time which threatens
catastrophe. It is a valedictory and an exhortation."
—Joshua Dubler, Society of Fellows, Columbia University; author
of *Down in the Chapel: Religious Life in an American Prison*

"We've been talking about turning everyday life and its challenges into a meaningful political strategy for ages. Finally *Common Preservation* succeeds in doing it. Engrossing."
—Ferdinando Fasce, author of *An American Family: The Great War and Corporate Culture in America*

"*Common Preservation* is simultaneously a handbook for understanding the emergence of social movements and a call to action for each and every one of us to join together and address the most imminent threat to continued human existence—human-caused climate change.... Longtime movement scholar, people's historian, and social activist Jeremy Brecher is just the right author at just the right time to engage with this topic. With a lifetime of participation in movements ranging from nuclear disarmament and peace to civil rights, gender equality, and labor, Brecher is well equipped to address these questions. At the heart of this book is a lifelong passion for progressive social change and a deep thirst for understanding how individuals on occasion come to realize their shared interests and coordinate their efforts to transform the world for the betterment of all.... Read. Discuss. Act."
—Todd E. Vachon, from the foreword

Common Preservation
In a Time of Mutual Destruction
Jeremy Brecher

Common Preservation: In a Time of Mutual Destruction
Jeremy Brecher
© 2021 PM Press.

ISBN: 978–1–62963–788–4
Library of Congress Control Number: 2019946105

Cover by John Yates / www.stealworks.com
Interior design by briandesign

10 9 8 7 6 5 4 3 2 1

PM Press
PO Box 23912
Oakland, CA 94623
www.pmpress.org

Printed in the USA.

Contents

Foreword

By Todd E. Vachon

Common Preservation is simultaneously a handbook for understanding the emergence of social movements and a call to action for each and every one of us to join together and address the most imminent threat to continued human existence—human-caused climate change. By identifying common patterns between iconic movements like the US civil rights movement and more obscure actions such as a local meat boycott by housewives in Staten Island, Brecher reminds us of how "doing history"—finding significant and meaningful connections— can help us act more effectively now and in the future. As your middle school social studies teacher likely told your class, "If we don't know our history, we are doomed to repeat our mistakes." The message from Brecher is more urgent: if we don't learn from our actions and develop new strategies for common preservation immediately, we are doomed to end history altogether.

Common Preservation addresses these central questions:

How might we come to see that our self-interest, indeed our self-preservation, depends upon our common preservation?

How might the billions of individual humans living on the planet today coordinate our efforts and reconstruct our patterns of actions to address the threat to our mutual survival?

Longtime movement scholar, people's historian, and social activist Jeremy Brecher is just the right author at just the right time to engage with this topic. With a lifetime of participation in movements ranging from nuclear disarmament and peace to civil rights, gender equality, and labor, Brecher is well equipped to address these questions. At the heart of this book is a lifelong passion for progressive social change and a deep thirst for understanding how individuals on occasion come to realize their shared interests and coordinate their efforts to transform the world for the betterment of all. Understanding these processes is more important than ever in this current era when we are facing global pandemic, global depression, accelerating climate crisis, and heightened struggles over justice and equality.

I have seen common preservation, and I know it can work. While I was in graduate school at the University of Connecticut, my fellow graduate workers and I had been accustomed to working for low pay and simply dealing with it as best we could. It was just the way things were, and everyone knew it when they accepted the offer to come to the university. Some took on extra jobs without telling their advisors, others found they were eligible for food stamps and used them to help provide for their family. But when the university began to unilaterally cut benefits and impose further economic hardships on graduate workers, a gap arose between their expectations and the realities they faced. Just struggling along through "grad school poverty" was no longer working. A small group of grad workers got together and shared our stories of individual efforts to cope with the hardships. We decided to speak with more of our co-workers about their problems, which increased awareness among graduate assistants that what we had been experiencing as individual problems were in fact shared by over two thousand other graduate assistants from all different departments. It was a collective problem that required a collective solution. We ultimately formed an organization to coordinate our actions and address the problem—a union.

Common Preservation shows that there is a pattern to the emergence of such collective solutions. For example, on March 15, 2019, 1.4 million students from over two thousand cities in 125 countries on six continents made history when they walked out of school. It was the latest in a series of global student strikes urging the governments of the world to act now on climate change. These widespread mobilizations were inspired by the weekly strikes held outside of the Swedish parliament by a lone sixteen-year-old named Greta Thunberg. Like Greta, students around the world expressed fear, anger, and disappointment that adults have not acted on climate change. Addressing a crowd in Santa Fe, New Mexico, eighteen-year-old Hannah Laga Abram said:

> We are living in the sixth mass extinction. Ice is melting. Forests are burning. Waters are rising. And we do not even speak of it.

Why? Because admitting the facts means admitting crimes of epic proportions by living our daily lives. Because counting the losses means being overpowered by grief. Because allowing the scale of the crisis means facing the fear of swiftly impending disaster and the fact that our entire system must change. But now is not the time to ignore science in order to save our feelings. It is time to be terrified, enraged, heartbroken, grief-stricken, radical. It is time to act.[1]

Throughout human history, the experience of personal harm inflicted by systems of exploitation and oppression has led many people to pursue individual acts of revolt. *Common Preservation* analyzes many instances, such as work-related strategies like working inefficiently, sabotaging machines in the factory, or breaking tools on the plantation. But these individual efforts were typically insufficient to surmount the powerful forces blocking social change and thus the existing conditions persisted. Some people began experimenting with forms of collective action, such as work slowdowns and stoppages. Many even began to see that their personal well-being was inextricably connected to their collective well-being as members of a class, racial group, or population. The results were the labor movement, the abolitionist movement, the underground railroad, the civil rights movement, the suffragist movement, and the women's movement. While economic inequality, racism, and gender disparities still permeate modern society, the collective efforts and coordinated actions of these many individuals through social movements have undoubtedly advanced the causes of workers, black people, and women and have thus transformed the world. The lessons learned from these and other movements provide the intellectual food that nourishes *Common Preservation*.

Part 1 of the book provides a refreshingly ideology-free exploration of some of the greatest social thinkers in modern history, ranging from Marx to Gandhi, from W.E.B Du Bois to E.P. Thompson. In what he calls "raiding parties," Brecher seeks out key insights from many streams of classic social thought to inform his common preservation framework. While readers may have varying opinions on some of the theories that are examined, Brecher's approach is undeniably succinct and effective in its summation of the big ideas and laser-like focus on just the points that are most relevant to his key research questions. Unlike most conversations with classic theorists, his book is surprisingly easy to read and provides a good primer for those not steeped in social movements literature, but also provides just enough depth that it is not too simplistic for more advanced readers.

In Part 2, Brecher develops his heuristic for common preservation. Drawing together the "tools" that were "raided" in Part 1, he takes us into his "workshop" to construct an original and compelling framework for understanding processes of social change; in particular, the transition of human actions away from mere individual acts of self-preservation toward collective acts of common preservation. At the center of Brecher's heuristic is an innovative use of Jean Piaget's concept of equilibration. Developed primarily for understanding the cognitive development of children, equilibration arises from a gap between established patterns of thought and action and new information that doesn't fit those patterns. Faced with such a challenge, people may develop new patterns that compensate for the gap. For social movements, the journey from an established pattern of behavior to a gap that leads to a compensation, which then establishes a new pattern corresponds with my own experiences as well as with my reading of major historical cases.

Part 3 of the book demonstrates how to apply the common preservation heuristic to the growing climate protection movement. Readers are taken on a guided tour of ongoing efforts to halt climate change, including the many failures thus far, and the possibility of an alternative strategy for climate protection, which Brecher calls "climate insurgency." In the Commentary section in the back of the book are detailed notes that elaborate on how the common preservation heuristic is used in the text. It is here that the real wisdom of the heuristic is revealed. Whether a longtime student of social movements, a regular movement participant, or just a curious reader, this application of the common preservation heuristic is certain to trigger at least one, if not several, "aha!" moments.

The guiding principle throughout *Common Preservation* is that human action is patterned, but, as Piaget said, these patterns or structures are "not eternally predestined either from within or from without." In other words, people construct and reconstruct their own patterns of action. The youth of the world today are confronting a world where the existing social patterns will amount to nothing less than collective suicide. Preventing the most catastrophic consequences of climate change is dependent upon our ability to coordinate our efforts, reconstruct our patterns of action, and challenge the powerful few that are driving and profiting from the unfolding crisis. It is going to take nothing less than a massive movement the likes of which the world has never seen—but whose underlying dynamics are revealed in scores of movements analyzed in *Common Preservation*. If done properly, this movement can simultaneously address many of the lingering social and economic injustices that are so inherently tied up in the struggle for climate protection. This volume helps us understand how such a movement might come to be and at the same time urges us to actively participate in its development. For the good of all of us. For our common preservation. Read. Discuss. Act. And together we just might "save the humans."

Acknowledgments

I thank those who have read drafts of this book, including Dan Sofaer, Michael Ferber, Josh Dubler, Evelina Dagnino, and Todd Vachon. I thank all the fellow denizens of the virtual global workshop from whom I have learned what is in this book—they must number in the thousands. This book is dedicated to Jill Cutler, who has lived with it for fifty years and edited more drafts than I can count.

An Ordinary Week in the Twenty-First Century

Look at the news. Most of what you see is about individuals, groups, and institutions seeking their own self-interest and self-aggrandizement. But dig deeper and you will also find something else: people coming together to seek their common well-being. Consider just one week in October 2009.

On the weekend culminating Sunday, October 18, 173 million people around the world gathered in three thousand events in 120 countries and literally stood up to demand that their governments eradicate extreme poverty and achieve the UN's Millennium Development Goals. The action, dubbed "Stand Up, Take Action, End Poverty Now!" was organized by the UN Millennium Campaign and NGOs around the world. Organizers credited the use of Skype and social networking tools with the rapid expansion of Stand Up. The 2009 action shattered the Guinness World Record for the largest mobilization of human beings in recorded history.

On Monday, October 19, two hundred people blocked work on the Mbombela Olympic stadium outside the city of Nelspruit in South Africa's Mpurnalanga province demanding the government honor its promise to build a school after community structures were torn down to make way for the stadium. In Mpumalanga, South Africa, two hundred and forty miners in the Two Rivers mine staged an underground sit-in when a manager dismissed four workers after a rock fell on a miner's foot; the four miners were rehired. A strike by French railway workers protested a reorganization of freight services that would eliminate the jobs of six thousand workers. Copper miners in Peru staged a two-day strike to protest legislation cutting their benefits and to demand a lower retirement age for miners; workers at the Spence copper mine in Chile struck for higher pay. In Ivory Coast, a strike of cocoa growers' cooperatives blocked cocoa deliveries to demand greater government support for their industry. And hundreds of angry farmers from across Europe besieged EU agriculture ministers and tipped over milk cans to oppose cuts in EU milk price supports.

On Tuesday, October 20, in Guragaon, Haryana, India, eighty thousand workers at sixty factories struck to protest the shooting of an auto worker trying to organize a union at Rico Auto Industries. In the English Midlands, a thousand climate activists gathered in the woods to prepare for an effort to shut down the Ratcliffe-on-Soar power station that resulted in fifty-seven arrests.

On Wednesday, October 21, the Italian newspaper *La Repubblica* reported that a hundred thousand women had signed an online petition against Italian prime minister Silvio Berlusconi, accusing him of offending women; many of the women included photographs of themselves with slogans like "we are not your concubines." In Ireland, fifty-five thousand government workers voted to strike against austerity pay and job cuts and the Irish Congress of Trade Unions announced a national day of protest against cuts in welfare payments and public sector wages. In Algeria, people living in the Diar Echams shantytown in Algiers confronted four hundred policemen and an armored vehicle in a demonstration protesting job and housing shortages. Striking workers at the Sudbury, Ontario, subsidiary of the Brazilian company Vale organized rallies in Toronto, New York, and Rio de Janeiro in support of their strike.

On Thursday, October 22, as part of a continuing struggle against the coup that removed Honduran president Manuel Zelaya, 150 people blocked a street in the north of Tegucigalpa to protest the suspension of negotiations to return Zelaya to office. In Brisbane, Australia, some climate activists shackled themselves to a conveyor belt while others formed a flotilla of sixteen kayaks to block a Taiwanese coal ship loading in Brisbane Harbor. In West Virginia, eight people were arrested for chaining themselves to a coal truck and lying across a key mining road in a protest against mountaintop removal mining. In the UK, 120,000 postal workers launched a two-day national strike against proposed changes in pay and working conditions. In Washington, DC, six hundred health care advocates demonstrated at a conference of the private health insurance organization America's Health Insurance Plans while seven families who had been denied care told their stories to the media. And in Toronto, Canada, 150 students at the Northern Secondary School spent their lunch break in a demonstration outside the school to protest the stationing of police officers in the school.

On Friday, October 23, parents from across Hawaii rallied at the State Capitol to protest a thirty-four-day furlough of teachers that would close schools for 170,000 children. In Nigeria, hundreds of women surrounded the home of a government minister and prevented him from leaving for the office in a protest against electrical power outages that lasted up to a week. In Thailand, workers struck the State Railway of Thailand, demanding repair work, provision of spare parts, and a halt to the stationing of policemen on trains. In Meghalaya state in India, opponents of uranium mining blockaded a road, then fifty of them slipped into a government building and pinned antinuclear black badges on ministers, legislators, and government officials. In Iran, in the midst of severe repression, protesters challenging election fraud began chanting antigovernment slogans at a media fair in Tehran until they were attacked by government supporters.

On Saturday, October 24, 5,400 events in 173 countries demanded that the world's governments cut greenhouse gas emissions to bring the atmosphere back to a safe level below 350 parts per million of carbon. Divers at the Great Barrier Reef in Australia and in the ocean off the Maldives raised banners reading "350"; skiers and snowboarders formed the number 350 on a mountainside in New Zealand; hikers raised a 350 banner on the tallest mountain in Antarctica. Around the shore of the Dead Sea, Israeli activists made a large 3, Palestinians a huge 5, and Jordanians a giant 0. Three hundred events in China ranged from performance art at the Great Wall to student programs at coastal beaches demonstrating the rise in sea level. CNN called the International Day of Climate Action "the most widespread day of political action in our planet's history."

These events are all very different. They grow out of different historical experiences, draw on different cultures, involve different goals, use different methods, and face different opponents. But there is also a family resemblance among them. They all involve people trying to solve their shared problems through collective action—a shift to what I will call "common preservation."

How does a shift to common preservation emerge? Why does it happen at some times and not at others? Can it have an effective impact on the problems people face? Can it lead to new problems? Can it contribute to addressing today's global problems like climate change, war, oppression, and economic injustice? If you want to know more, read on!

Introduction

This book is about change, but not just any kind of change. It is about change that improves capabilities—change that is often referred to as development. More specifically, it is about the development of new forms of action that enable people to cooperate to realize their collective ends. I call this the development of common preservation.

It is often said that the first law of life is self-preservation. But from time to time people shift from pursuing their own interests and well-being as individuals to strategies that use collective action to realize shared ends. Back in the seventeenth century the English visionary Gerrard Winstanley called this a shift to "common preservation." This book recounts a half century of my own efforts to understand and nurture common preservation. It codifies what I have learned in a set of tools that can be applied to diverse situations. It concludes by applying these tools to climate protection.

Often, though not always, a shift to common preservation takes the form of a social movement. Consider the story of Mrs. Ann Giordano, thirty-three, who lived in Staten Island, New York, and described herself as "just a housewife." She had never been particularly conscious of food prices; her kitchen didn't have enough shelf space for her to buy in large quantities. But one day in the spring of 1973 when she had put the groceries away there was still space left on the shelf. She vaguely wondered if she had left a bag of food at the store. Next time she came home from shopping, she looked in her wallet and concluded she had accidentally left a twenty-dollar bill behind. When she went back to the supermarket and found out how much her food was really costing, she suddenly realized where the shelf space had come from and where the money had gone.

Food prices were soaring, and millions of shoppers were having similar experiences. Giordano called some of her friends and discussed the idea of a consumer boycott—an idea that was springing up simultaneously in many places around the country in response to rising food prices. Soon an extensive grapevine of women was calling homes all over Staten Island, spreading word of the boycott. They called a meeting at a local bowling alley to which over one hundred people came on two days' notice, named themselves Jet-Stop (Joint Effort to Stop These Outrageous Prices), and elected captains for each district. Within a week they had covered Staten Island with leaflets, picketed the major stores, and laid the basis for a highly effective boycott.[1]

Giordano and her friends were typical of those who gave birth to the 1973 consumer meat boycott, "a movement which started in a hundred different places all at once and that's not led by anyone." As a newspaper account described it:

> The boycott is being organized principally at the grass-roots level rather than by any overall committee or national leadership. It is made up mainly of groups of tenants in apartment buildings, neighbors who shop at the same markets in small towns, block associations and—perhaps most typical—groups of women who meet every morning over coffee. All have been spurred into action by the common desire to bring food prices back to what they consider a manageable level."[2]

The 1973 consumer meat boycott was undoubtedly the largest protest in American history up to that time. A Gallup poll taken at the end of the boycott found that over 25 percent of all consumers—whose families included fifty million members—had participated in it. Large retail and wholesale distributors reported their meat sales down by one-half to two-thirds.[3] In a response to the protest, Republican president Richard Nixon ordered a freeze on meat prices.

Common Preservation

How could a problem that people like Mrs. Giordano initially experienced as a personal matter they discovered in their own kitchens be transformed into a cooperative effort to address a problem that they recognized they shared and needed to address in common? How could fifty million people in thousands of localities with no previous organization and only limited, local connections become a mass movement that engaged a quarter of the American population in a matter of a few weeks? How could the boycotters organize themselves over the span of a continent and across boundaries of race, class, and culture? How could they coordinate their action to have such a huge joint impact that a conservative president was forced to make a highly visible—if disingenuous—response?

The story of the 1973 meat boycott seems so far from our normal understanding and experience of "how the world works" that it can easily be regarded as a "black swan," an anomaly that occurs so rarely that instances can simply be disregarded. Yet far from being an anomaly, the emergence of new strategies of self-organization and self-transformation—in short, the emergence of common preservation—is a pattern that recurs over and over.

Sometimes it happens: different people are affected by the same problem. None of them can solve it alone. But they discover that by acting together in new ways they can create new solutions. Such cooperation in service of mutual well-being embodies a strategy in which people try to solve their problems by meeting each other's needs rather than exclusively their own. And as Kenneth Boulding memorably remarked, what happens is possible.

Not all examples are so sudden or so unexpected as the 1973 consumer meat boycott. Neither are they all so devoid of previous organization, leadership, or shared values and experiences. But nonetheless the emergence of common preservation often involves processes far different from conventional assumptions, for example, that such movements can only be produced by great leaders or large and powerful organizations.

My first participation in a movement for common preservation was the nuclear disarmament movement and especially the campaign to halt nuclear testing; it resulted in the 1963 Nuclear Test-Ban Treaty and helped bring about US–Soviet detente, the end of the Cold War, the nuclear nonproliferation agreement, the strategic arms limitation treaties, and an 80 percent reduction in strategic nuclear weapons. I witnessed opposition to the US war in Vietnam grow from protests by a few dozen students to Washington demonstrations with more than a million participants, mass disaffection, military mutinies, and ultimately a decision by the US to withdraw. I saw the opposition to the US invasion of Iraq produce "huge antiwar demonstrations" with fifteen million participants around the world that led the *New York Times* to conclude that there were "two superpowers on the planet, the United States and world public opinion."

More recently I worked with movements and organizations that had been isolated within national borders to reach out to each other in the face of economic globalization and create a movement of "globalization from below," a.k.a. the global justice or antiglobalization movement. I witnessed its "Battle of Seattle" halt the inauguration of the World Trade Organization; hundreds of other confrontations countering the globalization juggernaut; and the formation of the World Social Forum linking thousands of global justice groups in ongoing dialogue around the world. I saw the global climate movement, which started largely among scientists and diplomats, organize a global day of action with 5,200 rallies from Mt. Everest to the Great Barrier Reef.[4]

Other movements I watched from afar, occasionally lending a bit of support when the opportunity arose. I learned how Rosa Parks's refusal to move to the back of the bus grew into the Montgomery bus boycott, the sit-ins and freedom rides, the great campaigns in Selma and Albany, Georgia, the Civil Rights and Voting Rights Acts, and eventually to the election of the first African American as president of the United States. I saw the women's liberation movement grow from a handful of women raising questions about gender relations in the US civil rights movement to a force challenging sexism in every sphere of life and in every country in the world. I followed the emergence of the "flying university" protest movement in Poland, which helped give rise to the social self-defense movement KOR, the Solidarity trade union, the overthrow of Poland's communist regime, and ultimately the end of Communism throughout Eastern Europe and the Soviet Union.

More recently I wrote about what I called the US "mini-revolts of the twenty-first century," ranging from the Battle of Seattle to Occupy Wall Street and from the Fight for $15 to the ongoing community movements and teachers strikes in defense of public education. I slept in Zuccotti Park with Occupy Wall Street. I was arrested at the White House in the first sit-ins against the Keystone XL pipeline.

I've spent much of my life studying and writing about the history of social movements that to a greater or lesser extent embody common preservation. For example, I've written about the way forms of popular resistance like anti-impressment riots and tax evasion evolved into the revolutionary Committees of Correspondence which linked together activists across colonial boundaries, laid the basis for the American Revolution, and ultimately provided much of the political infrastructure for the new American government. And I've written about the way American workers over the course of two hundred years formed labor movements and engaged in strikes and mass upheavals that transformed American capitalism.

Despite the diversity of these movements, similar questions arise whenever new forms of common preservation erupt: How could something so novel emerge so rapidly and unexpectedly? How could people who were so isolated and divided come together in concerted action? How could people who had been so powerless have such an impact? Can social movements actually contribute to solving the problems that gave rise to them? Conversely, why do such movements sometimes go terribly wrong, producing new forms of domination, conflict, and disorder? These questions may seem simple, but they open up an inquiry that may require rethinking our assumptions about the way the world works.

Not all social movements represent common preservation. Not all common preservation is embodied in social movements. But social movements provide a prime set of examples for studying the emergence of common preservation and an important means for creating new common preservations.

A Heuristic for Common Preservation

My life coincides with the period in which we human beings began to threaten our own survival as a species. I was born just months before the first A-bomb was dropped on Hiroshima. I have lived to see today's threat of climate change and global ecological collapse. It has been, and continues to be, an era of mutual destruction. My quest has been to find ways to realize the common human interest in averting collective suicide.

Over the past half century, I have gradually developed a method of inquiry—a heuristic—for exploring common preservations and their emergence. "Heuristic" comes from the Greek for "find out"; it comes from the same root as "eureka"—"I found it." A heuristic is a method to help solve a problem. It has been described as the distillation of the best practices for navigating one's way through a complex system or situation. Heuristics aim to produce solutions that work, whether or not they can be proved. In this book I present a heuristic method, tell how it developed, and show some ways I have tried to use it.

Consider a workshop. It contains tools like hammers, saws, and pliers, and machines like presses, lathes, and drills. It also stashes old jigs, fixtures, and patterns. It has files of the blueprints from past jobs. It has manuals for the equipment and technical guides covering the procedures used and the products made in the shop. It has stock materials like lumber and metal waiting to be transformed. It has samples from past projects that illustrate ways that past problems have been solved.

The workshop also includes skilled and experienced workers with individual and shared know-how accumulated over the generations. That know-how is encapsulated in rules of thumb and best practices, as well as tacit knowledge that is only revealed in the action of hand and eye. The resources of the workshop are organized to make it easy for the workers to find what they need. And the workshop has ways to transfer the knowledge it has accumulated to newcomers through a mix of formal instruction, observation, practice, and storytelling.

When a novel job comes in, there is no preprogrammed solution to the problems it presents. The appropriate resources from the workshop have to be located, selected, modified, sequenced, and applied in new ways.

The knowledge accumulated in such a workshop is very different from a scientific theory or textbook that explains the physics or chemistry of wood or metal. Skilled craftspeople often have studied the science relevant to their work and know it can help them get a deeper understanding of the problems at hand and possible ways to address them. Good craftspeople are grateful for more theoretical scientists who provide knowledge that can make problem-solving easier and more precise. But they know that their job is different from a theorist's. Their methods won't produce an elegant theoretical model; but a scientific theory by itself is unlikely to produce a comfortable rocking chair or an effective machine tool.

The heuristic strategies and devices I've spent my life exploring include very different kinds of stuff—stories about past projects that have happy endings or that went awry, examples of products that solved the problem at hand successfully, rules of thumb that have often worked in the past, and even bits of theory that might come in handy. They include questions, models, ideal types, historical case studies, and examples of how all of these have been taken from one problem and applied to another. The result is unlike a deductive theory; usefulness and efficiency, not elegance and certainty, are its goals.

In writing this book, I have thought of myself as an experienced craftsperson, trying to pass along what I have learned about solving problems and constructing new common preservations in a collective virtual workshop that spans the globe. I do so by telling stories about past problems and efforts to solve them, presenting solutions that did and didn't work, describing procedures and rules of thumb that frequently seem to produce useful results, presenting some more formal ideas that have helped solve problems in the past, describing strategies that organize the search effectively, and trying to label these heuristic devices in ways that make it easier to reach for the right one at the right time.

The result is what one philosopher of science calls "advisory strategies."[5] These are neither descriptions nor explanations but rather guides to potentially fruitful ways to find new solutions. They are the product of "compiled hindsight," useful lessons extracted from the experience of the past.

Such a heuristic approach may be particularly suitable for subjects that are only quasi-regular, so that the best results come from capturing regularities without trying to force the irregularities into recalcitrant theoretical boxes. It provides a way to identify the patterns that do exist, while recognizing that there is a great deal that doesn't fit the pattern or can't be reduced to it. Such quasi-regularity is often typical of human history and human life. Surely it is typical of common preservation.

This book is not intended as either an autobiography or as a work of theory. It's not an autobiography because the real subject is not myself but what I've learned that might be helpful for constructing new common preservations for the era of mutual destruction. Yet the story is too intertwined with concrete history, experience, and action to provide a conventional theory distinct from practice and making strong claims to universal truth. Think of it rather as the narrative of the old codger who has spent his life in the back corner of the virtual workshop and who is now trying to pass on as best he can what he's learned about how to use its resources to meet today's urgent problems. I don't claim that my heuristic embodies the truth. I only claim that it has helped me understand and act on social problems, and that it may be worthwhile for others to test it and see if the same might be true for them.

Loops

However skilled the workers, they can't be sure the workshop's products will work under real-life "combat conditions." Their products have to go out and be tested in the world outside the workshop. Someone has to use them and see how well they perform. Then the results need to be reported back to the workshop. If there are problems, the original design must be modified and the resulting product tested again in practice. Such a "product improvement cycle" underlies our ability to find better strategies—including new common preservations.

The more I have studied the emergence of new common preservations, the more I have come to believe that they cannot be understood within a simple linear model of cause and effect; they depend on loops like the circuit of the product improvement cycle. Such loops communicate information about the effects of an individual's or group's action back in a way that the actors can use to improve their own action in the future. Such loops have been variously referred to as self-correction, feedback, learning by doing, regulation, and equilibration. Whatever they are called, they seem to involve a circular process that goes beyond linear causal chains to allow the results of past action to be "fed back" to correct and improve subsequent actions.

These loops allow the actors, paradoxically, to change themselves in order to preserve themselves. Common preservation often manifests this paradox of preservation through transformation—and often requires such "loopy" ways of thinking to resolve that paradox. It is among the many phenomena that require what have been variously called holistic, dialectical, nonlinear, nonreductionist, equilibratory, open-system, or cybernetic ways of thinking, ways that today are often put in the rubric of "complexity theory."

Unless they use some such loops, it is hard to see how people can identify problems in the world and respond to them. It is hard to understand how an apparently small change in the evaluation of a small bit of information—say, a change in the interpretation of possibilities or motives—may lead to dramatic change in the way individuals and groups act. It is hard to explain why major changes, for example the emergence of social movements, can appear so suddenly and unexpectedly, apparently out of nowhere. And it is hard to see how we can create the new common preservations we need to halt today's mutual destruction.

For that reason this book delves into the rather abstract "loopy" processes of change that make common preservation possible and comprehensible. But because such loopy ways of thinking don't fit conventional patterns of cause and effect, they may at first appear paradoxical or counterintuitive. I try to present what may be an unfamiliar paradigm in different ways with different kinds of examples to give readers a variety of points of entry to understanding it. As with any unconventional paradigm, it may take some perseverance to assimilate new ways of thinking. I hope the resolution of some of the puzzles and paradoxes of common preservation will make the effort worthwhile.

Development as Problem-Solving Self-Transformation

One of the discoveries of research about complex or nonlinear or loopy systems is that they allow the overcoming of entropy—the law of physics that all things tend to move from higher to lower states of energy and organization—at least for a limited space and time. They make it possible for entities to move toward more organized states—a process that has come to be called "self-organization."

I believe that common preservation can be understood as an instance of such self-organization. But it has two further features that go beyond self-organization in general.

First, common preservation is not just random increase in organization. It normally arises in response to some kind of problem or disequilibrium or gap. It is adopted in order to solve the problem, eliminate the disequilibrium, or reduce the gap. And in many instances common preservation is at least partially effective in doing so—the 1973 meat boycott did lead to a national freeze on the price of meat. This book will explore how that is possible.

Second, common preservation involves not just more of the same kind of organization, but a transformation of organization. It is therefore not just self-organization, but also self-transformation. Problem-solving, gap-closing self-organization and self-transformation is what underlies development—change that improves capabilities.

Most of what I've learned about common preservation I've learned from observing and participating in social movements and studying their history. But alongside that I've also conducted a scavenger hunt among thinkers from diverse fields. I've tried to compile what I've learned from both approaches into my heuristic. The dozen or so books I've written on social movements and social change have all been tacitly—though rarely explicitly—guided by my developing heuristic for common preservation.

Since the early 1970s I have been slowly working on a parallel track to make those tacit understandings explicit. In 2012 I published *Save the Humans? Common Preservation in Action,* which portrays the development of my approach to social movements as it grew out of observing and participating in them and studying their history.[6] It provides an introduction to many themes that are developed more fully in *Common Preservation.* This sequel presents my heuristic for common preservation directly. It tells how I discovered the thinkers who influenced it, how I extracted from them ways of thinking that I applied to the problems of common preservation, and how I applied those heuristic tools in a variety of ways and a variety of situations.

This book is not primarily about any particular problem but rather about tools that can be used to address a variety of problems in diverse situations. It is intended, to use a hackneyed metaphor, not to provide people with a fish but to teach them how to fish—not how to understand and act on one specific historical situation but how to go about understanding and acting on a wide range of distinctive historical situations. Its focus on heuristic tools may make it seem somewhat abstract at points. I hope the apparently abstract elements it delineates will gradually become clearer, richer, and more evidently useful as they are presented, developed, and applied in many different ways.

This volume is divided into three parts, each of which provides a different point of entry for assimilating my heuristic for common preservation.

Part 1, "Discovering the Tools," tells how my effort to understand and act on social problems led me to conduct intellectual raiding parties into rarified discourses on such matters as the nature of entities, relationships, and change. I explored the methodology of history, the dialectics of Karl Marx, the pragmatism of John Dewey. I plunged into the then-emerging paradigms of cybernetics and systems theory, especially the development-oriented version developed by Jean Piaget. I adapted ways of applying such paradigms to human society from historical sociologist Michael Mann and from related ideas developed by Gandhi and his interpreter Gene Sharp. Part 1 tries to extract something for the use of social movements from thinkers and traditions that might sometimes seem remote from contemporary social problems.

Part 2, "The Tools," provides in effect a tour of my workshop. It starts from the ideas of mathematician G. Polya, pioneer of modern heuristics, to develop a strategy for problem-solving that can be applied to social problems. It then lays out thirteen tools or elements of my heuristic. They include identifying and solving problems; thinking and doing; transforming means, ends, entities, coordination, differentiations, and power; and countering domination and disorder. It concludes with ways to forestall common preservations from turning into new forms of domination and disorder.

Part 3, "Using the Tools: Climate Protection," employs the common preservation heuristic to explore the efforts to halt climate change, their failure so far, and the possibility of an alternative strategy for climate protection I call climate insurgency. It illustrates how to apply the heuristic to a real-life problem. A series of notes (see Commentaries for Part 3, 317–41) indicates how the heuristic tools were used to construct the account.

My heuristic is the result of where I started out and the particular track I followed in creating it. No doubt others, following different itineraries, may come up with different and perhaps better ways of thinking about and pursuing common preservation. Nonetheless I hope you will find something in my method of inquiry that will be useful for yours. Best of all would be if you could combine mine with your own in ways that were better than either one alone. That's what I would consider success for this book.

To paraphrase the immortal words of Gregory Bateson, there is no trial-and-error learning without error. This story is driven forward by the inadequacies I found in my own ways of understanding and acting on the world and by my efforts to overcome them. I'm sure the ideas I propose in this book are still inadequate. I'm equally confident that you and others can take what I've done, find the flaws, and correct them.

I'm asking you to try.

PART 1
DISCOVERING THE TOOLS

CHAPTER 1

Discovering the Tools

On September 10, 2011, I got an email from my friend Marina Sitrin, who has been active in and written about "horizontalist" social movements in the US and around the world. She wrote, "It would be great to get together. September 17th is being organized as an 'Occupy Wall Street' day-week, so that might be fun."[1] If there ever was proof that even the self-proclaimed cognoscenti can't foresee the future, it may be my failure to hop on the train and get myself to Wall Street that day.

To the amazement of even its initiators, within a few weeks the occupation of a small park near Wall Street became the focus of a global movement, with occupations in six hundred US locations and simultaneous coordinated demonstrations by people in more than a thousand cities in eighty-two countries. During one week, the Occupy movements received an amazing 13 percent of all media coverage in the US. Media references to "economic inequality" grew exponentially. And despite the occupiers' sometimes unkempt appearance, 54 percent of Americans told pollsters that they had a favorable opinion of the Wall Street protesters, while only 23 percent had an unfavorable opinion.[2]

Less than two months later, violent police attacks drove occupiers in New York and around the country out of their encampments. Over the next year the occupy movement gradually declined, leaving many participants disillusioned. But its continuing impact was enormous. A December 2011 poll found that 50 percent of Americans—double the number in 2009—said they believe there are "strong conflicts" between rich and poor in the United States. Political pundits from both left and right attributed Obama's victory in the 2012 presidential elections in part to his adopting a political narrative previously popularized by the Occupy movement.

may be false—or it may cast what was believed before in a whole new light.[14]

That back-and-forth testing between concept and evidence, between pattern and instance, became a centerpiece of my heuristic.

I wanted to use history to address problems people were facing in the present, and again I drew on E.H. Carr's *What Is History?* to understand how to do so. Carr explains the purpose of history with a sort of parable. Jones, after drinking too much and getting into a car with defective brakes, runs over and kills Robinson, who was crossing the road at a dangerous intersection to buy cigarettes. An inquest at the local police headquarters examines the possible causes of the accident. Was it due to excess alcohol consumption, or poor car maintenance, or bad road marking? Just then some interlopers arrive who argue that Robinson was killed because he was a cigarette smoker. They are gently but firmly edged to the door and the janitor ordered under no circumstances to allow them to return.

Why? According to Carr, "the historian distills from the experience of the past, or from so much of the experience of the past as is accessible to him, that part which he recognizes as amenable to rational explanation and interpretation, and from it draws conclusions which may serve as a guide to action."[15] Rational and historically significant explanations are those that "could also be applied to other historical situations." In the case of poor Robinson, "it made sense to suppose that the curbing of alcoholic indulgence in drivers, or a stricter control over the condition of brakes, or an improvement in the siting of roads, might serve the end of reducing the number of traffic fatalities. But it made no sense at all to suppose that the number of traffic fatalities could be reduced by preventing people from smoking cigarettes."[16]

I embraced Carr's idea of history as a rational reconstruction whose rationality was based on its usefulness. I recognized that there were many nonrational factors in human life. But I wanted to mobilize rational responses to real problems, and for that purpose it was appropriate to emphasize the rational, purposive aspect of human existence.[17]

Carr emphasized that the culmination of the past—that which gives it significance—is not the present but the future: the historian must not only ask the question "why" but also the question "whither?"[18] As I put it in *Strike!*, the historian's work is important because "it contributes

A story like the development of Occupy Wall Street could be told as just one damn thing after another, a collection of facts presented without any organization. It could be portrayed as a fad; a result of sudden collective insanity; the product of charismatic leaders; an outcome of accidental, random events; or perhaps an act of God or the devil. It is not clear that such explanations would be useful, however, or verifiable.

Alternatively, it could be presented as the inevitable outcome of some linear chain of events, perhaps starting with the change in the distribution of wealth or the fall in Americans' incomes after the Great Recession or the issuing of a call by an obscure Canadian magazine. But when you actually try to make such an interpretation, you find that it is extremely difficult to fit the phenomena of movements like Occupy Wall Street to that kind of linear model.

Such movements seem to exhibit rapid, unexpected changes. New capabilities, goals, and attitudes develop in the process. Previously unconnected people start coordinating their activity in pursuit of common goals. They often do so without depending on guidance from an established structure of authority. Unarmed, nonviolent movements are often able to exercise power or influence despite the opposition of highly armed, violent opponents. And such movements often lead to broader changes in society despite the fact that they do not control any of the conventional levers of power that are normally presumed to determine social outcomes.

The process seems to be determined by an opaque mix of intentional human action and unintended side effects. Outcomes are context-dependent; factors and forces that appeared irrelevant can suddenly become salient. Seemingly small causes can have disproportionately large results: Occupy Wall Street might have vanished early on but for the citywide outrage police provoked when they lured supporters onto a lane of the Brooklyn Bridge and then arrested them en masse. Patterns can be observed, but then they change or vanish. Yet these phenomena are not simply random flux; within them are elements of development, even the emergence of new common preservations.

I've spent a good deal of my life trying to fathom such complex interactions. Mostly I've done so by participating in and studying social movements, but I've also conducted what I think of as "raiding parties" into the ideas of thinkers who might provide alternatives.[3]

The chapters of "Part 1: Discovering the Tools" describe those raiding parties and what I learned from them that has contributed to my understanding of common preservation. The story begins with my childhood discovery of W.E.B. Du Bois's *Black Reconstruction* and my growing interest in history, especially the history of social change and social movements.

From the writing of E.H. Carr and E.P. Thompson I learned something about how to do history. Understanding social movements and common preservation requires first of all looking at them historically, using evidence and argument to uncover the process of their development. But history in and of itself can be limited to a mere collection of facts recounted one after another but only as one damn thing after another. For history to be useful we need to find the significant connections that make it meaningful—in particular those that may help us act more effectively and wisely in the future.

From Ernest Schachtel's *Metamorphosis* I learned about the paradoxes of human development and was led to wonder how they applied to social movements and social change. Studying Marx provided an invaluable but also problematic vision of class, class conflict, and worker self-organization. The pragmatism of John Dewey provided a way of looking at human action as an aspect of how living beings adapt to their environment—and adapt their environment to themselves.

I was fascinated by the feedback cycles of Norbert Weiner's cybernetics and the self-regulation through interaction of Ludvig von Bertilanffy's theory of open systems. I drew on historical sociologist Michael Mann's ideas about power as rooted in social networks. From Gandhi and his great interpreter Gene Sharp I learned to view power as rooted in dependence, and see the apparently powerless as potentially powerful because of the mutual dependence that exists within a social system.

Many of these "loopy" ideas converged in the work of the Swiss developmental thinker Jean Piaget. From him I learned a way not only to describe but also to explain development. His vision of "equilibration" and its ramifying correlates became the guiding thread of my common preservation heuristic.

The study of such highly interconnected, interactive fields is now often referred to collectively as complexity theory, but also as systems, cybernetic, developmental, holistic, nonlinear, ecological, or dialectical approaches. They are all based on the principle that the parts cannot be understood independently of their interaction with each other and with the wholes of which they are part. This is not to say that either societies or social movements form complete systems—as I emphasize in "The Abolition of Society" below. But they do have systems properties that produce what have been called "system effects" and they cannot be understood if that is ignored.[4]

It is not enough to understand "society as a system," however. The fields from which phenomena like Occupy Wall Street emerge are composed of thinking and acting human individuals and groups who are pursuing their own ends, adapting their actions to their environments, and varying their own ends and their strategies for reaching them. Understanding the emergence of common preservation requires understanding not only the social field in which it develops but also the goals and strategies of the people who make it.

CHAPTER 2

Freedom Road

How do people who are isolated and oppressed join together to pursue their common interests? Where can they find the power to liberate themselves from their oppression? How can the way they do so be studied and understood? I got my first inkling of these questions from discovering the story of black Americans in the historical period following the Civil War known as Reconstruction.

I had picked up a copy of the novel *Freedom Road* by Howard Fast from my parents' bookshelf.[1] It told the fictional story of Gideon Jackson, a black slave who had escaped his plantation in South Carolina and joined the Union Army. When he returned home, he was elected to the legislature that would draw up a new constitution for the state. Fearfully he began participating in the proceedings and painfully he began learning to read and write. Working with blacks and some whites from across the state he helped draw up a new plan of government based on universal male voting, public education, and racial equality before the law. He helped his former fellow slaves and a number of poor white neighbors buy land from the plantation. The fictional Gideon Jackson was elected to the US Congress—as a dozen former slaves actually were.

Gideon Jackson early got wind of the plans of former slave owners to restore white supremacy by eliminating the federal troops who protected these activities. He observed the rising racist terrorism of the Ku Klux Klan. He tried in vain to halt the corrupt deal through which the southern white elite threw the 1876 presidential election in exchange for the withdrawal of federal troops from the South. He returned to his home plantation where he and his fellow landowners made a last stand against the armed bands that were reimposing white supremacy. They went down fighting, and all they had built was destroyed.

Even though I first read *Freedom Road* some sixty years ago, I can still recall the tears streaming down my cheeks as I turned the final pages. My youthful emotions were stirred by the inspiration and the tragedy. But I knew that *Freedom Road* was only a made-up story and only the story of one man. Some of it sounded too heroic to be true. Sometimes it sounded like the "anyone can make it in America" stories I later learned to associate with the novels of Horatio Alger. Some of it seemed to make these great accomplishments the product of one great man.

I wanted to learn more. A black acquaintance of my parents suggested I take a look at *Black Reconstruction* by W.E.B. Du Bois, which had been a prime source for Howard Fast's novel.[2] There I found a story, not a made-up one but one based on historical evidence.

Du Bois challenged the theory that "the Negro did nothing but faithfully serve his master until emancipation was thrust upon him" as simply false. But he also doubted that "the Negro" immediately "left serfdom and took his stand with the army of freedom." After all, most of the South's four million African Americans were isolated on country plantations, and nine-tenths of them could neither read nor write. "Any mass movement under such circumstances must materialize slowly and painfully."

What "the Negro" did was "to wait, look, and listen and try to see where his interest lay." When it became clear that Southern victory was far from certain, and that the Northern armies would not return fugitive slaves to their masters, "the slave entered upon a general strike against slavery." As they had done for generations, slaves ran away from their masters—but now they could run away to the relative safety of the Union Army.[3] Eventually half a million fled to the federal army, which gradually accepted them as a crucial workforce, and millions more were poised to join them. Two hundred thousand eventually became Union soldiers.[4] Du Bois concluded that "this withdrawal and bestowal of his labor decided the war."[5]

From this account I got an early glimpse of the process I would come to think of as the development of common preservation. I learned that even people who were the very symbol of extreme oppression were not just passive victims of their conditions but could, under appropriate circumstances, manifest a degree of agency, affect their situation, and even change the course of history. I learned that this required a process through which they gathered information about their changing circumstances, tested possible ways of responding, and eventually developed new strategies for action. It also involved a social process of self-organization in which separated and isolated people created new relationships among themselves. I learned that when they did so their individual powerlessness could be transformed into a collective force. And I learned that their collective withdrawal of their consent, cooperation, and labor gave them a power that the shackle and the lash could not overcome.

Du Bois's book also represented my first encounter with what has come to be known as "history from below." It gave me not only a starting point for thinking about how divided and oppressed people can come together for collective action, it gave me a glimmering of how history could contribute to that process. Du Bois wrote *Black Reconstruction* as a contribution to the struggle for black freedom in his own time. Far from being an academic exercise, it was written to dispel myths, distortions, and downright lies that supported white supremacy and that pervaded the history of Reconstruction as it was presented in schools, universities, and allegedly scholarly tomes. And by telling what African Americans had actually accomplished during the Civil War and Reconstruction, it provided a sense of the possibilities for even the most oppressed to serve as agents of their own liberation and the making of history. It gave me a vision of what history could be.

Yet Du Bois insisted that the contribution of history to liberation did not lie in replacing one political view with another, but in refuting bias and distortion with evidence and argument. The value of history was not as political propaganda for one or another side, but as a way to approach a deeper and more universal truth.

"What is the object of writing the history of Reconstruction?" Du Bois asked. It was not to justify or condemn one group or another. "It is simply to establish the Truth, on which Right in the future may be built." But the history of Reconstruction as told in the history books of his day "simply shows that with sufficient general agreement and determination among the dominant classes, the truth of history may be utterly distorted and contradicted to any convenient fairy tale that the masters of men wish." A "science of history" requires scholars who "regard the truth as more important than the defense of the white race" and will not encourage students to gather materials to "support a prejudice or buttress a lie."[6]

I knew I was not competent to evaluate the details of Du Bois's interpretations, let alone the context in which he placed them—a global struggle between capital and a working-class fatally divided by race. But I was happy to go forward with those interpretations as hypotheses posing questions about which I might learn more.

More important, Du Bois's work gave me a vision of the potential role of history that has inspired me all my life. My first book, *Strike!*, a history of the periods of worker revolt I called "mass strikes," closed with "Afterword: A Challenge to Historians."[7] In it I quoted the introduction to a book on the Flint sit-down strikes. "If there is any one paramount characteristic of books on American history, it is that they are not histories of the people." Histories of "the generals, the diplomats, and the politicos" were plentiful.

> This is no accident. It is part of the great conspiracy which consists in drawing an iron curtain between the people and their past. The generals, the diplomats, and the politicos learned long ago that history is more than a record of the past; it is, as well, a source from which may be drawn a sense of strength and direction for the future. At all costs, that sense of strength and direction and purpose must be denied to the millions of men and women who labor for their living. Hence, the record of their past achievements is deliberately obscured in order to dull their aspirations for the future."[8]

I added:

> The very memory of revolt is a subversive force. Societies, like individuals, are adept at forgetting those aspects of their past which do not fit their present self-image. For it is just those aspects of the past which preserve the threat—and the promise—of possibilities different from the present. Historians, far from preserving those memories, have generally served as a filter by means of which they are screened.[9]

From that day to this I have tried to use history—based on evidence and argument—as a way to raise that iron curtain.

W.E.B. Du Bois grew up in Great Barrington, Massachusetts, just across the border from my home in Connecticut. I remember in my youth there was an effort to publicly commemorate him there. Members of the Veterans of Foreign Wars, American Legion, Daughters of the American Revolution, and the John Birch Society campaigned against it and it was defeated. For decades his memory was almost as suppressed in his hometown as the memory of the African American role in Reconstruction before he recovered it.[10]

One day in 2001 I got a phone call from Karen Falcon, whom I had known since she was a child growing up on a nearby hilltop in my hometown. She had become director of the Jubilee School, a unique elementary school for black children in inner city Philadelphia. Her students had been studying W.E.B. Du Bois and they had decided they wanted to visit Great Barrington; would I help get their activities recorded on video? They picked me up in a battered school bus that had traveled from Philadelphia, and we drove to Du Bois's grave, which had been unmarked until 1994. The Jubilee School had planned a series of events, and we heard a speech by Du Bois's son and held a ceremony at the local black church.[11] Apparently their visit touched a chord. The next year the church began holding an annual Du Bois birthday celebration, a local historian produced a walking tour pamphlet with fifty local Du Bois sites, and a Du Bois River Garden and Park was dedicated. Soon Great Barrington would vote nearly two-to-one to put up signs on the roads coming into town noting that it was the birthplace of W.E.B. Du Bois.

I saw those signs when I visited Great Barrington in 2011. There was also a large sign marking Du Bois's birthplace. Stopping there, I picked up a handful of leaflets, maps, and guides to Du Bois history. Next we drove past the new, well-marked Du Bois Center. Nearby was a cemetery with signs that proclaimed it the site of Du Bois's grave. Downtown a large mural commemorated his life. The circle had been closed, and no longer was Du Bois a prophet without honor in his own hometown.

CHAPTER 3

Metamorphosis

The emergence of a movement among slaves in the midst of the Civil War wasn't just a matter of simple cause and effect like a stick hitting a ball; it represented a development from a state of disorganization and oppression to one of self-organization and resistance. The 1973 meat boycott, Occupy Wall Street, and other instances of self-organization involved development from an initial state to a more and differently organized one. But what is development? I got my first inkling of an answer not from history but from psychology.

When I was seven, an extraordinary woman named Dorothy Lee came to my little community in northwestern Connecticut. She was a Greek immigrant from that rarity, a Protestant Greek family, and one of awesome academic accomplishments. She referred to herself as an existential anthropologist, although in later years she became so alienated from academe that she started calling herself an ex-anthropologist. By the time I was eleven or twelve I had wholeheartedly adopted Dorothy as a mentor. She challenged me to think, feel, and experience. Her decision to resign a position at Harvard in favor of a marginal job in a far less prestigious university had a stunning impact on me, making me realize that one could act on one's values in ways that contradicted other people's expectations and even violated what some might consider common sense. The next year when I turned sixteen I dropped out of high school.

In my mid-teens Dorothy told me to read *Metamorphosis* by the German émigré psychoanalyst Ernest Schachtel.[1] It was an unlikely recommendation but one that had a profound impact on me.

Metamorphosis traces the changes in human affect, perception, attention, and memory that take place from birth to adulthood. It provided my first exposure to the concept of "development." Schachtel presented development as a kind of transformation that combined continuity and change. As he wrote in the foreword, "The human metamorphosis from birth to adulthood is much greater than that of man's nearest relatives in the animal kingdom."[2] Yet "any attempt to understand man must take into account not only the changes but also the continuities in his development, for the later stages still show the traces of the earlier ones" and "the condition of the newborn shows the seeds of, the *Anlage* for, the later developments."[3]

Each change, each new phase of development, emerges from the previous state of the being.[4] Ultimately all trace back to "innate structures and dispositions" which characterize "all human energies and capacities."[5] But it is a mistake to focus primarily on such origins. These innate features are repeatedly transformed in the process of development. The change from infant to adult in humans is dramatic, far more so than the similar change in related species.

The concept of development is of course a staple of biology. Caterpillars grow into butterflies and embryos grow into mature mammals. But the outcome of such development is much more constrained than that of humans. Every butterfly of a particular species acts pretty much the same way, whereas adult humans in America, China, the Arctic, or the Brazilian jungle act very differently, and even individuals within the same social group can vary considerably. This reflects the relative atrophy of instinct in humans and the relatively greater role played by culture and individual learning. The result might be called, to borrow a phrase from another sphere, "development as freedom."[6]

Schachtel's method was to combine how things are experienced and how they arise—phenomenology and genesis. It combined "careful, qualitative observation" of experiences and reactions and "genetic exploration" of how they developed through "interaction with the environment."[7]

But that left open the question of explaining development—how and why it occurred. Could it be simply the result of wired-in maturation? If so, how could mature human beings be so different in different cultures? Or was it simply the result of rearing, a product of the social environment? If so, how could people sometimes transcend, critique, and even transform their environment?

Schachtel's answer was that people are inherently active and potentially open to the world. From birth on people show "steadily increasing capacities for active searching for satisfaction and for active discovery and exploration." Far from being painful, the infant "enjoys these active capacities."[8] Many encounters are sought "not in order to abolish the stimuli or the excitation caused by them, and increasingly not in order to still hunger or thirst or as a detour on the way to a return to the comfort of sleep, but out of a growing urge to get in touch with and explore the world around the infant."[9] These traits allow man to take "a conscious part not only in his own, individual development," but "in the evolution of mankind."[10]

This contrasted sharply with the dominant view of human nature at the time. It is difficult to recapture today how deeply American thought and culture were permeated by the ideas of Sigmund Freud, or at least versions of them, in the era in which I grew up. Schachtel, though deeply immersed in the traditions of psychoanalysis, was also highly critical of some of Freud's key doctrines. In particular he rejected Freud's version of the "pleasure principle," with its assertion that "the fundamental movement of the living organism is toward an excitationless state of quiescence."[11] He rejected similar ideas, such as the view then common in psychology that an organism's objective is "drive reduction."[12]

I began almost intuitively using the concept of development in thinking about social change and the emergence of social movements and common preservations. I tried to find the "seeds" of actions and then the transformations that explain how they developed new, radically different forms.

Du Bois had done something like this in his interpretation of the rise of the self-liberation movement among slaves during the Civil War. He described sharing of information, running away from the plantation, and the withdrawal of efficiency as tactics that slaves used in normal times. As the Union armies entered the South, slaves adapted these tactics for the new situation in which slaveholder control was weakened. The result was what Du Bois characterized as the "general strike" of the black workforce and its gradual transfer of its labor power to the Union forces.

A similar process marked the consumer meat boycott of 1973. Housewives were used to "boycotting" an item as individuals if the price was too high. In many cases they were also familiar with phone banks and other organizing techniques that were used by churches, political parties, and other organizations. When they wanted to protest rising meat prices, they transformed their individual shopping decisions into a collective action, and they used familiar techniques to organize themselves to do so.

I also found that the concept of development could be used not just to understand the past but also to think about strategy for the future. I was active in Students for a Democratic Society (SDS) in the 1960s, and its original strategy reflected something like this idea of development. The SDS statement *America and the New Era* proposed a "revolutionary trajectory" in which small actions would cascade or snowball into larger ones that would finally lead to fundamental social change.

It noted the emergence of "local insurgent actions" like mass direct action and voter registration campaigns among black people, political reform movements directed against entrenched Democratic machines, political action for peace, and community-based attempts to reach underprivileged youth. It proposed as next steps organized protest in economically depressed areas, organizing nonunion workers, and involving slum-dwellers in politics.[13] "Reform programs" are not "mere palliatives" if they are "accelerated steps toward more and more radical demands." It is "not simply the current 'demand' by itself that tells the story: it is *toward* what it is leading that is important."[14]

My longtime friend and collaborator Tim Costello and I used something like this approach in our book *Common Sense for Hard Times*.[15] We wrote that even in normal times people use cooperative tactics like strikes, sabotage, and street action to solve shared problems and remedy immediate grievances. In the context of the deteriorating economic conditions of the early 1970s, such tactics were being used in a more concerted way, such as the meat boycotts, truckers' blockades, and strike waves we described in the book. We argued that only by expanding such action could people resist the destruction of their conditions of life, and that such an expansion could lead to a transformation of society.

We gave as an example the revolt of the American colonies against Britain. A decade before the American Revolution, American colonists viewed British rule as necessary, legitimate, and desirable. But they did use extralegal mass direct action for such purposes as halting the impressment of sailors, protecting local smugglers who violated customs laws, and preventing export of food when supplies were low.

When the British imposed the 1765 Stamp Act, increasing colonial taxes, the solution the colonists found was to "apply the existing techniques of popular resistance to the new problem." They boycotted British goods and forced tax officials to resign. The British government withdrew the Stamp Act, but replaced it with a new set of taxes. The colonials renewed their boycott, backed by unification of the thirteen colonies around a "Nonimportation Agreement." Local and colony-by-colony Nonimportation Associations gradually took over more and more of the functions of government. Meanwhile, the colonies reached out to each other through Committees of Correspondence which eventually organized the first Continental Congress. When colonists established their independence, the forms of organization they had developed in their struggle became the institutions of the new American government.[16]

In the early days of Occupy Wall Street I was asked to give a talk at the City University of New York and Occupy New School, "What Can 99-Percenters Learn from the History of Social Movements?"[17] I argued that "movements have to keep evolving their forms or they lose their initiative and dynamism." We could take inspiration in this regard from the lineage of movements in the Great Depression that "started with hunger marches and eventually helped spawn the great industrial unions in American industry." I recounted how hunger marches of the unemployed led to the formation of Unemployed Workers Councils. As government employment programs like the Works Progress Administration (WPA) grew, the Unemployed Workers Councils developed into the Workers Alliance, a hybrid of a trade union for WPA workers and a welfare rights organization. The Workers Alliance was short-lived, but as American industry began to revive the consciousness and networks it had created provided much of the informal social infrastructure for the rise of industrial unionism. I suggested that Occupy Wall Street should seek not the "right" form but "a progression of forms." Occupy Wall Street itself proved to be short-lived, but it indeed became the progenitor of a sequence of movements like Strike Debt and Occupy Sandy Relief, and a seedbed for movements ranging from the Fight for $15 to the Tar Sands Blockade.[18]

Each of these social movements reflected Schachtel's idea of "development" as I had initially encountered it in *Metamorphosis*. My application of ideas taken from a psychoanalyst (albeit a maverick one) to history was very different from the usual form of "psychohistory," which tries to use psychology to decode the inner drives of historical individuals. It launched me on a continuing effort to run raiding parties into unlikely fields to gain whatever insight I could for understanding social movements and common preservation. The booty of those raiding parties is displayed in the rest of Part 1.

In some ways, development appeared puzzling if not downright paradoxical. It seemed to imply that something turns into something else yet also remains the same. Entities were transformed yet also retained a continuous identity. Their development was in some ways determined, yet it led not to a fixed outcome but to one shaped at least in part by themselves.

Mostly I was left with questions: What does it mean to develop if the goal is not predetermined? How is development "rooted" in past? How is development different from normal ideas of causation? I've been trying ever since to develop a way of thinking that would clarify what development is and how it works.

CHAPTER 4

What Is History?

By my early teens I was participating in a variety of social movements. I joined peace marches, went to civil rights meetings, and lobbied my state legislator for conversion to a peacetime economy. I continued reading about social movements, trying to puzzle out a historical and developmental understanding of them. I read about the American, French, Russian, Mexican, and Cuban revolutions and about the women's, black, populist, and other movements in the US.

At Reed College in Portland, Oregon, I became fascinated by American labor history and continued to read everything I could find about it after I dropped out and went to the Institute for Policy Studies in Washington, DC. I started writing a book that I titled *Mass Strike in America* and that was published in 1972 as *Strike!*

I had only one brief history course in college, so I had to figure out how to do history on my own. I found guidance in E.H. Carr's little book *What Is History?* Carr disparaged the idea that historians first gather the facts, then draw conclusions from them. "For myself, as soon as I have got going on a few of what I take to be the capital sources, the itch becomes too strong and I begin to write."

> Thereafter, reading and writing go on simultaneously. The writing is added to, subtracted from, re-shaped, cancelled, as I go on reading. The reading is guided and directed and made fruitful by the writing: the more I write, the more I know what I am looking for, the better I understand the significance and relevance of what I find.[1]

The result was a kind of loop in which new information corrected existing patterns of thought and the modified patterns of thought guided a search for still further corrective information. I followed Carr's back-and-forth process in writing *Strike!* I plunged myself into the evidence, poring over yellowed newspapers, journals, and books. (I knew nothing as yet about archival research or oral history.) At the same time, I sought out ideas about how to interpret that evidence anywhere I could find them. I read previous labor historians and scholars from labor studies, economics, political science, and psychology. I studied and used ideas from liberals, conservatives, and Marxists, trying to fit their ideas to the ever-expanding body of evidence I was accumulating. The ideas had to be changed and changed again and new ones sought or invented. The result was far from perfect, but it beat either random raw facts or the ideas I had started with.

Such an approach might suggest how to construct history, but how could you evaluate what interpretations of history were or were not valid? I found a congenial approach in the work of English historian E.P. Thompson, whose *The Making of the English Working Class* influenced a generation of American labor historians. I first discovered Thompson's approach to historical method in the 1960s in the *New Reasoner* and the *New Left Review*, but his most developed discussion is in *The Poverty of Theory*. Thompson says that historical practice is engaged in

> an argument between received, inadequate, or ideologically-informed concepts or hypotheses on the one hand, and fresh or inconvenient evidence on the other; with the elaboration of new hypotheses; with the testing of these hypotheses against the evidence, which may involve interrogating existing evidence in new ways, or renewed research to confirm or disprove the new notions; with discarding those hypotheses which fail these tests, and refining or revising those which do, in the light of this engagement.[2]

A historical notion can be said to "work" if it has "not been *dis*proved by contrary evidence" and "successfully organizes or 'explains' hitherto inexplicable evidence." If it meets these tests, it is "an adequate (though approximate) representation of the causative sequence, or rationality, of these events, and it conforms (within the logic of the historical discipline) with a process which did in fact eventuate in the past."[3] These tests appeal both to the evidence, and to the "coherence, adequacy and consistency of the concepts" and to their "congruence with the knowledge of adjacent disciplines."[4]

According to Thompson, the purpose of what he calls "historical logic" is "to test hypotheses as to structure, causation, etc." and "to eliminate self-confirming procedures." It proceeds by "a dialogue between concept and evidence, a dialogue conducted by successive hypotheses, on the one hand, and empirical research on the other."[5] This logic—the evidence interrogated thus—constitutes history's "ultimate court of appeal."[6]

In *Strike!* I borrowed the concept of the "mass strike," which Rosa Luxemburg had developed for Europe in the early decades of the twentieth century, to understand peak periods of industrial conflict in the US. Luxemburg defined a mass strike as not just a single act but as a whole period of class struggle. "Its use, its effects, its reasons for coming about are in a constant state of flux." Political and economic strikes, united and partial strikes of individual sections of industry and general strikes of entire cities, peaceful wage strikes and street battles, uprisings with barricades—"all run together and run alongside each other, get in each other's way, overlap each other; a perpetually moving and changing sea of phenomena."[7] I wrote detailed accounts of six periods of intense industrial conflict in the US from the "Great Upheaval" of 1877 to the overlapping strikes that shut much of American industry after World War II, with a comparison to the intense labor conflict that was emerging in the early 1970s as *Strike!* was being written. I hoped that the six case studies would be illuminated by the mass strike concept and that the detailed evidence they presented would verify that concept's applicability.

Thompson pointed out that historical concepts are not necessarily the same as those of disciplines that study more static phenomena. Instead, they may describe processes.[8] Thompson gives the example of a "crisis of subsistence" in which "a poor harvest leads to dearth, which leads to rising mortality and the consumption of the next year's seed." A second poor harvest then leads to "extreme dearth, epidemics, a peak in mortality, and then a sharply rising conception-rate."[9] The concept of the mass strike I explored in *Strike!* was a "historical concept" in the same sense: a pattern that was repeated in different contexts. What the different periods of mass strike had in common was not particular facts but rather a common process which I explored in a section called "The Mass Strike Process." I tried to show that each of the periods I studied followed a similar developmental process. I also tried to show that the

character of mass strikes itself developed over time along with transformations in American economy and society.

Thompson said that historical concepts are generalized from many
examples. But he stressed that historical concepts cannot be applied
like classical scientific laws or like models into which the evidence is to
be fitted. Rather, they are "expectations" that "do not impose a rule" but
that do "hasten and facilitate the interrogation of the evidence."[10] They
are, in short, heuristic.

The knowledge provided by history cannot aspire to the same
standards as are claimed for natural sciences. Historical knowledge is
in its nature "provisional and incomplete (but not therefore untrue),"
"selective (but not therefore untrue)," and "limited and defined by the
questions proposed to the evidence (and the concepts informing those
questions)."[11] Historical knowledge "must always fall short of positive
proof" but "false historical knowledge is generally subject to *dis*proof."[12]

Thompson criticized the kind of "theory" that wasn't grounded in
history. I too found such theory unsatisfactory because the means to test
its fit with evidence were so limited. I concluded theory could easily be
lost in an endless sea of speculation without the discipline of the historian, who, as Carr put it, must "bring into the picture all known or knowable facts relevant, in one sense or another, to the theme on which he
is engaged and to the interpretation proposed"—including those facts
apparently contradictory to this interpretation.[13] I nonetheless periodi-
cally delved into "theory," seeking ideas and hypotheses to test against
evidence and for coherence—tests like those Thompson had prescribed.

I also tried to share this epistemological approach beyond the community of professional historians, to make it available as a tool for those
trying to understand their own social realities. In *History from Below:
How to Uncover and Tell the Story of Your Community, Association, or
Union*, I presented it as an extension of practices familiar in everyday life:

> You can't prove what happened in the past the way you prove an
> answer in mathematics; all you can do is construct the most likely
> account of what happened. It's like a courtroom, except that you
> often have to be satisfied with "the most probable account' even
> if it can't be proved "beyond a reasonable doubt."
>
> Keep testing each new thing you learn against what you already
> know. If something "doesn't fit" with the rest of what is known, it

to what we need to know to cope with the practical problems of the future."[19]

An example: most of the twentieth century had seen a growth in job security in the American workplace, but starting in the 1970s the trend began to reverse. My friend and writing partner Tim Costello saw the erosion of "steady work" as a transforming force in working-class life. In the early 1990s he began trying to figure out how to make contingent work the focus of an organizing campaign.

I remember sitting on Tim's porch in Boston trying to develop a strategy to counter the rise of contingent work. There wasn't much to go on. Then it dawned on us that most of the workers who made up the unemployed councils of the Great Depression, which I had written about in *Strike!*, probably were working intermittently whenever they could, so that they were really contingent workers; we reviewed their strategies and borrowed whatever we could from them. Some contemporary unions represented workers who moved frequently among employers, and we tried to learn from their practices. There were also nonunion organizations, such as the working women's organization Nine to Five, that had organized workers on a nonworkplace basis. None of these provided an off-the-shelf model, but they did offer starting points for thinking about possible strategies. Tim's strategy ended up including direct organizing of contingent workers, efforts to change union policies on contingent work, legislative reforms, and employer codes of conduct—all strategies drawn from the historical examples we had examined but adapted to the concrete situations faced by workers in a different time.

Although I have used historical methods, I didn't exactly become a historian of a conventional kind. My project has not been to seek knowledge exclusively of the past. From history I have primarily borrowed a method of inquiry. Historical method guides the common preservation heuristic presented in this book. The heuristic constructs an account through a back-and-forth loop between research and ideas; testing of concepts against evidence and of evidence in the light of concepts; a focus on processes; and an evaluation of significance based on applicability to other situations. I have tried to apply those methods both to understanding the past and to solving problems of the future. In doing so I have focused on one kind of historical phenomena, development.

I agreed with Carr that it is the future that gives history its significance, but on one point I disagreed with him passionately. Carr defended the idea of "history as progress" and devoted his final chapter to showing aspects of progress in modern history.[20] I believed that history was on a fundamentally wrong track, and that the problem was to get off that track and onto another one. As I put it in *Strike!*, "The new threats of nuclear and ecological disaster, combined with the more traditional effects of economic, social, and military crisis, mean that humanity—if it survives at all—will do so only through fundamental changes in its way of life."[21]

Hamlet once grumbled,

The time is out of joint, O cursed spite,
That ever I was born to set it right.

Make that "we."

CHAPTER 5

Re:Marx

Marxism had a strange and ambiguous place in the world in which I grew up. It was most familiar as the ideology used to justify a system of tyranny with aspirations to global domination. A few hardy souls tried to maintain or develop it as a serious theory of society or social liberation, but they were largely isolated from both the non-Marxist left and from most of those who called themselves Marxists.

Neither of my parents, despite their participation in labor, peace, and other progressive causes, had much interest in Marx. Nor, for that matter, did the US Communist Party or those I met who were close to it. It was a standing joke that many top Communist leaders had never read Marx's major work, *Capital*. While many in the British New Left came from a Marxist background and continued to work in a Marxist paradigm, few in the American New Left that formed much of my political environment from the 1960s on were serious students of Marx. I never called myself a Marxist or accepted Marx or Marxism as "correct." But I've spent a lot of my life learning from Marx and Marxists.

In this chapter I tell a little about my encounters with Marxism and why I never accepted what I understand to be the core of Marxist doctrine. In the following chapter, "Robbing Marx," I present some of the ideas I've gleaned from Marx for the common preservation heuristic. The third chapter on Marx, "Adventures of the Dialectic," considers the unresolved problems in Marx's "dialectical" approach to development that helped stimulate me to explore the other approaches discussed in Part 1.

As a budding radical, I inevitably stumbled on the writings of Marx and Marxists. I first discovered Erich Fromm's *Marx's Concept of Man*, then some of the early translations of Gramsci, then the work of Herbert

Marcuse. I read the *Communist Manifesto*, *The Civil War in France*, Engels's *Socialism: Utopian and Scientific*, and various other Marxist classics. Many of the historians I studied, such as E.P. Thompson, Gabriel Kolko, Christopher Hill, William Appleman Williams, and Louis Hacker considered themselves Marxists or seemed so to others.

In the late 1960s historian Gabriel Kolko, then working at the Institute for Policy Studies where I was studying, sent me in the direction of the Marxist writer Paul Mattick. In his youth after World War I, Mattick had participated in the German worker uprisings, then came to the US and worked as a machinist. He became an organizer of the unemployed, a writer on Marxist economics, and the leading US advocate for council communism, a Marxist tendency that advocated a movement led by workers' councils rather than political parties.[1] I worked closely with his son and intellectual heir, Paul Mattick Jr., publishing the magazine *Root and Branch*. Paul gave a graduate seminar on *Capital* which I took on a noncredit basis. It was a great intellectual experience to study *Capital* in the context of a strong living tradition of Marx interpretation. But it perhaps says something about my priorities that I chose to abandon the seminar to travel with Tim Costello interviewing young workers for our book *Common Sense for Hard Times*.[2]

I early gave up on trying to pin down "what Marx really meant." Indeed, I've been less and less sure that he recognized the potential for ambiguity and contradiction lurking in his own thought—let alone the diversity of contradictory and self-contradictory views that could be embraced by those who claimed to follow and interpret him. But such a fate may be inescapable for any truly innovative, multifaceted, and evolving thinker.

Whatever the evolution of Marx's own thought, historically Marxism has been identified above all with the *Communist Manifesto*. It was a source of inspiration for me as it has been for tens of millions of others around the world. For many years I reread it annually and still regard it as a touchstone.

Marx's long-term collaborator Friedrich Engels summed up "the fundamental proposition" which forms the "nucleus" of the *Manifesto* thus:

> In every historical epoch, the prevailing mode of economic production and exchange, and the social organization necessarily

following from it, form the basis upon which is built up, and from which alone can be explained, the political and intellectual history of that epoch; that consequently the whole history of mankind (since the dissolution of primitive tribal society, holding land in common ownership) has been a history of class struggles, contests between exploiting and exploited, ruling and oppressed classes; that the history of these class struggles forms a series of evolution in which, now-a-days, a stage has been reached where the exploited and oppressed class—the proletariat—cannot attain its emancipation from the sway of the exploiting and ruling class—the bourgeoisie—without, at the same time, and once and for all, emancipating society at large from all exploitation, oppression, class-distinctions and class struggles.[3]

I never found this "nucleus" credible. In a somewhat callow but not therefore invalid paper I wrote as a student at the Institute for Policy Studies in the late 1960s jejunely titled "Re:Markx," I argued that the actual course of social development was far from what Marx had predicted. The establishment by the working class of a socialist society in the economically most advanced countries "obviously has not occurred."[4]

Marx had adopted a false premise: "That social transformation can only be accomplished by the coming to power of a new class, that is, by revolution." The history of the transition from feudalism to capitalism, which Marx took as his paradigm case, belied this view. In some countries, such as France, this transition did involve a political seizure of power by the bourgeoisie, in others—notably Germany and Japan—"it was brought about by the old feudal ruling class itself, which retained its dominance while revolutionizing its own economic system to overcome its economic fetters."[5]

Much the same thing had happened with the socialization of modern capitalism. Marx identified the contradiction in capitalism as between the private ownership of the means of production and the increasingly social character of the production process. Only by socializing the economy could this contradiction be overcome. And in fact capitalist economies were reshaped by socialization—"carried out not by the working class but by the capitalists themselves, who have virtually abolished the classical capitalist market and substituted economic planning, while retaining their social domination." (This, of course, was written long before the era of neoliberalism produced a reversion toward classic capitalist markets and a decline of economic planning worldwide—a reversion that was rarely predicted by Marxist theorists and is difficult to reconcile with a progressive "series in evolution" culminating in a classless society.)

This example illustrated a deeper flaw: Marx's assertion of historical inevitability. "To the extent that the pronouncements of the *Manifesto* are given the status of scientific laws, they are clearly false—proven so by the scientific test of historical experiment."[6]

But if there was no law in history, perhaps there was a logic. The historic rise of modern productive techniques "posed a problem for Western societies." Typically, "the bourgeoisie *did* smash the older feudal societies." But this result was not inevitable. In some cases, for example Germany, they failed to do so, and the old feudal classes made the transition to modern society instead; in the case of Russia, both groups failed and the task was left to the workers and intellectuals; in Spain, the process never happened at all. These historical results, I concluded, "have a common logic which makes them intelligible, even though no law dictated them."

I saw this distinction between scientific law and historical logic as of practical significance. "At present, the United States is posed the problem of liquidating its disastrous commitment in Vietnam. This liquidation may be achieved by popular opposition to the war. It may be achieved by the establishment. Or it may not be achieved at all."

I saw such a nondeterministic approach as an alternative to "the optimism of the Marxist position" which had "led to disastrous attitudes," such as the view of German revolutionaries that "since socialist revolution was inevitable eventually, there was no real possibility that Nazism would develop instead." But I also saw it as an alternative to New Left tendencies toward "hostility to a historical view of man's situation" rooted in "an existentialist view of man's absolute freedom in the present." This led to "forms of action which go completely against the logic of history" and "make it impossible to develop strategies which utilize the logic of history."[7]

Historical inevitability "often served as a means of absolution from moral responsibility" for Marxists.[8] Without it, people are "again responsible." This responsibility was partly negative. If we plan a demonstration in which people are killed, we are partly responsible. If we follow a policy that results in a fascist coup, we are partially responsible. If we create a movement which ends up deliberately starving huge masses of people to death—as socialists did in Russia—"the blood is partly on our hands." But the responsibility was also positive. "The horror that is our present world will not cure itself automatically." It requires our action and something we might call statesmanship, "the ability to take social forces and shape them to one's ends," rather than merely reflecting them.

One could easily find Marxist texts in accord with the nondeterministic approach I was advocating; "men make history, but not under conditions of their own choosing" comes to mind.[9] But the very fact that Marx could so easily be interpreted in almost opposite ways led me early on to leave to Marxicologists the question of which were his "real" views.

My rejection of Marx's "fundamental proposition" notwithstanding, Marx and Marxism have been formative for me as for millions of others around the world. The very critique I made of it in "Re:Markx" used ideas about social dynamics that would have been unthinkable without Marx and the Marxist tradition.

Karl Marx hated what capitalism did to workers. Whatever the flaws of his theories, he continues to inspire because of his relentless encouragement of collective action by the oppressed. To his apparently determinist interpretation of history, he could have answered with his own words: "The philosophers have only *interpreted* the world, in various ways; the point is to *change* it."[10]

In the early 1970s I attended a lecture by Mattick. He had spent much of his long life studying Marxist political economy, and he spoke for what seemed like several hours delineating the entire theoretical edifice of *Capital*. (One young worker who attended was afterward heard to say, "I have only one question: Does he breathe?) Then, to my amazement, he closed by saying that none of this matters. This is all shit. "The political economy of the working class is the class struggle."

There's at least one Marx who would have agreed.

CHAPTER 6

Expropriating Marx

Stripped of the baggage of historical inevitability, Marx's work provides an extremely rich body of hypotheses to test against historical evidence. The failure of some—such as the prediction that the working class would transform capitalism into socialism—by no means renders the rest worthless. In *Strike!* I tested many of Marx's ideas about the development of capitalism, the formation of the working class, and the impact of capitalist crises on the conflict between classes; I found many of them well supported by the facts of US history.

Marx's presentation of the development of workers' movements and the forming of workers into a class are prime examples of the common preservation process. Furthermore, embedded within Marx's theory are more general ideas that can be readapted to purposes and contexts beyond class struggles.

Marx's idea of class exemplifies a more general idea of social differentiation and stratification. Marx's theory in *Capital* involves two kinds of differentiation. One is the division of labor. This in turn is broken down into the division of labor in society, between hunters and farmers, for example, and the division of labor in the production process of a single product, for example the collaboration of different crafts in making a vehicle. The other is the division between workers and capitalists, based on capitalists' exclusive possession of the means of production.

Thinkers before Marx analyzed differentiation through the division of labor. Adam Smith portrayed the division of labor as leading to an interdependence that benefitted all. Workers whose labor was specialized were more productive and received the blessing of Smith's "invisible hand." Social classes were similarly interdependent: workers provided capitalists with labor; capitalists provided workers with wages.

But Marx saw in such differentiation the seeds of antagonism. Each worker's freedom was restricted by their limited role in the division of labor. And, of course, for Marx workers had an antagonistic relationship to employers, both within capitalism in the struggle over wages and historically in the struggle between capitalism and socialism.

Marx did not abandon Adam Smith's idea that differentiation leads to interdependence. But he maintained that the inequality between capitalists who own society's means of production and workers who are excluded from them turned mutual dependence into unilateral dependence. Since workers don't own the means of production, they are forced to work for those who do. The power of capitalists over workers is the result of workers' dependence on the means of production and therefore on the capitalists who possess them.

The idea that differentiation breeds antagonism and dependence has been applied to many aspects of society besides economic class. For example, it provided a template for the "dependency theory" that examined the relation between imperialism and the societies it dominated. More recently, feminism highlighted the antagonistic dependencies between women and men.

Such an approach can also be applied to organizations. For example, the differentiation of organizations into leaders and led is often presumed to be necessary and beneficial to all. But it can lead, whether in unions or parties or churches or governments, to an antagonistic relationship in which power is concentrated in leaders and the rank and file are rendered powerless.

Marx's two forms of differentiation lead to two different kinds of problems for those who live under capitalism, which Marx distinguished in a brilliant passage in *Capital*. On the one hand, capitalism generates problems of domination—for example, the tyranny of the capitalist over the worker in the workplace. This class division implies "the undisputed authority of the capitalist over men, that are but parts of a mechanism that belongs to him."[1]

On the other hand, capitalism generates chaos and disorganization, notably what Marx calls the "anarchy of the market." The division of labor within society "brings into contact independent commodity-producers, who acknowledge no other authority but that of competition." Marx recognizes a tendency toward equilibrium among the various spheres of production, but "only in the shape of a reaction against the constant upsetting of this equilibrium"—through what today economists might call equilibration by feedback. He compared this to the war of all against all in the animal kingdom that "more or less preserves the conditions of existence of every species."[2]

This distinction between problems of domination and problems of disorder is applicable to many other areas of social life. In the nation-state system, for example, there are problems that have to do with the domination of one nation or people by another—a.k.a. imperialism. But there are also problems that have to do with uncontrolled interactions among nations, such as arms races and cycles of violence and revenge. And, as in Marx's analysis of capitalism, the two problems are often intertwined.

Distinguishing problems of domination and problems of disorder has been important for me in thinking about alternatives to the existing organization of society. If domination were the only problem, then the solution would simply be liberation; but liberation by itself can simply lead to disorder. Conversely, if disorder were the only problem, a central organizing authority would be the evident solution; unfortunately, history has shown that such an authority can easily become a new center of oppression. So adequate solutions to social problems must limit both domination and disorder by combining freedom and coordination.

The domination of employers over workers, combined with the general disruption and impoverishment workers experience as a result of the "anarchy of capitalist production," led in Marx's analysis to the process of class formation. In the *Communist Manifesto*, Marx gives a marvelous synoptic description of the formation of the working class through its struggle with the capitalist class, thereby illuminating the emergence of a new form of common preservation.

At first "the contest is carried on by individual laborers, then by the workpeople of a factory, then by the operatives of one trade, in one locality, against the individual bourgeoisie who directly exploits them." At this stage "the laborers still form an incoherent mass scattered over the whole country, and broken up by their mutual competition." But with the further development of industry, "the proletariat not only increases in number, it becomes concentrated in great masses, its strength grows, and it feels that strength more."

As the economic crises and other problems of capitalism deepen, "the collisions between individual workmen and individual bourgeois take more and more the character of collision between two classes." Workers begin to establish combinations in the form of trade unions. "They club together in order to keep up the rate of wages; they found permanent associations in order to make provision beforehand for these occasional revolts." Improved means of communication place workers in different locations in contact with one another, centralizing local struggles "into one national struggle between classes." Labor historians like E.P. Thompson have corrected and enriched this account, but its general outlines have remained persuasive.

For Marx, the formation of a class does not take place in a vacuum; it occurs not only through its internal development but also through its interaction—especially conflictual interaction—with other classes. Such an interactive framework is also necessary for understanding the development of other kinds of social groups. For example, the development of the nationalist movements in countries like India or Algeria is incomprehensible unless one looks at the impact of the emerging movement on the various interest groups that affect the colonial administration, the resulting evolution of colonial policy, and the impact of that in turn on the colonized people and their national movements.

I've absorbed these Marxist concepts into my own thinking and applied them in myriad ways. The idea of differentiations leading to antagonisms can be applied to sectarian religious conflict as aptly as to class. The distinction and interrelation between problems of domination and of disorder are as relevant to the nation-state system as they are to capitalism. The formation and development of social groups out of isolated individuals is as apparent for gender, racial, national, and other groups as it is for the working class.

Marx's account of the development of the working class, whatever its flaws, provides one valuable way of thinking about the emergence of common preservation. His analysis of differentiation provides a reminder that there are many interests besides common ones that will have to be addressed to overcome today's threats of mutual destruction. His delineation of the twin problems of domination and disorder should alert us to the need to address both.

CHAPTER 7

Adventures of the Dialectic

"The despair of necessity," Søren Kierkegaard wrote, "is due to the lack of possibility." When one is about to swoon with despair, the cry is, "Procure me possibility!"[1] The lack of belief in even the possibility of significant change buttresses the status quo. As my collaborator Tim Costello and I put it in *Common Sense for Hard Times*, "The sheer fact that people's experiences take place entirely within the existing society often makes the idea of any fundamental change in that society seem a mere fantasy."[2]

Much of the power and influence of Marxism results from its view of the world as a process of change. Objects may appear to be independent, permanent, and unchanging, but such an appearance is false. Rather, objects are constituted by each other and by the wholes or systems of which they are part. Furthermore, the relations between objects and within systems contain contradictions that inevitably lead to change.

These assertions define a paradigm of the nature of change in general, often referred to as the Marxian dialectic. That paradigm has had immense influence on thinking about social change, and it continues to have at least tacit influence even among many who do not consider themselves Marxists. I've long sought ways to use aspects of the Marxian dialectic while escaping some of its problems.

Dialectical ways of thinking have appeared in many different forms, from the early Greek philosopher Heraclitus to some versions of modern systems theory.[3] A vast and murky literature probes the "real" character of Marx's dialectic. Marx apparently never wrote down a mature statement of his own view of the dialectic, so interpreters depend either on his practice, his passing remarks, or the extensive interpretations of his collaborator Friedrich Engels.[4] Marx's views often appear vague or contradictory—and those of his interpreters even more so. But the Marxian dialectic is important, both because of the contribution it can make to understanding change and interaction and because for a century and a half it has underpinned so much thinking about social change.

Bertell Ollman, a well-known interpreter of the Marxian dialectic, points out that "understanding anything in our everyday experience requires that we know something about how it arose and developed and how it fits into the larger context or system of which it is part."[5] I early accepted the need to situate anything in relation to its history and context. The process of forming such an understanding I had come to refer to as "contextualization" or an "ecological shift," comparable to ecology's shift of biology's focus from individual organisms to the interconnected web of life.

Dialectical thinking provides a way to focus attention on change and interaction. It stands in contrast with several other ways of thinking about change. In premodern societies, the cosmos was often seen in terms of recurring cycles or as a degeneration from a previous golden age. In many religious and philosophical traditions, the only real reality is that which is unchanging; Plato, for example, evoked unchanging eternal forms as the highest reality. Starting around the time of the industrial revolution, ideas that portray the world as a continuing process of progress became pervasive; the "Whig" interpretation of history as progress and "social Darwinist" applications of Darwin's theory of evolution provide examples.[6]

It is not hard to construct connections between these paradigms and ideas about what is natural, necessary, and proper for society. Intellectual historians have seen affinities between Plato's eternal forms and society ruled by a hereditary elite. Similarly they have asserted a logical connection between the idea of conflict-free progress and a bourgeoisie seeking to legitimate itself against both a feudal aristocracy and an emerging working class. Nor should it be surprising to find advocates of revolutionary social change like Marx and Engels maintaining that change through conflict is the law of the natural and social world.

The Marxian dialectic involves some very broad assumptions about change and interaction that—like their contraries—appear impossible to verify by historical tests.

Conventional political thought often assumes what exists is normal and change is what must be explained. The Marxian dialectic tends conversely to regard change as normal and stability as merely a passing appearance. This assumption makes it difficult to explain stability, let alone retrogression. It has been said that Marxists are always at risk from the danger of looking at every situation as if it were about to dissolve. Further, the Marxian view tends to rule out a priori the possibility of conflict-free change and to imply that only revolutionary change is real. Crippling or even disastrous political conclusions can result from these unverifiable presuppositions—for example, that the inevitability of communism made the ascendancy of Nazism impossible.

The Marxian dialectic also arbitrarily emphasizes the interrelatedness of the whole over the distinct identity of the parts. In this perspective "the truth is the whole." Reality forms a system in which all elements are actually manifestations of "internal relations" within the whole.

The assertion that everything is related to everything is not false. But it provides no way to distinguish more and less significant relations. Marxism "solved" this problem by asserting that economic production and exchange are *the* significant relations and that the social classes that express economic relations are *the* significant social actors.[7]

This view provided Marxism a powerful tool to integrate the whole social field into a coherent totality. The problem is that it was too coherent—to the point of class monomania. A paradigm that started as a holistic approach often ended up producing an extreme reductionism in which all the complexities, ambiguities, and contradictions of social life were reduced to the class struggle between workers and capitalists.

As social movements increasingly focused on nonclass issues, ranging from the oppression of women to nuclear exterminism to the environment, the Marxist paradigm generated more and more anomalies. While heroic efforts at interpretation could still give it a degree of relevance and coherence, the effort seemed less and less justified by the payoff. Much social movement thought moved toward "postmodernism," in some versions of which the search for coherent wholes was itself excoriated and abandoned. But this approach did not obviate social movements' need for understanding social connections.

An additional problem results from the way the Marxian dialectic uses language and concepts to represent change and interaction—something I have had to grapple with constantly as a writer. As Ollman explains, the Marxian dialectic requires "expanding our notion of anything to include, as aspects of what it is, both the process by which it has become that and the broader interactive context in which it is found." Dialectics "restructures our thinking about reality" by "replacing the commonsense notion of 'thing' (as something that has a history and has external connections with other things) with notions of 'process' (which contains its history and possible futures) and 'relation' (which contains as part of what it is its ties with other relations.)"[8] A classic example is the way Marx transformed the economists' term "capital" from meaning money and physical means of production to meaning the historically developing exploitative relationship between workers and capitalists. It was this feature of Marxism that made Italian sociologist Vilfredo Pareto complain in exasperation, "Marx's words are like bats. One can see in them both birds and mice."[9]

Ollman notes that Marx does not present definitions of his concepts and records his initial shock at discovering that the apparent meanings of Marx's key concepts "varied with the context, often considerably."[10] Ollman and others have plausibly defended this as a valid way to deal with an interrelated and changing reality, and it may not be inherently illegitimate, but it sure can be confusing.

There is nothing wrong with using a noun to refer to a process rather than to an entity or substance. Such terms as "arms race," "class struggle," and "racialization" do just that.[11] Nor is there a problem using a noun to refer to an entity that undergoes change, as long as it is clearly defined as such: it's fine to use the noun "oak" to refer to the entity that begins as an acorn and ends as a mighty tree.

The problem comes when we take a term normally used to refer to an entity and use it to refer instead to a process. Thus "capital" might normally be defined as wealth used for production. Marx uses it instead to refer to something we eventually come to understand as the entire process by which surplus-value is extracted from labor in a society divided into owners and nonowners of the means of production.

There is nothing unacceptable about this concept—in fact, it is quite useful for understanding capitalist economies. Yet the strategy of using the language of entities to refer to processes does make problems, especially where, as in Marx, terms are rarely defined.

Marx's linguistic strategy can make the meaning of words very different for those operating inside and outside the paradigm. To outsiders, Marxists can sometimes sound like members of a cult guided by esoteric understandings accessible only to initiates.[12] For them, the presuppositions of that understanding are not assumptions but reality. This is a dubious strategy for organizing open, democratic, participatory dialogue to guide social action.

The absence of defined terms makes verification outside the assumptions of the theory difficult at best. As Ollman acknowledges, the results of Marx's investigations are "prescribed to a large degree by the preliminary organization of his subject matter."[13] Yet Marxism provides few means to test the validity of its "preliminary organization." When empirical data is inconvenient for the theory, the theory can often be readjusted to eliminate the inconvenience. The result is a theory that is self-validating. This is particularly true of the theory's most fundamental principles, such as the assertion that all is change, which is as unverifiable as the contrary assertion that only the unchanging is real.[14]

Over many years I've tried to learn as much as I could from Marx and the Marxist tradition but to translate its concepts into more explicit descriptions of processes. In *Strike!*, for example, I described class conflict as a process in which workers and employers battled, but not as one that could be reduced to the conflict of abstract entities like "labor" against "capital." Such a procedure leads, I hope, to clearer and more testable descriptions.

Marx's dialectic is a theory of development. As Engels put it, "the dialectical laws are really laws of development."[15] But Marxism is not the only theory of development. I've continued to search for ways of thinking about development that escape some of the problems of the Marxian dialectic. I've pursued approaches that don't take for granted the priority of either change or stability. I've sought ways of thinking that allow the identification of significant connections and relations without falling into either the triviality that everything is related to everything else or arbitrarily assuming that one set of relations is a priori more real or significant than others. I've looked for ways to understand structures, wholes, and systems that escape self-validation by allowing testing against evidence. And I've sought ways to talk about change and interaction that are accessible to open dialogue among people with different experiences and perspectives.

This quest has led me to explore ways of thinking ranging from pragmatism to cybernetics and from open systems theory to Jean

Piaget's equilibration to today's complexity theory. I hope what I've purloined from them can sharpen at least a bit the weapons we have to wield against the despair of necessity.

CHAPTER 8

Learning by Doing

How do people develop new ways of thinking and acting? Your answer to this question is likely to affect your interpretation of Black Reconstruction, the 1973 meat boycott, Occupy Wall Street, or the great periods of mass strike in American history.

Most answers tend toward one of two poles. At one, some leader, thinker, organization, or other outside force inculcates new ideas and behaviors in relatively passive people. At the other, what appear to be new patterns actually repose preformed in the actor, only needing to be evoked by appropriate circumstances. But there is a third alternative: that people can produce new knowledge of the world and new ways of acting on it as part of their action in the world. I learned about this approach, commonly known as "pragmatism," from its most famous exponent, the American philosopher John Dewey, but also from Rosa Luxemburg and others in the Marxist tradition who developed a form of Marxism "tainted" by pragmatism.

I had to face this question when I was writing *Strike!* Mass actions could be viewed as the product of great leaders, radical agitators, or powerful organizations. Or they could be seen as automatic, reflex reactions to wage cuts and tyranny on the job. While these approaches may have some elements of truth in particular situations, I have been unsympathetic to them as general interpretive frameworks for social movements and common preservations. If workers and other oppressed people were blank slates written on by radicals, leaders, and organizations, why were slaves, housewives, and other groups untutored by such external forces able to form movements like Black Reconstruction, the 1973 meat boycott, and the great mass strikes I described in *Strike!*? Conversely, if the workers or blacks or housewives revolted because of their essence or nature, why weren't they in revolt all the time?

I got a clue from the revolutionary thinker and activist Rosa Luxemburg. For Luxemburg, mass strikes and other social movements developed through a process of collective learning. This learning was not cut off from action, but instead was part of the same process. Learning occurred through social experiment. Each social act was a test, which the actors could evaluate and from which they could draw conclusions. For example, she portrayed the frequent demonstrations called by the Spartikusbund during the German Revolution of 1918–19 as tests to discover the temper and mindset of the masses.

Of course, as a good scientific Marxist Luxemburg knew the conclusion workers would ultimately have to come up with—socialist revolution. But she saw the process of coming to this conclusion as something workers had to produce for themselves.

Luxemburg wrote about mass strikes: "The modern proletarian class does not carry out its struggle according to a plan set out in some book or theory." The modern workers' struggle is "a part of history, a part of social progress." It is "in the middle of history, in the middle of progress, in the middle of the fight" that "we learn how we must fight." Working people "forge from their own consciousness, from their own belief, and even from their own understanding the weapons of their own liberation."[1]

In *Strike!* I tried to test this approach against the historical evidence of mass strikes in America. I noted many instances when workers learned lessons from their ongoing actions. I found, for example, "the action of one group of workers often serves as the triggering example to large numbers of others."

> The strike and defeat of the militia in Martinsburg, West Virginia started a chain reaction in the Great Upheaval of 1877; victory over the nation's most notorious industrial magnate in the first Gould strike was a major factor precipitating the struggles of 1886; similarly, the Great Northern strike laid the basis for the Pullman strike and the mass strikes of 1894; and it was the successful sitdowns of the rubberworkers that triggered the sitdown wave of 1936-7.[2]

Each exemplary action "demonstrated the power workers held because they could stop production" thus "infusing other workers with self-confidence and an appreciation of their own power."

In other cases it was defeat or the threat of impending defeat that drove home the need for a wider solidarity and more forceful tactics.

> The dramatic defeat of the Homestead strike of 1892 at the hands of the Carnegie Steel Company and the state militia had a great impact on workers throughout the country, laying the groundwork for the sense of class war that accompanied the 1894 Pullman strike and the intense solidarity revealed in that struggle. Similarly, the San Francisco general strike of 1934 resulted from the impending defeat of the longshoremen by the National Guard. And the solidarity that marked the General Motors strike of 1936–1937 grew largely from the experience of defeats in the preceding years in isolated plants in Toledo, Cleveland, and elsewhere.

Thus mass strikes revealed "an evolution based on lessons learned from the successes and failures of the recent past."[3]

I found grounding for this view of social change as collective learning through action from an unexpected source—John Dewey.[4] Dewey was regarded as the dominant American philosopher for much of the twentieth century; historian Henry Steele Commager described him as "the guide, the mentor, and the conscience of the American people."[5] He was widely viewed as the personification of democracy, which he characterized as "the one, ultimate, ethical ideal of humanity."[6] For many on the left, however, his philosophy of "pragmatism" represented liberalism as acceptance of the capitalist and imperialist status quo. One left-wing critic called Dewey "the leading philosopher of U.S. imperialism."[7]

John Dewey took the idea of evolutionary adaptation from Charles Darwin and applied it to human thought and action. His pragmatism envisioned adaptation not simply as acquiescence to the status quo, however, but as transformation of it. Dewey emphasized the adjustment of the organism to its environment—but he defined "adjustment" as including "an adaptation of the environment to the individual's needs and ends, rather than vice versa."[8] Call it adaptation by transformation.

Dewey portrayed thinking as a response to problems people cannot solve with their existing patterns of adaptation. Reflective inquiry comes to the fore when "there is something seriously the matter, some trouble, due to active discordance, dissentiency, conflict among the factors of a prior nonintellectual experience."[9] Some such presumption must underlie the procedure I intuitively adopt of starting any inquiry from a problem to be solved, and of explaining change in people's action as a response to a problem they face.

Dewey emphasized the close relation between thought and action. He viewed people's ideas as a means for them to act in the world. As one of his biographers put it, for Dewey "ideas were hypotheses or plans of action, the truth of which rested on their ability to 'work' in experience."[10] In a *Root & Branch* article more or less contemporaneous with *Strike!* I wrote, "Ideas, insofar as they are relevant to action, are essentially maps of the environment and plans for how to operate in it. They are generally accepted or rejected on the basis of how well the predictions based on them allow people to function in the world."[11] Though I associated this approach more with the version of Marxism I was absorbing from Luxemburg and the advocate of workers' councils Anton Pannekoek, it surely amounts to Dewey-style pragmatism.[12]

Dewey pointed out that people use the results of their action to improve their thinking; Dewey's approach to education, for example, is often summed up as "learning by doing." That requires a loop between thought and action, between theory and practice—what he called experiment and what would later be dubbed "feedback." Action expresses thought, but thought also changes as a result of action. This can be seen as an aspect of the more general tendency of biological organisms both to maintain their organization and to adapt to their environment.

The interpretation of pragmatism became pressing for me when I was writing *Strike!* and trying to understand the history of American trade unionism. Dewey's protestations to the contrary notwithstanding, "pragmatic adaptation" has often come to refer to acquiescence in the status quo. Historians of American trade unionism like John R. Commons praised the conservatism of what is often called "business unionism" as an expression of American "pragmatism." They argued that the success of trade unions as institutions within the existing economic system depended on their sloughing off utopian aspirations that could not be achieved within that framework.[13]

But this way of applying pragmatism seemed to me one-sided. It ignored the repeated breakdown of trade union adaptation. In periods of crisis, trade unions either collapsed altogether or at least lost the power to maintain workers' conditions of life at currently acceptable levels. With this breakdown of adaptation, a new adaptive process started up as workers searched experimentally for new forms of organization and action based on their own collective power. Mass strikes were a response to the breakdown of existing modes of adaptation and an attempt to find new ones. Far from being the product of utopian fantasies, they were an attempt to construct a pragmatic "adjustment" that would provide "an adaptation of the environment to the individual's needs and ends."[14] They represented adaptation by transformation.

The possibility that people could collectively learn in the course of action how to improve future action was important to me, as it was for both Dewey and Luxemburg. If people have to be instructed by some special group of leaders, intellectuals, party officials, or other authorities in order to change their ways, then those authorities are likely to be in a position to dominate them not only in the present but in the future. But if people can form their own collective subjects—think, learn, and act as a group—then perhaps they do not need an external authority to tell them what to do. They can learn what to do through their own experience. Of course, some people may think, learn, and act sooner than others and help lead the way for them; but that does not require a separate group with a special font of knowledge. The ability to learn and change collectively through action seemed to me a potential basis for human freedom and democracy.

I saw that capacity for social learning as also a means to keep social movements from going wrong. I grew up in the shadow of an "actually existing Communism" whose roots were in Marxism and the movement for worker liberation but which had produced a system of domination and tyranny in which actually existing workers were largely power-less and their freedoms largely extinguished. While numerous causes have been suggested for this disturbing development, I learned from Rosa Luxemburg that one of them was an elitism often lurking within the very communist and socialist movements that purported to seek freedom for workers and society as a whole.

In his foundational pamphlet *What Is to Be Done*, Lenin had written, "The history of all countries shows that the working class, exclusively by its own effort, is able to develop only trade-union consciousness"[15]—in contrast to a deeper "socialist consciousness." Then he quoted with approval the leading socialist theorist of the day, Karl Kautsky:

The vehicle of science is not the proletariat, but the bourgeois intelligentsia: it was in the minds of individual members of this stratum that modern socialism originated, and it was they who communicated it to the more intellectually developed proletarians who, in their turn, introduce it into the proletarian class struggles where conditions allow that to be done. Thus, socialist consciousness is something introduced into the proletarian class struggle from without.[16]

Luxemburg argued to the contrary that socialist consciousness is something that workers construct through their own struggles. It is only through a process of trial and error that they can gain improved understandings. As she put it in her polemic against the centralized party direction Lenin advocated in *What Is to Be Done*, "the only 'subject' which merits today the role of director is the collective 'ego' of the working class. The working class demands the right to make its mistakes and learn in the dialectic of history." She added scornfully, "The errors committed by a truly revolutionary movement are infinitely more fruitful than the infallibility of the cleverest Central Committee.[17]

I tried to develop this idea of collective learning "in the dialectic of history" on the basis of what I was discovering in my study of American mass strikes. In a 1973 symposium, *Strike!* was criticized for its approach to the "consciousness necessary for socialist revolution." I didn't try to question the teleological presuppositions of such a critique, but I did respond in light of the experimentalist approach I had learned from Rosa Luxemburg and my study of American working-class history.[18]

Such a consciousness consists in workers' "shared understanding that they can collectively initiate and control their own action to meet their own needs." Such an understanding "does not flow directly and automatically from the position of workers in production." Nor does it arise primarily from "the speeches, manifestoes, and other 'consciousness-raising' activities of the Left," though they may make some contribution to it. The working class can come to understand its power *"only by acting."* It is only in their own action that "workers can see the evidence of their potential power." It is only because workers strike that their "power to bring society to a halt" seems "more than a dream." It is only because workers stick together in struggles that their "co-operative take-over of society" is conceivable. It is only because they plan and organize their activities themselves that the "planned co-ordination of production by those who produce" can be imagined.[19]

While I gradually learned to supplement the teleological Marxist worldview and idiom in which these debates occurred with less deterministic ones, the idea of collective action as a series of experiments in which people learn through trial and error how to act more effectively has become a keystone of my common preservation heuristic.

CHAPTER 9

Feedback

In *Strike!* I described how people turned from individual to collective strategies when their current strategies weren't working. I recounted how groups of workers turned to wider forms of mutual aid both because of successes they interpreted as indicating that collective action was working and because of failures they interpreted as indicating that still wider solidarity was needed. Such development of new forms of action resulted from the information circuit that reported back to them the results of their past action. Around the time I was finishing *Strike!* I began discovering thinkers in a variety of fields who were exploring such "loopy" processes as part of a much more general pattern of what was coming to be called "feedback."[1]

In classical physics, things move because forces affect them. From Newton's time onward, the aspiration of science had been to find causal chains that explain the behavior of objects by identifying the forces that impinge on them. But around the time I was first beginning to try to understand social change, this "linear" way of thinking based on sequences of causation was starting to be challenged by "nonlinear" approaches based on the concept of feedback. Feedback became central to my understanding of how people and society change—including how they develop new forms of common preservation.

Long before the term "feedback" was invented, the underlying principle had popped up in fields ranging from windmill and steam engine design to human physiology. In *The Wisdom of the Body*, for example, the American physiologist Walter Cannon explained that organisms have a certain "steady state" to which they tend. If their temperature, or salt/water balance, or other variables rise too high or fall too low, that triggers mechanisms to counter the excess and return the body to its normal equilibrium or steady state.

"Homeostasis" is the term Cannon used for the stable conditions created by such processes. Consider, for example, a room with a furnace hooked up to a thermostat. The thermostat is a "control device" composed of a thermometer connected to a switch. If the temperature in the room falls below the thermostat's lower setting, the switch is triggered and turns on the furnace. When the furnace raises the room's temperature above the thermostat's upper setting, the switch is reversed and the furnace turned off. This homeostatic system will tend toward a certain equilibrium or goal or steady state—a normal temperature range for the room.[2]

The idea of feedback is now so ubiquitous that it is hard to realize how new it is as a general concept. Ironically, it was first fully developed in order to guide radar-directed antiaircraft weapons. A projectile might be aimed at its target, but meanwhile the target was moving and the projectile itself was affected by variations in the external environment, such as wind, and by slight imperfections in its own functioning, that diverted it from its intended path. The concept of feedback was developed in the process of solving this problem. Sensors would identify the actual positions of the projectile and the target. A control device would compare their actual locations to the intended trajectory of the projectile. If the two differed, the control device would calculate the amount and direction of correction needed. It would then activate some kind of effecter—a rudder or a side rocket, for example—to direct the projectile back to the required path.

The signal sent by the sensor was dubbed "feedback." Feedback was information—in Gregory Bateson's phrase, "news of a difference." The circuit that carried the information was called a "feedback loop."[3]

Mathematician Norbert Wiener, who developed the concept of feedback, invented the term "cybernetics" (now, oddly, used to describe almost anything having to do with computers) as a label for the whole range of phenomena controlled by feedback. He took the term from the Greek word for "steersman." The steersman of a boat observes its course and compares it with the course desired. The steersman then moves the rudder in a way that changes the course to correct or compensate for the discrepancy between the two. Others have called this idea "control theory" or "regulation."[4]

Such circular, "cybernetic" principles can be identified in many kinds of social processes. When, in the early 1960s, scientists discovered that nuclear testing was releasing radioactive strontium-90 that was lodging in children's baby teeth, threatening them with cancer and birth defects, some scientists rapidly disseminated the information to the public. Millions of people joined the movement for a nuclear test-ban treaty. Such a treaty became US policy, and soon most countries in the world had halted nuclear testing. Global common preservation had become a crucial means to national (and species) self-preservation. That happened because there was some kind of loop between an action (nuclear testing), its results (dangerous nuclear fallout), and modified action (protest and a test ban).

Such regulation by feedback makes it impossible to distinguish what is cause and what is effect, since within such a system cause and effect form a loop. This leads to phenomena that don't resemble a conventional causal chain. Of course, all the actions of the human body, the thermostat, the antiaircraft projectile, and the steersman follow the presumably universal laws of physics. But they are steered or controlled by a process that pursues a goal, purpose, or norm—in short, an end—that is not just a result of the blind impact of one object on another. Indeed, such cybernetic loops could be intentionally used to counteract unguided chains of cause and effect and thereby realize an end.

In a commonsense view of purpose, one conceives of a goal and then takes action to reach it. But a cybernetic loop operates through negation. Action is not taken directly to achieve the goal, but rather indirectly by reducing the deviation from the goal.[5] Similarly, cybernetics explains events not by describing their causes, but rather by the absence, removal, or counteracting of that which prevents them from occurring.

Many people find the metaphors of thermostats and guided missiles cold and mechanical. So let us return to the metaphor of a workshop for another image of the cybernetic feedback loop.[6]

If the workers in the workshop just make things according to their established plans and patterns, there is no way to tell if those products have deficiencies for meeting their purpose or if they could meet it better. Their products have to go out and be tested in the world outside the workshop. Someone has to use them and see how well they do their job. Then the results must be reported back to the workshop. For example, the denizens of the workshop may learn that a product breaks down whenever the weather gets too hot. They may learn this from the results of a consumer products testing lab, from angry letters of complaint from users, or from their own site visits to consumers.

In each case, the information must somehow get back to the workshop. The workers in the workshop then take out the original plans for the product and compare them to the condition that has been discovered. They try to identify what is wrong with the original plans. For example, the motor may generate heat and the product has no way to dissipate it, so that in hot weather it just gets hotter and hotter. Or a particular part may be extremely sensitive to heat and cease to function properly when it gets too hot.

The workers then try to find a solution to the problem. They may add a vent and fan to dissipate the heat. They may replace the oversensitive part with one made of a less heat-sensitive material. They may add to the product manual an instruction to shut the product down for ten minutes every hour in hot weather to let it cool off. The solution must somehow counteract or compensate for the problem.

Next the change is incorporated in the product's design—in the pattern from which it is produced. The workers implement the modified design to produce what they hope is an improved product.

Then the product must go back out of the workshop and be tested "under combat conditions." Does it still overheat or has the problem been fixed? If the problem has been solved, the workshop denizens need to find that out and incorporate the modified design in their future production. If the problem has not been solved, they need to go "back to the drawing boards" and try to come up with an alternative solution.

Such a "product improvement cycle" illustrates what I mean by a "feedback loop" that guides actors to produce actions that better realize their ends.

The concept of feedback has been used to design weapons, automatic machine tools, and highway systems; advocates of "systems analysis" hoped to use it to control human society as a whole. But Wiener, who coined the term feedback, rejected that approach. As historian of technology David Noble wrote, "Wiener insisted upon the indeterminacy of systems."

> His approach, reflecting a lifelong interest in biology and a morality based upon independent acts of conscience, was organic,

ecological, and human. He emphasized especially that living systems were open and contingent rather than closed and deterministic because the 'steersman,' the self-correcting mechanism, was human in social systems and thus moved not by formal logic but by skill, experience, and purpose.[7]

Warning against the dangers of modern technology running amok, Wiener advocated that the social application of the cybernetic concept should be "a constant feedback that would allow an individual to intervene and call a halt to a process initiated, thus permitting him second thoughts in response to unexpected effects and the opportunity to recast his wishes."

Wiener exemplified that idea in his own life, for example by publicly refusing to work on military projects. The "practical use of guided missiles can only be to kill foreign civilians indiscriminately. If therefore I do not desire to participate in the bombing or poisoning of defenseless peoples—and I most certainly do not—I must take a serious responsibility as to those to whom I disclose my scientific ideas."[8] Instead he turned his knowledge of control devices, honed on weapons production, to the design of prosthetic devices, which might help rehabilitate the victims of war.[9]

Wiener also wrote public warnings about the social implications of emerging technology, such as a 1947 letter to the *Atlantic Monthly* headed "A Scientist Rebels."[10] He wrote United Auto Workers president Walter Reuther warning of the dangers of industrial automation and proposing to cooperate in a campaign to assure that the radical advances in technology then looming would benefit rather than harm labor.[11] His actions reveal that "feedback" is not just a way that people can be forced to conform to society, but that it can serve as a means to help people change it.

While it was anticipated by many thinkers, including Aristotle, Darwin, Marx, Dewey, and Piaget, cybernetics provided a way to explain explicitly much that had previously been only vaguely intuited. As physicist, and early associate of Wiener, Heinz von Foerster put it, "cybernetics introduced a way of thinking which is implicit in so many fields" but "not explicitly referred to as cybernetics." Eventually cybernetics "melted, as a field" into many other fields. John Dixon, a founding member of the American Society for Cybernetics, said, "the word cybernetics dropped out, but Wiener's work continues under many other names. Look at the development of brain research, mathematical modeling, computers, networking. All of this you could claim is cybernetics."[12]

Like many others, I began using cybernetic concepts to try to make my own vague intuitions clearer and more explicit. In the case of the 1973 meat boycott, for example, I began to think about the everyday activity of shopping, the dawning awareness of price increases, the testing of others' responses to them, the shift to a collective strategy using a boycott, the initiation of the boycott, and the decision to extend it nationally as a result of its success, all as examples of feedback loops between action, evaluation, and modified action.

CHAPTER 10

Open Systems

Far from the world of American weapons laboratories, the Austrian biologist Ludwig von Bertalanffy was developing the concept of "open systems" as a way of thinking about organisms.[1] Walter Cannon had shown how organisms tend toward an internal equilibrium or steady state through the use of feedback loops. But Bertalanffy saw that internal homeostasis was only half the organism's story. In isolation, an organism would quickly die through suffocation, dehydration, starvation, or the accumulation of wastes. It is only able to maintain its norms or "state variables" by importing matter and energy from outside, from its environment, and by exporting waste material that would otherwise poison it. Bertalanffy called such a system, one which maintains its norms by means of interchange with its environment, an "open system."

The secret of such an open system is the semipermeability of its boundaries. Such boundaries selectively let certain matter and information in and out, but prevent other stuff from crossing. Such a system can counter the natural tendency toward disorganization, known as entropy. In the case of an animal, imported air (inhalation) prevents suffocation; imported water (drinking) prevents dehydration; imported food (eating) prevents starvation. Export (exhalation, urination, defecation) gets rid of poisonous waste materials. Fur keeps in heat by insulation; sweating gets rid of it by evaporation. Semipermeability, in short, is the quick of life.

The theory of open systems initially distinguishes between a system and its environment. But in many cases "the environment" turns out to be composed of other open systems. An individual cell, for example, is an open system, maintaining its own patterns by importing nutrients and exporting wastes through its semipermeable cell wall. But the environment of the individual cell is actually the organism of which it is part. And the science of ecology shows that the individual organism in turn lives in an environment that is actually the eco-system of which it is part, composed largely of other organisms and their products. So open systems may form a hierarchy in which each system includes sub-systems and is part of larger meta-systems. The theory of open systems thus becomes a theory of multilevel parts and wholes, both separated and connected by semipermeable boundaries.

This idea has gradually taken hold in biology as an alternative to what paleontologist Stephen Jay Gould described as the Darwinian tradition that reduces "all large-scale evolutionary phenomena to extrapolated results of natural selection working at the level of individual organisms within populations." The alternative recognizes "genes, organisms, and species as legitimate entities in a sequence of levels with unique explanatory principles emerging at each more inclusive plateau."[2] Such models try to understand nature as "a hierarchy of interdependent levels, each coherent in itself, but each linked by ties of feedback to adjacent levels." No level is "an ultimate reality and reference point for extrapolation"; all are "legitimate, interacting aspects of our natural world."[3]

Perhaps because it started with organisms, or perhaps because boundaries tend to be imagined in terms of spatial metaphors, open systems theory has tended to portray systems, subsystems, and meta-systems as nesting neatly within each other. But in fact, different systems and subsystems can overlap and their boundaries can cut across each other. A migrating bird may be part of a tropical ecosystem in one season and an arctic one the next. The penis is part of both the urinary system and the sexual system. A slime mold may form a contiguous unit at one time, disperse into physically separate parts connected only by communications links, and then come back together, all the time functioning as a single organism.

The open systems idea suggests obvious parallels to human social life. Human individuals can be conceived as open systems that pursue their own "state variables" by means of their interaction with the environment. (That can include, as Dewey emphasized, "adaptation of the environment to the individual's needs and ends, rather than vice versa.")[4] That environment is largely composed of the social groups and organizations of which individuals are part—themselves likely to be open systems.

But the application of systems models to society can also lead to misconceptions based on false analogies between different kinds of systems. Societies, for example, have often been compared to individual organisms. But there are problems with such a comparison. The groups and institutions that people are part of often overlap and cut across each other's boundaries, so that people are part of many different meta-systems.[5] That makes it problematic to regard "a society" as a bounded and integrated whole in the same way that an organism is.

Organisms are generally much more closely integrated than societies, with their parts much more intensely interdependent. Societies make radical, unprecedented changes in ways that individual organisms do not. Their goals are not genetically wired in like those of organisms. When organisms die so do their subsystems; when societies are dissolved, individuals, groups, and institutions that have been part of them may live on. Both organisms and societies may be open systems, but of very different kinds. It would be difficult to find an organism manifesting equivalents of the American Civil War or the transformation from feudalism to capitalism.

To deal with such differences, Bertalanffy proposed a meta-theory that would compare theories about different kinds of systems, to find both what they had in common and the features that made them different. He called it "general systems theory." I came to regard my own approach to social change as fitting into the general family of systems theories.

Like Norbert Wiener, Bertalanffy saw his theory as an alternative to, not an expression of, the drive to control human society from above. He closed his introductory essay on "The Meaning of General Systems Theory":

> Human society is not a community of ants or termites, governed by inherited instinct and controlled by the laws of the superordinate whole; it is based upon the achievements of the individual and is doomed if the individual is made a cog in the social machine. This, I believe, is the ultimate precept a theory of organization can give: not a manual for dictators of any denomination more efficiently to subjugate human beings by the scientific application of Iron Laws, but a warning that the Leviathan of organization must not swallow the individual without sealing its own inevitable doom.[6]

The use of systems ideas does not imply that everything is caused or can be explained by the system of which it is part. As international politics scholar Robert Jervis wrote, "Few if any realms of human conduct are completely determined at the systems level. Actors' choices are crucial."[7] This does not, however, mean "an absence of regularities." Systems may not completely determine actions and events, but even incomplete or weak systems produce what Jervis calls "systems effects." The common preservation heuristic uses systems ideas not to provide complete determination, but to alert us to such system effects.

According to systems theory, a multi-level open system reproduces its established patterns through the action of its subsystems. Some systems theorists seem to indicate that this allows only the two possibilities of reproduction and breakdown. But there is a third possibility: the subsystems within such a system may instead coordinate with each other—or with others outside the boundary of their own metasystem—to impose new patterns different from those of the currently dominant system.

Such coalitions can lead to change that neither simply reproduces the system's norms more effectively nor replaces them with total disorder. For me, open systems theory suggested a way to understand how systems can be changed "from below." And why shouldn't such changes include the emergence of new common preservations?

When I first started doing research on the history of the brass workers in the Naugatuck Valley of Connecticut, local people told me I'd never understand this place unless I recognized that in the olden days Waterbury was all sectioned off and people didn't mingle too well. Indeed, as I dug deeper into the city's history, I discovered that in the early twentieth century its working class was largely divided into segregated ethnic communities, each speaking its own language, living in its own neighborhoods, embedded in its own churches, clubs, stores, and other ethnic institutions, and isolated by its own traditions and customs. They formed bounded, not-so-permeable systems.

In the brass plants jobs were ethnically stratified, with the skilled machinist jobs overwhelmingly held by workers of British and northern European background, common labor jobs held by Eastern and Southern European and French-Canadian immigrants, and the "hot and heavy" jobs in the foundries held by African Americans. In the Waterbury general strikes of 1919 and 1920, interethnic cooperation was tenuous;

each ethnic group had its own union and held its meetings and rallies separately in its own language.

Two decades later, however, brass workers organized in inclusive industrial unions. A major objective was to establish seniority systems for job advancement that would eliminate ethnic and other favoritism. While ethnicity remained a factor in union politics, it was far less divisive in strikes and other union actions. Workers had learned that they would be powerless unless they stuck together across racial and ethnic lines. Industrial unionism also replaced a rather gradual gradient between skilled workers and bosses with a more defined division between workers and management. This complex transformation of boundaries was a critical dimension of the rise of industrial unionism and the transformation of the community's class structure.[8]

CHAPTER 11

The Abolition of Society

The conventional way to apply systems theory to human social life has been to define societies as systems—bounded entities whose various structures fit more or less tightly together to form integrated wholes. Marxists, Weberians, and many other sociologists accept one or another version of this framework. It was summed up by Walter Buckley in the compendium *Modern Systems Research for the Behavioral Scientist*: "Society" as a "complex adaptive system."[1]

I was already backing away from this unitary idea of "society" in *Common Sense for Hard Times*, but I didn't know how to formulate an alternative. It was a breakthrough when one day in a bookstore I picked up *The Sources of Social Power* by British historical sociologist Michael Mann.[2] Mann provided me an alternative vision: "Since the rise of civilization, human existence is structured primarily by power networks—states, markets, military organizations, and ideologies—whose boundaries do not necessarily or even normally coincide and which do not form the kind of system normally thought of as 'a society.'"[3] He goes so far as to say, "If I could, I would abolish the concept of 'society' altogether."[4] The development and interaction of such networks provided a different way to translate the abstract systems principles I had been struggling with into an interpretation of concrete social processes.

Mann starts from the idea that human beings have many goals and set up many networks of social relationships to pursue them. The networks established for raising children, for meeting material needs, for finding meaning in life, and for protecting against attack or pillaging others do not normally coincide; in fact, they are far more likely to overlap and intersect. Further, such networks tend to be "promiscuous," drawing on many kinds of economic, political, military, and ideological resources.

According to Mann, bringing about cooperation is the essence of a power source. "Collective power" arises when persons in cooperation can enhance their joint power over third parties or over nature.[5] As I had already concluded from my own experience and study of social movements, power originates in coordination.

Mann notes that collective power can be distributed unequally. The result is "distributive power"—the power of some people over others within a system of coordinated action.[6] It can range from the power of military commanders over their troops to the power of the wealthy over the poor to the power of masters over slaves.

Collective power itself tends to foster distributive power: "In implementing collective goals, social organization and a division of labor are set up. Organization and division of function carry an inherent tendency to distributive power, deriving from supervision and coordination.... Those who occupy supervisory and coordinating positions have an immense organizational superiority over the others."[7]

Another way to put this is that coordination provides collective benefits. People therefore comply with those who provide coordination. But those who control coordination may be able to extend their power to pursue their own interests rather than collective ones.[8] People may support a leader who proposes programs that are in their interest, but the leader may use their office to enrich themselves at the expense of their constituents, for example.

Collective and distributive power are usually intertwined. This helps explain why distributive power is so often acquiesced in by those who are distributed less of it. "The masses comply because they lack collective organization to do otherwise, because they are embedded within collective and distributive power organizations controlled by others. They are *organizationally outflanked*."[9] Though "anyone can refuse to obey," opportunities are often lacking for "establishing alternative machinery" for implementing their goals.[10] (We will see in the next chapter how such a refusal to obey can be parlayed into the "power of the powerless.")

How then can social change possibly occur? Mann proposes that the characteristic way that new solutions to social problems emerge is through neither revolution nor reform. Rather, a new solution develops in what he calls "interstitial locations"—nooks and crannies in and around the dominant institutions. Those who were initially marginal then link together in ways that allow them to outflank the dominant institutions and force a reorganization of the status quo.[11]

At certain points, people see existing power institutions as blocking goals that could be attained by cooperation that transcends those institutions. So people develop new networks that outrun them. Such movements create subversive "invisible connections" across institutional boundaries.[12] These interstitial networks translate human goals into organizational means. In short, they establish new patterns of coordination.

To link groups with disparate traditions and experiences, such networks use what are variously referred to as shared worldviews, paradigms, visions, frames, or ideologies. Such belief systems unite seemingly disparate human beings by claiming that they have meaningful common properties: "An ideology will emerge as a powerful, autonomous movement when it can put together in a single explanation and organization a number of aspects of experience that have hitherto been marginal, interstitial to the dominant institutions of power."[13]

The emerging belief system becomes a guide for efforts to transform the world. It defines common values and norms, providing the basis for a common program. When a network draws together people and practices from many formerly marginalized social spaces and makes it possible for them to act together, it establishes an independent source of power. Ultimately, new power networks may become strong enough to reorganize the dominant institutional configuration. If they do, common preservation has transformed society.

The rise of labor and socialist movements in the nineteenth century and of feminist and environmental movements in the twentieth century in many ways fits this model of emergence at the margins, linking, and outflanking. So, ironically, does the emergence of economic globalization.

Self-organization in marginal locations can be synergistic with transforming dominant institutions. The rising European bourgeoisie both created their own market institutions and fought to restructure the feudal political system to allow markets to develop more freely. Labor movements both organized marginalized workers into unions and forced governments to protect labor rights, which in turn facilitated the growth of unions, which thereby increased the pressure for extending labor rights.

Mann's approach to social change easily fits the one I was developing in my common preservation heuristic. It starts from a gap between people's goals and the existing organization of society. That gap leads actors to seek new patterns of coordination. They do so by constructing shared representations of their identity, goals, situation, and potential for action. These become the basis for coordinating actions that transcend the status quo and may eventually transform it.

Mann points out that the problems faced by humanity today—the familiar laundry list of ecological, military, and economic calamities—require fundamentally new solutions. They are not the problems which existing institutions developed to solve; therefore existing institutions are unlikely to be effective at solving them.

Mann says such maladaptation of existing institutions to emerging problems has been a common situation in human history. As a result, major social change usually comes from social locations that are interstitial to existing institutions. Such locations can exist precisely because society is not a unitary whole, but rather is composed of overlapping networks whose boundaries do not normally coincide.

In *Globalization from Below*, my collaborators and I explicitly used Mann's analysis to propose a strategy for the emerging movement we called "globalization from below." After paraphrasing "invisible connections" between "interstitial locations" as "linking the nooks and crannies," we wrote: "Social movements may lack the obvious paraphernalia of power: armies, wealth, palaces, temples, and bureaucracies. But by linking from the nooks and crannies, developing a common vision and program, and withdrawing their consent from existing institutions, they can impose norms on states, classes, armies, and other power actors."[14]

We called it the "Lilliput strategy."

CHAPTER 12

The Power of the Powerless

From the first time I read *Black Reconstruction*, I wondered how people who appeared powerless and dominated by others could gain the power to change their conditions. It was not only a question of how they could organize themselves, but also how they could overcome domination and assert their own power. It seemed a paradox—how could individuals, or even organized groups, succeed against powerful forces that controlled the wealth, the organization, the established authority, and above all the means of violence to use against them?

That question continued to preoccupy me as the antiwar movement struggled to end the US war in Vietnam. Although the movement refuted every argument for the war, organized protest demonstrations with a million or more people, and won over a substantial majority of the population, the war went on year after year. In part to gain more understanding of how popular movements could actually acquire the power they needed I turned to a study of American labor history.

Drawing on the history and traditions of workers movements, I came to see the power of employers over workers as the result of dependence. As I put it in *Strike!*, employers had power over workers because employers controlled the means of production and therefore workers depended on them for the jobs they needed to make a living. All workers share "a subordination to the control of employers," who have the power to make decisions that shape their daily lives.

The poet William Blake captured the intimate relationship between dependence and obedience. The king shall "call for Famine from the heath"

To cut off the bread from the city;
That the remnant may learn to obey.[1]

But *Strike!* argued that workers, collectively, had a potential counterpower over employers if they refused to obey. Employers needed workers to work in order to produce. "All the functions of their employer, indeed of society, depend on their labor." By withdrawing their labor and by refusing to cooperate with established authorities in other ways, workers "can bring any workplace, community, or even country to a halt."[2] By taking control of their own activity, "ordinary people" have "the power to reshape society."

This counterdependence was expressed vividly in Bertolt Brecht's "German War Primer":

General, your tank is a strong vehicle.
It breaks down a forest and crushes a hundred people.
But it has one fault: it needs a driver.[3]

The power of the general, however great it may appear, depends on that driver. More generally, those who dominate can do so only because others support or acquiesce in their domination. It is the activity of people that continually recreates the power of the powerful. But this relationship thereby creates a counterdependence—captured in the labor movement anthem "Solidarity Forever":

They have taken untold millions that they never toiled to earn
But without our brain and muscle not a single wheel can turn.

That dependence can be parlayed into power through the formation of a coordinated group, for example a union:

We can break their haughty power, gain our freedom when we learn
That the union makes us strong.

The scores of strikes I recounted in *Strike!* all demonstrated that becoming a collective actor and utilizing the dependence of their employers gave workers a power that they did not possess as individuals.

Satyagraha

My mother's brother died in World War II and she responded by becoming a pacifist and a Quaker. I remember as a young child asking her what she believed about politics and her reply that there had been a man in India named Gandhi who had developed a way to fight against things that were wrong without using violence. We had a copy of Gandhi's

My Experiment with Truth on the bookshelf and I looked at it once or twice, but for some reason it never captured my imagination, perhaps because it appeared to project an unrealistic politics based exclusively on morality.

When I was at the Institute for Policy Studies in the 1960s, I wrote a critique of Erik Erikson's book *Gandhi's Truth,* arguing that much of Gandhi's action in India could best be understood as an attempt to head off an anticolonial revolution by organizing nonviolent protests that remained firmly in the hands of the elite who controlled the Indian National Congress.[4] So it was a great surprise to me when I later discovered that Gandhi propounded an approach to power that complemented what I had gleaned from the history of workers movements and also the "loopy," nonlinear ways of thinking I was absorbing from systems theory.

In 1973, just after the publication of *Strike!,* the veteran pacifist activist-turned-scholar Gene Sharp published a monumental three-volume study called *The Politics of Nonviolent Action.* Sharp's approach was rooted in Gandhi's—but a far different Gandhi that the one I thought I knew. This Gandhi was not only about morality but also about power.

After closely following the massive strikes, general strikes, street battles, peasant revolts, and military mutinies of the Russian Revolution of 1905 that forced the czar to grant a constitution, Mohandas (not yet dubbed "Mahatma") Gandhi concluded, "Even the most powerful cannot rule without the cooperation of the ruled."[5] Shortly thereafter, he launched his first civil disobedience campaign, proclaiming, "We too can resort to the Russian remedy against tyranny."

Gandhi continued to develop his concept of civil disobedience as a means to empower people subjected to domination. Gandhi called his approach *satyagraha.* It was based on a theory of power: the powerful are dependent on the rest of society for their power. Governing people is possible "only so long as they consent either consciously or unconsciously to be governed."[6] Addressing India's British rulers, he acknowledged, "You have great military resources. Your naval power is matchless. If we wanted to fight with you on your own ground, we should be unable to do so." But if India's demands were not met, "we cease to play the part of the ruled." The rulers could "cut us to pieces" and "shatter us at the cannon's mouth." But "if you act contrary to our will we shall not help you," and "without our help, we know that you cannot move one step forward."[7]

In 1930 Gandhi drafted a declaration for the nationalist Indian National Congress which was passed by public meetings around the country. It called submission to British rule disastrous, a "crime against man and God." But "the most effective way of gaining our freedom is not through violence." If Indians could "withdraw our voluntary help and stop payment of taxes without doing violence, even under provocation, the end of this inhuman rule is assured."[8]

While independence was the goal, in 1930 Gandhi chose the British salt laws as the immediate target. The British colonial government forbade Indians to collect or sell salt, thus making Indians dependent on the Raj for this basic life necessity. In 1930 Gandhi led a march to the sea to harvest salt. Millions of Indians engaged in civil disobedience by harvesting salt in violation of British law; eighty thousand of them were jailed. The campaign marked a turning point in the campaign for Indian independence.

The British viceroy, Lord Irwin, described the campaign as "a deliberate attempt to coerce established authority by mass action." Therefore it was "unconstitutional and dangerously subversive." Mass action, "even if it is intended by its promoters to be nonviolent," was nothing but "the application of force under another form." The Indian mass action campaign was "exactly analogous to a general strike in an industrial country" which aimed for "the coercion of Government by mass pressure."[9] Gandhi agreed; the noncooperation movement "deliberately aims at the overthrow of the Government, and is therefore legally seditious."[10]

Gandhi explicitly recognized that such a movement was a matter not of "carrying conviction by argument" but of power. "The matter resolves itself into one of matching forces." Great Britain would defend her commerce and interest "by all the forces at her command." India consequently had to "evolve force enough to free herself from that embrace of death."[11] Ultimately it did.

Power in Systems

At the start of *The Politics of Nonviolent Action*, Gene Sharp characterized the conventional, commonsense, top-down view of power. People are "dependent upon the good will, the decisions and the support of their government" or "other hierarchical system to which they belong." Such power is "self-perpetuating, durable, not easily or quickly controlled or destroyed." It follows that "in open conflict such power cannot in the last analysis be controlled or destroyed simply by people but only by the threat or use of overwhelming physical might."[12] Power, in a word, is linear, with powerful actors causing the powerless to do what the powerful command.

Some Marxists have expressed similar views of power. Capitalists own the means of production, the true source of power, which gives them unilateral control of society, including the state and the means of violence. Therefore, workers under capitalism are powerless. But in practice Marx himself did not propound such a one-sided view of power. He portrayed the abolition of American slavery, for example, as something to which both Manchester cotton mill workers and Southern slaves themselves contributed. And he argued in *Capital* that workers must "put their heads together, and, as a class, compel the passing of a law" for a "legally limited working-day."[13]

What we may call "people power" approaches like Gandhi's, in contrast to unilateral, linear, top-down models, are based on a presumption of mutual interaction and mutual dependence. Power cannot be reduced to one force acting on another. Each actor has needs they depend on the other to fulfill; therefore each potentially has power over the other. Such power is nonlinear. It is based on actions by each that affect the other. The power of the powerless requires utilizing the interdependencies among different actors or subsystems—what Gene Sharp calls their "pillars of support."[14] Power cannot be understood without taking into account those interdependencies. Gandhi's insistence that even the most powerful cannot rule without the cooperation of the ruled was grounded in the systems principles of interaction and interdependence.

Many systems theories have little place for questions of power. They present a peculiarly benign view of how the world works. Admittedly, since parts interact with each other, each is constrained by the others, but in a reciprocal rather than a unilateral way. Through their actions parts maintain the whole, which in turn maintains the conditions on which each part depends. As in a living organism, maintaining the whole is in the interest of all of the parts. Acts that one element of a system uses to influence another are portrayed as benign "signals" rather than power-laden sanctions. Domination is simply not part of the picture.

A people-power view does not assume such a benign, nonantagonistic harmony among different elements of a system. Indeed, power is implicit in a system. A system like the British Raj could be highly unequal in the freedom and benefits it offered to British and Indians. So could a system based on owners of capital employing workers. In both instances there could be mutuality of dependence but opposition of interest.

Within such an antagonistic system, some subsystems can adopt the goal of changing the system rather than maintaining it. Such changes can range from modest adjustments, to radical transformation, to schism or dissolution.

In times of apparent quiescence, such a system might give the appearance of unilateral, top-down power. But its mutual dependence provides the basis for that power to be challenged by those subjected to it. What is necessary to change a system is for those subjected to power to utilize the dependence of their rulers on them.

Such dependence need not be symmetrical. Capitalists' control of property is very different from workers' control of their labor, but the latter can still challenge the former. Gandhi pointed out the contrast between British power based on military force versus Indian power based on the English need for Indian cooperation to rule. The result is what Gandhi described as a "matching of forces" but often of very different, asymmetrical ones.

Gandhi proposed to achieve liberation through a process of chipping away at the supports that maintained British rule. This strategy has an affinity with cybernetic explanation, in which a goal is reached by progressively reducing that which prevents it. Power results less from the ability to impose a result than from the ability to counter or remove resistances to it.[15]

For example, in the civil rights era many southern businessmen swung from "massive resistance" to encouraging acquiescence in desegregation because they feared the reactions of northern business investors to racist violence. The Kennedy administration moved to support civil rights, albeit tepidly, in part from its fear of foreign disapproval of US racism, especially in newly independent African countries courted by the Soviet Union. Democratic Party politicians were dependent on large black voting blocs in northern cities like Detroit and Chicago, but their support was jeopardized when Democrats in the South perpetrated and Democrats in the White House and Congress tolerated highly visible racial oppression. While the civil rights movement directly confronted the evil of southern segregation, it actually drew much of its power from the "indirect strategy" of putting pressure on the forces whose acquiescence made it possible for segregation to persist. Desegregation ultimately succeeded in part because such "systems effects" dismantled the obstacles to it.[16]

The threat to power-holders may be a specific and targeted withdrawal of cooperation. For example, student protesters in the antisweatshop movement made clear that their campuses would be subject to sit-ins and other forms of disruption until their universities agreed to ban the use of their schools' logos on products made in sweatshops.

Preaching People's Power

Gandhi wrote: "The rich cannot accumulate wealth without the cooperation of the poor in society. If this knowledge were to penetrate to and spread among the poor they would become strong and would learn how to free themselves by means of nonviolence from the crushing inequalities which have brought them to the verge of starvation."[17]

I have spent much of my life trying to propagate the knowledge that the powerful depend on other elements of society and that the apparently powerless can thereby develop the power to change their situation if they can learn to act collectively. That knowledge is relevant beyond issues of rich and poor and workers and employers. For example, in response to the huge 1969 Vietnam Moratorium demonstrations, I wrote, "Despite the apparent power of the men in Washington to make the crucial decisions, it is not they who keep the country going, who do its work and fight its wars." Rather, "it is the people—the same people who support two-to-one the withdrawal of all U.S. troops from Vietnam. If they refuse to work—if they strike—the war must end."[18]

In *Globalization from Below* my colleagues and I asked, "Why are social movements able to change society?"[19] The power of existing social relations is based on "the active cooperation of some people and the consent and/or acquiescence of others." Action ranging from going to work to paying taxes to staying off private property "continually re-creates the power of the powerful." This dependence gives people a potential power over society, "but one that can be realized only if they are prepared to reverse their acquiescence." Social movements can be understood as "the collective withdrawal of consent to established institutions." The movement against globalization from above can be understood as "the withdrawal of consent from such globalization."

I am now trying to use a similar approach for climate change. In *Against Doom: A Climate Insurgency Manual* I wrote, "The powers that are responsible for climate change could not continue for a day without the acquiescence of those whose lives and future they are destroying." They are only able to continue their destructive course because others enable or acquiesce in it. "A movement can impose its will without weapons or violence if it can withdraw that cooperation from the powers that be."[20] Fear of such withdrawal can motivate those in positions of power to change.

Of course, a collection of frightened, isolated, confused individuals will find it difficult to engage in such concerted action. So in order for "people power" to express itself effectively, people must organize themselves, gain the conviction that their action is necessary and right, and discover their power in action. That requires a social process that "joins people together in a social movement, clarifies common interests, exposes the false arguments of the opposition, establishes a claim to moral and legal legitimacy, and engages in actions that reveal the potential power of the people."

The fundamental strategy for climate protection is to "withdraw the support of the people from climate destruction." The climate protection movement uses nonviolent direct action, a.k.a. civil disobedience, to express "popular refusal to acquiesce in the burning of fossil fuels" and to "force a transition to climate-safe energy." It defends such action as "both the right and the duty of the people" and "proclaims climate destruction" to be "illegal and unconstitutional." It mobilizes both "those who are willing to engage in activities the authorities claim to be illegal" and "the wider population who support their objectives." It seeks to create "an irresistible momentum of escalating popular action for climate protection."[21]

Whether such a movement will succeed depends, to use Gandhi's phrase, on a "matching of forces."

CHAPTER 13

Equilibration: The Secret of Development

In 1972 I audited Paul Mattick Jr.'s course on Marx's *Capital*. Paul's mother, Ilse Mattick, was a professor of child development steeped in the work of the Swiss developmental thinker Jean Piaget. In trying to explain Marx's theory of social development, Paul pointed out similarities to Piaget's theory of child development. I asked what to read and was referred to a standard textbook on Piaget. Intrigued but also puzzled, I started tackling some of Piaget's own voluminous and difficult writings. I assimilated his ideas selectively, trying to extract what I could for understanding social movements and common preservation.[1]

Although often thought of as a child psychologist, Piaget actually wrote extensively about biology, the history of science, and epistemology as well. Piaget used many ideas I had already gleaned from various versions of systems theory.[2] But systems theorists often seemed preoccupied with how systems maintain themselves—with homeostasis. Piaget's primary concern was development—particularly the metamorphosis in human intelligence between infancy and adulthood. His general theory of development incorporates elements from many ways of thinking we have already presented in earlier chapters, including historical methodology, Darwinism, pragmatism, Marxism, general systems theory, cybernetics, and complexity theory. He defined development as not merely change but improvement in the patterns of thinking and acting that make it possible to realize goals that one could not reach before.

William James once described the minds of infants as a "blooming, buzzing confusion." Their ability to act on the world is limited to a few uncoordinated patterns; their coordination with other infants is so limited that today we often call it "parallel play." Piaget's theory of development was meant to explain how, from such a beginning, they become adult human beings, highly and complexly organized in their thinking, acting, and coordinating with other people.

The development of social movements presents intriguing parallels. Those who will become members of a movement often start with disjointed thoughts and perceptions based on their idiosyncratic individual and group experiences, they do not act collectively, and they are unable to communicate with each other and coordinate their actions. In the process of becoming part of a movement they develop ways to collectively create and share ideas, engage in collective action, and coordinate their action to realize common purposes. Because Piaget intended his general ideas about development to apply in realms far beyond child cognitive development, I wondered if they could they help illuminate the development of social movements and common preservation.

Piaget's way of thinking illuminates some of the thorniest questions about why and how common preservation is possible. How can people act intelligently without being able to articulate how they do so? How can a persistent, apparently stable structure suddenly change?[3] How can radical change nonetheless retain a degree of continuity with the past? How can the failure of existing patterns of thought and action end up resulting in better ones? How do isolated, disconnected individuals develop coordination and become a collaborating group? How can people organize themselves without someone ordering them to do so and telling them how? How can organization sometimes lead to more rather than less freedom? How can people come to think and act not only in new ways but also in ways that are better for solving the problems they face today and new problems they may face in the future?

My five chapters on Piaget delve into his thought in what may at first appear extravagant depth because it is central to the common preservation heuristic. It provides much of the base for parts 2 and 3 of this book. Its keywords, like "equilibration," "assimilation," "accommodation," and "compensation" are essential terms and concepts for our workshop. The chapters delineate equilibration; explain how it is produced through a combination of assimilation and accommodation; show how equilibration makes development possible; apply equilibration to the development of social movements; and suggest some implications of Piaget's ideas for common preservation.

Piaget is a notoriously difficult writer, and there are numerous stumbling blocks to understanding him. As two of his translators wrote,

Piaget was "a great thinker but an inconsiderate if not downright awful writer."[4] His theory constantly evolved over more than sixty years, and much of his writing is an argument with his own previous views.[5] He deals simultaneously with a wide span of material, from concrete historical and psychological data to highly abstract theory. His work has been systematically misinterpreted, especially in the United States, as a theory of biologically determined stages of human development. He has also been falsely portrayed as believing that human development is an individual rather than a social matter—the child as "the scientist in the crib." Piaget operated in his own unique paradigm, making it difficult to get inside his way of thinking. All the parts of his theory are interrelated, making it hard to understand any part until you have understood the rest.[6] He developed his own technical language for presenting it, which furthermore changed over time. Despite the highly conceptualized character of his writing, his intuitions, as one of his most profound interpreters wrote, "often outstripped his ability to realize them concretely."[7] My chapters on Piaget are not a scholarly attempt to explicate "the real Piaget" but rather a report on what my raiding parties have brought back for use in understanding social movements and social change.

Nobody finds Piaget's ideas easy to assimilate at first, but the good news is that, in my experience, Piaget's core intuitions can be grasped and applied far more easily than the details of his ever-evolving theory can be mastered. I've found them irreplaceable. In my chapters on Piaget I focus less on conclusions he attempted to prove than on possibilities for common preservation that his way of thinking might open up.

What Is Equilibration?

Piaget got a job early in his career working on child intelligence tests, and he observed from the kinds of mistakes that children made that they think very differently from adults. He became preoccupied with explaining how a child's thinking changed into that of an adult. This development was more than just a random variation; it was a change from a less to a more adequate way of understanding and acting on the world.

This change couldn't be exclusively the result of an innate, wired-in biological program; children didn't develop normal capabilities if they were deprived of experience and activity in the world. Yet it wasn't just the result of experience or teaching applied to a blank slate, either; no amount of experience or teaching could get a five-year-old child to reason like an adult. It seemed that the child's own activity somehow led, over time, to the transformation of its way of thinking. But how?

Piaget's answer was that development takes place through what he called equilibration. (He also uses a number of other terms, including "compensation," "regulation," "coordination," and "construction" to mean more or less the same thing.) "Knowledge does not proceed either from experience with objects alone or from an innate program preformed in the subject but results, instead, from a succession of constructions producing new structures."[8] He developed a very abstract, very general theory of how equilibration works, grounded in what he called "laws of the general coordination of actions." It is this aspect of his thought that I found useful for thinking about the development of social movements and the emergence of common preservations.[9]

"Equilibrium" is nothing more than a Latinate word for "balance"; equilibration is simply the process of establishing an equality or balance. It is an action that reduces the gap or disparity between the ends of an actor and the situation in which they find themselves. Like Wiener's term "feedback," Piaget's term equilibration does not express a previously unthought-of idea, but it brings together under one term processes that have been known by many different names in different contexts. It can help us identify patterns whose similarity is not initially evident.

Let me try to give an intuitive sense of what I aim to capture with the term "equilibration." Imagine yourself an infant learning to stand up and walk. At first when you try to stand up, you simply topple over. Gradually you learn that if you start to topple in one direction you must adjust some part of your body in another direction enough to compensate for your imbalance. Such a balancing process is what Piaget calls "equilibration"; learning how to do it better he calls "improving equilibration."

Now if you now want to walk, you must move your leg away from your balanced standing position. To keep from "losing your balance" you again have to compensate by moving some other part of your body as well. As you walk, each body movement must take the others into account—the movement of different body parts must be coordinated. And to stay in balance the body as a whole must coordinate with the direction of gravity by adjusting its various parts.

Of course, learning to stand and walk are biologically determined tasks that every normal child will accomplish. But now consider learning to stand and walk upside down on your hands. While some previous

it. The bear man searched the scientific literature and queried many experienced bear scientists but could not find a single account of a similar behavior by a black bear.

While we cannot know for certain the process that led the bear to produce this behavior, we can try to reconstruct it. The bear acted on a familiar pattern: investigate something that smells like it might be food. But the feedback from its action brought an unpleasant surprise: the pain of a barb in its flesh when it crossed the barbed wire. When it approached the wire again, it posed itself the problem of how to cross it without getting a painful prick. In some way, we are not privy to how, it came up with the possibility of avoiding the barb by pressing the wire to the ground. It created a new solution to a problem by modifying its action to compensate for an obstacle. That's equilibration. If it was able to apply that solution to other situations—say, the barbed wire around a farmer's field—that would demonstrate development.

Why do people equilibrate? The reasons need to be investigated in any particular case. It may be to avoid the consequences of disequilibrium: people may correct their posture so they don't fall down, put money in their bank account so they won't be overdrawn, or advocate for solar power to reduce the threat of global warming. It may be to gain benefits from equilibration: the child who can stand up can reach that high shelf with the tempting toy. There may also be more intrinsic motives, either instinctive or learned: disequilibrium may be experienced as an undesirable state in itself, and there may be feelings of pleasure and satisfaction in establishing new equilibria.[11]

Piaget uses equilibration to explain the development of living beings ranging from the musculature of the mollusks he collected as a child in Alpine streams to the logical deductions made by late adolescents. Critics have questioned whether equilibration is too vague to be meaningful, whether it is anything more than a metaphor, and whether it is of any use for explaining concrete phenomena like human language or the evolution of philosophy.[12] My answer is that Piaget provides the best general explanation of development I have been able to find, and, as we will see, addresses many of the specific aspects of development that are necessary for common preservation. His explanations also have implications for how to encourage that development.

I have used Piaget's general pattern of equilibration in myriad ways to explore the development of new forms of common preservation in social movements. In *Strike!* I showed how at many times American workers discovered that as individuals they were unable to achieve their goals, whereupon they turned to organizations like unions and collective action like strikes to do so—equilibrating the imbalance between their goals and their established patterns of action.[13] In *Global Village or Global Pillage* and *Globalization from Below* I described how established strategies adapted to a national framework failed in the face of globalization, and how popular organizations and movements began to develop new forms of global cooperation in order to function in the new globalized environment. In *Climate Insurgency* I recounted how twenty-five years of lobbying and public education failed to bring about national commitment and global agreement for climate protection, and how a climate protection movement using civil disobedience, nonviolent direct action, and disruption of the fossil fuel industry emerged to fill the gap. In each case the details of my analysis were of course drawn from the concrete historical evidence, but the interpretive framework drew heavily on Piaget's explanation of development through equilibration. Equilibration underlies the approach to the development of common preservation presented in part 2 of this book.

CHAPTER 14

Assimilation and Accommodation: The Secret of Equilibration

Piaget started out studying biology, and the biological concept of adaptation is reflected in all his work. Like Dewey, he considered thinking to be one form of the general process by which organisms adapt to their environment.[1] His theory of equilibration is designed to explain how that process works.

Equilibration reflects the paradox of development: a being maintains itself yet turns into something very different. Both living organisms and human individuals and groups maintain their organization yet also adapt to their environment. Piaget calls the organization maintenance process "assimilation" and the adaptation process "accommodation." Assimilation combined with accommodation can lead to development.

Pattern and Change

Assimilation is the action by which any system or organism incorporates elements of the environment into its own patterns or structures. "When a rabbit eats cabbage, he is not changed into cabbage but, on the contrary, the cabbage is changed into rabbit."[2] This is similar to Bertalanffy's idea of an "open system" that maintains its own structure (stays rabbit) by importing material from the environment (eating cabbage and changing it into rabbit). Assimilation might involve external action (finding and eating the cabbage) or internal action (digesting the cabbage into elements that can be made into rabbit).

To understand assimilation, imagine an organism, a person, a group, or a system—let's say, for example, a workshop.[3] It has an organization or framework or structure. It has a number of patterns or schemas or plans that relate means and ends—plans of action to realize a goal. It acts on an object, say, turning leather into a pair of shoes. The goal is successfully realized; information returns to the workshop via a feedback loop and confirms that the goal has been realized. The workshop acts again according to the same plan and again produces another pair of shoes. In each repetition of the action the object—the leather—is assimilated to its plan and intention. The action of the workshop is in equilibrium with the goal of that action. As long as it is not deprived of leather the workshop can go on realizing its norms or steady state—making shoes.

To understand accommodation, imagine that the same entity is in an environment that has changed, for example by having access only to tougher leather. The workshop goes through the same procedures, but because the environment has changed its actions no longer achieve its goal. Its tools can no longer cut and shape the leather properly. Feedback representing a gap between the result of action and its goal is reported back to the workshop. It may continue repeating the same action, but if it does so it will find out repeatedly that its actions are failing to achieve their goal.

To realize its intent, the workshop has to vary its action. It may try new materials or purchase new tools or try different procedures. The variations it performs may be selected completely at random, or they may be guided by more or less certain conjectures about what variations would be most likely to succeed—a process we will examine more extensively in Chapter 15. If the revised action fails, other variations will need to be tested to reach the goal. If a new variation compensates for the divergence of the original action from its goal, the subsequent action will realize the goal. Thanks to the new materials, tools, or procedures, it will produce a new pair of shoes. If such a new variation is repeatedly successful, and the workshop adopts it as its standard operating procedure, the workshop has successfully accommodated to its environment, even though that environment has changed.

In such a process, continuity and change are interdependent. Each action includes assimilation to an existing pattern, but also accommodation of that pattern. Paradoxically, an existing pattern preserves its continuity by modifying itself.

A system that assimilates and accommodates is different from a "closed system" like a pendulum or a solar system that maintains equilibrium through a static balance of forces. It is also different from a homeostatic system in which feedback simply reestablishes a preexisting balance—a steady state or equilibrium. The goal of a homeo-static system is to return to a previous equilibrium. Equilibration also aims to realize equilibrium, but it does not necessarily restore a pre-existing equilibrium. Its goal is to establish an equilibrium—be it old or new—that overcomes the existing disequilibrium, gap, or problem. It accepts a new equilibrium as a success.

Assimilation and Accommodation: The 1973 Meat Boycott

Common preservation is the development of coordinated action for shared ends. Social movements are historical expressions of the emergence of common preservation in particular times and places. To understand their emergence, whether gradual or sudden, two questions need to be answered:

First, why did something new emerge? In an equilibration approach the answer is likely to be the discovery of a disequilibrium or gap: actions that are guided by existing patterns produce outcomes that differ from the actor's intent. So they act in new ways to overcome the gap.

Second, why was that new mode of action a social movement embodying new common preservations? In an equilibration approach the answer is likely to be the recognition that the gap cannot be closed by existing patterns of action, but that the gap may possibly be closed by new forms of common preservation.[4]

To see how a Piagetian approach to development works for a concrete instance of common preservation in a social movement, let us go back to the story of Mrs. Ann Giordano and the 1973 meat boycott recounted in the introduction.[5]

As you may recall, Mrs. Giordano regularly went shopping for groceries, a relatively simple action pattern combining transportation, selection, payment, and other elements for the goal of acquiring food. She did this over and over successfully, assimilating the journey, the shopping, and the paying to her own goal and plan. Normally it went without a hitch—assimilation without a need for significant accommodation.

One day, however, she discovered she had space left on her kitchen shelf—a quite literal gap. Her first explanation was that she had left a bag of groceries at the store. Next time she discovered another gap—the shortage of money in her wallet. She then began an inquiry to discover why these discrepancies were occurring. The answer was the rising cost of food.

As a result of rising food prices, millions of people were having similar experiences. No doubt many of them tried to restore equilibrium by buying less meat; but that probably led to other problems, such as complaining husbands and children.

With such individual solutions failing, the condition was established for a search for something different—a more radical accommodation of their established patterns. The evident fact that other people were experiencing the same problem made it possible to reinterpret the problem as a collective rather than just an individual one. That implied the possibility of forming a common purpose and addressing the problem through collective rather than purely individual action.

The search for a form of collective response led many people in many different milieus around the country to the bright idea of a consumer boycott. For some, boycotts may have been a form of action they had participated in or heard or read about that they realized they could apply in this different context. For others, a boycott may have initially seemed to be doing what they were doing anyway—buying less meat—but doing so as a collective rather than an individual act. In either case the meat boycott involved taking an existing pattern and modifying its context, goal, and form.

Two very different systems of thought converged in the meat boycott as a solution to the problem of excessive meat prices. One came from the economic idea of a balance of supply and demand. If demand could be reduced, prices would fall. The purpose of the boycott in this view was to reduce demand and thereby lower prices. The other approach came from the idea of political power. It defined the boycott as a protest. If enough people participated, their collective action would pose a threat or provide an opportunity to those in a position to make decisions, and thereby induce them to take action to reduce meat prices. In either view, the search for a solution led to the possibility of developing collective power through collective action, group formation, and common preservation. Participants began acting together because they thought it might increase their power to realize their ends.

There was no preexisting organization among the diverse individuals and milieus being affected by the meat price increases; people had been facing them alone. So they began to test the hypothesis that a collective response might be possible simply by making random phone calls to ask others if they would be willing to participate in a boycott. This initiated a new pattern of social interaction.

Preexisting groups like tenants of the same building, consumers who shopped at the same grocery store, and block associations were modified to serve as vehicles for the movement. Women met every morning over coffee—turning the conventional kaffeeklatsch into a vehicle for social action.

Isolated individuals were becoming a coordinated group—a new entity or whole of which they were part. In Staten Island the initial activists called a meeting and gave their emerging entity a name to express their new collective identity. They coordinated their action by assigning individuals specific roles. They began to draw others into their emerging movement through leafleting and picket lines at grocery stores. Seeing others in action led many previously uninvolved in the boycott in turn to accommodate their own patterns by internalizing this new way of thinking and acting and beginning to act on it themselves.

The boycott strategy was initially successful, even forcing the president of the United States to declare a freeze on meat prices. Lacking a further strategy for meeting its participants' needs, however, the movement soon lost momentum. Participants stopped coordinating their activity and returned to more individual strategies.

The combination of assimilation and accommodation became the means for solving problems and closing gaps that I applied in the heuristic for common preservation presented in part 2.

CHAPTER 15

How Development Works

Assimilation and accommodation help explain why development is possible, but to understand and nourish common preservation we need to know in more detail how development occurs.

Development presupposes individuals, groups, organizations, systems, subjects, or other entities that can use feedback loops to compare the results of their action to their goals. It requires that they can correct these gaps between action and goals by varying their action. That makes it possible for them to assimilate and accommodate—to maintain their organization and to adapt it.

Development takes place through repeated cycles of interaction between an entity and its environment.[1] We can break down Piaget's cycle of improved equilibration into four stages: the preexisting pattern, the discovery of a gap, the change that corrects that gap, and the incorporation of that correction into the initial pattern.

Guiding Patterns

Piaget calls the general pattern of an action through which an actor assimilates the environment a scheme, schema, or structure. Such a pattern has general features which are present every time the pattern is applied.[2] These patterns are coordinated wholes that establish a relation among their parts or subsystems. They are organized to realize an end or goal. They guide the actor's action and thought. Their elements must coordinate with each other and with the pattern as a whole to achieve the end. An infant's scheme "to stand up" involves coordinating many muscles in a way that raises the body and counteracts the force of gravity. The production of a chair or shoe in a workshop requires a pattern or plan that coordinates the different activities of workers and machines. The organization of a political demonstration requires strategizing, publicity, logistic planning, transportation, internal communication, production of signs and art, and preparation for possible disruption.

If all these patterns or subsystems work together harmoniously the actor or system maintains its internal equilibrium. If the action guided by an established pattern consistently reaches its goal, the actor is in a state of equilibrium with their environment. The environment is consistently assimilated to the guiding pattern and no significant change in the pattern is required for the action to succeed. Therefore, there is no motive for development.

Gaps

Interaction with the environment can lead, however, to disequilibria or gaps, in which the result of an action is different from the actor's intention or goal. According to Piaget such gaps are the origin of development. "Progress in the development of knowledge must be sought in disequilibria as such." Disequilibria "alone force the subject to go beyond his current state and strike out in new directions." They provide an "essential motivational factor."[3] It is the child who starts to teeter over who learns how to stand upright by adjusting parts of their body to gravity. It was the housewives who couldn't afford meat for their families who organized America's largest protest.

Compensation: Closing the Gap

News of a disequilibrium or gap reaches an actor through feedback. The actor can of course simply go on repeating the failed action. Or they can give up trying to reach their goal. But they may instead launch on a process of accommodation—modifying their action to overcome its failure.

Such accommodation can simply adapt an established pattern to work in a different concrete situation. "The scheme to grasp, for example, does not apply in the same manner to very small and very large objects."[4] It needs to be accommodated differently to hold a pin and a beach ball. But accommodation can also involve a change in the guiding pattern as a whole, or even substitution of a different pattern— people complaining about meat prices see others boycotting and begin to do so themselves.

That equilibration process starts with one or more cycles in which feedback is compared to intentions and the gap or disequilibrium between them is identified. Such a gap can be ignored, denied, or regarded as inevitable. Alternatively, it can be redefined as a problem to be solved. That in turn can initiate a search for a solution—what Dewey calls an inquiry.

In order to succeed, such a search must identify a modification that eliminates the gap. Piaget calls modifications that overcome such gaps "compensations." A compensation is "an action in a direction opposite to a given effect which thus tends to cancel or to neutralize the effect."[5] A simple example: as a bicycle begins to tip in one direction, the rider compensates by leaning in the opposite direction, thus reestablishing equilibrium. A successful compensation constitutes the solution to a problem.[6]

"Compensation" is a way of expressing the cybernetic idea of pursuing a goal by counteracting that which deviates from it. The steersman compensates for the gap between where the boat is currently headed and where the steersman wants it to go by moving the rudder to create counterpressure that shifts the boat toward the intended course. Millions of people boycotting meat pressured President Nixon to freeze its price.

Compensation is the basic process underlying equilibration. Compensation makes it possible to maintain stability and pursue goals in a changing world. Compensation can just be a small adjustment, but it can also involve the construction of new and very different patterns that may transgress existing ones. Remember the *capoeiristas* who had to suppress their normal patterns and develop new ones to walk on their hands. Or the women who had to unlearn patterns of gender subservience and develop the women's liberation movement in order to overcome confinement to narrow social roles.

How does an actor discover or invent a modification that will actually compensate for a gap? At one pole, they may do so simply by trial and error. They can randomly change their plan of action, try the change out as an experiment, and evaluate its feedback to find out whether the changed action succeeds or fails. Such an approach resembles Darwin's natural selection by random variation and subsequent selection of those variations that succeed. Learning by trial and error can be observed in preverbal children, animals, and other open systems. It continues to guide a significant proportion of adult action.

However, the search for improved action can instead be guided. This requires regulation by some kind of higher-level process in which the elements of action and its environment are represented.

Even without conscious thought, action can be tacitly guided at a meta level. A rabbit that is hungry may respond by searching randomly for food, but it is unlikely to respond by randomly wiggling different parts of its body in turn. Searching for food implies the goal of finding food and a whole repertoire of behaviors to accomplish it. The rabbit may not have a conscious concept representing the search for food, but some such scheme is implicit in its action—the action implies some things, such as intent to find food, and not others, such as intent to scratch an itch. Otherwise the rabbit would just move parts of its body randomly in response to its hunger.

From an early age, human infants engage in actions that express organized patterns and seek to realize goals, but which do not depend on representations that are distinct from the actions themselves. Indeed, some of Piaget's most provocative experiments show that children can perform acts such as navigating a wire maze with great skill without being able to describe accurately how they do it.

As they move beyond infancy, human beings begin to develop a symbolic or semiotic function, the ability to represent the world through signifiers like delayed imitation, pictures, and above all language. Piaget observes that such representation allows equilibration to be carried to a whole new level. It allows people to represent their own thinking and the actions it produces. That lets them perform what Piaget calls operations: interiorized actions conducted on representations of objects.

Interiorizing actions—performing them symbolically on virtual or imaginary objects—makes it possible to discover what the results of an action would have been without actually performing it. You can know—without conducting the experiment—that putting equal weights on the two pans of a scale will lead the two pans to move to the same level. People thereby can learn without correction by trial and error in the real world: the trials can be performed "in their heads" on mental representations. This allows "precorrection" of errors. The design department of the workshop doesn't have to shape and assemble actual pieces of wood or metal in order to plan a new product; it can draw lines on paper that represent them and perform mental experiments to see how they will work. Of course, it still might be wise to test such conclusions in the real world because there is no other way to know for sure that they are really adequate to reach the goal.

Operations themselves can become the object of other operations. Such thinking about thinking Piaget calls "reflective abstraction." It is "a reconstruction on an upper level of what is already organized in another manner on a lower level."[7] Someone who engages in reflective abstraction is "reflexive" in the sense that they reflect on themselves or represent their own operations.

Reflective abstraction includes at least some of what people mean when they speak of "consciousness" and "self-consciousness."[8] It is by representing their own action that someone becomes capable of mental operations—a.k.a. thinking. And by representing their own mental operations they become capable of self-consciousness.

Reflective abstraction allows people to guide their inquiries through "thought experiments." These fall on the continuum between pure trial and error and perfect precorrection. They are often based on guesses, hypotheses, and conjectures—what the founder of modern heuristics, the mathematician G. Polya, called "bright ideas." The range of these guesses may be progressively narrowed down, as in the guessing game of "Twenty Questions," where answers to questions like "is it an animal?" and "is it square?" can reduce the scope of further inquiry. Of course, such narrowing can also block future guesses that are "outside the box."

The continuum from trial-and-error learning to full precorrection assorted well with my own observations of how new compensations arise in social movements. That can range from unplanned, "spontaneous" outbursts that suddenly reveal new possibilities for action to strategic actions planned with the precision of a military operation.

New forms of action do not generally start from a completely thought-out plan. Rather, they originate from a response to a concrete situation. But as people reflect on the actions they have taken, they come to a new understanding of themselves and their potentials. They may in turn incorporate that understanding in future action. As Akron rubber workers began in the early 1930s to participate in quickie sit-down strikes to challenge immediate grievances in individual departments, they gained a new understanding of their collective power over production and their capacity for cooperation. That in turn led them to engage in massive company-wide factory occupations.

Development: Applying the Compensation

A pattern that has been changed to close a gap can be applied not only to the original problem it was modified to solve; it can subsequently be generalized to other objects, other tasks, and other contexts. It therefore represents an improved capability—a.k.a. development.

In contrast to homeostatic systems that reproduce a predetermined equilibrium, Piaget's idea of equilibration portrays an ongoing process that "leads from a state near equilibrium to a qualitatively different state at equilibrium by way of multiple disequilibria and re-equilibrations."[9]

At any given time there are established patterns or schemes or structures, but they are always subject to further equilibration. For example, a new improvement may come into conflict with other established patterns, requiring a new round of assimilation and accommodation to resolve the conflict. Thus, "the being of structures consists in their coming to be, that is their being 'under construction.'"[10] And since equilibration leads from one structure or pattern of coordination to another, it is essentially a process of reconstruction, recoordination, or even self-transformation. Such a process is often described today as "self-organization."

The equilibration cycle suggests a way of explaining emergent properties like the tendencies toward solidarity, self-assertion, and self-management I found in mass strikes. When we accommodate a pattern that has failed to meet a practical necessity in a particular instance we may thereby also initiate a new pattern that may better compensate for other gaps between means and ends.

CHAPTER 16

Equilibration and Social Movements

If the equilibration cycle—from established pattern to gap to compensation to establishment of a new pattern that in turn produces new gaps—underlies development, then we should be able to use it to illuminate the development of social movements and common preservation. It should help answer questions like how can patterns of action long persist and then suddenly change? Why do people shift from individual to collective strategies, from self- to common preservation? How do social movements emerge? How do they change their goals? Their strategies? Their forms of action?

Guiding Patterns

Let's take as the starting point for interpreting development the pre-existing equilibrium or scheme or guiding pattern. Such patterns have goals and multiple features that have been adapted to work with each other and work as a whole to realize their ends by changing an actual or virtual object. We'll begin with an example we have examined before, the 1973 meat boycott. The relevant preexisting pattern was that shoppers went to grocery stores and bought food to feed their families. They had expectations about what various items would cost and spent their money to meet their needs.

Let's next look at Occupy Wall Street. While OWS eventually engaged people in all walks of life, its early participants were primarily people in their late twenties and early thirties who had devoted considerable time to higher education and expected an appropriate future career based on that.[1]

Finally, let us look at the climate-protection movement between the 1980s, when climate scientists became certain that humans were causing global warming, and the failed 2009 Copenhagen climate summit. Every year the nations of the world met for the "Council of Parties" to the UN Framework Convention on Climate Change (UNFCCC). Every year thousands of civil society organizations gathered for the event, lobbied the delegates to act on climate change, and conducted visible public events around the world like bike rides and concerts to draw public attention to the issue.[2] These actions represented assimilation to established patterns of international negotiations and popular support for environmental protection.

Gaps

In each of these cases, "standard operating procedure" ran up against obstacles or disequilibria or gaps that prevented the established guiding patterns from realizing their ends.

In the case of the 1973 meat boycott, the gap was the rising cost of meat.

In the case of Occupy Wall Street, converging aspects of a global economic crisis undermined the expectations of young Americans in the anterooms of their careers. Crucial was the crushing accumulation of student debt. The 2008 recession also meant greatly reduced job opportunities for educated youth. More broadly, the recession and rapidly growing inequality was reducing the life prospects of the great majority of Americans, creating a reservoir of discontent available to respond to exemplary actions.

The goal of the climate protection movement was a binding global agreement and national legislation to reduce greenhouse gas emissions sufficiently to prevent an increase in global temperatures of more than 2°C. The 2009 Copenhagen Climate Summit ended in a fiasco that indicated no such binding agreement was likely for years to come, and the subsequent defeat of climate legislation in the US Congress established that the world's leading greenhouse gas emitter would continue with a "business as usual" destruction of the earth's climate. Assimilation to the existing strategy for climate protection continued but it only produced repeated failure.

Compensation: Closing the Gap

News of these gaps reached the actors via some form of feedback. Shoppers discovered they could no longer afford meat. Future Wall

Street Occupiers experienced debt, unemployment, and the lack of a course forward in life; they connected these experiences to growing poverty alongside conspicuous wealth and to the public policy that aggravated these trends, summed up in the oft-repeated slogan "Banks got bailed out; we got sold out." Climate protection activists increasingly recognized the continuing ineffectualness of conventional modes of climate action, climaxing in the failure of the Copenhagen Summit.

In all three cases, the recognition of failure led to a search for a modified strategy. In the meat boycott and OWS, this meant a shift from individual to collective action. For the soon-to-be meat boycotters, this was first expressed in phone calls, breakfast meetings, and other kinds of outreach and dialogue. For the soon-to-be Wall Street occupiers, it was manifested in a flurry of electronic communications, a call published in the anticonsumerist magazine *Adbusters*, personal testimony and photos posted to a website called WeAreThe99percent, and a series of meetings in New York City.

Climate activism was already a movement in which people took it for granted that effective action had to be collective; participants had established patterns of working together over the years. In this case, the shift in strategy was not from individual to collective action but to a different kind of collective action.

A search was then required to identify what kind of collective action might overcome the obstacles that were leading to failure—what might compensate for the gap between goal and accomplishment. New compensations were often modifications of familiar practices—accommodation of an existing pattern of assimilation. The idea of a meat boycott probably arose in part from a practice people had already adopted through necessity—buying less meat. It was a modest step to transform this from an individual necessity to a means of collective action. No doubt many people were also familiar with previous boycotts; again, it was a small step to apply this idea to their new circumstances. Occupy Wall Street was preceded by a series of occupations in Madison, Wisconsin, New York City, and most visibly of all the massive occupation of Cairo's Tahrir square that had led to the fall of the Mubarak dictatorship. The shift to a direct-action strategy for the climate protection movement was preceded by a series of small-scale, local direct-action campaigns against fossil fuel infrastructure projects, many of them motivated more by local environmental threats than by global warming.

The Keystone XL struggle in particular grew out of such campaigns and joined them together into a national confrontation between the movement and the Obama administration.

As people began acting together, their experience provided a new kind of feedback that revealed their existence as a group. From this they began to construct representations of themselves as a group. The meat boycotters began creating organizations like Staten Island's Joint Action to Stop These Outrageous Prices (Jet-STOP). Occupy Wall Street only defined itself as a group and an organization when hundreds of people arrived on Wall Street, retreated to Zuccotti Park, held their first general assembly, and prepared to camp out for the night. The direct-action climate movement was expressed in hundreds of different organizations, regularly joining together in action and creating a general sense of identity as "the movement" or "blockadia" without ever taking the form of an overarching organization.

In each of these cases, an existing pattern was accommodated to compensate for its previous failures. And reflection on the new form of collective action and its impact led the emerging collective actor to new self-understanding.

Development: Applying the Compensation

Each of these equilibration cycles led to additional cycles that produced either further development or dissolution.

The meat boycott succeeded in forcing the president to freeze meat prices, but at a level that its participants regarded as already too high. Merely continuing the boycott had little promise of further effect. It was not clear how an escalation of the same tactics could achieve more. Many movements under such conditions revise their objectives to utilize the organization and power they have created, but there was no obvious way for this to happen with the meat boycott. Although it occurred in the midst of a crescendo of wildcat strikes, informal job resistance, and civil disorders of various kinds, its participants were unable to form junctures with them.[3] As a result, the boycott petered out and the organization that had been created out of collective action soon dissolved.

Occupy Wall Street evolved rapidly through a series of cycles. It mobilized a wide swath of the New York working class in support, warded off political and police attacks, inspired Occupy movements in six hundred cities in the US, stimulated a global day of action with mass demonstrations in one thousand cities in eighty-two countries, built alliances with a wide range of labor and political groups, and led to a sea change in public and media attention to the issue of inequality. OWS was driven out of Zuccotti Park two months after the initial occupation. It continued as an informal network for a year or so, but eventually dissolved. Its impact continued to reverberate in new forms. It directly spawned new initiatives like Strike Debt and Occupy Sandy Relief. The Fight for $15 movement for a fifteen-dollar minimum wage drew much of its spirit and many of its participants from the national Occupy movement. In 2013, President Obama declared rising income inequality as "the defining challenge of our time" and in 2016 Senator Bernie Sanders nearly won the Democratic nomination for president on a platform that proclaimed, "The issue of wealth and income inequality is the great moral issue of our time, it is the great economic issue of our time, and it is the great political issue of our time." It is hard to imagine this transformation of American political discourse without the impact of Occupy Wall Street.

The climate direct-action movement came together in a protracted struggle against the Keystone XL pipeline. That struggle mobilized a large number of people to engage in direct action; transformed the national politics of climate protection; and ultimately led President Obama to refuse to authorize the pipeline. That was followed by a largely unsuccessful effort to influence the Paris climate summit. It was clear to movement organizations and activists that a major popular intervention was necessary if there was to be any chance of implementing the vague commitments of the Paris agreement, let alone strengthening them enough to adequately protect the climate. The result was a worldwide coordinated direct action campaign against major fossil fuel infrastructure projects known as Break Free from Fossil Fuels. No doubt this will lead to further rounds of reevaluation and action—further rounds of development.[4]

The heuristic presented in part 2 uses such an equilibration cycle to organize inquiry into social movements and common preservation.

coordinations can be used in modified form, many other new ones must be constructed. In fact, a fascinating study of upside-down movement in the Brazilian martial art capoeira shows that inborn reflexes like the vestibulo-spinal reflex must actually be "turned off."[10] So effective equilibration may require transforming some patterns and extinguishing others.

Equilibration is not limited to balancing one's own body. Consider, for example, a young child presented with a weighing scale and a set of identical weights. You put several weights on the right pan of the scale, which immediately tips downward. You ask the child to use the weights to make both sides of the scale level. If they are mature enough, they will probably put some weights on the left pan. If the scale doesn't move to a level position, they will add more weights until it does. If the left pan goes down and the right pan goes up, they will take away weights from the left pan or add weights to the right pan until the scale is level.

If the child is grown up enough, they can also do this equilibration mentally, "in their head." They can count the weights in the right pan and figure out without trying it that putting the same number of equal weights in the left pan will bring the scale to a level position.

Such equilibration can take place whenever two different items like the weight of the opposite sides of the body or the two pans of the weighing scales can be made equal by increasing one or reducing the other. If the strings on two guitars are "out of tune," their pitch can be equilibrated by tightening the ones that are too low and loosening the ones that are too high.

Equilibration closes a gap or overcomes an obstacle or solves a problem—a discrepancy between what is and what is intended—by changing an existing pattern of action. If a new and improved pattern can be applied to other instances it demonstrates development: individuals and groups are now able to achieve goals they could not reach before.

A few years ago, a biology grad student we dubbed "the bear man" strung a strand of barbed wire between some trees on the hillside above my home. Inside he put odoriferous (and to us humans noxious) bait to lure the black bears that wandered through the forest. At a community meeting to report his findings he described a bear that had crossed his barbed wire, investigated the bait, and turned to leave. As she approached the barbed wire she paused and gazed at it. Then she placed her paw on the wire, pushing it down to the ground, and scrambled over

CHAPTER 17

Equilibration and Common Preservation

What blocks common preservation from being realized through equilibration? How can those blockages be overcome?

Equilibration among individuals and groups requires both assimilation and accommodation. If an individual or group assimilates everything to its own viewpoint and acts on its own plans and intentions without accommodating to those of others, it expresses what Piaget terms "autocentricity."[1] By this term Piaget by no means implies selfishness or conceit, but rather a failure or inability to coordinate viewpoints. It can be overcome by the process Piaget calls "decentering."

Conversely, if people submit without resistance to whatever is imposed on them from outside, they are manifesting what Piaget calls "social constraint." They exhibit only accommodation to others with no accommodation by others to them. Overcoming social constraint requires reciprocal assimilation and accommodation.

In sum, if people don't accommodate at all to each other but just go on "doing their own thing," that is assimilation without accommodation—autocentricity. If they instead do whatever others tell or force them to do, that is accommodation without assimilation—social constraint. Neither would be able to equilibrate their action to produce coordination or cooperation.

We can illustrate autocentricity, social constraint, and decentering with a thought experiment. Let's assign a classroom of kids some tasks that require coordination. For example, we could ask students in the class to each select a building block and then have them all put their blocks together to construct the tallest building they can. To probe autocentricity we can give each student a different building plan to follow. The likely result is that each individual will bring their block and start trying to build the building, but that they will be unable to do so. Each is autocentrically following their own plan and they have no way to adapt their plans into a common plan. They are likely either to fight over whose plan to follow, decide to disobey the rules, or give up in frustration.

Now let's try a variation. We again ask the kids to take one block each and build the tallest building they can. This time let's ask them each to make up their own plan in their head or on paper about the best way to do so. Then let's appoint one child to be a dictator. The others have to submit to their orders. What is likely to happen? The kids go to get their blocks, but the dictator starts to give each of them orders about what to do. When a child starts on an action, the dictator interferes and orders them to do it a different way or to do something else instead. For example, the dictator tells a child who starts putting down a block on the floor for a foundation instead to put it on top of another block. The kids can't act on their own plans because the dictator interferes. They are forestalled from assimilating the objects—the building blocks—to their own schemes or patterns.

Autocentricity and social constraint block equilibration and prevent the development of collective coordination. Autocentricity interferes with interaction that could lead to mutual assimilation and accommodation—the kids can only follow their own plans without regard to others and therefore cannot jointly create new coordinations. Social constraint not only prevents the kids from executing their own plans, but it prevents them from interacting in a way that would let them modify their plans to form a common plan. The kids can't work out solutions through give-and-take because they have to wait and submit to the dictator's orders.

People overcome autocentricity by mutually assimilating each other's patterns and accommodating their own. The kids could compare their plans, see that they were incompatible, and modify their individual plans to form a joint plan. People overcome social constraint by disobeying it individually or collectively—the kids could refuse to obey the dictator's orders and start assimilating and accommodating to each other's plans. In both cases they are overcoming the barriers to equilibration. If they are able to incorporate their new practices in their ongoing thought and action they have developed into a coordinated group.

We can find similar patterns in the formation of social movements and other collectives that develop out of individuals and groups that initially could not collaborate because of autocentricity or social constraint.

We described above how in the early decades of the twentieth century, the working-class communities of Connecticut's Naugatuck Valley were sharply divided by ethnicity.[2] These separations, combined with rivalry over jobs and vigorous employer opposition, help explain why, despite significant grievances, workers were unable to organize unions in the Valley's factories.

Though they are difficult to trace, there undoubtedly were some attempts to build bridges across ethnic boundaries. The Scovill Manufacturing Company labor spy file includes a card describing a "dangerous Italian" who is "organizing an international dance." But in general, each ethnic community and workforce remained something of a separate world, an exemplar of autocentricity. In June 1919, the boundaries were pierced and thousands of workers at area factories began walking off their jobs. They came from a score of ethnic groups and had little common organization. They held out for nearly a month until the major companies announced substantial wage increases and the workers returned to their jobs.

The 1919 strike kicked off a flurry of organizing within and across ethnic groups. Thousands of workers joined one of two unions established to organize the unskilled immigrant workforce. Both unions had sections for Italians, Lithuanians, Poles, Russians, Portuguese, French, and other groups, but they were able to formulate six common demands and designate a multiethnic leadership that negotiated with the employers and municipal officials. Mass meetings were followed by a general strike in 1920 in which as many as sixteen thousand workers participated. In Piaget's terms the workers had conducted a significant decentering, changing from poorly communicating, fractious ethnic groups to a cohesive force. Ethnic tensions remained, but through coordination and accommodation the workers were able to transcend ethnic autocentricity enough to function as a collective actor.

Social constraint, like autocentricity, can take many forms. The Italian teenage girls employed at Lesnow Bros. shirtwaist factory in New Haven in the early 1930s worked under the close surveillance of their employers. They were also under tight control by their families. When male, mostly Jewish garment workers from New York picketed their plant to demand a union, the girls were told by both their bosses and their parents to have nothing to do with them. The young women had already conducted their own work stoppage in the plant to protest a change in the piece-rate system. Then one of them, a teenager named Jennie Aiello, said she was going to go out and talk to those men. She did, and the young women of Lesnow's began working with them to organize a union.

I interviewed Jennie and some of her workmates half a century later. Jennie's friend Anna Scafardi recalled, "She was the one that went out first, talked to us. As much as we were afraid, I followed her, we kept talking to everybody, and we got in." Jennie met opposition from her family. Her younger brother Nick recalled, "They had some kind of dispute someplace. And she had took me 'for a walk.' But she didn't tell my father that it was her time to be on the picketline." When I asked Jennie about opposition from her family she replied, "I didn't care what they say, what they didn't say. I lied like hell, but I went to meetings."

The young Lesnow women along with the skilled male workers went on strike, shutting down the company completely. Eventually Lesnow signed an agreement for a union shop and a 10 percent wage increase. It turned out to be the breakthrough that started the unionization of tens of thousands of shirtwaist workers through the entire northeastern United States. Mutual assimilation and accommodation among different workers combined with their resistance to authority overcame multiple forms of social constraint.

All of these once divided or dominated groups—the kids building a tower, the brass workers coming together to cooperate across ethnic lines for a strike, the teenage garment workers defying both their employer and their parents to organize a union—formed a collective able to coordinate their action for a common purpose in order to affect their world.

The coordination of actors together with disobedience to authority may have a familiar ring. They are the same combination we found providing the "power of the powerless" in the satyagraha of Mahatma Gandhi. To succeed, a movement for common preservation must overcome both the disorganization of the actors and the power of the authorities.

Collective Subjects Transforming the World

Assimilation and accommodation can lead to the construction of a subject—what Piaget defines as an entity "able to transform the world physically or virtually." Such a subject may be either individual or inter-individual—collective.[3] The development of a coordinated group like the student tower-builders and the brass and garment industry strikers represents the construction of a collective subject. For Piaget, "individual operations and cooperation form one inseparable whole." What Piaget calls the "general coordination of actions" is "common to inter- and intra-individual actions and operations."[4] Individuals to achieve goals must coordinate actions, like the child who coordinates eyes and hands to grasp an object it sees. An equivalent "coordination of actions" is required for different people to work together to realize an objective.

In a small sailboat one person may manage the tiller with one hand and the sail with the other. Alternatively, one person may manage the tiller and another person the sail. But in either case the same coordination will be needed between tiller-handling and sail-handling to get the boat to its destination. One case is "intra-individual," the other is "inter-individual," but they both exhibit the "general coordination of actions." The sailing duo coordinating the tiller and sail are transforming the world by moving their boat toward their destination; they therefore constitute a collective subject. So did the American farmers who showed up at public meetings and eventually turned themselves into the American revolutionary army which drove the British out of North America.

At the core of the general coordination of actions is the idea of compensation or correction for deviation from goals by an action in an opposite direction that cancels that deviation. Collective compensations can be constructed out of individual ones by modifying and combining individual actions and operations. For example, one student can compare two plans and decide how to combine them to make a plan for a building. But two students working together can compare and discuss both plans and make a joint plan from them. In a workshop, one person can use a series of drafting and machining tools to plan and make the parts of a product. But using the same principles of coordination a group of workers can make the parts of the same product simultaneously. Individuals may know how to bargain with their neighbors or their family members; as union members they can combine their skills to negotiate with their employers. Individual housewives knew how to minimize the meat they purchased; by doing the same thing but doing it collectively they produced the nationwide 1973 meat boycott. All these actors of course had to accommodate their individual means of action to one another in order to produce a collective action, but they were able to do so because the principles of the "general coordination of actions" were the same.

A subject, whether individual or collective, must be constructed. In the infancy of the individual, according to Piaget, "there is no subject." There is no differentiation between subject and object. Gradually the subject's actions are "differentiated, diversified, and coordinated together." As long as interactions between subject and object are made up of "isolated, uncoordinated actions," there are "neither objects nor a subject." "To the extent that these interactions give rise to coordinations" then there is a "construction of the subject."[5] When a child's hands and eyes begin to coordinate, for example, they become able to transform the world by deliberately moving an object from one place to another. If their ability to do so persists, they constitute an active subject.

Collective subjects, similarly, are constructed by engaging in coordinated action to affect the objects with which a group interacts.[6] When a group of workers gradually construct a method to prevent speed-up by setting maximum output rates on piece rate jobs, they have become, in Piaget's sense, a collective subject. So do oppressed peasants who form secret local guerilla groups that gradually develop the capacity to link up and coordinate their actions over regions or entire countries. So do the denizens of a workshop when they work out ways to collaborate to produce a joint product.

Individual subjects emerge out of their own activity and experience. As a result, they start from their own narrow perspective—Piaget's "autocentricity." In order to construct a collective subject, people need to assimilate and accommodate to each other's viewpoints—Piaget's "decentering."[7] That allows individuals to transcend the idiosyncratic results of their personal development and become part of a community that can function as a collective subject: "The subject's activity calls for a continual 'decentering' without which he cannot become free from his spontaneous intellectual autocentricity. This 'decentering' makes the subject enter upon, not so much an already available and therefore external universality, as an uninterrupted process of coordinating and setting in reciprocal relations."[8]

According to Piaget, to internalize an "external universality" is to accept "social constraint." Conversely, failing to engage in mutual assimilation and accommodation with other viewpoints embodies the "unconscious autocentricity of the individual," that is, "the mental attitude of young children who do not yet know how to collaborate or to coordinate their points of view."

Unlike individual subjects, collective subjects are composed of elements—people—that are already subjects themselves. So the construction of collective subjects does not require the long development Piaget describes as prerequisite for mature thought in individuals. Rather, it involves features that facilitate coordinated action, such as communications channels, networks and other social relationships, and shared mental operations and representations.[9]

Piaget's explication of decentering illuminated what I had discovered in the course of studying mass strikes and other social movements. Group formation and collective action do not necessarily start from a concept of the group as a group. A collection of people will often act in concert in response to a common problem without first having a strong consciousness of themselves as a group. As participants observe themselves acting in concert, they begin to take note of what they have in common, and to construct a conception of themselves as a collective subject or actor. Their action may be rational and purposive from the start, but consciousness of themselves as a group may only develop subsequently by an act of reflective abstraction. It is their actual ability to coordinate their action to realize their ends that constitutes them as a collective subject since, as Piaget says, any entity is a subject to the extent that it is able to transform the world physically or virtually.

I found this approach useful for constructing an account of the rise of what is often called the global justice or antiglobalization movement and which I referred to as "globalization from below." I described how economic globalization was creating problems for a wide range of people and movements around the world. In response to these problems, countermovements began from many diverse starting points, "ranging from local campaigns against runaway plants to union organizing in poor countries, and from protection of indigenous peoples to resistance to corporate-engineered food." As they began to act on their objectives, participants started asking each other for solidarity and support. The resulting cooperation started to construct a collective subject as many participants began "recognizing their commonalities and beginning to envision themselves as constructing a common movement."[10] Only as a result of such a shift to common preservation did globalization from below as an entity fully emerge.

Piaget's portrayal of decentering, overcoming social constraint, and forming collective subjects became a key element of my heuristic for common preservation. It sketches a process of self-organization that can make the emergence of new collective subjects, and of new common preservations, possible. Equilibration may not explain in some ultimate, philosophical sense why there is freedom or action or life, but it can help us understand how human beings can improve their action in certain regards without their improvement being either "wired in" or imposed "from outside." As Piaget put it, "Man can transform himself by transforming the world and can structure himself by constructing structures; and these structures are his own, for they are not eternally predestined either from within or from without."[11] Human action is patterned, but people construct and reconstruct their own patterns.

Piaget contrasts autocentricity and social constraint with an "ideal equilibrium" in which the relation of individual and group is not based on either.[12] Ideal equilibrium—"the reciprocal preservation of the whole and of the parts"—means "cooperation between individuals who become autonomous by this very cooperation."[13] People who meet, discuss, and decide by free consent can be autonomous; people who simply accept ideas imposed by others, or who act without regard to what others think, cannot. Such an "uninterrupted process of coordinating" allows collective subjects and the individual subjects who compose them to develop new forms of action that may overcome existing gaps and conflicts.

Even when Piaget's more speculative intuitions do not provide a secure basis for drawing conclusions, they often open up vistas for fruitful exploration. Piaget's "ideal equilibrium," for example, suggests that there may be an alternative to either atomic individualism or social domination—a free coordination in which individuals voluntarily share knowledge and coordinate their action to achieve individual and common goals. This suggests the possibility that we are not faced with an ineluctable either/or between domination and disorder: improved patterns of coordination may reduce both. It may well be impossible to fully realize such ideal equilibrium, but that doesn't mean that the quest for free coordination is simply a pipe dream or an impossible utopian fantasy.[14] Why shouldn't we be able to move toward it by "improving equilibration"?

Conclusion to Part 1

There are times when self-preservation doesn't work. It can even lead to self- or mutual destruction. When self-preservation cannot solve our problems, we can try and see what common preservation will do.

Common preservation is a shift from pursuing our own interests and well-being as individuals and established groups to strategies of collective action to realize common ends.

In a time when we are threatened by mutual destruction, I wanted to know how common preservation happens and how to encourage it. How do people move from strategies of self-preservation to those of common preservation? How do they form a concerted group capable of taking collective action? How can they use such action to affect for the better the problems they face?

I looked for answers wherever I could find them. I sought them primarily by observing and participating in social movements. That story is told in my book *Save the Humans? Common Preservation in Action*. In addition, I also conducted "raiding parties" on the work of thinkers who I hoped might also contribute to a better understanding of social movements and common preservation. Part 1 of this book presents the results.

The Pattern of Development

If humans and other living beings were entirely self-sufficient, we would have no needs that require action to meet. But as indicated by Dewey, Bertalanffy, Mann, and Piaget, among many others, human individuals and groups, like other living beings, are able to live only by meeting our various needs through action on and interaction with our environment.

To meet those needs, as Piaget points out, we develop patterns of action built up over time from biological, species, historical, social, and individual experience. Those guiding patterns coordinate various means to realize our ends and thereby fulfill our needs.

On the basis of those patterns we act. Our actions have results—intended and unintended. As Norbert Wiener described in the theory of cybernetics, we receive information about those results through feedback. We compare this feedback about the results of our action to our intent. If there is a gap between the two, we can correct our action to close the gap. That correction need not restore previous conditions; it can create a new solution that is different and better than previous patterns.

But where does the correction come from? As Piaget indicates, faced with a problem, a gap between the intention of our action and its result, we can search for a modification of our action that has the characteristics that will compensate for the gap—a search Dewey calls an "inquiry." The search may be random, selectively guided, or somewhere in between. It may be relatively passive, a scanning of the environment for something that looks like it might work. Or it may be quite active, seeking, uncovering, combining, testing, and evaluating information that may contribute to a solution. Such a search progresses by taking a known pattern and modifying it to compensate for the gap. That is assimilation combined with accommodation.

However convincing the results of mental operations may be, the proof of the modified pattern is in its ability to produce new and useful actions. Thought experiments must be tested in the arena of life itself. If the correction works, it can be incorporated in the pattern that will guide future action—development has occurred. If not, the search for new corrections must be renewed.

The Development of Common Preservation

This pattern of development helps explain in a general way how development—not merely change, but improvement that makes it possible to realize previously unreachable goals—can occur. But how can that explain a shift to common preservation? In chapter 17, "Equilibration and Social Movements," we saw how variants of this pattern of development led to the emergence of new common preservations—the 1973 consumer meat boycott, Occupy Wall Street, and the direct-action climate protection movement. Here I will give two other examples that illustrate how variants of the development pattern can lead to new strategies of common preservation.

Du Bois's investigation of the emergence of collective action by black slaves during and after the Civil War identified a radical shift of strategy in the face of new conditions. To gain some power over their conditions in normal times, slaves deliberately broke tools, worked inefficiently, and attempted to run away, though rarely with success; they also tried to win favor with owners and overseers by compliance with their demands. But in practice these patterns often failed to ensure better subsistence or less brutalization, let alone freedom.

As union armies occupied the South and made clear that they would not return fugitive slaves to their masters, one strategy, running away, began to achieve its intent—escape from hunger, an end to whippings and other brutalities, and liberation from slavery. The word-of-mouth "feedback" from the experience of those who fled to union lines indicated that it succeeded. And so the pattern of only occasionally trying to escape was replaced by one of escaping whenever the opportunity arose. Half a million slaves compared remaining on the plantation with the dash for freedom and chose the latter, with millions more poised to join them. The ex-slaves, now turned workers and soldiers, organized themselves to withhold their labor from the Confederacy—what Du Bois dubbed their "general strike"—and to support their everyday life behind Union lines. They thereby became a political force that provided the basis for Reconstruction—the first black participation in the political system of the South.

In *Strike!* I conducted similar inquiries about the participation of workers in mass strikes. Workers often expressed needs for secure employment, acceptable wages, protection of their health and safety, control over work time and work processes, and freedom from arbitrary authority. Often they tried to achieve these goals by advancing within companies and the labor market as individuals or by controlling certain jobs for their ethnic, gender, racial, or other group. These strategies were often unsuccessful, however, primarily because individual workers were largely powerless relative to their employers. So at certain points—for example when conditions deteriorated, or when opportunities for effective collective action improved—workers turned from individual to collective strategies to overcome the gap between objectives and results. Often small experiments—cooperation in limiting production quotas, for example—suggested the possibility of collective action as a means to increase workers' power. So did examples like strikes and other visible action conducted by others elsewhere. The end result might be collective action like slowdowns and strikes and collective organization like informal work groups, unions, and wider social and political movements.

Common Preservation in Action

People move from individual to common preservation primarily in the hope that they can better accomplish their ends. But why is it plausible that collective action can achieve things that individual action can't? And what leads people to believe it can?

The problems that generate new common preservations are generally the result of a lack of power. Slaves were powerless before masters; workers needed the jobs their employers could provide; housewives could not control the price of beef; opponents of climate change had little influence on huge fossil fuel corporations and the governments they controlled. How could they acquire the power they needed to counteract that power?

Power, as Michael Mann indicates, results from cooperation. The ability to coordinate the action of various people multiplies its force. Mann describes as networks the great variety of means through which people coordinate their action for common purposes. Networks form and grow by connecting initially isolated individuals and groups into a concerted force—linking the nooks and crannies.

But how is this of any use in the face of the power of slave owners, bosses, and fossil fuel corporations? The answer, according to Gandhi and Sharp, is that power depends on the consent or cooperation of others. Slave owners are powerful, but their power depends on the obedience of slaves. Employers are powerful, but their power depends on the labor of their workers. Consumers depend on meat companies to supply their tables, but conversely meat companies depend on consumers to buy their products. Fossil fuel companies can purchase politicians and acquire permits, but they can't build power plants and pipelines if millions of people block their construction projects.

Both the powerful and the powerless are part of a system of mutual dependence. The powerful are dependent on the rest of society for their power and cannot govern without the cooperation of those they govern. But the withdrawal of cooperation in itself has little effect when conducted by isolated individuals—as a foreman in a Naugatuck Valley brass plant put it, "If a man won't work, I'll just send for another man." It is by combining cooperation among those facing a problem with the withdrawal of cooperation from those perpetuating the problem that common preservation can make change for the better.

It is going to take a lot of development, in particular development of common preservation, to get out of the tangle of mutual destruction we're in. Part 2 translates the development of common preservation into a heuristic to help guide inquiry when common preservation has occurred—or when it is needed.

PART 2
THE TOOLS

CHAPTER 18

The Tools

All the ideas gathered in part 1 went into the formation of my thinking about social problems and social change. But like old metamorphic rocks they have mingled and interacted so much that their components may be almost beyond recognition. And new features have emerged that are not to be found in the originals.

As I worked on research and action problems over the past few decades, I would often rummage through these ideas, trying them out in various circumstances to see if they would help identify significant problems or develop new solutions. I assimilated them as tools for my workshop and accommodated them to the jobs at hand. Out of them—as well as from my own observation and experience—I gradually developed a heuristic for common preservation.

Heuristics are methods to help solve a problem, commonly informally. They are ways of thinking that are worth trying out in particular situations to see if they are useful for "interrogating the evidence." They are tools for the workshop of common preservation.

Part 2 sums up what I have found useful for understanding common preservations and for conducting thought experiments for new ones. From compiled hindsight, thought experiments, and actual experiments, it identifies patterns that help explain why the development of new common preservations might be possible; what can block them; and how those blocks can be overcome. This heuristic presents patterns that can be applied—and modified—to understand the emergence of common preservations in the past and to guide their emergence in the future.

We know from history that new common preservations really do emerge from time to time. And we can observe a general pattern in the social movements described in this book:

People experience a problem they can't solve using their current patterns of individual and combined action. They may try to deny or ignore the problem, or they may despair and give up trying to solve it. But sometimes they seek new solutions that require new patterns of action. They test new ways of acting that require new forms of coordination. They begin to share information, ideas, and plans. They debate the implications of past experiments and the likely result of new ones. They come up with further modifications of their action patterns and test them in turn. They are often stymied by failures of their experiments. But their combined effort may give them new power to solve their problems. It may also create new problems—problems that may in turn require new common preservations.

What accounts for this pattern? How and why does it happen? The answers are of practical significance. Understanding why common preservation, and the emergence of new common preservations, is possible at all can help us see why they do not arise in particular situations, and will shed light on what might be done to reduce the obstacles to their emergence. Identifying the kinds of problems that require new common preservations for their solution, such as disorder and domination, helps clarify what potential solutions might be. Showing the "fit" between problems and their solutions helps identify what kinds of possible solutions may be worth testing. Seeing why new solutions may in turn produce new problems may help find ways to forestall such untoward results.

How to Solve It

I don't remember it myself, but there's a story in my family that at a certain stage I, like many children, drove everyone crazy by asking "why?" all the time. Finally a grownup relative asked me why I asked "why?" all the time. "Why," I'm told I answered, "is the word I use to find things out." Like every child who asks a question, I had invented heuristics.

Many years later on a shelf of discarded books I chanced to pick up a tattered copy of *How to Solve It: A New Aspect of Mathematical Method* by the mathematician G. Polya. It was originally published in 1945 and is now recognized as a classic, perhaps the first modern book on heuristics. Directed primarily to math teachers, it provides a set of procedures and questions designed to elicit "mental operations typically useful for the solution of problems."[1]

To my surprise, I found Polya's heuristics helpful for the problems I was attempting to solve. It gave me a way to understand and organize the unguided groping that I went through in my own mind as I approached a problem. But it also gave me a way to think about the problem-solving process more generally. It provided a way to take the rather abstract ideas presented in Part 1 and apply them to concrete problems. From it I got the idea—embodied in this book—of organizing the mental operations I typically found useful for understanding, engaging in, and encouraging common preservation in the form of a common preservation heuristic. Its purpose would not be to provide cut-and-dried answers to my questions about common preservation, but rather a way to investigate them. It follows Rilke's advice to "love the questions" in the hope of living "into the answer."[2] If we are to survive, we will need to live our way into common preservation.

As a historian, I found Polya's heuristic provided a way to think about what happened when people in the past faced problems and attempted to find solutions to them. It helped me reconstruct the process by which American colonists came up with the idea of affecting British colonial policy through a boycott of British tea, and how American housewives a couple of centuries later came up with the idea of boycotting meat as a way of affecting American economic policy.

As a person concerned with today's social problems, I found in Polya's heuristic a strategy for searching for solutions. The method Tim Costello and I used to search for a strategy to organize contingent workers, for example, pretty much followed the methods laid out by Polya.

Polya warns that finding "infallible rules of discovery" will "never be more than a dream."[3] Solving problems is a "practical skill" like swimming. It is acquired by imitation and practice.[4] It even involves "unconscious work" and a dimension of luck.[5]

As with Dewey, Piaget, and others in their tradition, Polya's approach starts with identifying a gap—in a math problem, the "unknown." It is "an unsolved problem, an open question." It can be represented as "a gap across which we have to construct a bridge."[6]

Polya's core strategy is to take a pattern with which a problem solver is already familiar and apply it to the problem at hand. "Look at the unknown! And try to think of a familiar problem having the same or a similar unknown." This is what anyone is likely to do when faced with a problem.

> Are you hungry? You wish to obtain food and you think of familiar
> ways of obtaining food.... You wish to construct a triangle and
> you think of familiar ways of constructing a triangle. Have you
> a problem of any kind? You wish to find a certain unknown, and
> you think of familiar ways of finding such an unknown, or some
> similar unknown.[7]

In Piaget's terms, you look for a familiar pattern you can apply to the
new problem—a pattern to which you can assimilate the problem.

Such an approach comes naturally to anyone who is "seriously
concerned with his problem and has some common sense." But such a
person may not be able to express what they are doing "in clear words."
Polya's heuristic is intended to make that possible.[8]

Of course, each problem is different, so the method that solved a
previous problem must be modified to solve a new one. Indeed, Polya
advises, "If you cannot solve the proposed problem, try to solve first some
related problem."[9] If we can find and solve such a problem, "We have a
model to follow."[10] Only beware the danger that we may "stray so far
from our original problem that we are in danger of losing it altogether."[11]
To speak Piagetian, we must accommodate our patterns without changing them so much that they become irrelevant to the problem at hand.

We generally have to start by feeling our way toward a solution. As
we understand the problem better and assemble relevant ideas and
information, we can begin to see what is necessary for its solution and
devise a plan that lays out the areas of research, the operations, and the
tools that will be necessary to solve it.

I found Polya's discussion of solving practical problems particularly
appropriate to historical and social questions. He points out several ways
that practical problems are different from conventional mathematical
problems. Practical problems typically involve many "unknowns," many
different conditions that the solution must meet, and vast amounts of
potentially relevant data. A plan for a dam, for example, must specify a
wide range of dimensions, materials, and locations. It must meet multiple conditions, such as producing electric power, providing water for
irrigation, controlling floods, protecting the environment, and taking
as little time and money as possible to construct.

Practical problems require "much knowledge which has not yet
reached a precise, scientific level." The solver of practical problems has

"a multitude of data and conditions: we take into account as many as we can but we are obliged to neglect some."[12] This is very like the historian or the social movement strategist who must select out of a diverse mass of facts the most relevant ones, but who can never take everything into account.

Problem-solving for Polya involves both intuitive and formal reasoning. We may grasp a point either by concentrating upon it "till we see it so clearly and distinctly that we have no doubt that the step is correct" or we may derive it "according to formal rules." Both "insight" and "formal proof" have their place in problem-solving.[13] "Our non-mathematical knowledge cannot be based entirely on formal proofs. The more solid part of our everyday knowledge is continually tested and strengthened by our everyday experience."[14] I felt supported by Polya in my view that formal, propositional argument and more tacit, intuitive, experienced-based practices can complement each other for solving problems.

Problem-solving involves what Polya calls "heuristic" or "plausible" reasoning.[15] The conventional demonstrative syllogism states, "If A, then B." If B is false, then A is false. A "heuristic syllogism" states "If A, then B is more likely." If B is true, then we conclude not that A is true, but that A is more likely. The degree of credibility remains a judgment call, and it can never amount to certainty.[16]

What E.P. Thompson calls "historical logic" is based on such "plausible reasoning." As I wrote in *History from Below*, you can't prove what happened in the past the way you prove an answer in mathematics; all you can do is construct the most likely account of what happened. It's like a courtroom, except that often you have to be satisfied with "the most probable account" even if it can't be proved "beyond a reasonable doubt."[17]

I found Polya's ideas complemented Piaget's and provided a way to make them operational—to use them to guide action. Polya, like Piaget, portrays thinking as mental action.[18] A problem is essentially a gap that we need to bridge. The solution is a construction that closes the gap. The process involves mobilizing the relevant facts and combining them in new ways. This "adapting and combining activity" is "organization"[19] or, as Piaget might say, assimilation, accommodation, and coordination. This results in a reorganization of the way we conceive the problem—in Piaget's terms, an accommodation of our initial pattern.[20] The modified pattern constitutes an organized whole that closes the gap and thereby solves the problem.

Polya, like Piaget, portrays internalized operations and dialogue with others as instances of the same "functional nucleus." Polya describes thinking not only as mental action but also as "mental discourse, as a sort of mental conversation of the thinker with himself."[21]

I use Polya's ideas to reconstruct how people changed their patterns of thought and action in the past. I start by examining the problems they faced and why their existing patterns couldn't solve them. Then I look for evidence of other experiences or observations they may have drawn on to solve the problem. In *Strike!* I puzzled over how the sit-down strikes emerged so rapidly in 1934 in Akron's rubber industry. I asked myself questions such as, if workers have never organized a union, have they perhaps organized a church social group? (Many of Akron's rubber workers were active church members and union meetings often resembled religious revival meetings.[22]) If they've never stopped a rubber factory, have they perhaps stopped a baseball game? (The first sit-down was said to have happened at a baseball game to protest an unpopular umpire.) Did they hear from a foreign relative about factory occupations in a distant land? (Poland had recently had coal mine occupations, and many rubber workers came from Polish families.) In other words, I looked at what patterns they might know about that they could have adapted to meet their current needs.

I also looked at what accommodation of those patterns was necessary to apply them to the problem people faced. How did women have to modify a kaffeeklatsch to turn it into a consciousness-raising group or a meat boycott organization? This approach doesn't prove how the innovative action was constructed—after all, there could always have been another process that we don't have the evidence for. But it does provide a plausible reconstruction of how and why new action emerged.

I use this same approach for thinking about how people can solve the problems they face in the present. I start by identifying people who face an unsolved problem. I ask, what have they done in other circumstances? Then I think about how they could vary familiar actions in ways that might solve the problem. For the past few years, for example, I have been preoccupied with the question of how organized labor could change its approach to climate change. One way I tried to illuminate this was to prepare a "Historical Analysis of How Labor Changes on Key Issues" with case studies of civil rights, the Iraq War, single-payer health care, globalization, and immigration.[23] I drew on these experiences to develop strategies that might help labor transform its approach to climate. Such a result does not prove that labor will in fact change in that way, or at all. But it does indicate paths by which it plausibly might do so.[24]

Polya urges that after solving a problem, students look back at the completed solution, "reconsidering and reexamining the result and the path that led to it" in order to "consolidate their knowledge and develop their ability to solve problems."[25] This is an example of the process that Piaget describes as "reflective abstraction." It can lead to "compiled hindsight." It's what I'm trying to do in this book.

A Historical and Developmental Method

The heuristic uses the historical method described in E.H. Carr's *What Is History?* This involves a kind of loop in which new information corrects existing patterns of thought ("received interpretations"), further gaps of fact and interpretation are identified, and the modified patterns of thought guide a search for still further corrective information to eliminate old and new gaps of fact and interpretation.[26]

The heuristic develops, tests, and uses what E.P. Thompson in *The Poverty of Theory* calls "historical concepts." These describe processes that may occur in a variety of different contexts. For example, historians have identified in different times and places a "crisis of subsistence" in which a crop failure leads to famine, epidemics, rising death rates, consumption of next year's seed, and then after sharp population reduction a rising birthrate. Our heuristic identifies many such patterns in the development of common preservation.

The thirteen heuristic tools presented in this part classify various forms of equilibration. There is nothing magical or inevitable about thirteen tools. No doubt they could be partitioned differently to give more elements or combined to give fewer. There may be some equally important elements I haven't thought of. All I can say is I kept adding elements for many decades, but the list here has remained stable for two decades or more while I have applied it to a wide variety of problems. If you can expand or improve it, all the better.

The various elements of my heuristic are not independent. Rather each represents a different but related approach to the same phenomena. For example, the same subject or problem could be looked at in terms either of boundaries or of coordination. You could ask, how much do boundaries impede coordination? But you could also ask, does coordination cross boundaries? The questions are not identical, but they do overlap.

Indeed, any one of the approaches could probably be extended to include all the others. For example, coordination or representation or disorder could be the theme into which all parts of an interpretation could be integrated. But that would reduce the power of the heuristic tools to call attention to and help organize diverse aspects of a problem or field.

The elements of the heuristic are intended to be a bit more than just a random pile of tools. They are selected and adapted to be complementary means to fulfill their function of understanding and furthering common preservation.[27] They are designed to combine in such a way as to enhance or complete each other. They are as well organized and comprehensive as I have been able to make them.

Using the Tools

In part 2, I take you into the workshop and show you how I put the heuristic tools into use. I hope you'll try out some of them for yourself and see if you can use them to address the problems that concern you. I wish I could put the tools in your hands and coach you in using them, but that is beyond what can be done in a book. But I can give you some idea of the general patterns I follow and reconstruct the operations I typically employ.

I start by developing some preliminary sense of the purpose of my inquiry and the questions I want to answer. This introduces a subjective element right from the beginning, since the interest that drives the inquiry is rooted in personal and collective needs and experience.

I gather initial information. I look to see how others have approached the same subject. Then I look at the preliminary information I have accumulated and ask whether I could see, find, or construct a pattern that reminds me of any of the tools. Alternatively, I might look at the tools and see if some of the initial information may fit into the patterns provided by one of them. Such a start aims to find or create what Polya calls a "bright idea."

Whichever way I start, I next select a heuristic tool that may help organize the information. For example, if I were trying to understand the development of a national union federation from separate unions in different crafts or different localities I might select "transforming coordination" to develop and test. As it happens, the early labor federation the National Labor Union did develop in the mid-nineteenth century in order to create greater labor strength in response to "feedback" from the failures of local and individual craft unions that resulted when industry went national.

Next, I gather and examine a wider range of information. Is there any evidence that might fit into the patterns of the selected tool? If so, I can start to build up a trial hypothesis or "first cut" by adding other information to the developing pattern. Then, to paraphrase E.H. Carr, the initial draft is "added to, subtracted from, re-shaped, cancelled," while the further research is "guided and directed and made fruitful by the writing." Through this process the hypothesis or model—for example of how coordination got transformed—grows more and more concrete and specific. This back-and-forth is the active part of the heuristic—it is not just a matter of coming across and recognizing patterns, but of active search and construction.

As I go back to pore over more information, I search for facts that may fit into my developing scheme poorly or not at all—or even contradict it. If I found such "bad news" or "disconfirming evidence" I would follow one of two courses. I might abandon the pattern and try out another one. Or I might try to modify or accommodate the pattern so that it assimilates both the old information and the new.

I would continue testing my tentative interpretation against new evidence and the views of others, modifying it as necessary.

If I got stuck with a contradiction I couldn't resolve or a dead end I couldn't move beyond, I might temporarily shift my focus to another topic, question, problem, or tool. That would advance another part of the inquiry, and it might give additional information or insight for the unresolved exploration, confirming, challenging, or elaborating it.

Eventually I would have to test all the different results against the evidence and against each other. I would mutually modify (assimilate and accommodate) them to form a coherent, non-self-contradictory whole that accords with the facts. I would test them against other theories and the findings of related fields. In the case of a historical narrative, I would similarly test for plausible fit between earlier and later actions and events.

This approach can be used both to make plausible explanations of the past and to identify plausible strategies for the future.

For the past, we would identify entities able to make an impact on the world, their problems, and their existing capabilities. If we find them modifying their capabilities in ways that solve their problems, and that would be unlikely unless they were modified for that purpose, we can reasonably conclude that they were intentionally made to solve those problems.

For the future, we can start from the same identification of entities, problems, and capabilities.

We can try to find ways to apply or modify the capabilities that *could* lead to solutions to the problems. This may require transformations and subsequent reorganizations through a series of possible but underdetermined, unpredictable stages. If we can find such a sequence of problem-solving modifications of which our actors are capable, we can say they represent a plausible solution to the problem and make it credible that the subjects or actors could solve the problem. That may make it more worthwhile to investigate, test, and pursue such solutions.

Of course, the account I've given here is more orderly, conscious, and rational than what happens in practice. While the inquiry is occurring, the inquirer is unlikely to have full consciousness and clarity about what they are actually doing; nor is their subsequent memory of what they did likely to be completely accurate. The account here is a rational reconstruction of the process, which is unlikely to be a perfect reproduction of what actually happened.

How would you go about evaluating whether an interpretation— your own or someone else's—is a good one? You need to see if there is an equilibrium or fit between the interpretation and the knowable facts; if the facts "destabilize" the interpretation by not fitting it well, the gap indicates that more work needs to be done to accommodate the account to the available evidence. You also need to see if the different elements of the interpretation contradict each other, or if as a whole the account is incoherent; if so, it is due for a rethink. The more an interpretation accords with the knowable facts and the less it contradicts itself, the better it can be relied on as a guide for action.

The Tools

This chapter, "The Tools," has described the common preservation heuristic and how to use it. The next two chapters will deal with very general processes that make common preservations possible. "Identifying

Problems" characterizes new common preservations as responses to problems—disequilibria or gaps that can't be overcome by currently established means. "Solving Problems" presents the capacity for equilibration—gap-reducing coordination—that is shared by living beings, but takes a particular form in human beings, as the means by which problems are typically solved.

The next two chapters look at the problem-solving equilibration process in terms of its relation to purposes. "Transforming Means" describes the way people change their strategies, for example by a shift from self-preservation to common preservation. "Transforming Ends" looks at the way purposes themselves can change in the course of the equilibration process.

"Transforming Representation" examines the complementary roles of tacit "thinking without thinking" and explicit representation and communication through language in the emergence of new common preservations.

The next four chapters consider the way new common preservations can emerge through different kinds of change in the relations among individuals and groups. "Transforming Boundaries" examines the role of boundaries and entities and their changes in the emergence of new common preservations. "Transforming Coordination" explores how new patterns of joint action emerge, how they can increase participants' power, and how that can provide a motive for new common preservations. "Transforming Differentiation" examines the division into different roles that accompanies coordination and the problems it can present for common preservation. "Transforming Power" distinguishes equally and unequally shared power, shows the origin of power in dependence, and examines the multilateral and mutable character of the power that results.

The last four chapters address how common preservations can counter various types of problems that arise in systems of parts and wholes. "Countering Disorder" explores how common preservations can address the problems that lead to failures of coordination and unintended side effects and interaction effects. "Countering Domination" considers how common preservations can deal with unequal power rooted in unequal dependence. "Countering Disorder Combined with Domination" examines how common preservation can address multiple power centers that create chaos through competition to control people and resources. "Forestalling New Disorder and Domination" discusses how to proactively limit future problems by incorporating the means of countering them in new common preservations.

"Conclusion to Part 2" sums up the heuristic patterns proposed for understanding and encouraging common preservation.

This heuristic continues to evolve, and I hope it will continue to do so. I hope if you find it useful you will not only apply it to new problems but further modify it to make it work better.

CHAPTER 19

Identifying Problems

The emergence of new common preservations requires that many people abandon their current strategies and shift to new ones that depend on complex new relationships with other people. The process may be costly and the results uncertain. People are unlikely to make such a shift unless they share serious problems that give them a strong motivation to do so. Therefore new common preservations normally represent a response to a problem.[1] To probe the origins, character, and implications of problems we use our problem identification tool.

The idea of a problem is illustrated by the story I was raised on about a little boy who never spoke. He grew to be two, then three, then four, and his parents grew more and more worried. Then suddenly one morning he remarked, "There's not enough salt in the oatmeal." His parents, astonished, exclaimed, "You can talk!" The boy replied, "Of course I can talk." "Why didn't you ever talk before?" "Because up to now everything has been satisfactory."

A problem is a situation that someone considers unsatisfactory. John Dewey interprets a problem as a disturbance in the normal ongoing process of life.[2] It provides the starting point for inquiry that might lead to adaptive action. Jean Piaget interprets a problem as a gap. It is something that existing patterns of thought and action cannot assimilate without changing themselves or the world. Such a gap creates an imbalance or disequilibrium. Disequilibrium, far from being abnormal, is the human condition. And it is what drives equilibration—the search for solutions to problems that will create a new equilibrium.

Problems present themselves in a variety of forms. As needs: there is something we need and don't have, the lack of which impedes our functioning. As desires: we want something that we don't have. As ethical violations: something is morally wrong. As norms: someone violates our beliefs about how someone in their position should behave. As failures to meet expectations: our experience contradicts what we anticipated, and now we don't know what to expect. As preferences: we compare what exists to some other possible state and find it lacking.

It is tempting but fruitless to seek a single formulation to which all such gaps can be reduced. These different kinds of gaps—of needs, wants, values, norms, expectations, and preferences—are not fixed or rigidly distinguished. As E.P. Thompson put it, "Inside every 'need' there is an affect, or 'want', on its way to becoming an 'ought' (and *vice versa*)."[3] What they have in common is a gap between means and ends or a conflict among different means or different ends.

Problems can be disregarded, denied, or despairingly accepted as unchangeable reality. But they can also be viewed as gaps between what exists and what could be.[4] They can thereby be transformed into needs to be fulfilled, obstacles to be overcome, interests to be realized, or mysteries to be resolved. They can thus provide motives: conditions of individual and collective actors that incite them to action.

Some problems can be solved by individuals. Some can be solved by collectively applying existing social patterns. But some can only be solved by transforming existing social patterns. It is problems that can't be solved in some other way that lead to new forms of common preservation.

When the boy with too little salt in his oatmeal complained to his parents, they may simply have passed him the salt cellar. But suppose he had been living in India under British rule. The British salt monopoly laws forbade Indians to make salt, thus keeping the price prohibitively high for many Indians. Solving the boy's salt problem may have required new forms of action and new forms of coordination among different people's actions—for example, the massive salt marches, initiated by Gandhi, to make salt in defiance of British law.

The idea of a problem to which people respond by creating new solutions can serve as a heuristic for understanding the emergence of new common preservations. In writing about the economic globalization of the late twentieth century, for example, I repeatedly used the emergence of a problem as the starting point for understanding the emergence of new social patterns.[5] The plunging economic growth rates and plummeting corporate profits of the 1970s led corporations and their intellectual servants first to advocate economic nationalist and Keynesian solutions, then to promote globalization and neoliberalism. National governments and national economic regulation made a problem for corporations seeking to lower their costs through globalization; they promoted new institutions like the World Trade Organization to solve it. The established corporate patterns of vertical and horizontal integration became a problem in a global economy with vague and shifting market boundaries; to solve the problem, corporations moved to a core-ring structure in which all but core functions could be outsourced anywhere in the world.

New problems and new solutions were not limited to corporations and their supporters, however. Collapsing commodity prices created problems for poor countries; they responded by trying to act collectively through the United Nations to establish new trade arrangements embodied in a "New International Economic Order." Corporate-led globalization presented a problem to workers and unions, who found themselves thrust into a competitive "race to the bottom." After the failure of economic nationalist strategies, many of them turned to new forms of international labor solidarity to resist the race to the bottom.

A wide range of people, from consumer advocates to AIDS activists to local food producers, faced problems as a result of global competition and new global trade rules. Their established strategies were oriented toward national economies that were being disintegrated. Yet they were poorly connected to other people around the world who faced the same problems, and from potential allies who faced different problems but ones that had the same causes. The diverse set of problems caused by globalization eventually led to the emergence of globalization from below, also known as the global justice or antiglobalization movement, and such new organizational responses as transnational advocacy networks and the World Social Forum. Thus the problems created by globalization led to a process of problem-solving or equilibration that produced new common preservations.

The tool for identifying problems can be used not only to understand the past but also to understand our current situations and their potential development—including the potential to solve their problems through new common preservations. I can give a few examples from my own experience.

In the 1970s I noted that working people's own knowledge and insight were not getting adequately reflected in the emerging field of labor history, and conversely the knowledge that was being created by the "new labor history" was rarely reaching working people and their communities. The identification of these problems led me to establish the Brass Workers History Project, a participatory, community-based labor history project that involved brass workers in Connecticut's Naugatuck Valley in recounting and interpreting their own experience, and then to disseminate a book and a movie about them to a local and national working-class audience.

When the Naugatuck Valley brass industry collapsed, working people and their institutions faced devastating unemployment and disruption of community life. They appeared powerless to respond. Some of them began to identify this powerlessness as a central part of their problem. They recognized that it was caused in part because there was no vehicle through which they could attempt to influence the forces that were overwhelming their communities. In response they formed a community coalition called the Naugatuck Valley Project to combat plant closings and deindustrialization.

In the 1980s, the Connecticut economy crashed. Among a welter of explanations, one critical problem was identified: the lack of investment in the state's small businesses. I helped create the Connecticut Community Economic Development Fund to provide community-based businesses with capital and capacity building.

As the George W. Bush administration began the buildup for a war against Iraq, the devastating consequences that it would cause became increasingly apparent. The identification of this problem led to a global mass movement culminating in worldwide demonstrations with fifteen million participants. But the growing power of the movement revealed the problem that the US veto in the Security Council blocked international action to halt the war. The identification of this problem led to a global effort to promote a UN General Assembly "Uniting for Peace" resolution against a US attack on Iraq—an effort that was only defeated by US threats of retaliation against countries that supported it.[6]

When China proposed a new labor contract law that would for the first time provide significant protections for Chinese workers' labor rights, foreign corporations that operated in China tried to gut the law. This problem was identified through monitoring of the Chinese press and leaking of internal corporate documents. Knowledge of the problem was disseminated through an international information campaign. This campaign identified the probable effect of the law's defeat—downward pressure on labor conditions throughout the world due to China's "wild west" employment practices. The outcome was an international campaign by labor and human rights groups that helped save the most important provisions of the law.[7]

In each of these cases, a problem or disequilibrium led to a process of problem-solving or equilibration that ultimately produced a new common preservation.

People who solved a problem in the past are likely to have used something resembling our problem identification and problem-solving tools to do so. Historians can examine the problems people faced in the past, probe the process by which they became aware of them, and explain how they did or did not respond. We the living can identify problems we face in common, inquire into their causes and dynamics, and conduct thought experiments in search of solutions.

While human beings have always had problems, there are two things new about the problems of our era. Our species has developed the capacity for self-annihilation. And global forces pass with less and less difficulty across national boundaries. As a result, problems are increasingly global and species-wide. So solutions cannot be just for restricted groups. No restricted group can solve the problem of providing a secure future for itself without solving the more general problem of providing a secure future for everyone. Self-preservation requires common preservation.[8]

CHAPTER 20

Solving Problems

Individuals and groups may identify problems, but how do they find solutions? How do they create new and better ways of acting—including new common preservations? How can we the living use problem-solving techniques to better solve our own problems? Our problem-solving tool can help us understand how people in the past have gone about solving their problems; how we can investigate their efforts; and how we can solve our problems better.

Problem-Solving as Equilibration

People can create new problem-solving common preservations because we are equilibrators. We can vary our action to close the gaps between our ends and the conditions we face. Among the ways we can vary our action is to coordinate it with others in new ways that better realize our common ends.

If people's behavior were to be completely determined by the social system in which they live, or by those in positions of social power, or by uncontrolled social forces, they would not be able to create new common preservations. But life isn't like that. Living beings guide their action themselves. They act to realize their own ends.

We, like other living beings, are not simply dictated to by our environment; we also impose our own patterns on the environment. We can pursue goals despite changes in our environment by modifying our actions to compensate for those changes.

That doesn't mean that our actions are fully determined by some unchanging program within us, however. We not only change our environment, we also change ourselves. We preserve ourselves by changing our environment; but we change our environment by changing ourselves.

This capacity to equilibrate belongs not only to individual living beings, but also in some degree to the groups they comprise, some of the products they fashion, and the ecosystems of which they are part.

Many social theories assert that individuals and societies gravitate toward some kind of equilibrium, a balance of forces. The structural-functionalism of Talcott Parsons, for example, held that to survive and maintain equilibrium with respect to its environment, a social system must maintain its "latent pattern."[1] The possibility that it could maintain equilibrium by transforming its patterns was apparently not even considered. Such an approach is notoriously inept for dealing with social change. In it what appears to be change must be reduced to the realization of a predetermined equilibrium or status quo.

Equilibration as I understand it, following Jean Piaget, is very different from such equilibrium models. In this approach, the default state of individuals and groups is likely to be *dis*equilibrium. Whatever equilibrium there is results not from a static balance of forces, but from an active process of compensation that overcomes imbalances. Indeed, it is disequilibrium that motivates the effort to establish new and better equilibria. Problems are the parents of solutions.

Such equilibration is possible because of feedback loops. Feedback loops are circular flows of information that use the results of past action to guide future action. A feedback loop allows an entity—whether an organism, an individual, a group, or even an artificial device—to guide its action to realize its ends. It compares information about the results of action with that action's intent. If that comparison indicates a discrepancy between the desired ends and the existing situation, the entity acts to counteract or compensate for the gap. It then compares the result of its new action with the ends it sought to realize. If that action has not successfully achieved its objective, the entity uses the information—the feedback—from its action to correct its subsequent action so as to close the gap and align its means and ends more effectively. Indeed, it may not just correct its current action; it may incorporate the correction in its patterns to improve its action in the future. That is development.

The cybernetic idea of guidance through a feedback loop spells out the intuitive idea of trial-and-error learning, which occurs through the correction of error. Error represents a gap between what is intended and what actually results; improved action reduces that gap. Pragmatism regards such gaps as problems to be solved. In cybernetics they are known as deviations from goal that are corrected by feedback. Piaget calls them disequilibria, to be resolved by equilibration.

We can often observe trial-and-error learning without being able to fully account for how it works. In intelligent animals, trial-and-error learning is easy to observe but hard to explicate; the same can be true for humans. It's not just wired-in instinct; some kind of cognitive unconscious or "thinking without thinking" must be at work. Such tacit learning can contribute to the emergence of new common preservations. We can identify and make use of such capacities, even if they are produced by means that we don't yet understand.

Nor are problem-solving capacities limited to trial and error. People can mentally represent their situations and their own action virtually using language and other representations. They can organize these virtual representations or reflective abstractions in their minds. They can conduct thought experiments on these virtual objects. They can thereby conduct trials and identify errors mentally without having to actually conduct them in the world of practice. They can equilibrate their thinking to help equilibrate their action. And through language they can share their representations and their thought experiments with others.

Equilibration provides a template for understanding the emergence of new common preservations. For example, African American civil rights groups organized for decades to support legal challenges to segregation. Despite some victories, the segregation of schools, lunch counters, and transportation in the South continued unabated. The experience of continuing segregation illustrates feedback. African American communities reflected on, discussed, and evaluated their past action by comparing its effects to the ends for which it aimed. Disappointment with the results led to experiment with new modes of struggle. Those in turn led to the militant direct-action phase of the civil rights movement in the 1950s and 1960s.

This process—problem-solving, correction, or equilibration—works in a paradoxically negative way. A cybernetic system realizes a goal not so much by calculating how to reach it, but by progressively reducing the deviation from it. Gregory Bateson pointed out how cybernetic explanation contrasts with conventional causal explanation: "We consider what alternative possibilities could conceivably have occurred and then ask why many of the alternatives were not followed, so that the particular event was one of those few which could, in fact, occur."[2] Such explanation is nondeterministic in the sense that actors could have decided to act differently, and if they had, different results would have been possible.

Action realizes an intent by counteracting or compensating for the divergence from that intent. A dog that chases and catches a rabbit attains the goal of catching a rabbit; but it does so by eliminating the distance that initially separated it from the rabbit. A very different example of the same point is military theorist Liddell Hart's idea of an "indirect strategy"—one in which an enemy is defeated not by applying superior force, but by weakening and fragmenting its capacity to act.

Equilibration by one actor can lead to disequilibrium or even destruction for another. But counteraction does not necessarily imply antagonism. Violence and war are counteraction, but so are offering mutual cooperation and making a deal.[3]

Equilibration can help explain the emergence of social movements, mass strikes, and similar forms of social action. In the case of the women's liberation movement, for example, the pervasive strategy of female advancement through higher education left women's social subordination intact and led to innumerable experiences of personal frustration with discrimination on the job and relegation to the role of being "just a housewife." The feedback from those experiences led hundreds and eventually millions of women to shift to a strategy that challenged prevailing social roles.

The action of living beings is not just random; it is organized into patterns.[4] These patterns represent the general features of an action. They are built up in and inherited from the past—biological, historical, and personal. The particulars of particular situations are assimilated to them. So each act is both a particular act in a particular context and an instance of a broader pattern.

The guidance of action by patterns means that learning is not simply a matter of a stimulus mechanically reinforcing one or another response. Rather, a subject must assimilate the "stimulus" to their own patterns and accommodate their patterns to make them more effective. Such patterns make it possible for individuals and groups to be active, rather than merely reactive. When something happens to them, their response is determined not just by the impinging event, but also by their own patterns.

The same general patterns may be applied over and over again, but they must be applied in ways that fit particular situations. They adapt or accommodate to particular situations on the basis of feedback about their past effectiveness. This can happen biologically through the Darwinian process of natural selection or in humans through trial-and-error learning and reflective abstraction.

Such patterns can be more or less fixed. Even the simplest organisms have some capacity to change behaviors that are not producing their intended results, but most of their behavior is wired-in genetically, leaving only a limited opportunity for variation and learning. Their behavior is primarily guided by instinct—fixed patterns developed by evolutionary adaptation. In more intelligent creatures, instinct is less rigid and more subject to modification by learning. They can make use of accumulated hindsight, drawing lessons from past experience to improve their ability to act effectively not just in the present but in the future. They not only change what they do; they learn from the feedback from their own action to change it for the better.

In human beings, instincts have partially atrophied and the patterns that guide human action are more the product of learning. The result is the enormously greater variability of human action. People can combine patterns, break them down into components, modify them, abandon them, and invent new ones. People who once made jungle huts can make skyscrapers; people who once made war can become peacemakers—and vice versa. While instinctive patterns like eating and copulating remain, the range of human actions among different individuals, societies, and eras is so great that instinct can't explain very much of the variation. While many other species engage in common preservation, their patterns are largely set by instinct.[5] Because their instincts have atrophied, humans can develop new common preservations.

The loop connecting initial patterns, actions based on them, feedback of the results, and an improved pattern can help explain both the apparent stability of social patterns and their periodic transformation. Each application of a pattern is both an expression of the continuing pattern and a new act, distinct from all others. It is therefore both a preservation of the pattern and a change. In a cybernetic interpretation, preservation and transformation are not opposites, but different aspects of the same process. Entities maintain themselves by changing and change in order to maintain themselves. The women who initiated and joined the women's liberation movement made a change that transformed the world. Yet in doing so they drew on their established purposes and on established patterns of action they modified for the new strategy—kaffeeklatsch morphed to consciousness-raising group. This represented, from one perspective, a radical change in strategy, but it also represented a continuity both of means and of ends.

Equilibration may seem to imply a gradual process of adaptation with no sharp discontinuities. But that is not necessarily so. The harder gaps are to close, the larger the changes in practices and goals necessary to address them—the less assimilation to existing patterns works and the more accommodation of those patterns is necessary. In such cases, equilibration takes the form not of minor adjustment but of transformation.[6]

Transformation, however, does not mean total change with no elements of continuity. Even the most revolutionary action makes use of existing social patterns, seeks to realize some preexisting values, and tries to preserve the continuity of human life, even while it challenges a wide range of existing conditions. Consider the Bolshevik party led by V.I. Lenin that promoted the 1917 Russian Revolution. Bolshevism represented a transformation but also a continuation of the Russian revolutionary tradition dating back to the nineteenth-century Decembrists and the Narodniks. Lenin was constantly trying to adapt Marxist theory to the conditions of Russian society and the contemporary world crisis. After the Russian Revolution he explicitly compared the Bolshevik cadre ruling Russia to the aristocratic class that had ruled it before. Chinese Communist revolutionary leader Mao Zedong drew much of his military and political strategy from the history of Chinese peasant revolts and the martial arts practices of Tai Chi. Even the most radical movement to "turn the world upside down" seeks to transform the world but also preserves it.

When modest adjustment won't work, yet people haven't created a successful transformation, they can often experience a period of flailing, in which old patterns don't work but new ones haven't been discovered. They can search for new patterns without immediate success. There can therefore be a period of accumulating discontinuity before new solutions are found.

Often old patterns have to be extinguished for new ones to take hold. We find ourselves "between two worlds, one dead, the other powerless to be born."[7] Sometimes prevailing patterns have to be deliberately dismantled or destroyed. In such cases there is a dramatic quality to equilibration: whether new equilibrations will be discovered or will prevail hangs in the balance.

Equilibration does not offer a sharp dichotomy between "revolution" (a complete rupture of past and future patterns) and "reform" (changes that occur within the continuity of a dominant pattern). Consider, for example, the black civil rights movement that emerged in the South in the 1950s. From one perspective it embodied a sudden, radical, and unexpected transformation. In a few short years, an oppressed and apparently acquiescent population astonished the world with demonstrations, sit-ins, and mass civil disobedience and made electrifying political, economic, and social changes in the American South.

Yet a deeper look reveals the continuities within the black community. The struggle for liberation had roots going back to slave rebellions, black participation in the Civil War, and Reconstruction. The black churches, often portrayed as the very emblem of black submissiveness, expressed as well as repressed an aspiration and an ideology of freedom and maintained an organizational structure able to resist pressures from the white community. The emerging freedom movement drew on the music, language, spirit, mass participation, and leadership traditions of the black church, but used them for a purpose and in a way that was largely novel and that was initially opposed by many church leaders—and which turned the South upside down.

Using the Problem-Solving Tool

We can use our problem-solving tool to explore how people have tried to solve problems in the past. For example, as a historian of the climate movement I have tried to reconstruct how climate scientists came to become public advocates for climate protection (see part 3). Initially the feedback from their measurements and calculations revealed a gap between the expectation of a stable climate and the reality of intensifying global warming. Their scientific representations indicated that this, if not corrected, would cause devastating effects. They defined global warming as a problem that needed to be solved. But, in their role as researchers, they did not have the ability to correct it. So they began expanding their role to inform policymakers of the problem and what was necessary to solve it. After years of such efforts, feedback revealed that this strategy was not working. So many climate scientists decided to "go public" and participate in public action and even civil disobedience as a way to mobilize more effective forces to combat climate change.

We can also use our problem-solving tool to develop strategies to combat problems we have identified in the present. In 2009 the long-anticipated Copenhagen climate summit broke down in wrangling and discord. The US Congress abandoned efforts to pass climate legislation. As described in chapter 39 below, I tried in a discussion paper called "Climate Protection Strategy: Beyond Business-as-Usual" to lay out a plausible solution to this problem. I advocated an independent global climate movement that could hold all countries and corporations accountable, force them to compete in a global race to cut greenhouse gases, and make the transition to a low-greenhouse-gas economy as serious a priority as war production was during World War II. Whatever the strengths and weaknesses of this strategy, it illustrates how such strategies can be constructed using our problem-solving tool.

Encouraging new common preservations often involves nurturing elements of the problem-solving process. Indeed, much of my own work has been directed to closing feedback loops so that people can see the results of their action and modify their patterns accordingly. For example, the participatory Brass Workers History Project in Connecticut's Naugatuck Valley used a book, a documentary, and public programs to present the history of nonelite groups back to nonelite groups—with the hope that they might make use of what the project had learned from other workers. In my book *In the Name of Democracy: American War Crimes in Iraq and Beyond* and the accompanying War Crimes Watch website I tried to create a feedback loop that would lead at least some Americans to grasp that, if they wanted to move toward a more secure world based on constitutional democracy and international law, they needed to support the application of constitutional and international law to their own leaders.

You can't use equilibration to predict the future, because historical development cannot be reduced to a chain of causes and effects that determine that future. Instead, the feedback from an action may loop back to the actor, who can use it to correct the pattern that guides their actions, leading to a very different result even in otherwise identical circumstances. What an equilibration-based approach can do is identify established patterns, the problems they may come up against, and the range of solutions that may be available to address them. Such a way of thinking may be more useful than deterministic or statistical prediction for people who are trying to decide how to act in response to their problems. It can help us find better solutions—including, for example, new common preservations.

CHAPTER 21

Transforming Means

The equilibration of ends and means can lead to new strategies of common preservation. Our transforming-means tool can help understand how strategies change—and how to change them.

Each of us evolves a strategy for living in the world. It is pieced together from what we learned as children, what we have observed others doing, what we have learned from our own experience and the ideas we have of what might work in the future. Such strategies can be quite conscious plans and decisions, or they can be largely a matter of unconscious habit, just repeating what an individual—or their social group—has "always done."

People use such strategies as individuals, for example by getting a particular kind of education to get a job. Individuals use participation in groups as a strategy, for example by participating in a union to get a raise. Work groups, ethnic groups, classes, genders, and many other kinds of groups use and modify their strategies to advance their interests. Whole societies can pursue strategies of economic development, or imperialism, or westernization.

Such strategies do not exist in a vacuum but in interaction with people's actual conditions.

Strategies that are well adapted to real social conditions work—people find their activity meaningful and useful in getting what they need and want. But when realities change, the old strategies may stop working; accepted practices no longer "make sense" or achieve the ends of those who are pursuing them.[1]

This idea of transforming strategy is close to the concept of adaptation in the pragmatism of John Dewey. I applied this approach in *Strike!* to explain the emergence of mass strikes. I wrote that mainstream labor historians rightly emphasized the "evolutionary adaptation" of trade unions to the existing structure of American society. But this adaptation had repeatedly broken down. At that point, "a new evolutionary process starts up as workers search experimentally for new forms of organization and action." Mass strikes are "essentially the result of the breakdown of existing modes of adaptation and the attempt to find new ones." They are therefore "pragmatic" rather than "utopian." But pragmatism properly understood "envisions adaptation not simply as an acceptance of the status quo, but as a transformation of it."[2] Adaptation, in short, is not a mechanical process caused by change in external conditions but a result of workers' own active quest for new solutions—solutions that could involve changing themselves and changing the world.

Adaptation or the emergence of new strategies can be understood as a type of equilibration. In the case of mass strikes, people acting on the basis of their established patterns discovered that those patterns ceased to solve their problems, usually because changing conditions rendered them ineffective in reaching goals.[3] This led people to try new forms of action, such as new forms of solidarity and rebellion. If they succeeded, the initial pattern might be modified and the new form of action become normal. If the new actions failed, they might be abandoned, or they might lead to still further modification of previous patterns. The new patterns seen in mass strikes are the result of such processes. And as radically different from previous actions as they may seem, they result from transformative modifications that still preserve a degree of continuity with previous practices—they embody, in short, development.

Equilibration of means to ends can similarly be used to interpret the response of American labor to globalization in the late 1980s.[4] In the decades following World War II when American productivity led the world, American labor unions provided strong support for trade policies that would open up foreign markets through reciprocal reduction in tariffs. But by the 1980s the intensification of globalization created new problems for American labor. Strategies that had evolved to provide institutional stability for unions and a rising standard of living for workers grew less and less effective in the face of corporations willing and able to close US operations and move them abroad. Initially organized labor shifted to conventional economic nationalism and protectionism. But this strategy did not succeed in reducing the effects of globalization on American workers. So gradually a new strategy based on countering the "race to the bottom" by transnational organizing and public policies designed to "raise the bottom" emerged. This changing response to globalization illustrates how, under changing conditions, feedback combined with reflection may lead to the transformation of strategies.

Today our actions are generating feedback—war, impoverishment, environmental destruction—that tells us our strategies are failing to achieve our goals. Indeed, they are generating the doomsday threats of global warming, nuclear annihilation, and other forms of self- and mutual destruction. In my book *Save the Humans?* I argued that none of our individual or collective goals can be realized without a transformation of our means—a shift to a strategy of common preservation rather than the futile pursuit of self-preservation.[5]

CHAPTER 22

Transforming Ends

Means can change through equilibration to realize established ends. But ends as well as means are part of the feedback loop that produces equilibration. Can ends themselves be equilibrated? Or do they lie outside the equilibration process? Can the emergence of new patterns of common preservation result from and produce new goals? Or must new common preservations be merely new means to realize goals that are already established? Our transforming-ends tool shows why and how people can use equilibration to construct new ends.

At any one time ends may appear simply as given. But a deeper investigation usually shows they have emerged through individual and shared history and natural history. Ends too can be shaped and reshaped by equilibration.

Ends do not exist in isolation from other ends. They are part of an overall network or nexus of ends. Some ends are more important than others. Some are means for realizing others. Many of the links among ends are circular, so that they depend on each other for their realization.

The successful pursuit of ends requires that they be coordinated with other ends, and that in turn may require that established ends be accommodated to each other. In short, ends must be ordered and coordinated—equilibrated.[1]

As people face new conditions, address new problems, and try new strategies, their overall network or nexus may change. Feedback from experience may lead an end to be elevated or abandoned because the effort to achieve it was judged more or less beneficial. A new goal may emerge because it is necessary to reach an established one; it may subsequently become a goal for its own sake. Conversely, an established goal may be abandoned or become inactive because it is too costly to reach, or because it interferes with a more important one, or because it is no longer necessary for reaching some other goal that it was originally adopted to realize.

The history of workers' movements illustrates this process. Workers have goals. But when their ability to realize those goals is stymied, they have to reconsider either their goals or their means to reach them. A goal that is impossible may be abandoned: many workers in the Great Depression gave up on the idea that they might someday become independent entrepreneurs, and therefore they became more open to collective action with other workers. Or new goals may be adopted as means to achieve established ones: workers discover that the need for a decent wage cannot be met by individual striving but requires solidarity among workers, which they may subsequently adopt as a goal in itself because it proves generally to lead to a better life.

Strike! emphasized such emergent ends. Workers might start with purely individual goals for better wages, economic security, and dignity on the job. But to realize these they had to pursue other goals, such as solidarity and organization. The pursuit of those goals led in turn to new experiences and new traits. Solidarity, for example, may start simply as a practical means to win better wages and working conditions in a particular situation. But in the course of struggles it may become a value in itself, an end to be pursued in its own right, and therefore a desirable basis for reconstructing society. *Strike!* presented this process as the key to the emergence of new goals in the course of mass strikes and as a reason that mass strikes could potentially lead to social transformation.

Ends take many forms. They may express needs that are required for survival or functioning, wants that are experienced as feelings of desire, values that embody a hierarchy of motives, norms that reflect ethical principles, and preferences that rank one condition relative to others.

The equilibration of ends can help make possible the emergence and consolidation of new common preservations. Common preservation may initially aim simply to help reach an existing goal. It may begin as a means to self-preservation. But if common preservation proves itself as a strategy, it may become more than that. It may become the normal and preferred way of dealing with problems as they arise. Under such conditions, common preservation can become an end in itself, one that is recognized as necessary for both individual and collective survival and well-being. For example, workers often begin to cooperate in response to a specific grievance, but remaining united may thereupon become a goal in itself. Other goals that interfere with their solidarity may then be put aside or the need for them met in some other way. As a union activist who helped organize the Yale University technical and clerical workers local put it, before we had the union we would protest particular grievances, but eventually we decided to form a union so that in the future we'd be organized to fight for whatever we wanted.

The motives that lead people to pursue particular ends are immensely varied. Some are undoubtedly rooted in biological instinct. The hunger mechanism, for example, clearly motivates people to seek and eat food. But in humans even instincts are subject to a high degree of modification: many people will starve rather than eat human flesh and some will fast to the death in service of a higher cause.

Some ends result from the mechanisms of human attachment, in which strong emotions become associated with people, objects, or ideas.[2] People will sacrifice their own interests for those of a beloved; some will die for a principle or a flag. Such ends may also have biological roots, but their expression in human history has been infinitely varied. They also change over time, as seen in such phenomena as religious conversion and falling in—and out of—love.

Some ends have been assimilated from other people. This may result from observation and imitation. Or it may be inculcated by education, indoctrination, or fear. Such internalized ends may form the basis of action or may be given mere lip service.

The coordination of ends takes place in close connection with the potential for their realization. New ends can emerge as a result of new opportunities and capacities. The abolitionist leader and ex-slave Frederick Douglass once said that the slave with a cruel master craves a kinder master; the slave with a kind master craves no master at all. Labor historian David Montgomery once said that what workers want is a function of what they believe they can realistically get. The goal of global domination developed by the neoconservatives of the George W. Bush administration emerged in part due to their belief that such a goal had become realistically achievable because the major forces that had limited US power, the Soviet Union in particular, had vanished.

Conversely, goals may be given up as too costly, that is, too damaging to other goals, or as unrealizable. Most American corporations in the 1930s wanted a union-free environment, but in the context of the sit-down strikes they decided they would be better off accepting some kinds of unions than having to engage in continuous and devastating class conflict.

People may give up goals that are means to other goals because they find alternative ways to reach them. After World War II, American workers in the unionized sector largely abandoned the goal of public provision of health care because most won health insurance coverage through their employers.[3]

Conversely, new goals may be adopted as necessary means to achieve established goals. For example, Leon Trotsky explained in his *History of the Russian Revolution* that, in the period preceding the Russian Revolution, workers had become committed to the eight-hour day. While they did not initially aim to make a revolution, they gradually concluded a revolution was the only way to win and defend the eight-hour day. They therefore adopted revolution as a goal.[4]

The emergence of new ends to realize existing ones underlies the basic theme of this book. We live in an era in which all sane human ends are put in jeopardy by the threat of mutual destruction.[5] A wide range of individual and group ends, starting with survival, are impossible to achieve under current historical conditions unless we address such problems as environmental destruction, military omnicide, global impoverishment, and political and social oppression. So correcting those problems must itself become an end for all who wish to achieve the goal of survival and well-being for themselves and those they care about.

Today even self-preservation cannot be reliably protected by individuals and restricted groups acting on their own. Transforming ends from self- to common preservation is therefore the necessary condition for realizing our other goals.

CHAPTER 23

Transforming Representation

Some things can stand for other things. That is representation. While debates about the nature of representation are rife in philosophy, linguistics, psychology, literary theory, and other fields, my purpose here is not to delve into these issues, but rather to address a practical question: How can change in representation contribute to common preservation?

Representations can be changed. And a change in the way people represent a situation can change the way they respond to it. If people change their representation of a problem from an individual to a shared one, for example, it may facilitate their shift from self- to common preservation. Our transforming-representation tool is designed to interrogate how representation can change.

Representations don't always require the use of language or other overt signs—they can be tacit.

Piaget's remarkable experiments on "the reach of consciousness" show that even children who have mastered language are able to conduct highly skilled activities that they are nonetheless unable to describe accurately in words.[1] Even for adults, a great deal of action is guided by patterns that are not fully represented in or directed by language or other signs; nonetheless, these patterns are effective in accomplishing their objectives.[2] Malcolm Gladwell's 2005 book *Blink* indicated the value and effectiveness of such tacit "thinking without thinking."[3]

In early childhood we develop an additional mode of representation—language and other language-like systems of signs such as pantomime and mathematics. This allows us to conduct operations—virtual mental actions—on representations of objects, ourselves, and our own action.

Representation by language can be used not only for internal thinking, but also for external communication. Language makes it possible for people to share their representations of their own actions and of the world. Indeed, human language must be acquired by each individual from others before it can be used internally, however much the potential to do so may be preestablished genetically. While animals and infants can communicate through gestures and the manifestation of internal states, the human use of language lets people share their internal mental operations—what they are doing "in their heads."

Representation can be used to conduct what Piaget calls reflective abstraction. People can take what is already organized at one level and represent it at a higher level. The higher level is like a map and the lower level like the territory it maps. Yet the higher level is not just a mirror-like reflection of the lower; a person can reconstruct the representations at the upper level and conduct thought experiments on them. They can also use what they have developed at a higher level to go back and transform what they have previously organized at a lower level—it is as if the map can reconstruct the territory.

Feedback is representation. It is news about something that has happened. Even simple feedback processes involve representation of a kind. In a sense a fish's sleek body "represents" the properties of hydrodynamics that have been selectively bred into it. The patterns that guide an animal's or an infant's action are representations of those actions. Thinking with language is not an alternative to the feedback cycle, but an elaboration of it. In place of a simple comparison between intention and result, thinking with signs allows feedback loops to include incredibly complex, interacting, developing, multileveled representations and virtual operations on them.

Thinking is likely to involve a mingling of tacit and explicit processes, some accessible and some inaccessible to consciousness. Some thought processes can be the object of others. They are constantly affecting, testing, and revising each other. This process goes on within and between people and their environments. It might be described by Gregory Bateson's phrase "ecology of mind."

Representation by language allows "thought experiments" on virtual objects that can go beyond the here and now and test possibilities without having to carry out actual experiments. We can ask ourselves, "What would happen if . . . ?" And we can use our knowledge to provide a probable answer, though one that is never certain without testing in practice. We can identify patterns and design effective actions without always having to conduct trials and suffer errors. We can equilibrate not only external situations but also those we represent in our own minds.

Mental representation makes it possible for us to learn not only from our own experiments but also from observation. We can treat an action that was not taken by us as if we had taken it ourselves and observe the consequences. A great deal of knowledge, from astronomy to history, operates through such observation of "natural experiments." And a great deal of social action draws on the observation and imitation of what other people are doing. Occupy Wall Street self-consciously imitated the Wisconsin Uprising and the occupation of Tahrir Square. The seemingly mysterious spread of sit-down strikes or flying squadrons in periods of mass strike, sometimes described as "spreading by contagion," is often the result of observation and imitation—part of the "mass strike process" I described in *Strike!* This dynamic can be used intentionally through "exemplary action" intended to stimulate others to act. Big Bill Haywood described in his autobiography how in a period of intense class conflict he promoted confrontation with the intent of triggering a revolt like the Great Upheaval of 1877.

Because people can represent not only their own action but also their own thought processes, they can think critically about their own thinking and that of others. This provides a way to correct contradictions among different observations and the patterns into which they are fitted. For example, when I was investigating the deindustrialization of Connecticut's Naugatuck Valley, I discovered that the region's employers had blamed its economic decline on workers' excessive wage demands— and that a large proportion of the community, including many workers themselves, accepted this explanation. At the same time the employers were milking the local plants and investing the money elsewhere. In our book and documentary *Brass Valley*, we portrayed the employers' deliberate disinvestment from the region's aging brass industry. The book and movie were widely distributed and discussed in Naugatuck Valley communities, and over subsequent decades this critical perspective gradually entered the local discourse on deindustrialization, so that now public discussion will often include the role of corporate disinvestment strategy in the demise of the valley's brass industry.

The ability to represent one's own thought processes can play a crucial role in the transition from self-preservation to common preservation. It makes possible an "ecological shift" in which elements initially considered in isolation are re-represented as parts of a larger pattern or system of interaction. *Strike!*, for example, portrayed workers shifting from interpreting their situation in a purely individual context to seeing it in terms of conditions they share with other workers. *Global Village or Global Pillage* described the American labor movement's shift, albeit incomplete, from viewing globalization in an economic nationalist "unfair foreign competition" frame to a global "race to the bottom" frame. Such an ecological shift can provide a new understanding of problems and possibilities which in turn can suggest new forms of common preservation as the solution.

The ability to mutually share our representations and our virtual operations on them makes possible a "decentering" in which one's own initial viewpoint is re-represented as only one viewpoint among others with which it can be coordinated. *Strike!* described workers reinterpreting their own viewpoints in the light of their interaction with the viewpoints of others—for example, putting their conflict with another ethnic group in the context of employer manipulation. *Globalization from Below* told how multiple, isolated national movements interacted with each other in ways that increasingly led to a common perspective. This process was greatly accelerated by the emergence of the intensified interaction of the World Social Forum. Such decentering and coordination of viewpoints is often a critical feature of the emergence of new common preservations.

Language allows people to engage in cooperative thought experiments—sharing the process and results of actions on representations. This in turn makes it possible for people to guide their action jointly—to deliberately coordinate the action of different people to produce a combined result. A great deal of what social movements do is to construct such representations, conduct virtual operations on them, and then try those operations in practice. Over the course of a quarter century, for example, the Naugatuck Valley Project, a community organization in western Connecticut I worked with and wrote about, identified problems ranging from plant closings to gouging landlords to kids with no place to play, discussed and developed possible solutions, and tried them out in practice.[4]

Strike! showed workers facing oppression and developing both tacit and explicitly verbalized understandings of what to do about it. The book emphasized the role of tacit knowledge and learning in working-class action. It argued that people could act intelligently without necessarily being able to articulate explicitly their underlying reasoning. But it also portrayed workers expressing to each other their understandings of their situations, debating alternative plans of action, conducting individual and joint "thought experiments" regarding the likely effects of different courses, making explicit plans to coordinate their action, and reconsidering past conclusions in the light of an action's results. It described, for example, groups led by a cobbler and a railroad machinist in Sedalia, Missouri, in 1884, who met "night after night, discussing the condition of workers and how to change it, debating various labor philosophies and their implications for immediate action." From these groups came the leaders of future strikes in the area.[5]

Building Bridges: The Emerging Grassroots Coalition of Labor and Community described how separate social movements discovered their need for each other and their ability to cooperate, how that experiential learning led to explicit formulations and further concrete experiments in cooperation, and the development of labor-community coalitions as an enduring feature of American life. *Globalization from Below* showed how frustration with the failure of established forms of action in national frameworks led both to trial-and-error experiments with new forms of global action and explicit verbal formulations of the nature of globalization and what to do about it.

The proposal in *Save the Humans?* for a human survival movement, and the proposal in *Climate Insurgency* for a global nonviolent climate insurgency, illustrate thought experiments intended to construct new strategies. They took representations abstracted from past actions and tried to combine them in new ways to address the novel situation we face today. We can share such thought experiments and, if they seem promising, try them out.

Common preservation involves critical thought, shifts in ways of thinking, the sharing of ideas, and other expressions of representation through language. But is not just a matter of ideas and abstract thought.

The emergence of common preservation is a historical and social process embedded in people's entire way of living. It involves words, but it also involves experiences, actions, and feelings. Tacit and explicit knowledge, learning, and communication are mingled in its emergence. Transforming representation is part of that process.

CHAPTER 24

Transforming Boundaries

For new patterns of common preservation to develop, often boundaries have to change, and sometimes new entities have to emerge. They are able to do so through a process of equilibration. We can use the transforming-boundaries tool to probe how boundaries are established and maintained, how they change, and how we can change them.

In social movements, isolated individuals become part of a group and act in concert. The history of mass strikes provides many examples of the transformation of people from isolated individuals to part of a movement or group. The boundaries between craft, occupational, ethnic, and racial groups fade as their members began to act on their common interest as a class. Conversely, communities that had seemed united can become divided by class conflict into separate warring groups; descriptions of general strikes in San Francisco, Seattle, and elsewhere for example often portray the breakdown of everyday social, ethnic, and even family units and their replacement by formal and informal groupings based on class. As movements and organizations subsequently evanesce, such connections may dissolve, and previous boundaries may reassert themselves.

I recounted in a previous chapter how the fourteen-year-old Italian garment worker Jenny Aiello defied both her family and her bosses by helping organize a union and a strike at the Lesnow Brothers shirtwaist factory in New Haven, Connecticut, in 1933.[1] The emergence of worker organization at Lesnow involved at least three significant shifts in social entities and the character of their boundaries. First, the young workers began to act in concert and to see themselves as a group. Second, Jenny and her friends penetrated the boundary between themselves and the organizers outside the plant. Third, the boundary between the young immigrant women production workers and the male cutters was lowered enough that they were able to cooperate in the strike and form one union together. The outcome of the strike was the first union contract for shirt makers outside New York City; before the end of the year twenty thousand shirt workers in New York, Connecticut, and Pennsylvania had won union contracts.

Common preservation is an activity of distinct entities—otherwise it would simply be self-preservation of a single entity. Yet, if those entities were entirely isolated islands, they would never be able to act together for common ends. Understanding common preservation requires resolving the apparent paradox of entities that seem separate yet also connected.

The science of ecology provides one way to think about distinct entities that are nonetheless also parts of larger wholes. Individual organisms and particular species are part of ecological niches and a wider biosphere whose interactions cut cross individual and species boundaries. The dispersion of strontium-90 produced by nuclear testing and the spread of DDT in the food chain revealed by Rachel Carson's *Silent Spring* showed not only the connectedness of the environment but its importance for human well-being and its vulnerability to human disruption.

The Marxist tradition provides another way to address the paradox of separate elements that are also parts of wholes or systems. An old philosophical saw holds that "Everything is what it is and not another thing."[2] But in Marx's dialectical thought, "objects," or "entities," far from being separate "things," are in a constant state of change that leads apparently distinct things to turn into their opposites. What seem like isolated and competing individual workers, for example, can turn into a unified working class.[3] People are part of and determined by society, but they are also distinct individuals—"social individuals." Human individuals are part of nature but distinguished by the fact that their action is guided by consciousness (whatever that might be). The truth is in the whole, but the whole is determined by the contradictions among the parts.

Marxist dialectic tries heroically to overcome what seem like insuperable either/ors. But it can be disconcertingly slippery. If things are always turning into their opposites, is there any way to hold meanings steady long enough to test them against evidence?

Ludwig von Bertalanffy's ideas about open systems and semipermeable boundaries provide another way to explore both boundedness and connectedness as well as both stability and change. While his general systems theory originated with biological organisms, it focused on the most general features of systems, which included human individuals, groups, and minds.

In general systems theory, boundaries are patterns that impede the passage of something—"zones of lowered permeability."[4] Boundaries make possible systems: entities that maintain some degree of patterning by means of the interaction of their parts. Without boundaries, systems would be dissolved by the flux of the universe.

In a closed system—think of a pendulum or the solar system—opposing forces balance each other so that the pattern of the whole is maintained. But such a closed system can persist only because it is walled off from anything in the environment that might disturb its equilibrium. We know that in practice friction leads pendulum clocks to run down and that the solar system will eventually go out of balance and the planets fly together or apart.

Bertalanffy described a different kind of entity he called an open system. An open system actively compensates for variations in the environment through the interaction of its parts. Such a system can maintain patterns and pursue goals amid the flux of the universe. In Piaget's language, a closed system expresses an equilibrium; an open system requires equilibration in order to persist.

The secret that makes an open system possible is a boundary that is semipermeable—that lets some but not all things pass. It allows the import of energy and information that can counter the tendency to entropy. It blocks the import of disorder that would disorganize the system. And it expels poisons and waste products that would disrupt the system.

Organisms, people, social groups, and institutions are obvious examples of such open systems. All are able to counter the forces of entropy and maintain some degree of order and stability amid flux by patterns that vary to counter the effects of a changing environment. All preserve their stability through boundaries, but their boundaries are only relative, not impermeable.

Boundaries define entities or wholes. But no entity is an island, entire unto itself; "each is part of the Main." Every boundary of an open system is a semipermeable membrane, through which some but not all things penetrate. The semipermeability of boundaries allows open systems to interact with their environments in spite of their bounded-ness. Semipermeable boundaries make life itself possible, since they allow organisms to import energy, materials, and information needed to sustain life while excluding or expelling that which would disorgan-ize or kill them.

Open systems are quasi-independent. They control much of their own action. Their boundaries insulate them from the unmediated impact of their environment. Their feedback loops allow them to vary their own action in ways that are shaped by their own patterns, not just by the causal impact of their environment. Indeed, they are often able to affect their environment. But at the same time they are dependent on their environment for meeting their needs and realizing their ends. The great bulk of a nation's economic activity may take place within its borders, for example, yet it may be heavily dependent on certain imports from abroad.

The idea of open systems resolves some of the paradoxes of common preservation. Human beings can be both bounded and connected with the world beyond themselves. They can be relatively independent and also part of social groups and natural environments. They can be par-tially dependent and also originators of their own action.

Open systems can form a hierarchy. The environment of one open system can consist of one or more other systems. Conversely, many open systems contain subsystems that maintain their own stability and patterns. Semipermeable boundaries can separate a system from and at the same time connect it with the larger systems of which it is a part.

Systems sometimes nest neatly within each other. In biology, cells nest in organs, organs in organisms, and organisms in biological niches that in turn are part of larger natural systems. Such nesting may also characterize some human phenomena. Human groups may nest in spatial hierarchies: neighborhoods in towns, towns in regions, regions in nations. Or they may nest in organizational hierarchies: platoons in brigades, brigades in divisions, divisions in armies.

But the image of nesting is often too neat for representing human relations. Neat nesting is the exception rather than the rule among bounded social entities. More often human systems overlap. Individuals belong to many organizations; organizations include individuals who are also members of other organizations. Entities can be bounded yet spatially dispersed: ethnic groups, religions, and families may be spread in global diasporas yet retain strong boundaries between themselves and outsiders. Corporations, language communities, and social movements operate across national boundaries. To grasp the actual contours of human social life and organization, open systems theory has to allow for such overlap and dispersal.[5]

Michael Mann's *The Sources of Social Power* presents an alternative to the model of "nesting" systems. As Mann summed up his approach, "Societies are constituted of multiple overlapping and intersecting sociospatial networks of power."[6] Because people have multiple goals, they form multiple networks of cooperation. These networks cut across the boundaries of what are conventionally thought of as separate societies.[7]

Transformation of boundaries is an important aspect of many kinds of social change. In early modern Europe, nation-states unified independent principalities while they also fragmented the Roman Catholic Church and the Holy Roman Empire into separate national religious and political jurisdictions. In the wake of the American Revolution, colonies established independence from the British empire, but also became subsidiary parts of the new United States of America. More recent examples include the reduction of boundaries among European states through the evolution of the European Union and their subsequent elevation through Brexit and other changes; the breakdown of Yugoslavia into its component states; and the boundary-crossing convergence of social movements represented by globalization from below. In periods of mass strike, the boundaries among ethnic and religious groups may become less salient, while boundaries between different classes became more formidable. Each of these examples represents an equilibration of the organization and boundaries of entities.[8]

The idea of open systems, corrected by an emphasis on overlapping and intersecting networks, provides a way to deal with some of the complexities of real historical situations. It can help us explore overlapping phenomena like class, race, gender, family, nationality, location, ethnic identity, and others without having to reduce some of them to other, purportedly more real or fundamental, ones. It can help us explain how social activity organized in one way, say by ethnicity and race, can rapidly be transformed by social movements and mass strikes to being organized another way, say by class or gender. And it can help us understand how the seemingly impregnable boundaries of nations could, in the era of globalization, be subverted increasingly easily by corporations, communications, and transnational social movement networks.

The idea of multilevel systems with semipermeable boundaries is exemplified in the convergence of social movements I called "globalization from below." Movements and organizations once strongly enclosed by national borders and sectoral objectives increasingly linked across national boundaries and supported each other's efforts, often assimilating some of each other's objectives and strategies in the process. Yet these movements retained distinct identities even while functioning in some ways as parts of a single movement.[9]

As the example of globalization from below shows, the transformation of boundaries and the emergence of new entities can be an intentional process. For example, *Global Village or Global Pillage* advocated a "Lilliput strategy" as a deliberate linking of distinct organizations, movements, and constituencies in different countries to form a network that could function as a global movement to resist the race to the bottom. By transforming their mutual relations, these groups could—and in fact did—create a new concerted historical entity, generally known as the global justice or antiglobalization movement, with its own organizational embodiments like transnational advocacy networks and the World Social Forum.

The idea of multilevel open systems also guided the exploration in *Global Visions* of alternatives to either a top-down globalized "new world order" or a return to atomistic or predatory nationalism. "In place of the current concentration of power in dominant states and transnational corporations," globalization from below proposes a "redistribution of power both upward and downward to a global but decentralized multilevel system." Globalization from below's "simultaneous emphasis on local empowerment and on transnationalization" may seem "contradictory, even paradoxical." But in fact the two directions are interdependent. "Diversity and local empowerment" can be "goals for global institutions," rather than "barriers to their development."[10] This vision was influenced by Piaget's idea that both domineering centralization and atomistic self-aggrandizement can be reduced at the same time by a decentering process that moves toward a more ideal equilibrium.

A similar emphasis on changing the nature of boundaries underlies my effort to envision a human survival movement.[11] The people of the world are divided from each other by many kinds of boundaries, in spite of our common interest in common preservation. We don't need to eliminate all boundaries. But we do need to lower those that prevent us from cooperating with each other to create a viable basis for the continuation of human life on earth.

CHAPTER 25

Transforming Coordination

However great their individual capacity to act, and however strong their common interests, people cannot pursue those interests collectively unless they can coordinate their action. Common preservation requires coordinated action for the common benefit of the actors. Indeed, it is the potential benefit of acting in concert that gives people a motive for shifting to new common preservations. Our transforming-coordination tool explores the barriers to coordination and how they can be overcome.

Coordinated actions are guided with reference to each other and their combined effect. Just as successful action requires that an actor adapt their action to its object, so coordination requires that the coordinating actors mutually adapt their action to each other. To construct new coordinations, people must reciprocally represent each other's patterns of action. They must vary their own action patterns so as to produce joint action intended to accomplish a joint goal. As Piaget puts it, coordination requires mutual assimilation and accommodation. Coordinators must mutually equilibrate.

Coordination can increase the range of conditions that can be counteracted and reduce the cost of doing so. Coordination creates collective power beyond that of the separate individuals whose actions are coordinated. It's a sociological truism that "persons in cooperation can enhance their joint power over third parties or over nature."[1] Coordination also makes those who benefit from that power dependent on it and on each other.

Consider the struggle against the Keystone XL pipeline described in part 3 of this book. Opposition to the pipeline began with Cree, Dene, Métis, and other indigenous peoples in Alberta. These tribes, each with their own organization and traditions, began to coordinate with each other to oppose the pipeline. They formed a wider coordination with dozens of other organizations around the province to bring lawsuits and call for a moratorium on tar sands development.

Meanwhile conservative ranchers, urban progressives, environmentalists, and farmers along the route of the proposed pipeline formed a coalition called Bold Nebraska which began coordinating with pipeline opponents in Alberta. Bill McKibben, a leader of 350.org, reached out to both groups and organized a US environmentalist coalition that developed a very different but complementary set of tactics and demands, sitting in at the White House to demand that President Barack Obama deny a permit for the pipeline. Along the route of the proposed pipeline activists formed a Tar Sands Blockade that prevented construction of the pipeline by disrupting construction sites. Native Americans and western ranchers held a five-day encampment in Washington, DC, that they dubbed the "Cowboy Indian Alliance." Each of these groups had its own traditions, values, motives, and means of action, yet by coordinating their action with each other through a variety of meetings, networks, communications, and tacit mutual adjustments they were able to create the conditions that led President Obama to deny the pipeline the permit it needed to go ahead.

Achieving a goal or compensating for a gap through inter-individual coordination constructs what can be called a collective, concerted, or inter-individual actor or actors-in-common. Becoming part of a collective actor does not prevent individuals from also continuing to be individual actors. Nor does it require entirely abandoning individual perspectives and interests. But it does require that actors mutually vary their patterns in order to adapt to the patterns of others.

A group is a collective actor to the extent that it is what Piaget calls a subject—actually able to transform the world physically or virtually. Coordinated action can thus be the starting point, rather than the result, of group formation. The work groups described in *Strike!* often recognized themselves as groups—for example, as "guerilla bands at war with management"—only after they had already begun to resist management in practice. Similarly, working people often recognized themselves as part of a class only after and as the result of observing and participating in large-scale mass actions.

Coordination does not require formal organization; there can be, as the subtitle of a recent book put it, "organizing without organizations."[2]

Millions of people have participated in peace rallies, demonstrations, and meetings without ever signing a membership card for an anti-nuclear or anti–Vietnam War organization. Organizations have come and gone, split and merged, yet their participants continue to act collectively. In mass strikes, hundreds of thousands of people have organized themselves to act in concert, sometimes over the length and breadth of a continent and across the lines dividing occupations, races, ethnicities, genders, and established organizations, often using many different organizations or none at all to do so.

This concept of coordination explains why social movements can engage in concerted action over such a wide field without anyone giving anyone else orders about what to do. Recognizing the needs of the movement, each participant adjusts their action both to those needs and to the other participants.

People have many different wishes, needs, and goals, and therefore they form varied patterns of coordination to realize their various ends. The prevailing patterns of coordination have developed over time in response to the past needs and problems of individuals and groups.

Coordination may take varied forms. It may be self-coordination among members of a group, or it may be at the direction of a distinct individual or group. It may be ad hoc or institutionalized. It may be diffuse, as in a market or a common language, or it may be highly centralized, as in an army or bureaucracy. It may be voluntary, coerced, or a combination of the two. It may be direct, as when a group of people join together to lift a heavy object. Or it may be indirect; in a market, for example, an individual simply exchanges commodities with another individual, but by doing so becomes part of a wider set of interactions that provide both the benefits and the constraints of coordination.

Economists distinguish three ways coordination can be organized: command, as in an army or bureaucracy; feedback without direct communication, as in what economists call a "perfect market"; and decentralized sharing of information and intentions, as in a network.[3]

In command systems, control of coordinated activity is assumed by a particular individual or group. The coordinator holds authority over the activity of others. Authority can be conceived as an agreement of those who are subject to the authority to obey those who exercise it.[4] Such obedience may be free or coerced or a combination of the two. Coordination by authority is proactive: coordinated action is first planned by one party and then implemented by another. This type of coordination prevails in corporations, governments, armies, and what economists generally refer to as "hierarchical organizations."

In systems with multiple actors who do not know each other's intentions, coordination may be produced nonetheless by individuals and groups adjusting their actions to the *effects* of other's actions. In what economists define as "perfect markets," for example, individuals act in response to the cumulative effects of buying and selling without knowing each other's intentions.[5] They are coordinated by the famous "invisible hand" of the market. Such coordination is decentralized and reactive: decisions are made in response to the unplanned cumulative effects of previous actions.[6]

In knowledge sharing systems, people may coordinate their actions by providing each other information about their capabilities and intentions and then mutually adjusting their plans on the basis of that shared information. Such coordination is characteristic of a nonhierarchical, nonauthoritarian group. Some economists have begun referring to this pattern of coordination as a network. Such coordination is decentralized but proactive: decisions are made by individuals and groups based on knowledge of the capabilities and intentions of others. Such networks are based on loops that convey information back and forth among the nodes of the network.

Each of these forms of coordination implies possible corresponding problems. Markets are prone to disorder. Command easily leads to domination. Networks tend to unmanageable complexity. Life without coordination, however, would be nasty, brutish, and short.

Human coordination may develop through the simple feedback of trial-and-error learning. Alternatively, it may develop through a collective process of representing needs, goals, problems, and conditions and constructing thought experiments in how to address them. That process requires communication and the construction of shared representations of objects and actions. It requires what Piaget calls "decentering" or the reciprocal assimilation and accommodation of viewpoints. In everyday speech we call it "give-and-take."

Coordination may be highly fluid, as it often is in the earlier stages of social movements. But it may become increasingly stable, developing from a single act to a tacit pattern to a rule. Patterns of coordination that persist or reproduce themselves over time become social structures or institutions. They may be maintained simply out of habit, tradition, or recognized self-interest, but they may also be reinforced by some kind of sanctions. They may be integrated into a system of law accepted as binding. They may be incorporated as units within still larger patterns of coordination. The presence of coordination or institutionalization by no means implies an absence of conflict; conflict is common and sometimes endemic among coordinated and institutionalized patterns.

Workers' coordination has often begun with strikes and protests against particular acts of abuse. Such actions may become traditions: in the Akron rubber plants, workers developed a pattern, and eventually a norm, that when one worker had a grievance with a foreman, their workmates would sit idle at their workstations until the grievance was settled. These practices were reinforced by stigmatization and other sanctions against violators. Eventually unions coopted this process, limited it, and controlled it through the contractual grievance procedure. Workers' coordination also became subject to the wider coordinations represented by the labor movement as a whole, government regulation, labor law, and the development of labor-management cooperation.

In an institution, people act and coordinate, not as a result of their personal patterns and objectives but as a function of their roles. So patterns of action may continue even though they do not express the actors' own personal desires. Armies go on fighting wars their soldiers know are already lost; corporations go on pouring carbon into the atmosphere even though their executives know it will lead to catastrophic global warming that will destroy their own children's environment. Such roles express a kind of alienation.

Established roles may change in either of two ways. A collective actor may modify their patterns. For example, a nation may act collectively to pass laws that restrict gender discrimination. Alternatively, the individuals or groups who compose a collective actor may change their own patterns in ways that partially or completely dissolve the established coordination of the whole. Participants in the women's liberation movement refused to make coffee in the office, wait for men to open doors for them, abandon careers when they got married, and stay in oppressive marriages, dramatically undermining the unequal coordinations of a sexist society through noncooperation.

Strike! portrayed capitalism as a system of coordination based on the authority of managers in the workplace and blind interaction in the market. Through the mass strike process, workers create new forms of coordination with each other. Such coordination could take place locally in workplaces and communities; through imitation of actions taken by others elsewhere; through informal committees and networks; and through formal organizations like labor unions. By coordinating their action, workers could augment their power.

Economic globalization represented in part an expanded coordination of markets; economic activities in one location interacted with "foreign" ones in ways that they hadn't when national boundaries were less permeable. Economic globalization also represented an expansion of command coordination within corporations that reorganized to function across national borders. Paradoxically, by devolving all but core functions to formally independent suppliers, the same corporations also replaced some command coordination with markets. Globalization from below was composed of new patterns of coordination, primarily networks, formed by social movements in response to globalization from above.

Many of the social experiments with which I have been involved produced new coordinations. The Naugatuck Valley Project, for example, coordinated the actions of religious congregations, unions, and community groups in a region to challenge plant closings and the effects of deindustrialization. The North American Federation for Fair Employment coordinated a variety of community organizations, advocacy groups, and unions on a continental scale to change the rules governing contingent work. The Uniting for Peace campaign created a tenuous coordination among antiwar activists around the world, some governments and political structures, and several coalitions of governments to use the UN General Assembly to halt the impending US attack on Iraq.

Common preservation is linked to coordination in two ways. To realize the goals of common preservation, action must be coordinated. And it is the benefit of such coordinated action that makes common preservation worth pursuing.

Creating new coordinations is often a crucial strategy for creating new common preservations. The creation of new coordinations in the past makes it plausible that we can develop further forms of coordination to help solve our problems in the future. A human survival movement, for example, would constitute a new set of coordinations. It would require the formation of common objectives. And it would require ongoing assimilation and accommodation—give-and-take—to realize them.

CHAPTER 26

Transforming Differentiation

Some differences among people, such as eye color and chromosomal gender, are determined from birth. But most differences are less determined by what people are born with than the world they are born into. Height depends in part on genes, but also on nutrition. Whether you are a secretary or a tycoon, a slave or a master, a worker or a manager, is much more a result of social roles than biology. We can use our transforming-differentiation tool to identify how such differences developed and how they might be changed.

Where there is coordination, there is also differentiation into different roles. Differentiation can occur in activity: some fish while others hunt. Differentiation can occur in space: one region produces bananas while another produces Christmas trees. Differentiation can occur in time: people dig iron ore out of the ground, process it into pure metal, and cast it into a frying pan or a cannon ball. When differentiation persists, it establishes a division of roles.

As Adam Smith pointed out long ago, if some hunt while others fish, the result is likely to be more skillful hunters and more skillful fishers together catching more prey. But differentiation can be a double-edged sword. Smith pointed out that an extreme division of labor may also degrade the capability of workers to a narrow set of skills. Marx added that it can generate inequality, and even domination, as some roles become more powerful and better rewarded than others. Michael Mann argued that differentiation can make people unequally dependent on each other. And it can allow organizations to follow the decisions of those who control important positions, rather than the will of the members as a whole.

The collective power that results from differentiation can be one of the benefits of a new common preservation. But those benefits may be unequally distributed. Through differentiation, even what was a common preservation can become a new form of exploitation. And it can create differences of interest that serve as obstacles to new common preservations. If workers win a wage increase but with sharply different wages for different occupations, for example, they may find it harder to agree on common goals in the future.

Those granted greater knowledge, control, and authority may use them to accumulate a still larger share of knowledge, control, and authority. If such differentiation persists the result can be domination.

Roles can be changed by equilibration. As individual craft production gave way to larger-scale factory-based production during the industrial revolution, factory owners took over control of production and its coordination. Society became differentiated into workers and capitalists. With the rise of corporate capitalism, management became professionalized and managers who ran businesses were increasingly differentiated from owners who had title to the enterprises but usually didn't run them.

Equilibration of differentiation can also be seen within labor organizations. Worker organization often started with informal coordination within and among work groups that showed little lasting differentiation between leaders and led. As these relationships became institutionalized in labor unions, however, individual and collective leaderships became increasingly differentiated from the "rank and file." This differentiation was often justified as necessary for effective action. It often led, however, to a divergence of interest between those in different organizational roles. In *Strike!* I tried to explain the highly visible divisions between leaders and members of trade unions in terms of this process of differentiation.

The differentiation of work functions can result from the deliberate policy of managers within workplaces and firms; early modern capitalists imposed such specialization over the vehement opposition of the guilds. It can arise through the market; the greater productivity resulting from subdividing jobs rewards greater specialization. Or it can be created by common agreement within a network; for example, when various groups concerned with contingent work came together to create the North American Federation for Fair Employment (NAFFE), they established specialized action groups to take leadership in each program area.

Differentiation makes those who benefit from it dependent on it and on each other. Without employers, workers are unemployed. Without workers, employers can't produce. Therefore differentiation of roles can provide a basis for differences of power.

If roles are easily cast off or exchanged, the impact of their differentiation is limited. But if differentiation continues over time, people's roles can become part of the way they are defined by themselves and others.

Roles may also come to be treated as features of institutions rather than of the people who fill them. Individuals may come and go while the roles remain the same. Conversely, as long as they accept an institutional role, individuals may act in alienated ways that conflict with their own interests and beliefs.

If different roles give different amounts of authority over an institution, the institution may be diverted from common purposes to the purposes of those in authority. If different roles confer different rights and responsibilities, the ends of some people may be sacrificed to those of others. Different rights and responsibilities generate different interests and may therefore generate conflict.

Differentiation of authority is likely to be particularly great if it is based on roles that oversee and direct the process of coordination itself. The differentiation between a carpenter and an electrician may have modest impact on opportunity and power, but the differentiation between a supervisor and a rank-and-file worker can have substantial effects. Such oversight roles put their holders in a position of greater knowledge and power.

While the differentiation of roles is inherent in coordination, it can be deliberately contained and reduced. The experiments with worker ownership I studied at Seymour Specialty Wire and Cooperative Home Care Associates attempted, with varying success, to increase the role of workers in managing their own jobs, thereby establishing more equal roles in the workplace. Network structures like NAFFE's limit role differentiation and allow ongoing redefinition of roles.

We can use our transforming differentiation tool for thought experiments to develop new strategies based on common preservation. When Tim Costello was delivering oil for Metropolitan Petroleum in Boston, he ran for Teamsters shop steward on the platform of redefining the steward as merely the convener of an assembly of the drivers who would make and implement decisions for the local union as a whole. Tim's and my many subsequent proposals for new forms of worker organization often involved reducing the sharp differentiation between union officials and the rank and file, for example by devolving functions of grievance handling, bargaining, and strike organization from a small group of professional leaders to shop committees and action groups.

Today our differentiated social roles leave most of us without either power over or responsibility for social processes as a whole. Those processes are leading to mutual destruction, but it's no one's "job" to fix them. While we no doubt need the benefits of some role differentiation, we all must share responsibility for the whole. We need a common role of sharing responsibility for common preservation.

CHAPTER 27

Transforming Power

In a general sense, power is the capacity to accomplish a result. We have the power to abolish hunger or to destroy the world with nuclear weapons. But power is often used in a narrower sense as the capacity to make someone else do what they would otherwise not choose to do. It is the power of some people over others.

Such "coercive" or "distributive" power can help some people and prevent others from realizing their own ends. Powerful actors—corporations and states, for example—can impose their own interests and deny those of other, less powerful actors. And they can coerce less powerful actors to do their bidding. We can use our transforming-power tool to identify how such power originates, how it is maintained, and how it can be overcome.

Unequal power can be a barrier to common preservation by preventing cooperation for common ends. People may want to cooperate with others, but coercive power may deter or prevent them from doing so. The need to counter such power can also provide a motive for developing new common preservations. The ability to equilibrate makes it possible to counteract coercive power through new common preservations.

We saw in "Transforming Coordination" above that collective power is the result of coordination. Coercive or distributive power is the result of dependence.

Individuals and groups—like other open systems—are inherently dependent on what is outside their boundaries to achieve their goals. Those who rely on coordination to realize their goals are, in addition, dependent on the coordinated group—the collective actor. Differentiation of functions and roles creates an additional dependence on others who can do what you can't do.

Such dependence provides the basis of coercive power. If I cannot achieve my goals without assistance or at least acquiescence from you, I am dependent on you and you have a degree of potential power over me. That potential power becomes real if you make use of my dependence to coerce me—to make me follow your will rather than my own.

Dependence is by definition a characteristic of individuals and groups as open systems. But as I began to study systems theory, cybernetics, and genetic structuralism, I was struck by how often they lack a concept of power. There seemed to be no place for conflict between the interests of the parts or those of the parts and the whole. But open systems are inherently dependent on their parts and on larger systems of which they are part, providing a potential basis for power.

The multilateral character of dependence in open systems provides a basis for change that is rarely noted by systems theorists. Power relations can be equilibrated because dependence is rarely if ever unilateral. Subsystems may be able to realize their goals by violating the system's established order. If—as in the case of human beings—those subsystems can represent and communicate alternative possibilities to each other, they can construct a shared alternative. Those devoted to the prevailing system may attempt to prevent them from realizing that alternative. But because dependencies are multilateral, those seeking such an alternative may be able to establish alliances—new coordinations—that permit them to implement it despite that opposition.

Of course, dependence does not necessarily have to be parlayed into power. A parent may be in a position to starve a child to death but never use or even threaten to use that power. Workers may have the capacity to strike but never brandish it, let alone use it. To exercise actual power, an actor must use or threaten to use dependence.

As Marx pointed out long ago, workers as individuals are dependent on employers because employers control capitalist society's means of production; people who do not possess the means of production have no way to gain a livelihood except by selling the one thing they have, their capacity to work, to those who do.

But, conversely, employers are dependent on workers as a group. It is the labor of workers that realizes the employers' goal: the expansion of their wealth. This dependence provides workers a potential power over their employers. If they collectively withdraw their labor—for example by soldiering or striking—that potential power can be realized.

Just as employers are dependent on workers as a group, so all who wield power are in reality dependent on others. Generals are dependent on privates and on the governments that fund their armies; politicians are dependent on voters, campaign contributors, and parties; governments are dependent on the compliance of their citizens and on recognition of their legitimacy by other countries. Utilizing such dependence can provide power. As *Strike!* put it, "Ordinary people—together—have potentially the greatest power of all." For "it is their activity which makes up society." If they refuse to work, the country stops. "If they take control of their own activity, their own work, they thereby take control of society."[1]

The idea that power is based on dependence contradicts a commonsense view that power rests on violence—that, as Mao Zedong put it, power grows from the barrel of a gun. One may kill a person, it is true, in the same way that you kill an animal. But killing a person doesn't really give you power over that person, it merely renders them no longer a person—try making a corpse obey your will. Of course, if someone can threaten you with violence you are dependent on them for your well-being or survival. So vulnerability to violence is a subset of dependence, not an alternative explanation of power. Power over another consists in being able to make them follow your will rather than exclusively their own. And that is made possible by the utilization of dependence.

The ability to use dependence is rarely available without the cooperation and acquiescence of many other actors. No matter how much power the powerful may have, they are always dependent on others to realize their goals. This is why those who are not in positions of institutionalized power can sometimes make change through concerted action.

Reflecting on the Russian Revolution of 1905, Gandhi wrote that even the most powerful cannot rule without the cooperation of the ruled.[2] Gene Sharp, who analyzed hundreds of historical examples in the three volumes of his *Politics of Nonviolent Action*, concluded that the basis of nonviolent action is that "the exercise of power depends on the consent of the ruled who, by withdrawing that consent, can control and even destroy the power of their opponent."[3] Even in war, victory frequently results not from physical annihilation of the enemy but from the withdrawal of the population's support for the war effort ("loss of morale"), defection of political supporters of the war, withdrawal of allies, and change in policy by ruling groups in response to the presence or threat of such factors.

Dependence may be direct, as in the case of employers and workers. But in societies with multiple institutions, patterns of dependence also tend to be multiple and often indirect. A corporation, for example, depends on the labor of its own workers, but also on customers, investors, suppliers, a supportive legal structure, protection against threats from rivals, favorable public policies, and many other conditions dependent in turn on varied forms of social coordination.

To be effective, an actual or threatened withdrawal of cooperation must be coordinated among individuals and groups whose support or acquiescence is important for the powerful. For that reason, action for social change often requires alliances and the parlaying of different forms of dependence into a coordinated expression of power.

Movements can use strategies that threaten power-holders through specific and targeted withdrawal of cooperation. For example, in the antisweatshop movement, student protesters made clear that their campuses would be subject to sit-ins and other forms of disruption until their universities agreed to ban the use of their schools' logos on products made in sweatshops. In the aftermath of Occupy Wall Street, a campaign called Occupy Debt defined refusal to pay debts as a form of civil disobedience against an immoral and oppressive financial system. Its strategy was to utilize the dependence of financial institutions on repayment by their debtors to force changes in private and public debt policy.

In addition to such targeted threats, the withdrawal of cooperation may generate fear of a more general social breakdown, what is often called "social unrest." For example, in the late 1990s, under heavy pressure from the World Bank, the Bolivian government sold off the public water system of its third-largest city, Cochabamba, to a subsidiary of the San Francisco–based Bechtel Corporation, which promptly doubled the price of water for people's homes. Early in 2000, the people of Cochabamba rebelled, shutting down the city with general strikes and blockades. The government declared a state of siege, and a young protester was shot and killed. Word spread worldwide from the remote Bolivian highlands via the internet. Hundreds of email messages poured into Bechtel from all over the world demanding that it leave Cochabamba. In the midst of local and global protests, the Bolivian government, which had said that Bechtel must not leave, suddenly reversed itself and signed an accord that included every demand of the protesters. There is little doubt that it did so out of fear of social unrest.

Today's uncontrolled power centers—including nation-states, particularly the world's only superpower, military establishments, corporations, markets, and powerful political interests—pose a threat to human survival. But these power actors are actually made up of, and dependent on, the very people whose future prospects they threaten. The key to countering their domination is to make use of that dependence. That is how new common preservations can realize their objectives, in spite of those who oppose them.

CHAPTER 28

Countering Disorder

When individuals and groups do not or cannot coordinate their action, so that their action does not express their common purposes, the result is disorder. When some people make use of the unequal dependence of others to coerce them into acting in ways they otherwise would not choose, the result is domination.[1] This chapter presents our countering-disorder tool; the next our countering-domination tool; the following one explores how to combine them.

Much of what goes on in the world cannot be explained as the result either of deliberate intent or of blind causal forces. Rather, much results from the interactions of deliberate human actions, their unintended consequences, and natural forces—a mixture of "praxis" and "process."[2] An economic crisis, for example, grows out of deliberate human actions—selling stocks, demanding payment of loans, and the like. Yet the interaction of these actions with other forces produces a result that is not willed, or sometimes even foreseen, by anyone.

When the actions of individuals, groups, and organizations are poorly coordinated, their combined effect may result not in the achievement of their goals, but rather in a disorder in which nobody achieves much of anything. Actions deliberately or inadvertently counteract each other.

It is not hard to understand why there can be disorder. As Gregory Bateson put it in his essay "Why Things Get in a Muddle," there are many more ways for things to be disorderly than orderly.[3] If many individuals, groups, and institutions are pursuing their own goals and interests, their action is unlikely to be well coordinated unless something influences it to be so.

The normal situation of the working class under capitalism illustrates such lack of coordination. Individuals and groups often pursue their own interests without coordinating with others. Unions of workers in different trades, companies, and industries function as isolated units. Even within the same union, rank-and-file workers are often unable to coordinate with each other because the channels of communication and the control of action run exclusively to the top rather than directly connecting workers with each other.

As a result of such dis-coordination, action is often futile or even counterproductive. Workers compete with each other for jobs and advancement, thereby undermining their own power. Different groups are unable to pool their potential power, leaving them at the mercy of their employers.

Another form of disorder can occur when people act to achieve a result but inadvertently produce other results as well. These are unintended consequences of their action. As E.H. Carr wrote, "It is difficult to believe that any individual willed or desired the great economic depression of the 1930s. Yet it was indubitably brought about by the actions of individuals, each consciously pursuing some totally different aim."[4] Similarly, global warming is being produced as an unintended result of burning fossil fuels in cars, factories, and homes. No one is burning oil, gas, or coal in order to warm up the atmosphere, yet that is the result of actions that are only intended to warm houses, manufacture products, get from place to place, make a living, or make a profit. Raising the price of a commodity may increase the vendor's immediate profit, but it may also reduce the demand for the commodity. Brutality toward a slave may produce immediate submission but also a resolve to run away or rebel.

In a more complex pattern, an intended effect can also result in subsequent secondary interaction effects that were not intended. A ball skitters off the side wall of a billiard table and accidentally hits another ball. Apparently harmless chlorofluorocarbon (CFC) gasses produced as refrigerants, once released in the atmosphere, rise to a level where they are changed by the sun's rays into chemicals that destroy the earth's protective ozone layer. Such unintended interaction effects occur because human actions take place not in a vacuum but in a larger context or system.

Unintended consequences may even form a self-reinforcing loop—a vicious circle. No one intends an arms race, but if each country is determined to produce more or better weapons than its opponent, the result is not the superiority each pursues but rather a self-perpetuating cycle of escalations.[5] In such patterns, the dynamics of deliberate human action may actually mimic those of blind, unguided natural processes. For example, uncoordinated human action may produce bifurcations and phase changes like those studied by complexity and chaos theory.[6]

Unintended consequences may result simply from lack of knowledge about the effects of one's actions. The impact of CFCs on the ozone layer or of fossil fuels on the earth's climate were little recognized until fairly recently. But lack of knowledge of consequences is often the result of the way consequences are distributed. The stockholders of a global corporation that destroys the environment in a distant land as a side effect of drilling for oil are unlikely to experience the destruction. The local people whose livelihood is destroyed may be well aware of the side effects of the drilling but be unconnected to the decision-making process that controls it. Slaves may successfully conceal the determination to resist or escape that their owners' brutality is producing. In such cases no feedback loop connects those taking action and those experiencing its side effects.

Economists discuss unintended consequences under the rubric of "external effects" or "externalities" because they involve costs or benefits that are "external" to the entity that produces them. For historians, unintended consequences reflect the "irony of history," in which human action so often has an impact far different from what the actors intend.

Unintended consequences may lead to self-defeat or even self-destruction. Burning of fossil fuels may destroy the atmospheric balances on which human life depends. Efforts by one community or country to become more competitive economically by reducing wages and environmental protections may provoke even greater reductions by others, leading to a competitive "race to the bottom" that drives down conditions for all. Nuclear weapons designed to deter attack may provoke accidental war and consequent omnicide. Such patterns of self-destruction are reminiscent of the mechanical sculpture *Homage to New York*, installed briefly in the Museum of Modern Art in New York, which over the course of twenty-seven minutes systematically dismantled itself into a pile of junk.[7]

Action that undermines an actor's own intentions embodies a kind of alienation. Marx's famous analysis of the alienation of labor presents workers as engaging in work that is not determined by their own purposes but by those of an employer and ultimately by the capitalist system's inhuman drive to accumulate capital; at the extreme of such alienation, slaves may literally forge their own chains. Such alienation can be built into a social pattern like capitalism or slavery or even into a material object. The mill that Akron rubber workers used to produce tires also produced mangled arms; today's fossil fuel–based system of production and consumption cannot function without producing the greenhouse gasses that threaten the society, species, and ecosystem on which it depends. An organizer with the group Jobs with Peace described a meeting in a Minnesota church basement promoting a state economic conversion law where a worker stood up from the audience and expressed such alienation: "I work at a factory where we produce parts for nuclear weapons. I have a wife and two daughters that I support. I carry their pictures in the top of my lunch box. Every day I look at them for lunch. I know that I'm providing for their current needs while at the same time I'm helping to destroy their future." He added, "Thank God for what you're doing." Then he started to cry.[8]

Countering disorder requires equilibrating not just the actions of individual actors but also their patterns of interaction. It requires creating new coordinations. That may involve many elements of equilibration, such as creating new feedback loops, new means of communication, "thought experiments" to test possible action, new forms of regulation, new modes of counteraction, changing boundaries, agreement on plans for cooperative action, new limits on acceptable behavior, and means to evaluate the actual results.

For example, countering global warming required new feedback loops that monitor the effect of human activity on global climate. At first such loops just involved scientists; the result was that knowledge about global warming was cut off from those in a position to affect it. The scientists next drew in global policymakers through the UN but discovered there was not enough public support to implement the changes they knew were necessary. The feedback loop now must be extended to include the world's people—the true victims of global warming and the only force able to counter it. And humanity must find new ways to counteract the processes destroying our climate and place new limits on global warming's perpetrators.

The creation of new channels of communication is often a feature of the process of overcoming disorder. The communication network created by the Committees of Public Safety in Britain's American colonies—of which Paul Revere's midnight ride stands as an icon—provides a classic instance. The creation of new kinds of internet-based communications networks to coordinate political action are an up-to-date example.[9]

Public research and debate often use "thought experiments" to propose and test alternatives to disorder. For example, the debate in the 1990s on a "new financial architecture" for the global economy produced a wide range of plans for countering the irrational bubbles and busts of financial markets and the maldistribution of resources they produced. The failure to implement those plans found its reward in the Great Recession of 2008.

Public policies have often been used to counter unintended side effects and interaction effects. During the 1930s minimum wage laws and other "fair labor standards" were legislated at a national level to counter the "race to the bottom." Labor unions organized workers and developed industry-wide bargaining to reduce labor costs as a factor in competition through a common wage floor. More recently, the European Union developed a "social dimension" with many such standards to forestall a race to the bottom in an integrating Europe—a strategy largely abandoned in the era of neoliberalism. The fight for international labor rights and standards pursued a similar strategy in the era of globalization. The North American Federation for Fair Employment (NAFFE) sought to counter the insecurity of working-class life that resulted from the growth of contingent work by helping contingent workers become an organized force that could impose new rules on workplaces and labor markets.

Countering disorder may require institutionalizing patterns of variable actions that can compensate for varying conditions. An example is the system of government budget surpluses and deficits propounded by Keynesian economics to counter the variations in the business cycle. Another is the agricultural policy known as the "ever-normal granary"—instituted by Joseph in biblical times on behalf of Pharaoh—under which excess products are stored following a bumper crop and released to market after a bad harvest.

New common preservations to counter disorder often involve limits on acceptable behavior. These may simply be shared norms, such as the "netiquette" agreed to by people who participate in a common internet network. They may be embodied in new agreements like the Montreal Protocol ban on CFC emissions. They may involve binding rules or laws, such as the arms control agreements of the 1970s that for several decades effectively restricted the most provocative interactions of the nuclear arms race.

All of these new common preservations are ways to promote improved coordination, both for its positive benefits and to reduce the disorder that results from unintended side effects and interaction effects. All are ways to increase collective power by coordination. All emerge through new equilibrations.

Unintended side effects and interaction effects can be difficult to change because people resist giving up the benefit of their own action's intended effect. Fixing them may therefore also require changing or finding a substitute for those actions. If people destroy the local ecology because they are seeking oil for energy, they need to find a less destructive way to drill for oil or an alternative source of energy or a way to make do with less energy. If people build weapons to enhance their security, ending an arms race is more likely if other ways can be found to protect their security, such as mutual disarmament or resolution of contested issues.

The disorder of ecological destruction, wars, and global economic chaos threatens us all. A human survival movement will use our countering disorder tool to impose new ways to coordinate human action for our common preservation.

CHAPTER 29

Countering Domination

Sometimes people are unable to solve their problems because powerful individuals or groups prevent them from doing so. Then it is not enough for common preservations to improve coordination. They must also stop the powerful from impeding joint action. This is the function of our countering-domination tool.

If the dependence among actors is equal, it constitutes balanced interdependence. The parties are equally free to coordinate or not to coordinate their action. But where dependence is unequal, some actors have more power, at least potentially, than others. Those in some roles have a greater opportunity to realize their goals than others. They also have a greater opportunity to counter the efforts of others to realize their own goals. This leaves those whose goals can be blocked dependent on those who are in a position to block them. The weaker can then be coerced into actions they would not freely choose because the more powerful use their power to make noncompliance painful and costly. If this power is used on a continuing basis, the result is domination.[1]

Dominant actors can often use the dependence of others to parlay their power into still greater power. They may use resources they command to employ supervisors to control those dependent on them; cultural producers to influence their minds and emotions; political, communications, and other mediating institutions to ameliorate or deflect their grievances; and guards, police, and soldiers to threaten them with violence.

Not all potential dependencies are used as effective power at any given time. If workers are unorganized, have no tradition of striking, and do not view themselves as a potential collective actor, their potential power over their employer is only latent. But their employers are dependent on them nonetheless. Utilizing dependence—for example by organizing and threatening to strike—makes latent power actual. Domination can be countered by utilizing dependence.

People counter domination by creating new common preservations. Workers form informal work groups, unions, and strike committees. Nations form coalitions against aggressors. Oppressed groups threaten to collectively withdraw their cooperation or to disrupt their oppressors.

Despite their diverse forms, these common preservations all work by withdrawing from the powerful the cooperation on which their domination depends. Such withdrawal may be direct, as when workers strike their employers or victims of discrimination hold a sit-in that halts business as usual. Or it may be indirect, as when supporters boycott a company that is being struck or one country restricts trade as a sanction against another that commits aggression or oppresses its own people.

In complex modern societies with many complex, overlapping forms of coordination, dependencies are often complex and mediated. Direct strategies make use of the capacity of those adversely affected by unequal power to directly coordinate their efforts for their common preservation. But indirect strategies can make use of the multilateral character of dependence and power. As a result, power struggles often involve complex and evolving alliances and coordinations among different groups.

Countering domination generally involves reducing or eliminating the imbalance of dependence in either of two ways. Those who are dominated can develop the ability to coordinate their own activity without depending on those currently in power: for example, workers in a workplace may organize themselves independently of management to gain more control of their conditions at work. Community members may form a consumer coop that eliminates their dependence on corporate supermarkets.

Conversely, those who are dominated can also impose limits on those in authority. Human rights protections and democratization can limit the power of government officials. The rules governing institutions like the World Bank and the IMF can strip them of some of their functions and authority. Armies and police agencies can be cut down to size or disbanded. The ability of corporations to conspire to cooperate against the public can be impeded by antitrust policies. The abolition of a powerful actor is the most restrictive limit; for example, the abolition of monarchy reduces a king's power to zero; the abolition of slavery eliminates the power of slaveholders over slaves.

Countering domination often starts with coordination of those affected to form a collective actor. For example, workers organize unions; countries organize alliances for collective security; social movements dispersed among nations construct networks for globalization from below.

Groups may try to change the overall balance of dependence by reducing their own dependence. The national movement in the North American colonies before the American Revolution, for example, organized a boycott of imported British goods in part to reduce the colonies' dependence on them and thereby increase their freedom of action. Thomas Jefferson advocated for a large class of independent, land-owning "yeoman" farmers as a way to reduce the white population's dependence on the wealthy and the state. Gandhi's program to encourage Indian villagers to produce their own "homespun" cloth was intended to reduce their dependence on imports from their British imperial rulers. Union strike funds relieve workers of the threat of immediate destitution when they walk off their jobs.

Conversely, groups may try to reduce the power of their opponents. The 1980s divestment campaign against apartheid South Africa tried to weaken the regime by driving down the value of its assets and currency. The campaigns against dictatorships in Chile, Argentina, and Brazil aimed to delegitimize the rulers and therefore reduce their ability to command.

Groups may try to form alliances with others on whom the powerful depend. Sometimes these are strategic alliances designed to last over time, like the Blue-Green Alliance of the United Steelworkers union and the environmentalist Sierra Club to promote "green jobs." Some may be more short-term, like the support committees that often develop around particular strikes.

Groups may also try to disrupt the alliances of their opponents. Union anticorporate campaigns, for example, attempt to isolate corporations from their investors and supporters in the business community, government, and the public through exposure, negative publicity, disinvestment, and other forms of pressure.

When a group seeks to challenge domination, the result is typically what Gandhi called a "matching of forces." When this involves subordinate and dominant groups, the matching is often asymmetrical—for example, dominant actors may use their control of wealth or police power, while subordinate actors may use withdrawal of labor or consent. If underlying power relations have indeed changed, the outcome is likely to be a new balance of power.

Once parties recognize a new balance of power, there is likely to be some kind of tacit or actual negotiation to establish a new modus vivendi. Often both parties find it advantageous to settle, even if they are not fully satisfied and hope to continue the conflict in the future. Even surrender often ends with some kind of negotiation in which new power relations are acknowledged and a basis is established for life to go on.

Union/management bargaining, civil rights movement negotiations with local "power structures," and the roundtable discussions that ended some of the communist regimes in Eastern Europe illustrate the process of formal negotiations. There can also be a tacit bargaining process in which parties change their behavior in ways that are mutually understood as a basis for halting overt conflict. The detente in the Cold War during the 1970s involved many such tacit tit-for-tats. Such a modus vivendi may alternate with acute conflict in the pattern Mao Zedong characterized as "Fight fight, talk talk."

Many of the social experiments with which I've been involved have tried in one way or another to counter domination. They have generally done so by linking those harmed by domination and their allies into new configurations that could make use of the dependencies of the powerful to change the balance of power. The Naugatuck Valley Project linked local unions, churches, and community organizations to gain leverage over corporations that threatened to shut down factories in the valley. In "Terminating the Bush Juggernaut" I proposed that governments, civil society, and social movements join together to impose nonviolent sanctions on the US to force an end to its war of aggression against Iraq.[2]

Many threats to human survival are perpetrated or perpetuated by powerful actors who resist the changes that would ameliorate them. Governments refuse to disarm; corporations refuse to stop producing greenhouse gasses. A human survival movement represents the widest of human interests, and therefore will be able to do much through persuasion. But at certain points countering domination will almost certainly also require a matching of forces.

CHAPTER 30

Countering Disorder Combined with Domination

Domination and disorder are often combined. Marx characterized capitalism as combining tyranny in the workplace with anarchy in the market. The powerful often treat the opportunity to dominate the powerless as the booty of rivalry among the powerful—acquiring more subjects or workers to exploit. Conversely, the powerful use their domination of the powerless to increase their power vis-à-vis their powerful rivals by acquiring more productive capacity or more soldiers for the competitive struggle. Countering disorder combined with domination requires new common preservations that correct both together, rather than simply shifting the balance from one to the other—and it requires its own countering-disorder-combined-with-domination tool for the purpose.

The movement against the nuclear arms race had to disentangle just such a mingling of disorder and domination. Many people campaigned against nuclear weapons per se. But the weapons turned out to be symptoms of broader patterns of power. The military establishments that wielded them were institutions that coordinated the activity of millions of people and made use of their power to influence government and other institutions; similarly, governments exercised authority over large populations, using their control of resources and allegiance to propagate nuclear overkill. The nation-state system defined each government as sovereign in a way that prevented any higher authority from limiting war making or imposing disarmament. Both highly integrated forms of coordination like armies and nation-states and the anarchic disorganization of interstate relations helped make the problem of nuclear war intractable. The combined result was an uncontrolled arms race.

Contemporary political discourse generally seeks the solution to social problems in either more government or more market. But neither state nor market guarantees adequate solutions to disorder and domination. Both market and state can include elements of disorder—the anarchy of the market and of the sovereign nation-state system. Both can include elements of domination—imperialism, authoritarianism, exploitation, and corporate self-aggrandizement. Solutions require not so much replacing one with the other as countering the tendencies toward disorder and domination in both.

Counteracting combined disorder and domination requires a set of interlocking equilibrations. The dominated have to organize themselves as collective actors. This is more difficult when the dominated are enclosed within the boundaries that divide conflicting institutions and obey the authority of those who rule them. They then may identify with and follow the leaders of their government or their employers in the struggle against other governments or employers. The formation of new common preservations that cross boundaries of conflicting institutions is often a critical part of the process of social change—and is often stigmatized as disloyalty or subversion.

Such emerging collective actors then must find ways to use their combined power to counter the power of the conflicting power centers that formerly divided them and that they now confront collectively. This often involves a series of tests in which a matching of forces mobilizes and demonstrates the collective power of the dominated. A series of internationally coordinated struggles over several years by social movements on several continents against the proposed Multilateral Agreement on Investment led in 1998 to the abandonment of negotiations for the treaty.

The new collective actors must then establish means to restrict or abolish the formerly dominant players or hold them accountable on an ongoing basis. This is the process of democratization, in which states, enterprises, and other institutions become accountable to those they rule and others they affect.

The new collective actors also need to establish a means of imposing coordination on the conflicting power centers. This requires some kind of coordinating process or authority that jointly regulates them and their interaction and to which they are accountable. The new actors-in-common must use their power to force rival power centers to submit to that higher coordination. In other words, power from below must make them submit to authority from above.

This, however, opens the opportunity for the higher coordinating process or body to become a new source of domination in its own right. Therefore those affected by it must use their power to hold it accountable on an ongoing basis.

Such measures may seem paradoxical because they devolve power both downward and upward. But the paradox is only apparent. What is actually happening is that one kind of power, the power of domination, is being reduced at each level, while another kind of power, the power of mutually beneficial coordination, is being increased at each level. Antagonistic self-aggrandizement is being replaced by common preservation.

The development of the US Constitution provides one example of this process. Under the weak Articles of Confederation, the newly independent states of North America competed and failed to act together or jointly regulate their commerce. The proponents of a more centralized government saw a powerful federal system as a means to allow coordinated action and regulation. They organized at the grassroots level across state lines to force the states to call a Constitutional Convention and eventually to ratify the constitution it produced. The result was a reduction in power of the individual states and the devolution of power upward to the federal government.

Many Americans feared that the expanded power of the federal government could create the basis for domination by a new monarchy. They therefore insisted on election of officials, procedures for impeachment, reservation of many powers to the states, separation of powers with checks and balances among branches of government, and other means to limit concentration of power and hold the federal government accountable to those it ruled.

Further, those concerned about excessive federal power insisted on a Bill of Rights that would protect the freedom of individuals and groups to speak and act on their own behalf. Thus, the centralized coordinating power was designed to increase rather than reduce the freedom of those it protected at the base. This protection was considerably expanded after the Civil War through the application of the Bill of Rights to the states. The Thirteenth Amendment, abolishing slavery throughout the US, further illustrates how an increase in centralized power can simultaneously represent a great leap forward in human freedom.

The Bill of Rights not only restricted the power of the federal government. It also guaranteed the right of the people to organize themselves and act on their own behalf. It thus allowed them to counter the emergence of new dominations and disorders. However imperfect the resulting system, its formation illustrates the process by which disorder combined with domination can be overcome.

The same apparently paradoxical shift of power upward and downward can be seen in the formation of the European Union. The powers of individual nations were curtailed by the formation of progressively stronger central powers. The result was the suppression of war and many destructive forms of economic conflict.

At the same time, individual human rights and the rights of social groups were protected throughout the EU. The principle of "subsidiarity" meant, at least in theory, that decisions would be taken by those most directly affected, and that power would be exercised at higher levels only when higher-level coordination was needed to realize common goals.

While nation-states lost some of their power in this system, lower-level groups such as regions and ethnic groups might increase theirs. The result was again a devolution of power both downward and upward.

The system included means, such as elections, the EU parliament, and courts, designed to hold higher levels of the system accountable. In reality, however, these were largely ineffectual in limiting the power of the EU executive, and the system as a whole was largely dominated by corporate interests. This "democracy deficit" undermined the system, which today is in crisis.

Industrial unions empowered workers while imposing order on major US industries. From the late nineteenth century till the emergence of managed capitalism during and after World War II, workers were confronted by huge and domineering corporations engaged in desperate competition for survival, growth, and supremacy. Whatever concessions particular corporations might have chosen to make to labor, they were forced by the competitive process to drive their labor costs to the lowest possible level.

Industrial unions, starting with the United Mine Workers in the late nineteenth century, responded by organizing workers across each industry, regardless of their occupation or particular employer. They used the power of the strike to establish leverage over individual employers. Then they used that power to force employers to establish industry-wide bargaining processes to impose uniform standards.

These processes might take the form of tacit "pattern bargaining." Or they might involve the formation of employer associations—ironically, often at labor's insistence—through which all employers in an industry engaged in joint collective bargaining with their entire combined workforce. Labor's goal—to a considerable extent achieved in the mid-twentieth century—was to eliminate labor costs as a factor in competition, allowing wages to rise for all without putting one or another employer at a competitive disadvantage. The result was that workers' power and well-being were augmented at the bottom through their organization vis-à-vis their own employers, but also at the industry level through industry-wide collective bargaining. How much this system would actually advance workers' interests turned out to largely depend on how much workers could control their own representatives.

Workers' strategy to win the right to organize in the US in the 1930s combined upward and downward devolution of power. Workers used direct action and local alliances to impose labor rights on individual employers. At the same time they demanded national legislation that would protect labor rights for all. The result was the National Labor Relations Act (Wagner Act—widely known as "Labor's Magna Carta"). It created a new central authority, the National Labor Relations Board (NLRB), which forced employers to bargain collectively with their employees and to desist from interfering with their rights.

This centralization of power greatly strengthened rank-and-file workers vis-à-vis both their own employer and their industries as a whole. There were few mechanisms to hold the NLRB accountable to workers, however, so that over time it became more subject to employer influence and even at times an instrument for limiting workers' power.

Today we find ourselves confronting a combination of domination and disorder that threatens the survival and well-being of our entire species. We face vast concentrations of power in such forms as global corporations and nation-states. At the same time we suffer from horrendous disorder in the form of unregulated markets, international conflict, and environmentally devastating side effects of uncontrolled human activity. We face nuclear-armed, accumulation-blinded, out-of-control power actors battling each other to dominate the world's people and resources. A movement for human preservation will have to counter disorder and domination—by increasing global coordination and by making it subject to democratic accountability from below. The two go hand in hand.

CHAPTER 31

Forestalling New Disorder and Domination

New common preservations always risk producing new disorders and dominations. As William Blake wrote:

> The iron hand crushd the Tyrants head
> And became a Tyrant in his stead.[1]

Our forestalling-new-disorder-and-domination tool helps explore how common preservations might engender new disorders and dominations and how they can be forestalled from doing so.

A movement that starts by seeking equalization of power or realization of common interests may end up pursuing domination or unintentionally causing disorder. Consider the way the French Revolution eventuated in an emperor, an empire, and the Napoleonic Wars. Apparently liberatory movements like the American and Russian Revolutions likewise issued in aggression, war, and empire. In a less dramatic way, the civil rights and antiwar movements become embroiled in conflicts with other movements that undermined the ability of each to realize its goals. Indeed, improved coordination within a group can lead to intensified conflict with those outside. The Native American Iroquois Federation was highly successful in reducing conflict among its member tribes; but that unity augmented their ability to dominate their neighbors.

We can anticipate and forestall disorder and domination by incorporating the means of countering them on an ongoing basis. This was the objective of the "self-limiting revolution" proposed by Adam Michnik and other activists in the Polish KOR and Solidarity movements. They sought a process that would transform Polish society, but one that was "self-limiting" because it eschewed "violent upheaval and forceful destruction of the existing system," which they believed would likely lead to seizure of power by a new authoritarianism. Rather, Michnik called for an "unceasing struggle for reform and evolution that seeks an expansion of civil liberties and human rights."[2] Along similar lines I have advocated a "constitutional insurgency" for climate protection based on the constitutional right to a stable climate but which would nonetheless be bound by constitutional obligations to respect the human and civil rights of others.

Such forestalling can apply the same methods used to solve existing problems but introduce them proactively. "Precorrection" in the solutions to social problems can be made possible through thought experiments on representations of hypothetical situations.

New common preservations can lead to disorder in various ways. The new collective actors may fail to coordinate with others they encounter as they develop. The solution is to construct new coordinations with those they interact with. New common preservations can establish boundaries so rigid that they block the further development of new coordinations. The antidote is to design each new common preservation to lay the basis for a further decentering process that enables further coordinations to overcome emerging gaps. This depends on an open dialogue that seeks wider common interests and improved patterns for their realization.

New common preservations can likewise lead to new dominations. The differentiation of roles within a group can lead to domination by leaders. To take a relatively benign example, labor movements that proffered workers self-liberation have produced bureaucratized, leadership-dominated institutions that can prevent workers from acting in concert to pursue either their own or broader social interests. Less benign is the way in which revolution and communism resulted in a system of party domination and Stalinist tyranny. Such developments can be forestalled by limiting the authority of leaders on the one hand and retaining the capacity of the rank and file to coordinate their own activity on the other.

Some solutions only generate the original problem over again in a new form. When a leader has become a tyrant, replacing the tyrant with a new leader while leaving everything else the same is a formula for a new tyranny. Curing inflation by inducing a recession will not, other things being equal, keep future business cycles from producing fresh rounds of inflation and recession down the road.

Forestalling new dominations and disorders requires rules and practices that permit people to recoordinate their action and reconfigure social roles. It requires not so much a once-and-for-all correction of existing problems as an ability to make ongoing corrections—less a system that realizes perfect freedom and order than a continuing process of countering deviations from them. That depends on feedback loops that allow ever-renewed change in compensations. Both the concerted actors seeking to change the world and the new common preservations they introduce need such ongoing equilibration to prevent new disorder and domination.

It is therefore important to seek solutions that are likely to forestall the emergence of new problems or make them easier to address when they do arise. Establishing periodic elections, rather than simply installing a new leader, was a brilliant way to forestall tyranny. And introducing "built-in stabilizers," such as government budget surpluses that reduce demand in times of boom and budget deficits and unemployment compensation programs that increase demand in periods of recession, provided a way to counter the tendency toward cycles of boom and bust on an ongoing basis.

To avoid new disorder and domination, new patterns of coordination must not foreclose the possibility of actors subsequently creating still other patterns. People must retain access to the means of acting and coordinating action. In practice, this means that people must remain organized at the grassroots and that communication and surveillance must remain diffused, accessible, and mutual. It requires collective actors whose members are able to initiate new forms of coordination both with other members and with those outside their current patterns of coordination.

That capacity is most likely to be retained when organizations take the form of networks of relatively autonomous parts. In such networks people retain the capacity—the ability and legitimate right—to coordinate their own activity. At the same time, they retain the capacity to initiate further coordination on a wider scale.

Tim Costello and his colleagues designed the North American Federation for Fair Employment (NAFFE) as a "structured network" designed to facilitate coordination without permanent centralized authority. It promoted the formation of action groups that served as its principal centers of initiative and coordination. As Tim's and my study of NAFFE argued,

> The network form allows a coordinated social movement composed of relatively autonomous groupings. It eschews a sharp distinction between organizers and the rank and file. It is difficult to monopolize the flow of communication within networks or to block its flow across organizational boundaries. Networks are resistant to leadership domination; their leaders are largely dependent on persuasion, rather than on control of scarce organizational resources or some form of muscle. When authority is delegated, it quickly expires, and is only renewed in the presence of active trust.[3]

The World Social Forum similarly created a "space" in which ongoing recoordination is facilitated. This allows both new coordinations among those already linked and the extension of the coordination process to new groups. Each Forum has attracted and welcomed a variety of new constituencies from around the globe, some of them previously hostile to the WSF or some of its participants.

Such decentralized action must at the same time provide vigorous pursuit of collective interests. If decentralized action is ineffective as a means to pursue collective interests, participants are likely to replaced it with more centralized forms.

Role differentiation secretes asymmetrical access to power. Therefore there will always be a need for means to reconfigure such differentiations and redistribute the powers and benefits that accompany them. This involves the ongoing de-stratification of social roles. For example, "job enlargement" and the principle of the all-round craft worker can counter the overspecialization of jobs. Similarly the application of the "subsidiarity principle" can devolve political decision-making to the lowest practical level to counter the overconcentration of power. And property rights can be unbundled and redistributed by means such as land reform and common ownership with leases and other time-limited assignment of limited use rights.[4]

Where authority to speak and act on behalf of a group is delegated, those granted authority need to remain accountable. Means to hold them accountable include the traditional structures of democracy, such as elections, recall, transparency, and the like. It also includes such emerging additions to democratic practice as mandated impact statements, affinity groups, and participatory budgeting. Indeed, the means of democratic participation and accountability are only in their infancy and need far greater development. Because new ways of circumventing such accountability will also continue to be invented, accountability cannot replace but can only supplement the ongoing capacity of people to recoordinate their activity themselves. As the abolitionist orator Wendell Phillips put it, "Eternal vigilance is the price of liberty."[5]

While some degree of institutionalization may be inevitable, institutional rules must include means for putting institutional rules into abeyance and returning to a state in which change in or elimination of existing patterns of coordination and differentiation is possible. Amendment clauses in constitutions and sunset clauses in legislation illustrate "meta-rules" providing for deinstitutionalization.

Such a strategy of ongoing correction is not the only possible strategy. It is also possible, for example, to envision and try to realize an ideal society in which all inequalities have been eliminated, all power resides in society as a whole, all social processes are socially planned and controlled, and all people spontaneously pursue the common good.

While the idea of such a society may have a role to play as a regulative ideal, it presents serious problems as a concrete objective. Coordination will always involve conflicts between individual and collective needs and aspirations. Role differentiation will always secrete distinct interests. The interaction of different social practices will always generate results that are not controlled by human intention. Individuals will always be tempted to form new patterns of action and coordination that benefit them but may disrupt or burden others. The futile attempt to realize utopia—in society or in social movements themselves—has often led to immense frustration and even destructive forms of repression and conflict.

That is no justification for passivity or despair. The fact that unintended consequences, out-of-control social processes, inequalities, and conflicts of interest cannot be completely eliminated is no argument against trying to reduce them to a minimum—and keep them at a minimum. It is no argument against trying to eliminate what might be called "surplus alienation," alienation that is greater than necessary. And more to the point, it is no argument against trying to reduce those alienations that threaten the existence and well-being of our environment, our species, and ourselves.

People rightly fear that the effort to introduce new common preservations may lead to new tyrannies and disorders. The incorporation of self-correcting patterns that forestall such results is crucial for the success of new common preservations—and for persuading people to believe in the possibility of their success. Proposals for new common preservations are likely to win sufficient support only if they include means to ensure that they don't lead to new disorders and dominations as bad or worse than those they attempt to cure.

Conclusion to Part 2

Common preservation often seems impossible. People are too selfish, too divided, too dominated, too hopeless. Yet we know that new common preservations do emerge repeatedly in human history. How?

As each of us lives our life, we use a set of established patterns. But sometimes a problem arises that we are unable to solve either as individuals or through established social patterns. The problem may be unsolvable because those affected by it can't or don't coordinate their action effectively. Or it may be unsolvable because some powerful individual or group blocks its solution. In either case, we can't realize our ends without new patterns of action.

Faced with such a problem, we may resort to denial or despair. But we may also look for new solutions. We can use trial and error, varying our patterns and testing the results. Or we can construct mental representations of our situation and our existing patterns of action and conduct thought experiments intended to find new solutions. Those solutions can then be tested in practice.

New common preservations originate in a recognition that certain problems can't be solved by prevailing patterns of thought and action. But that must be followed by a recognition that other people are affected by similar problems. Such recognition may be expressed in tacit cooperation with others developed through trial and error. It may involve sharing representations and jointly conducting thought experiments on them. In many cases it involves both.

We are able to construct new common preservations because we are equilibrators: we are open systems, guided by feedback loops, able to counteract deviations from our ends, relatively unrestrained by instinct, able to use language and other signs for thinking and communication, and able to coordinate our action through mutual assimilation and accommodation.

These biological and human capacities taken together make possible the emergence of new social patterns that are not biologically wired-in—including new common preservations. Feedback loops allow us to discover gaps between our intent and the result of our action. By trial and error we are able to test new actions and discover their results. And with the use of language, we can conduct such trials virtually, "in our heads." We can also imagine a wide range of alternatives to test virtually and in practice.

As open systems with semipermeable boundaries, we are able to interact with other people. We can form concerted actors that themselves are open systems with cybernetic feedback loops, able to act together to compensate for deviations from our goals. For us humans, the atrophy of instinct and the use of language to share information and thinking greatly increase our capacity to do so.

The capacity to assimilate the intentions and actions of others, and to accommodate to them, makes it possible for us to coordinate our actions. Both trial-and-error learning and thinking shared through language make it possible to develop new, improved coordinations—ones that increase the benefits from action.

This equilibration process applies not only to means but also to ends. As we learn to solve our problems in new ways, new goals become important for meeting our needs and some old ones become less important, superfluous, or counterproductive.

The potential benefits from improved coordinations give people a motive for pursuing them. But if coordination benefits only some, not all, participants, those who do not benefit will have no reason to participate. New common preservations are more likely to emerge when they realize the benefits of coordinated action in ways that benefit all participants. Some people may be reluctant to make problem-solving changes because they fear what they might lose as a result. But people can develop new ways of acting that solve problems while preserving their deepest interests or meeting their needs in other ways.

People may meet obstacles to their efforts at problem-solving equilibration. Powerful individuals and institutions may block necessary changes out of their own self-interest. Yet such obstacles have often been overcome. Because power originates in social coordination, even the most powerful are dependent on the collaboration and acquiescence of others for their power; the apparently powerless can counter the power of the powerful by withdrawing the collaboration and acquiescence on which they depend. This is the secret that underlies the power of social movements to make social change.

Coordination of different people's action produces power that goes beyond that of individuals. So does differentiation of action into different social roles. But such power may produce problems—including many of the problems to which social movements respond. The prevailing patterns of social coordination and differentiation may produce disorder. This results from allowing side effects and interaction effects that are not subject to control by those they affect. Solving the resulting problems requires construction of new patterns of coordination for concerted action to achieve common objectives.

Conversely, the prevailing patterns of coordination and differentiation may produce domination. This results from the unequal distribution of control over coordination and its benefits. Solving the resulting problems requires changing or dissolving existing patterns of coordination through which domination is exercised.

In the equilibration process, people develop new capacities and new goals. But those in turn can become the basis for new problems and further transformations. The power of social movements itself can be the source of new dominations and disorders. A coordinated group can differentiate into powerful leaders and a disempowered rank and file. It can become the vehicle for dominating others outside the group. Or the actions of different groups may cancel each other out or produce side effects and interaction effects that lead to vicious circles of self and mutual destruction. What begins as common preservation can end as tyranny or chaos.

Fortunately, such results can be forestalled by building the means of further equilibration into the way we solve our problems. To forestall the restoration of domination, social movements need to incorporate the principle of ongoing recoordination to ensure that the control and benefits of concerted action are equally accessible to all. To forestall new forms of disorder, social movements need to extend the practice of recoordination to side effects and interaction effects that result from their growing power, and to seek coordination with those outside the initial group of actors-in-common.

In sum, common preservation can be considered an equilibration in which people solve a problem and overcome an imbalance through new patterns of coordinated action that compensate for the gap between their ends and their established means or among their established ends. The heuristic tools are means for understanding and nurturing their ability to do so. When they succeed the result is the development of common preservation.

Common Preservation vs. Mutual Destruction

In this interpretation, people move from self-preservation to common preservation primarily in the hope that they can better accomplish their ends by doing so. But why is it plausible that collective action can achieve things that individual action can't? And what leads people to believe it can?

The problems that generate new common preservations are generally the result of a lack of power. Slaves were powerless before masters; workers needed the jobs their employers could provide; housewives could not control the price of beef; opponents of climate change had little influence on huge fossil fuel corporations and the governments they controlled. How could they acquire the power they needed to counteract that power?

Power, as Michael Mann points out, results from cooperation. The ability to coordinate the action of various people multiplies its force. Therefore people can acquire greater power by acting together—by pursuing common, rather than purely individual, ends. Mann describes the great variety of means through which people coordinate their action for common purposes as networks. Networks form and grow by connecting initially isolated individuals and groups into a concerted force—linking the nooks and crannies.

But why does this mean anything in the face of the power of slave owners, bosses, and fossil fuel corporations? The answer, according to Gandhi and Sharp, is that power also results from dependence. Slave owners are powerful, but their power depends on the obedience of slaves. Employers are powerful, but their power depends on the labor of their workers. Consumers depend on meat companies to supply their tables, but meat companies can't gain wealth if consumers stop buying meat. Fossil fuel companies can purchase politicians and acquire permits, but they can't build power plants and pipelines if millions of people blockade or refuse to pay for their construction projects.

Both the powerful and the powerless are part of a system of mutual dependence. The powerful are dependent on the rest of society for their power. That is why, as Gandhi put it, the powerful cannot rule without the cooperation of those they rule. But the withdrawal of cooperation in itself has little effect when conducted by isolated individuals—as one boss put it, "If a man won't work, I'll just send for another man." It is through the combination of cooperation and the utilization of dependence through the withdrawal of cooperation that common preservation can make change for the better.

Part 2 has elaborated the patterns and subpatterns of the development of common preservation into a heuristic designed to help guide inquiry when common preservation has occurred or is needed. Part 3 will use that heuristic to probe the development of the movement for climate protection and a possible strategy for countering human self-destruction through destruction of the climate.

PART 3
USING THE TOOLS: CLIMATE PROTECTION

CHAPTER 32

Climate Protection as Common Preservation

The purpose of part 3 is to show how the common preservation heuristic can be applied to understand and act on real-life problems.[1] It uses the common preservation heuristic to explore the efforts to halt climate change, their failure so far, and the possibility of an alternative strategy for climate protection I call climate insurgency.[*] The notes in the Commentary section (page 313) are marked with an asterisk and elaborate on how the common preservation heuristic is used in the text. Part 3 is not intended as a comprehensive or persuasive presentation of my approach to countering climate change; readers seeking such an account should consult my three books and many articles on the subject.

The scientific confirmation of human-caused global warming late in the twentieth century presented humanity with a problem.[*] The earth's climate had been extraordinarily stable for the thousands of years in which civilization developed. Now that stability was being thrown into disequilibrium. A gap opened between the climate we had come to expect and the climate we are actually facing now and in the future.

This gap created a problem that would eventually affect every human being. But at first the rest of us could only learn about it from information reported by climate scientists. The consequences could be predicted but not yet experienced.[*]

Human-caused climate change results from greenhouse gases (GHGs) produced by burning fossil fuels. The human failure to halt climate change results not from anyone's intention to heat the planet, but from a variety of strategies by individuals, groups, and institutions intended to provide for their needs, ends, and survival.[*] The paradoxical result of such efforts at self-preservation is mutual destruction. It results from an inability to coordinate our actions to meet our needs.* Like a ghoulish parody of Adam Smith, the invisible hand of self-interest is guiding us as individuals, groups, and institutions to produce the GHGs that are destroying humanity—including the GHG emitters themselves. This paradox is a form of alienation, in which our own efforts to pursue our self-interest and self-preservation result in a self- and mutual destruction that neither we nor anyone else intends.* It already is undermining the stability of our lives, and if not halted it may threaten the survival of our species.

As we saw in chapter 28, "Countering Disorder," such unintended consequences are the expectable result of a disordered system in which individuals and institutions are unable to cooperate to correct the untoward consequences of their actions and interactions.*

The solution to climate catastrophe—the way to end this common threat—is a form of human cooperation that halts global warming by halting the burning of fossil fuels and takes other measures to restore the balance of the earth's climate.* Producing that change will require a deliberate self-transformation of humanity that not only prevents the burning of fossil fuels but also transforms economic, social, and political life—the world order—to function without them.*

Such a transformation may seem far-fetched. But as we noted in the introduction to this book, from time to time people do shift from pursuing their own interests and well-being as individuals to strategies that use collective action to realize common ends. They discover the failure of the strategies they are pursuing to provide for their well-being. They also discover that other people are facing the same problem. Under such conditions they may in fact shift to strategies of common preservation to meet their needs and realize their ends.*

Climate change is surely a case where pursuing narrow self-interest—whether by pumping oil and gas out of the ground to make a profit or by opposing limits on coal mining in pursuit of national economic advantage—is resulting instead in mutual destruction. It is also a case where we can see that others—indeed, all the world's people—face a similar threat. As a result, millions of people around the world have already taken one or another form of action to halt climate change—they have started to replace mutual destruction with common preservation.[2]*

So far, however, our efforts to halt global warming have failed. Thirty years of human effort to protect the climate have not even slowed down its destruction. Touted international summits from Rio to Bali to

Copenhagen to Paris have left us with no binding agreement to limit GHG emissions. Despite the indicators of apocalyptic climate change—including floods, droughts, heat waves, extreme storms, Arctic melting, desertification, wildfires, epidemics, and mass migration—the emission of GHGs continues to rise and is projected to go on rising, leading to still more devastating climate change.*

Notwithstanding the sincerity of its individual participants, the official governmental climate protection process has been little more than a charade in which world leaders, governments, and business pretend to address climate change while pursuing policies that pour ever more GHGs into the atmosphere. The entire process reveals a collection of self-serving, self-aggrandizing institutions whose leaders have been unable to cooperate even for their own survival. Call it self-annihilation in the service of self-preservation.*

Even before the election of President Donald Trump, the US Department of Energy was predicting that global GHG emissions would increase 40 percent by 2040.[3] There are already 400 parts per million (ppm) of carbon in the atmosphere, far above the 350 ppm target often identified as the safe upper limit.

In this part we use the common preservation heuristic to try to develop an alternative strategy for climate protection. That strategy involves, first, recognizing that we need to cooperate with each other to provide for our common survival. Second, it requires the formation of a collective actor—we will call it a climate insurgency—through which we can pursue our common interests and our common survival. Third, it requires using the power of that collective actor to impose the changes that are necessary to halt the emission of the GHGs that are destroying our climate.

Part 3 interprets climate destruction in the light of other problems that have required common preservation as a solution.* It presents the movement for climate protection as the process—far from complete—of humanity's self-correction and self-transformation in response to a life-threatening gap. It is a story of compensation for error and development of new capabilities.*

Chapter 32, "Climate Protection as Common Preservation," argues that climate protection requires a shift to common preservation. It describes the efforts so far to protect the climate as steps in a learning process that can possibly but not necessarily lead to a solution to climate destruction by a self-transformation of humanity from mutual destruction to a strategy of common preservation.

Chapter 33, "The World Order of Climate Destruction," describes some of the basic patterns that have prevented common preservation for climate protection. They include such key elements of the world order as the division of the earth and humanity into sovereign nation states; the right of private property owners to burn fossil fuels and emit the GHGs that are destroying the climate; the forms of disorganization, unintended consequences, and barriers to collective action that arise from the market; and the power of fossil fuel producers and users and the widespread dependence on them. These elements present obstacles to human self-organization for climate protection.

Chapter 34, "Official Climate Protection from Rio to Paris," lays out the history of a quarter century of failure to reduce GHG emissions. It portrays this failure as the expectable result of a process dominated by fossil fuel interests, nation-states, property owners, and markets whose leaders are intent on pursuing their own interests even at the expense of common survival.

Chapter 35, "Development of the Climate Movement: Self-Organization," describes the rise of a global climate movement independent of the institutions that have blocked climate protection. It examines in particular the emergence of 350.org, which fits many of the patterns described earlier in this book for the rapid development of new common preservations, including new shared objectives, networks that cut across established boundaries, and new forms of cooperation. It describes how the global climate movement has become a vehicle for previously isolated people around the world to engage in joint action.

Chapter 36, "Development of the Climate Movement: Countering Power," describes the self-transformation of the climate movement in the twenty-first century. It focuses on the struggle to prevent the construction of the Keystone XL pipeline, which unified previously disconnected people and organizations; utilized mass civil disobedience to resist the building of fossil fuel infrastructure; and engaged fossil fuel proponents in a "matching of forces" that turned the climate issue into a contest of popular power.

Chapter 37, "Climate Insurgency: A Plausible Strategy for Common Preservation of the Climate?," provides a thought experiment designed to test a strategy for transforming the climate-destroying features of the world order through a global nonviolent constitutional insurgency. It argues that laws protecting climate destruction and the institutions that enforce them are themselves in violation of the most basic human and constitutional rights and government duties to the public trust, and therefore possess no legitimate authority, and should be disobeyed in the interest of climate protection. It proposes how to use people power to enforce the human and constitutional right to a stable climate.

Chapter 38, "A Common Preservation Program for Climate Protection," lays out the rapid elimination of fossil fuel emissions necessary to protect the climate and the transformations in the world order needed to support them. It focuses in particular on the changes in national institutions necessary to support the transition to a fossil-free economy and the changes in global institutions necessary to support national transitions. It presents these as a program to be implemented by the climate insurgency.

Chapter 39, "Climate Protection through Common Preservation," presents the overall process by which the failure of climate protection could plausibly be overcome by the development of common preservation.

"Afterword: From Climate Insurgency to a Human Survival Movement," proposes that the climate insurgency can serve as the leading edge of a developing movement for human survival through common preservation. That movement can use the climate insurgency as the starting point for building a wider and still more transformative movement that addresses problems of war, injustice, poverty, ecological destruction, and others that grow out of the mutual destruction of our present world order.

Each of these chapters shows a different way to use the common preservation heuristic. "Climate Protection as Common Preservation" applies the heuristic to construct an overview of how to solve a problem through a shift to common preservation. "The World Order of Climate Destruction" uses the heuristic to identify the basic social patterns that block the solution of a problem. "Official Climate Protection from Rio to Paris" uses the heuristic to construct a historical narrative that explains the successes and failures of efforts to solve a problem. "Development of the Climate Movement: Self-Organization" employs the heuristic to construct an account of the formation of a new social movement. "Development of the Climate Movement: Countering Power" utilizes the heuristic to probe the self-transformation of a movement to create new means of achieving its goals. "Climate Insurgency: A Plausible Strategy for Common Preservation of the Climate?" shows how to use the heuristic to construct a strategy for social change. "A Common Preservation Program for Climate Protection" indicates how to use the heuristic to develop a program for the transformation as an aspect of society. "Afterword: From Climate Insurgency to a Human Survival Movement," shows how to use the heuristic to help transform a movement's goals. This interpretation was constructed using the heuristic tools by means of the method described in "Using the Tools" in part 2 of chapter 1.

Part 3 draws on my own experience as a participant in climate protection efforts and on the three books of my "climate insurgency trilogy," where many of these themes are explained and documented more fully.[4]

It may be too late to save civilization or even humanity from climate annihilation. But if we can limit climate change to 2°C instead of 6° or 8° or 12°, the effort to do so will be worth it.

CHAPTER 33

The World Order of Climate Destruction

Why is humanity producing its own doom? Why is that destruction so difficult to stop? The explanation lies in the way human beings organize our life on earth—our world order.[1] This chapter uses the common preservation heuristic to construct a historical and developmental account of the disordered system, our contemporary world order, from which and into which the climate catastrophe emerged.*

The elements of the world order that account for global warming trace back to the beginnings of the modern world, when several intertwined and evolving patterns came to characterize human activity.* One was a nation-state system based on sovereign states—power centers that assert absolute sovereignty over a defined territory and its population and engage in interstate diplomacy, domination, conflict, and war. Another was a system of property rights that gave property owners the right to pollute. A third was a system of competitive market exchange that compelled property owners to "accumulate or perish."[2] These were joined in the nineteenth century by a thousandfold increase in the burning of fossil fuels, which became the basis of modern economies and the contemporary world order.

The nation-state, private property, and market systems emerged gradually out of the feudal order in medieval Europe, and parallel developments were occurring in other parts of the world as well. Because they dominate the world today—and because they are the patterns primarily responsible for the production of global warming—they can provide a starting point for our inquiry. Human life can't be reduced to these institutions; there are still also families and clans, communities, regions, religions, subcultures, voluntary associations, bioregions, and many other overlaid patterns of human organization. But the nation-state, property rights, market, and fossil fuel energy systems have shaped the use of fossil fuels over the history of the modern world.

The nation-state, property, market, and fossil fuel systems are the primary patterns of disorder and domination that will need to be transformed by climate insurgency in order to end the burning of fossil fuel and the climate destruction it causes.

Nation-States

The destruction of the earth's climate has been presided over by nation-states. Those states have the legal and constitutional responsibility to protect their citizens, but instead they have colluded with each other to allow the destruction of their own people and those of every other nation. They have engaged in a mock effort to reduce GHG emissions while continuing and even expanding the burning of fossil fuels.* States and their leaders have acted in this way not only out of their own institutional and individual self-interest, but also because of the constraints they face from the prevailing patterns of property ownership, international competition, and the power of the fossil fuel industry.*

While the nation-state system can seem as universal as the law of gravity, in fact it is neither eternal nor unchanging.* It developed from a very different system, feudalism, and today is being modified though hardly abolished by globalization. The nation-state system established the framework in which global warming developed and in which it is being perpetuated.

Medieval Europe was governed by a multilevel political system in which monarchs shared power and legitimate authority with feudal lords below them and the Holy Roman Emperor and Roman Catholic Church above. A "patchwork of overlapping and incomplete rights of government" was "inextricably superimposed and tangled."[3] It was a prime example of overlapping boundaries and interpenetrating entities.*

Within this system, monarchs began to assert supreme authority within their territories. They developed cadres of officials to manage the state. At the same time, markets, trade, and a class of capitalists gradually emerged. The budding capitalists found a territorially centralized state increasingly useful for protecting property rights at home and abroad, while monarchs found capitalist wealth an important source of revenue for their emerging states.* By the seventeenth century, the medieval multilayered patchwork of political power had been superseded by a system of territorial states exercising a monopoly of authority against church and feudal authorities within their territories and sovereignty against emperor and Pope. This system of territorial states whose rulers assert absolute sovereignty and independence has characterized the world order ever since. It is sometimes known as the "Westphalian system" after the Treaty of Westphalia (1648) that supported the absolute sovereignty of monarchs.*

This transformation included several simultaneous aspects that can be illuminated by our heuristic tools. It was a transformation of entities and boundaries—witness the increasing importance of nations and their boundaries and their increasing impermeability to higher religious and political authorities. It was a transformation of coordination—national bureaucracies, for example, grew at the expense of papal and imperial ones. Merchants and monarchs developed, if not common preservation, at least a symbiotic relationship of mutual support, albeit combined with mutual jostling. The system of territorial states became the predominant mental representation of the organization of humanity. The shift from feudal to national organization created a whole new network of dependencies, which in turn made possible altered patterns of power.*

Economic conflict, imperial domination, and war—in short, disorder and domination—were constitutive features of the system of sovereign nation-states. States required wealth to pay for military and imperial operations lest they be unable to dominate others and instead be dominated by them. Successful states generally developed strategies of economic development designed to increase taxable wealth by increasing production.[4] States were compelled to accumulate wealth and power for their own self-preservation and self-aggrandizement.

Initially only very restricted classes and elites had any influence within the emerging territorial states. Gradually those excluded began to demand representation in the state. The idea of democratic self-government arose in conflict with monarchical domination and usually took the form of demands that state rulers be selected by the people, who would thereby be transformed from subjects to citizens. In the "age of democratic revolutions" from 1760 to 1800, revolutions and insurrectionary movements in North America, France, Great Britain, Latin America, and elsewhere replaced existing states with more democratic ones or forced existing states to provide vehicles for popular participation, thus transforming the pattern of domination.* Nonetheless, states generally continued to play the role of preserving "public order," including a highly unequal distribution of economic and political power, by using force and violence to suppress challenges to it.

The people ruled by early modern states were often ethnically diverse, geographically scattered, and culturally unconnected with their rulers—a German could be king of England, for example. Starting around the late eighteenth century, however, nationalist movements began seeking to align states as territorial power centers with nations as communities of people who asserted common linguistic, racial, ethnic, religious, ideological, or historical bonds. In the nationalist view, humanity was assumed to be divided into distinct peoples. Each people was entitled to form a nation, which in turn was entitled to a monopoly of political authority within a given territory. The sovereignty of states, originally conceived as the "divine right of kings," was redefined as a right of peoples. This transformation involved both the redrawing of political boundaries and the reconceptualization of nations as entities.

From both a nationalist and a democratic perspective, the nation-state was increasingly defined as the embodiment of the will of the people—meaning the citizens of the nation. The nation was generally presumed to possess a collective identity and a national interest which included the common interests of all ethnic and religious subgroups and of different social classes. This was in effect an ecological shift, in which separated individuals and interests were reconceived as parts of a whole. Nations were conceived as a people sharing a common identity and common interests—what Benedict Anderson has described as an "imagined community."[5]*

Even in democratic countries, however, most people remained excluded from control over economic institutions. In the nineteenth and twentieth centuries, movements arose among the excluded groups and classes to extend democratic control over markets and enterprises either directly or via the state. The purpose of these movements was to transform class-differentiated economic power and counter economic domination through collective action.* Some governments used their authority to establish welfare states and to regulate the behavior of economic actors, markets, and the economy as a whole. In communist countries the state became the possessor of productive wealth, ostensibly for the benefit of the people but often for political and economic elites that controlled the state apparatus. Many states used their political authority to extend power over the economy for government aggrandizement and economic nationalism.* To varying degrees economic coordination was transformed by supplementing or replacing the market by economic planning and a "command economy."* Since the 1970s, neoliberal economic doctrine has advocated and often imposed restriction of the economic role of the state, but the state role in the economy remains a contested zone. These varied developments have led to new configurations of both domination and disorder.

Since World War II, the nation-state system has ostensibly been modified by the global authority of the United Nations. That authority, however, has remained subordinate to the power of nation-states. And while in theory each nation-state is sovereign, in fact, effective power within the nation-state system is largely concentrated in a few dominant nations. The United States and its allies dominated this system during the twentieth century, but their hegemony is now being challenged by China and other rapidly developing nations. The product of the nation-state system continues to be disorder manifested in an unremitting struggle for domination.*

The nation-state system has helped cause and perpetuate climate destruction. National sovereignty gives states the authority to determine what can or cannot be emitted into the atmosphere in their territories; it is states that authorize the emission of climate-destroying GHGs. The sovereignty of nations ensures that common human interests are trumped by the authority of states—allowing governments to destroy the global atmospheric commons without restraint from higher authority. The system of sovereign nation-states generates a competition in which each state must encourage the exploitation of nature's resources or face loss of power and wealth within the world order. The direct and indirect dependence of states and their officials on dominant economic actors—notably industries that produce and use fossil fuels—often makes governments subordinate to those with an interest in perpetuating climate destruction. In the absence of adequate democratic control, states often extend their authority to become vehicles for imposing climate destruction on society. In short, the nation-state system combines disorder and domination to produce climate destruction.

The lack of vehicles for expressing and implementing common global interests impedes the world's people from pursuing our common interest in climate protection.* Conversely, transforming the nation-state system is an essential part of protecting the climate. That won't require the abolition of the nation-state, but it will take modifications I will lay out in the final chapter of part 3.

Property

The earth was not created with labels saying who owns what. Property rights are a human institution that can assign, among other things, the right to burn fossil fuels and destroy the earth's climate.

Systems of property rights exist in most societies, in part to control conflict over who can use what resources. But rights to property may be distributed in many different ways, and property rights are far more complex than a simplistic view of private property that asserts, "I can do whatever I want with what is mine." Property ownership consists of what legal scholars often describe as a "bundle of rights." The rights to access a piece of property, to exclude others from it, to determine its use, to have the benefits of its use, to modify it, to destroy it, and to convey it to others can be distributed among different individuals, groups, and institutions.* Property can be private, public, or common; held individually or jointly; held for oneself or in trust for another. Even the most privatized "fee simple" property ownership involves obligations such as paying taxes and not violating the rights of your neighbors.*

Property rights are claims that can be enforced by courts, executive officials, or popular action. In modern societies around the world, the arbiter of who has what property rights is normally the state. It determines the bundle of property rights, regulating conflict among social players and forces. Without governmental systems of laws and law enforcement, contemporary property ownership would be meaningless. The determination of who owns what and the "security of property" depend on the state. Property rights are ultimately determined by the power of the jostling forces that control the state. The state, conversely, is largely dependent on property owners for both economic and political support.*

Property systems bring together differentiation, power, and dependency. They largely determine the distribution of wealth and the composition of classes. They differentiate between rich and poor, workers and capitalists, landowners and the landless. They are crucial means for exercising power in most societies. Such differentiations can be considerable: a 2017 Oxfam study found that eight individuals own as much combined wealth as half the human race.[6]

Human life depends on the resources of nature and the products of past human activity, that is society's wealth.* Under the property systems of the contemporary world order, society's wealth is mostly private property; most of the rest belongs to states. Property rights make individuals and society dependent on those who possess society's wealth for jobs, products, and almost everything else. If society's wealth is controlled by a limited group, those excluded will have to acquire the means of living from those who possess it. Those without access to the means of production will have to work for those who control those means. And those who possess wealth will have power over the collective action of other groups and of society as a whole.

In Europe in the feudal era, rights to use and control the most important form of property—land—were distributed among a hierarchy of lords and vassals, with nobody exercising absolute control of any piece. Members of rural communities held common rights to use land, water, flora, and fauna. No one could sell a parcel of land because no one person owned it.

The emergence of capitalism involved the gradual transformation of property rights. As property ownership became increasingly private and feudal forms of coordination atrophied, markets became more and more necessary to coordinate production and consumption. The property rights bundle was reconfigured so that land and other forms of property could have a single owner and therefore be "alienable," that is, subject to buying and selling. Fee simple ownership, in which owners have relatively unrestricted rights to a piece of property, became increasingly prevalent. The illusion of property rights as something unitary, rather than as a bundle of separable rights, grew.[7]*

Modern property law made it possible to own a piece of private property and sell it at will. The feudal "bundle of rights" was redistributed, but not as a symmetrical transfer of the same rights from one class to another. For example, the owners of land no longer held authority over those people once attached to it as serfs. Conversely, community rights to glean, hunt, and otherwise make use of the fruits of the land were not transferred to another group but divided up among private owners and the state.*

The reassignment of the property rights bundle had consequences that were unintended and not even imaginable at the time. In particular, the right of ownership and use included the seemingly innocuous right to burn something you own and to let the resulting emissions dissipate in the atmosphere. This right eventually would lead to the greatest challenge in human history.

Property rights change, even within capitalism.* Landowners once had rights to the space above their land "all the way up" but the arrival of airplanes put an end to that. One of the most venerable forms of property, slavery, was simply abolished—though it took a global abolitionist movement and an American civil war to do it.

Property law evolved to limit corporate liability and allow separation of ownership and management.[8]* Business firms evolved from individual proprietorships and partnerships to limited liability corporations, which organize an ever-increasing proportion of the world's economic activity.* American court decisions even granted such corporations the legal status and rights of living persons.

Running companies became the province of professional managers, who might well not be the owners. A growing proportion of people became corporate employees. In the 1930s, the rights of such corporations were restricted by their duty to bargain collectively with their employees.* By the mid-twentieth century a small number of giant corporations, integrating all aspects of production from raw materials to the consumer, dominated major markets in each major country.* In the era of globalization corporations have themselves gone global and have become part of concentrated global networks. According to a 2011 study, there are 43,000 transnational corporations, but 147 of them own 40 percent of transnational corporate wealth and 737 of them control 80 percent of it.[9]

Private property rights lie at the heart of climate destruction. Property law generally allows property owners the right to use their property as they see fit—including the right to spew greenhouse gases into the atmosphere and thereby disrupt the equilibrium of the earth's climate system. Property rights also allow them to make the major social investment decisions that foreclose the possibility of a transition to a climate-safe economy.*

Of course, the right of property owners to pollute the environment is not absolute. It is limited by environmental laws, zoning laws, the police power of the state, and the right to prevent a public nuisance. The right to do harm to others is limited by criminal and civil law. Under the public trust doctrine, essential natural resources including the atmosphere are the common property of the people, which the government cannot authorize private parties to privatize or harm. In practice, however, courts often find that private property rights of polluters trump all such considerations.[10]*

Our current system of property rights represents a form of domination; it gives property owners the power to do things to the rest of us to which we would not voluntarily agree. More specifically, it gives those who possess fossil fuels and the infrastructure to burn them the right to wreak unlimited destruction on the rest of humanity. Correcting that will require transforming their domination.

The unlimited right to use private property is fast becoming the right to make humanity extinct by destroying the climate on which it depends. Protecting earth's climate will require a struggle to limit the right of private property owners to destroy it. It will not require the abolition of property or even of private property. But it will require the transformation of the property rights system that authorizes and protects climate destruction.

Markets

Markets play a crucial role in climate destruction. Markets are where fossil fuels, the infrastructure that allows them to be burned, the energy they produce, the labor power that produces and uses them, and the stocks and bonds of fossil fuel corporations are bought and sold.* They are where their profits are realized. They provide the incentive for maximizing profit by using fossil fuels. They provide the "market signals" that would penalize those who might use less destructive but more expensive ways to produce energy. Their vulnerability to crisis and collapse generates fear that reducing fossil fuel use may result in economic catastrophe.*

While markets of one kind or another go back thousands of years, in feudal Europe markets were quite limited; most economic activity was controlled by feudal lords, whose peasants produced for them directly, or by local guilds of craftsmen who prevented competition through their monopoly control of their crafts and the goods they produced. This mixture of feudal command and guild networks provided the coordination between different branches of production and use. As this feudal economic organization atrophied, markets developed to provide an alternative form of coordination.*

Markets have long reached far beyond the realm of material objects. Slave markets sold human beings. Labor markets sold the productive capacity—time, effort, and skill—of workers. Land came to be bought and sold like any commodity. Financial markets exchanged money for promises of repayment with interest; they channeled current wealth into speculative investment to produce greater wealth in the future. Services were provided in exchange for money. Capital markets bought and sold shares of corporations.

Market-based economies developed their own dynamic patterns, composed of intentional actions but not resulting from any common plan. Companies produced in order to sell their products in the market; consequently "market signals" came to guide production. The unsteady "invisible hand" of the market produced price fluctuations, speculation, shortages, and gluts. Competition meant that each company tried to reduce its costs. This incentivized "externalizing" the negative conse-quences of production—for example, by using technologies that released destructive pollution into the environment where its burden would be borne by others. Market control of production compelled private enter-prises to pursue their own private interests at the expense of common interests—even common interests they themselves shared.*

The emerging system of markets and capitalists had an ambiguous relation to the system of territorial states.* Many capitalists traded inter-nationally, but most also developed close ties with their "home" states, each providing support to the other. According to historical sociologist Michael Mann, by the time of the industrial revolution, "capitalism was already contained within a civilization of competing geopolitical states." Each of the leading European states "approximated a self-contained eco-nomic network," and economic interaction was largely confined within national boundaries—and each nation's imperial dominions.[11] States shaped international trade, often aiding national businesses by eco-nomic policies, war, and empire. By the twentieth century, Europe and its offshoots such as the United States—what came to be known as "the West"—controlled most of the world market.*

Market-based economies gave rise to cycles of boom and bust with devastating recessions and depressions. From the 1930s through the 1960s "Keynesian" macroeconomic policies were used to counter these cycles, but they became less and less effective over time.* They were used less thereafter until the multi-trillion-dollar countercyclical stimulus used to combat the Great Recession that started in 2007.

Starting in the early 1970s, as the "golden age of capitalism" gave way to an era of global economic stagnation and crisis, corporations and their political supporters increasingly strove to create a world safe for enterprises to go anywhere and do anything they wanted without "interference" from governments, unions, and civil society organizations. Corporations radically expanded "offshoring" of production to foreign countries with cheaper labor costs; work became strung out over many countries in a "global assembly line"; financial markets and institutions went global; and governments scrapped economic regulation and labor and environmental protections to become "more competitive."[12]*

The result was a global "race to the bottom" in which workers, communities, and whole countries bid against each other to provide the cheapest labor, the weakest social and environmental protections, and the largest corporate subsidies.* The process became known as "globalization" and the doctrine and public policies that promoted it as "neoliberalism."

In the neoliberal global economy, what came to be known as "financialization" shifted resources from the real economy to financial speculation. The financial sector's share of total US corporate profits rose from 25 percent in the early 1980s to more than 40 percent twenty-five years later. Globalization, neoliberal policies, and financialization deepened global economic crises, culminating in the 2008 financial meltdown and the extended period of general economic decline in world markets known as the "Great Recession," the most severe and extended economic downturn since the Great Depression of the 1930s.

Markets drive climate destruction. It is the need to make a profit in the market that leads companies to extract and burn coal, oil, and gas. It is the same need that leads other companies to use the energy thereby produced. The instability of markets undermines efforts to protect the climate by generating the fear that climate protection could lead to economic collapse.

Climate protection therefore requires counteracting "the logic of the market."

Fossil Fuels

Up until the industrial revolution, the main sources of energy were humans, animals, water power, wind power, and firewood. At the end of the eighteenth century, Britain, the cradle of the industrial revolution, faced a problem: depletion of forests led to an energy crisis. Burning coal was adopted as the solution.* Between 1750 and 1900, coal mined for fuel in Great Britain increased from less than 5 million tons a year to 240 million tons a year.

The burning of fossil fuel became the basis of modern economies. Between 1800 and 2000, worldwide energy use grew eighty- to ninety-fold. Since the early nineteenth century there has been a thousandfold increase in the consumption of fossil fuels.[13]

Historian John R. McNeil describes the growth of fossil fuel energy as "the most revolutionary process in human history" since the domestication of animals. Today humans use fifty to one hundred times as much energy per capita as before the extensive burning of fossil fuels.[14] One gallon of gas does the equivalent work of 350 to 500 hours of unassisted human labor.[15] Fossil fuel energy is a key component of food production, transportation, manufacturing, communications, housing, and virtually every other feature of modern life.

The expansion of fossil fuel use was essential to the series of industrial revolutions, from machine production to today's computer-based technologies, that immensely increased human productive capacity.* Indeed, burning of fossil fuels may account for a substantial proportion of the growth in wealth frequently attributed to industrialism.

Fossil fuels became both the means and ends of international competition. They allowed states to build the warships, airplanes, and other engines of war they used to fight to dominate the lands where fossil fuels were found. Conversely, wars were fought in large part to gain access to fossil fuels.*

The colossal wealth and power produced by fossil fuels—as well as their capacity to destroy the earth's climate—has been concentrated in a few score companies.* Just ninety private and government-owned fossil fuel companies (along with a few cement companies) are responsible for nearly two-thirds of all carbon emissions since 1750—with half of them produced in the past twenty-five years. Nineteen of the world's fifty leading corporations are fossil fuel–producing companies and utilities. They account for 48 percent of the revenues and 46 percent of the profits of the top fifty companies in the *Fortune* Global 500.[16]

The growth of fossil fuel energy was an unplanned process. It had multiple unintended side effects that transformed and continue to transform the human and natural worlds. It created immense concentrated wealth and power for the industries that produce fossil fuels and their owners.* It allowed them to exercise de facto hegemony over the world's economic and political institutions, largely shaping the energy, diplomatic, and even military policies of nations and securing themselves wide support from other corporations, property owners, and often workers and citizens-at-large. And it made individuals, institutions, and humanity as a whole dependent for their way of life and even their survival on fossil fuels and the industries that controlled them.

Climate Destruction and the World Order

The burning of fossil fuels has an unintended side effect: global warming. For the climate system to be in balance, the heat created by sunlight hitting the earth must radiate back out of the atmosphere. But if too much heat is trapped by carbon and other gases in the atmosphere, the average temperature of the earth must rise. This "greenhouse effect" is like a blanket warming the planet. According to NASA, "97 percent of climate scientists agree that climate-warming trends over the past century are very likely due to human activities."[17]

The earth has already warmed nearly 1.5°F since the industrial revolution, when fossil fuels started to be burned on a large scale. GHGs already in the atmosphere will cause another 1.5°F increase. Unless we reverse current trends, there will be a 4°–9°F increase by the end of century. Unpredictable "tipping points" may make that far worse.

The effects of global warming can seem contradictory, producing snowstorms as well as heat waves, downpours as well as droughts. That is because global warming destabilizes and disrupts the earth's entire climate system, leading to opposite extremes. Results already include:

- heat waves
- droughts
- wildfires
- crop failures
- floods
- hurricanes
- tornadoes
- food shortages and price spikes
- water wars

- mass migrations
- extinction of plant and animal species

Until the 1980s, these side effects were not only unintended; they were uncertain. Yet over the past thirty years the causal connection between greenhouse gas emissions and climate change has become ever more certain, and the resulting devastation has become not only certain but manifested around the globe. In response there has been a global effort to establish policies and agreements to reduce GHG emissions on the part of governments, business, and civil society. But that effort has been ineffectual; GHG emissions have continued to soar. Humanity as a whole has been unable to counter the greatest threat in its history.

Any society would have an incentive to use fossil fuels. Leaving aside their inconvenient side effects, they allow people to produce far more of what they want with far less effort.

While in theory other economic and social systems might also burn large amounts of fossil fuels and thereby create atmospheric warming, actually existing climate change has been caused by the features of the actually existing world order. In addition to the reasons other forms of society might decide to burn fossil fuels, our actual world order exhibits features that make a reduction in fossil fuel use far harder.

The system of sovereign nation-states provides governments the authority to permit the emission of the GHGs that are destroying the climate. It allows them to disregard any responsibility to protect the future of humanity as a whole. It renders the institutions representing global human interests powerless or captive. It promotes economic and military competition that leads each country to pursue purported national interests in refusing to limit its GHG emissions. It divides the world's people and provides us apparent interests in national self-aggrandizement that override our common interest in climate protection.

The distribution of the bundle of property rights in a world order based on private ownership of the means of production lets individuals and corporations pour GHGs into the environment without effective restraint.

The competitive structure of markets creates a motive to accumulate wealth, which provides a drive (beyond mere consumption) for profit maximization of businesses, which in turn maximizes the use of fossil fuels for energy. Without such a drive, the use of fossil fuels purely for consumption would no doubt have been less. And fossil fuel use could have been restricted without threatening business failure or economic contraction. In this era of globalization and neoliberalism, product, labor, capital, and financial markets have become increasingly global and decreasingly subject to nonmarket regulation. The institutions representing public interests have been progressively dismantled, leaving these market dynamics to control with little restraint.* The immense wealth and power of the fossil fuel industry has effectively blocked efforts at climate protection.*

Any strategy to combat climate change must take these features of the world order into account.

CHAPTER 34

Official Climate Protection from Rio to Paris

It looked like the start of a new common preservation.

Over the course of the 1980s, converging lines of evidence established with growing certainty that the earth's temperature was rising because of the GHGs humans produced by burning fossil fuels. In 1988, the international community of climate scientists persuaded the World Meteorological Organization and the United Nations Environment Program to establish the Intergovernmental Panel on Climate Change to investigate and propagate the scientific facts about global warming.

Public response was rapid. Polls conducted in the US, for example, found that by 1988 most Americans said the greenhouse effect was very serious or extremely serious and that they worried a fair amount or a great deal about global warming.

In 1990, the UN General Assembly initiated negotiations for an international treaty to protect the climate. In 1992 at the Earth Summit in Rio de Janeiro nearly all the world's nations signed the United Nations Framework Convention on Climate Change (UNFCCC). It appeared that the world was well on its way to common preservation of the earth's climate. It seemed to confirm climate writer Bill McKibben's expectation that "if we get this set of facts out in front of everybody, they're so powerful—overwhelming—that people will do what needs to be done."[1]

Global warming appeared to be a problem that could be corrected. "What needs to be done" seemed pretty obvious. National governments needed to agree to make modest annual reductions in the total amount of greenhouse gases that were emitted into the atmosphere. Global negotiations had recently produced the Montreal Protocol, an agreement to phase out another pollutant, chlorinated hydrocarbons (CFCs), that had been causing a hole in the ozone layer. Greenhouse gases seemed controllable through similar measures taken by the same kinds of institutions.

Unfortunately, the two cases turned out to be very different. While industrial processes that emitted CFCs were relatively inconsequential and easily replaced, the burning of fossil fuels was the lifeblood of the modern economy. And the fossil fuel industry had a huge stake in its right to emit GHGs and possessed far more power than CFC producers to secure that right. Nonetheless, climate protection advocates assimilated the Montreal Protocol as a model means requiring only modest accommodation for climate protection.*

While advocates hoped that the Rio summit would actually start preserving the climate, it merely established a framework for negotiations but did not reduce GHG emissions. It thereby established a pattern that has persisted right down to the 2016 Paris agreement. In the quarter century from Rio to Paris, dozens of international conferences and various signed global agreements have failed to forbid the emission of one particle of greenhouse gas.

Governmental and intergovernmental climate protection produced faux common preservation. While they talked the climate protection talk, most of the world's governments were actually walking the climate destruction walk. The entire process has been little more than a charade in which world leaders, governments, and business pretended to address climate change while pursuing policies that pour ever move GHGs into the atmosphere. It was a process led by a collection of greedy, advantage-seeking institutions whose leaders were unable to cooperate even for their own survival.*

As a result there was no vehicle for imposing the common interest of humanity in climate protection on nations, corporations, and other institutions. From the outset of the purported climate protection process the most powerful actors pursued narrow national and economic interests at the expense of global climate protection. Nations claimed sovereignty rights as the basis for rejecting any agreements they did not believe served their economic interests. Fossil fuel corporations claimed property rights that they could not be enticed or forced to give up; they successfully fought for their right to go on destroying the climate and the human future. They were backed by a large segment of the world's "business community." Neoliberal doctrine was used to block any policies that might "interfere" with the market; dubious "market-based" policies were propounded as the "solution" to global warming with little evidence that they could be effective in practice.

In 1988, before UN climate negotiations even began, the US oil and auto industries and the National Association of Manufacturers formed the Global Climate Coalition to oppose any mandatory actions to address global warming.* Fossil fuel industry opposition of course expressed the most blatant self-interest. But the industry was able to impose that interest on others through its enormous wealth and power. The Global Climate Coalition spent millions of dollars on advertising against international climate agreements and national climate legislation. The power of the fossil fuel industry—including its wealth—was based on the dependence of individuals, communities, industries, and nations on the energy it controlled. That dependence also gave the industry hegemony over governments, other businesses, and even labor unions.* That power was ultimately legitimated and maintained by the property rules that gave private companies control over the energy lifeblood of society.

In 1990, the UN General Assembly initiated negotiations for a climate treaty. By the third session, however, the parties were at loggerheads. An "activist" coalition composed mostly of European nations and environmental organizations called for an agreement that would require every nation to implement targets and timetables for GHG reductions. A "go-slow" coalition led by the United States, the world's largest emitter of carbon dioxide, opposed any mandatory cuts. The role of economic competition in justifying this position would be formalized in the US Senate's unanimously passed Byrd-Hagel Resolution, which rejected any international climate agreement that did not require developing countries to make emissions reductions or that would seriously harm the US economy.

The developing countries' position in the negotiations was that the GHG problem was solely the responsibility of the developed countries that had created the problem. Limiting developing countries' carbon emissions was unacceptable because it would impede their development. If developing countries participated in any scheme limiting GHGs, the developed countries should pay for it.

According to physicist and historian Spencer Weart, industry-induced doubts about global warming and consequent lack of US support for climate protection efforts "gave other governments an excuse to continue business as usual."* Politicians could claim "they advocated tough measures" while "casting blame on the United States for any failure to get started."[2]

The sacrifice of climate protection to narrow economic interest was not limited to governments and business. For example, in February 1997, the executive council of US labor federation AFL-CIO issued a statement on the UN climate change negotiations. The statement noted the devastating impact that globalization had had on American workers and unions. It put that impact in the frame of rivalry between the United States and other industrialized and developing countries and applied the same frame to climate protection: "We believe the parties to the Rio Treaty made a fundamental error when they agreed to negotiate legally binding carbon restrictions on the United States and other industrialized countries, while simultaneously agreeing to exempt high-growth developing countries like China, Mexico, Brazil and Korea from any new carbon reduction commitments."[3] That will create "a powerful incentive for transnational corporations to export jobs, capital, and pollution," the statement continued.

The statement urged the United States to insist on "commitments from all nations to reduce carbon emissions" and "a reduction schedule compatible with the urgent need to avoid unfair and unnecessary job loss in developed economies." It did not propose alternative ways to combat global warming.

The failure of climate protection was disguised in the Kyoto and subsequent agreements by a policy framework that conformed to current economic shibboleths but had little chance of slowing GHG emissions. The problem was defined as "externalities": emitters had been allowed to put GHGs into the atmosphere for free; the results were costs like climate change that other people had to pay. The Kyoto solution was to "put a price on carbon"—make polluters pay for the negative effects of their emissions.* The cost of polluting could be increased by a "sin tax" on carbon emissions. In response to the higher price of fossil fuel energy people would shift from GHG-producing purchases to less polluting ones.

The US pushed an alternative "cap-and-trade" system that allowed polluters to buy permits to pollute and created a market in which to buy and sell those permits. The result was a system in which nobody was required to stop emitting greenhouse gases; all they had to do was purchase permits to emit. That was the theory; when this system was actually tried in Europe, more permits to pollute were given away free to polluters than the amount of GHGs they were already emitting. Subsequent experiments with cap-and-trade and carbon taxes have produced ambiguous results at best.

In the three decades between Rio and Paris, these basic patterns scarcely changed. The much-celebrated 2016 Paris summit abandoned even the aspiration for a binding international agreement limiting GHG emissions and replaced it with a system of voluntary national pledges with no enforcement. Scientists expect that even if all countries meet their Paris climate pledges the earth will heat up at least 6.3°F. Perhaps the most significant change since the Paris summit is President Donald Trump's replacement of US "go-slow" climate protection policies with deliberate expansion of fossil fuel extraction and burning.

Climate scientists did identify the problem of GHG-caused global warming. They did identify the solution: a rapid reduction in GHG emissions. The failure of humanity to implement that solution results in large part from the features of the world order described in the previous chapter.

The system of sovereign nation-states made it possible for each government to pursue its own self-interest without regard to the effects on the rest of the world—or even on itself. No higher authority represented common human interests or put effective restraint on individual or groups of nations. Even the Intergovernmental Panel on Climate Change—widely viewed as the representative of world scientific opinion expressed in the interest of the world's people—was explicitly inter*governmental*; it was largely composed of government-employed scientists and its influential *Summary for Policymakers* must be approved line-by-line by all of the more than 120 participating governments. The policies demanded by many states were explicitly based on their economic objectives in competition with other states; possible mutual benefits played little role in their calculations. The pursuit of national self-interest over the common human interest in climate protection exemplified the disorder and domination embedded in the nation-state system.

The prevailing system of property ownership gave property owners— whether private or governmental—the right to create climate havoc by burning fossil fuels. It led other property owners to support the property rights of the fossil fuel industry, even though the consequences would ultimately be the destruction of themselves, their posterity, and their enterprises.

A globalized, unregulated market also provided nations incentives for continuing GHG emissions. Nations strove to gain economic advantage for themselves and their associated enterprises by maintaining and expanding the burning of fossil fuel. They feared that the chaos of markets might mean that climate protection measures would lead to economic collapse. They acted on the basis of neoliberal shibboleths to advocate "market-based solutions" whose effectiveness for reducing fossil fuel emissions at the necessary pace was to say the least, unproven.

The fossil fuel industry itself used its economic and political power to persuade or at least confuse public opinion and directly sway political decision makers. It used its influence to dominate the policies of corporations, the media, and many other institutions. It used the dependence of individuals, institutions, and governments on the resources it controlled to force them to obey its dictates, lest they "freeze to death in the dark."

In short, climate protection was defeated as a result of strategies of self-preservation and self-aggrandizement that conformed to the pattern of the prevailing world order. The new challenge of climate change was assimilated to the existing ends of existing entities. Despite the news of ever-growing threat brought by scientific feedback loops and climate disasters, there was inadequate accommodation to the new realities. Instead there was a PR response—a charade of common preservation. Meanwhile, the patterns of disorder and domination that ensured greater warming were left intact.*

This story has parallels to the threat of nuclear holocaust in the Cold War era. Governments initially told their people that nuclear weapons would protect them against enemy attack. When that lost its credibility governments started negotiations for nuclear disarmament. When that failed to assuage a terrified humanity, countries escalated their purported objective to total and complete disarmament. Meanwhile, they continued to pursue nuclear overkill with a vengeance.

But their efforts had an unintended consequence.* Governments' pursuit of the arms race, combined with their advocacy for disarmament, led to their own discrediting and the rise of a popular movement to force them to fulfill their promises. While it never succeeded in banning the bomb, the peace movement did force the major nuclear powers into detente and an 80 percent cut in strategic arms.*

The failure of official climate protection led governments to escalate their official climate protection objectives, so that the Paris climate agreement called for (but took no effective measures to achieve) a global warming limit of 1.5°C. As we will see in the next chapter, official promises to protect the climate, combined with the utter failure to do so, had already led to the emergence of a new, independent climate protection movement—a peoples' self-organization against climate destruction—long before the dubious Paris pledges.

CHAPTER 35

Development of the Climate Movement: Self-Organization

Notwithstanding the combination of futility and reassurance provided by governmental climate protection leaders, efforts to reduce GHGs proliferated around the world. Educational campaigns urged consumers to "go green." Al Gore's 2006 documentary *An Inconvenient Truth* concluded with a list of actions individuals could take to reduce their GHG emissions, such as turning off electric lights when they left a room. Cities, states, provinces, regions, and corporations initiated climate action plans. Most nations developed climate protection policies of one kind or another.

As the evidence of climate danger grew, more and more people began to think that climate protection was too important to leave to scientists and politicians. Over time, a nongovernmental climate protection movement emerged. At first it was closely intertwined with official governmental efforts, but over the years significant elements of it differentiated to become more independent.*

Originally the effort was largely an extension of existing environmental organizations, but it came to include almost every imaginable constituency. It grew less by design than by new constituencies becoming conscious of the threat of climate change and drawing together to make new collective responses. While it always involved a combination of formal NGOs and less-formalized networks, it became increasingly decentralized and fluid. Although the movement originally concentrated on education, lobbying, legislation, and electoral action, over the span of a quarter century its focus shifted to more direct confrontation with governments and industry.*

Climate protection from below grew out of constituencies and cultures with divergent or even contradictory strategies, modes of action

and organization, ideologies, and interests. It would be an unlikely can-
didate for a common preservation movement if its recruits did not also
face a common danger. As climate protection from above ever more
clearly failed to avert that danger, climate movements developed not
only in response to climate change itself, but to the official climate
protection process and to each other.*

In 1987, as climate negotiations were gearing up, environmental
organizations around the world created the Climate Action Network
(CAN), which served both as a vehicle for global coordination and information exchange and as an advocate in its own right, demanding that
countries live up to their responsibilities and focusing global public
opinion on their failure to do so. CAN became the official vehicle for representing NGOs within the UNFCCC process. CAN embodied a drawing
together of climate protection "from above" and "from below" in one
complex, ongoing interaction, without strong boundaries or differentiation between the two.

In the lead-up to the Copenhagen summit a sector of climate activists critical of mainstream climate policies and organizations differentiated itself as a "climate justice movement." While its primary organizational expression, Climate Justice Now!, was absorbed back into CAN
and eventually dissolved, "climate justice" remains a significant stream
within the climate movement.*

As national governments equivocated about climate protection, city
governments around the world stepped in and pledged individually and
through a variety of organizations to meet climate targets and timetables.* Young people, indigenous people, religious communities, and
some segments of organized labor created climate protection organizations or drew their existing organizations into the climate protection
movement.

Meanwhile, millions of people around the world watched in horror
as the news of climate change spread—and as world leaders failed to
do anything effective to counter it. Yet most people remained passive
victims of climate change, isolated, misinformed, and manipulated.*

While climate change affected billions of people around the world
and millions of them were concerned about it, there was no vehicle for
most of them to do anything about it outside the official governmental
process of national legislation and international negotiations—nor was
it obvious how there could be one. Then a group of college students

invented such a vehicle. It was a textbook example of the emergence of a new common preservation through self-organization, interstitial emergence, and linking.*

At Middlebury College in Vermont, a group of students who were taking a course with economics professor Jonathan Isham started meeting in dining halls and dorm rooms over breakfast and evening beers to discuss how they could take action on global warming. Other students began joining the informal sessions. In February 2005, the group started meeting every Sunday night, dubbing itself the Sunday Night Group; this assemblage participated in a variety of small-scale actions around global warming. Its frame was that "climate change is a defining issue of our time and needs to be addressed."[1] Nature writer Bill McKibben was an early supporter of the group.

The group had no president, secretary, or treasurer. *Fight Global Warming Now*, a book written in 2007 by McKibben and six veterans of the Sunday Night Group, noted, "To the degree that leaders emerge, it is a result of natural leadership associated with a person's skills or talents around a project, or the time he or she has at the moment, rather than titles or positions."

McKibben's 1989 book *The End of Nature* had urged action to protect the climate, but seven years after its publication McKibben felt that policymakers were still ignoring the evident threat while carbon poured into the atmosphere at an ever-increasing rate. In 2006 McKibben and the Sunday Night group led three hundred people on a five-day walk across Vermont, culminating with one thousand participants for the final march into the capital.* They were startled to learn that it was the largest US climate demonstration up to that time.

The Middlebury team developed an experimental testing approach that characterized a series of subsequent initiatives.* They decided to "go national" by using social media to ask people to organize "Step It Up" climate rallies around the United States on April 14, 2007. Echoing the analysis of the IPCC and the targets and timetables of the Kyoto agreement, the group demanded that Congress enact policies that would cut US carbon emissions 80 percent by 2050. McKibben told an interviewer that the purpose was "to start a people's movement about climate change. And to shift the debate on Capitol Hill in a more ambitious direction."*

The group started with little money and only a vague idea of how the actions it was promoting would come together. The concept was simply to invite diverse people to participate on their own terms. "For three months, our small team was crammed into one room at our headquarters in Burlington, Vermont. Day after day, from this little corner of the country, we peered into our laptop screens and witnessed the self-assembly of a nationwide movement."[2] As new groups organized, "digital pins" populated a "digital map." Tens of thousands of people went online to "post announcements, share ideas, debate tactics, exchange resources, and inspire one another with their passion and creativity." The result was what the organizers described as "a Web-based collaborative effort that allows anyone involved to add their own flavor to the project." People became part of the movement just by organizing an action or showing up for one.

McKibben recalled, "We thought, maybe, we could organize a couple of hundred of these actions." But by mid-February they had surpassed the 650 mark. There were "sororities and retirement communities and national environmental groups and churches and rock-climbers and you name it—people were simply waiting for the opening to make their voices heard."* On April 14, there were 1,400 actions in all fifty states, ranging from skiers descending a melting glacier to divers demonstrating climate change effects under the ocean.

The Middlebury team and a small crew of fellow travelers based in countries all over the world, including South Africa, India, and New Zealand, decided to take the pattern established by Step It Up and go global.* NASA climate scientist James Hansen had recently written that if humanity wishes to preserve a planet "similar to that on which civilization developed and to which life on Earth is adapted," CO_2 in the atmosphere will need to be reduced "from its current 385 ppm" to "at most 350 ppm, but likely less than that." The now-global organizing team named their new initiative "350.org." That transformed climate discourse and action from increasingly arcane debate over national targets and timetables to a simple formula for what needed to be achieved by all parties acting together. 350.org redefined the problem as one of common preservation, rather than national advantage.* It called for global demonstrations on October 24, 2009, shortly before the Copenhagen climate summit. That day saw more than 5,200 actions in 181 countries, from Mt. Everest to the Great Barrier Reef, in what CNN declared "the most widespread day of political action" in the planet's history.

The self-assembly of 350.org exemplifies self-organization. Initially people were isolated and divided from each other by their existing patterns of life. They pursued self-preservation for themselves or entities like states and corporations of which they were part and in which they were enclosed.

The formation of a new movement for common preservation was possible because people recognized that they had a problem; that they shared that problem with others; and that they needed each other's help to solve it. Their effort fit the pattern of Michael Mann's interstitial emergence of new solutions followed by the linking of interstitial nooks and crannies. The new movement had to overcome disorder: the disorganization, isolation, and division that prevented people from joining together to pursue their own common interests—in this case, their common survival. They had to transform boundaries, create new entities, and develop new network-based forms of coordination. They had to transform their autocentric representation of their situation via decentering. They did so by identifying new possibilities for action; testing them experimentally; evaluating the results of their actions; and continuing to seek new forms of action that would increase their capacity to solve the problems they faced. Their virtual and actual experiments led to the development of new capacities for problem-solving and action.

Like other developing social movements, 350.org has often been criticized for its fluidity and lack of structure. Its founders, however, maintained that what they described as "decentralized networking" is "exactly what we need to fight global warming," that is, "a sustained and lively social movement." Rather than "restricting communications to messages flowing up and down (as in a traditional hierarchy)," we have to "allow people at the 'ends' of our networks to connect and information to flow in every direction." For the Step It Up day of action, "we made sure that individuals across the nation could connect to each other online on our 'organizer forum,' a chat room and discussion board on the site where people could brainstorm and tackle problems together." (Later they would make their own organizing software available for all comers to adopt.)

This decentralization involved a highly fluid form of organization. They advised, "Don't fret about structure. Far more than we need new organizations, we need nimble, relevant, strategic, and often temporary groups of people who can come together and do what needs to be done at the moment—and then do it again, with a whole different bunch of people, a few months later." Subsequently, 350.org would carry its "decentralized networking" into its campaigns against the Keystone XL pipeline and for divestment from fossil fuel corporations but use it in a much more sustained way than its one-shot Days of Action.*

While the success of efforts like Step It Up and 350.org have often been attributed to the internet and social networking tools, the organizers emphasized that those tools are not a substitute for face-to-face community. "The actions themselves didn't happen online—they were real-life, on-the-ground affairs, with neighbors coming together in the flesh to demand change." And as we have seen throughout this book, the self-organization of isolated and divided people—from the slaves in the Civil War South to the housewives of the meat boycott—could be accomplished long before the internet was even a gleam in anyone's eye.[3]

Despite such developments in organization and mobilization, the Copenhagen fiasco left the climate protection movement at a loss.* There was no apparent way to get either nations or world leaders to commit seriously to climate protection. In response, 350.org continued experimenting with various kinds of action. With Greenpeace and other groups it organized a Global Work Party October 10, 2010 (10/10/10), in which millions of people around the world installed solar panels, erected wind turbines, and planted community gardens. Global support was mobilized for local campaigns like one opposing fracking in the Delaware River basin and another to stop the World Bank from financing a large coal-fired power plant in Kosovo. 350.org tried to penetrate media silence about climate with global viral distribution of a rap song on climate change. It successfully encouraged some corporations to withdraw from the US Chamber of Commerce over its opposition to climate protection. It allied with the emerging Occupy Wall Street movement and launched a campaign for divestment from fossil fuels that has led the holders of trillions of dollars of assets to pledge to divest.

Yet neither 350.org nor the rest of the independent climate movement was sure how to exercise power or influence events. How could they force states, let alone the system of states, to shift their course to cooperate for climate protection? How could they restrict the right of property owners to do whatever they wished with what they claimed to own? How could they counteract the market incentives to continue and increase GHG emissions? And how could they counter the power of the fossil fuel industry to perpetuate its business plan of destroying the climate?

CHAPTER 36

Development of the Climate Movement: Countering Power

The climate movement could lobby, demonstrate, march, even organize 5,200 simultaneous actions in 181 countries—but the burning of fossil fuel went on unimpeded. The world order, and its resistance to climate protection, seemed barely affected. What the actions of the climate movement appeared to demonstrate was the powerlessness of the world's people to protect their future.

The feedback of movement ineffectiveness generated despair, but it also generated a search for ways to directly confront the fossil fuel juggernaut. That led to the next phase of the movement's development: a strategic shift to direct action confronting the property rights of fossil fuel emitters and defying the authority of governments protecting those rights. That in turn required and generated new ways of defining the problem, new forms of coordination, the assimilation of and accommodation to new constituencies, the transformation of the existing environmental movement, a transformation of public opinion, and new ways of exercising power.

Historically, action to protect the environment has often involved disobedience to established authority. But in the twenty years from the confirmation of GHG-caused global warming to the struggle over the Keystone XL pipeline, civil disobedience on behalf of climate protection was only sporadic. In 2002 Greenpeace launched one of the first actions, a shutdown of Esso gas stations in Luxembourg to protest the company's "continued sabotage of international efforts to protect the climate."[1] In 2005, Mountain Justice Summer disrupted corporate meetings and blockaded facilities to halt mountaintop removal mining in Appalachia, culminating in the arrest of climate scientist James Hansen, actress Daryl Hannah, Rainforest Action Network director Mike Brune, and twenty-six other protesters.[2] Starting in 2006, "climate camps" in Britain, Denmark, Canada, France, Ireland, Belgium, Wales, and Australia, drawing on the experience of the "peace camps" of the 1980s, combined trespassing and squatting with workshops on organic farming and alternative economics. Direct action and civil disobedience have steadily become more common and more central to the climate protection movement since the turn of the millennium.

Direct action for climate protection entered a new phase in 2008 when the TransCanada Corporation applied for a permit to build the Keystone XL (KXL) pipeline, which would carry eight hundred thousand barrels of bitumen daily 1,700 miles across the US border to refineries in Texas.

The Alberta region where the tar sands originate was the home to Cree, Dene, Métis, and other indigenous First Nations. While some Native people welcomed the jobs and economic opportunities that came with the tar sands extraction, many were vehemently opposed, especially as the devastation to land and water—and the consequent destruction of traditional subsistence hunting and fishing—became increasingly blatant and residents began to exhibit high rates of cancer and autoimmune diseases.[3] In the face of such horrific feedback, tribes opposed to the mining joined with dozens of other organizations across Alberta to call for a moratorium on tar sands projects and file suits to halt specific projects.[4] Intertribal gatherings and the Indigenous Environmental Network (IEN) began constructing anti-KXL alliances with other indigenous groups around North America.

The KXL pipeline was slated to pass through Nebraska's iconic Sand Hills and over the Ogallala Aquifer, which if contaminated would pollute the water supply for much of the Great Plains. A new organization called BOLD Nebraska pulled together a coalition of conservative ranchers, urban progressives, environmentalists, and farm advocacy groups to oppose the pipeline.[5]

Initially the opposition to tar sands extraction and the KXL pipeline, like many local campaigns against the extraction of extreme energy, grew out of local environmental and health concerns and attracted little attention beyond the affected local areas. Then James Hansen, head of the NASA Goddard Institute and widely regarded as the leading climate scientist in the United States, wrote in his blog that tar sands "must be left in the ground." Indeed, "if the tar sands are thrown into the mix it is essentially game over" for a viable planet. That statement defined tar sands extraction not solely as a local issue, but also as a key element of the global climate crisis.*

One person who took note of Hansen's blog post was Bill McKibben, who had recently taught a Middlebury College class on social movements. The class had read Taylor Branch's three-volume study of Martin Luther King Jr. and the civil rights movement.* McKibben had already concluded that it was time for the climate movement to turn to civil disobedience. What particularly struck him about the KXL pipeline was not only that it threatened the planet but also that because it crossed a US border it required approval by the president of the United States, who could deny a permit for it without action by the climate-deadlocked US Congress. In June 2011, after checking with the initial pipeline opponents in Alberta and Nebraska, McKibben and a group of other movement leaders sent out a letter calling for a month of civil disobedience actions at the White House to demand that President Obama deny the KXL pipeline a permit. It constituted a classic Gandhian challenge—a matching of forces.

Although the effort grew out of 350.org, its initiators set up a new organization called Tar Sands Action "so we could have a broad front supported by many groups."[6] Over a two-week period more than 1,200 people were arrested in the ongoing protests. McKibben later wrote that "establishment, insider environmentalism found itself a little overtaken by grassroots power"; the movement had "gone beyond education to resistance."[7]

The White House sit-ins led to a cascade of consequences. Ten large environmental organizations sent a joint letter to President Obama supporting the demonstrations and opposing KXL. Ten Nobel Peace laureates, including Desmond Tutu and the Dalai Lama, asked Obama to block the pipeline.[8] A million comments flooded the State Department comment line. The sit-ins constituted an exemplary action that led many institutions and individuals to consider—and act on—their own responsibilities for climate protection.* And they led many people to consider the possibility of action that went beyond the established "legitimate" channels of lobbying, electoral participation, and legal protest.*

The campaign against the KXL pipeline also brought divisions. Nonviolent direct action created what Dr. Martin Luther King Jr. called "creative tension," through which a community is "forced to confront the issue." Back in 2010, TransCanada had signed a coveted "project labor agreement" with the Teamsters, Plumbers, Operating Engineers, and Laborers unions offering preferential hiring and union conditions on the KXL pipeline. The four union presidents issued a statement saying that the project would "pave a path to better days and raise the standard of living for working men and women in the construction, manufacturing, and transportation industries."

The unions' position illustrated not only the dependence of workers on their employers for jobs but also the hegemony of the fossil fuel industry over much of organized labor. In 2009, North America's Building Trades Unions (NABTU) forged a partnership with the oil and gas industry to develop North American energy sources called the Oil and Gas Industry Labor-Management Committee (OGILMC). Sean McGarvey, president of NABTU, is president of the OGILMC and Jack Gerard, president of the American Petroleum Institute, is secretary-treasurer.[9] The API has been a major financial sponsor of building trades conferences.[10]

The media rushed to portray the pipeline as pitting the labor movement against the environmental movement; NPR's headline was "Pipeline Decision Pits Jobs against Environment." There was, however, opposition to the pipeline within organized labor. The Transport Workers Union (TWU) and the Amalgamated Transit Union (ATU) issued a joint statement saying, "We need jobs, but not ones based on increasing our reliance on Tar Sands Oil." The statement called for major New Deal–type public investments in infrastructure modernization and repair, energy conservation, and climate protection as a means of "putting people to work and laying the foundations of a green and sustainable economic future for the United States." Terry O'Sullivan, president of the Laborers' Union (LIUNA), cracked back: "It's time for ATU and TWU to come out from under the skirts of delusional environmental groups which stand in the way of creating good, much-needed American jobs." The divided AFL-CIO first maintained public neutrality on the pipeline, then gave it tacit support, and finally publicly lobbied Obama to authorize it.[11]

In November 2011, fifteen thousand people surrounded the White House with a mile-and-a-half-long "solidarity hug." A presidential veto of the pipeline seemed a very long shot, however. A *National Journal* poll of three hundred energy insiders found that more than 90 percent of them believed the KXL would get its permit.[12] Four days after the "solidarity hug," however, the White House announced that the State Department needed another year to study the issue. The legal and extralegal popular action against the pipeline had unexpectedly divided the political establishment.

Nonetheless, the KXL pipeline continued to be supported by the enormous power of the fossil fuel industry, which in turn received powerful support from the US Chamber of Commerce and other representatives of American business. In December 2011, Republicans in Congress tried to force President Obama's hand by submitting legislation requiring a decision within sixty days. Major environmental organizations and other KXL opponents conducted an inside-the-Beltway lobbying campaign against it, backed up by a grassroots mobilization. The legislation passed the House 234 to 193; McKibben estimated that the fossil fuel industry had spent $42 million to win the vote.[13] The powerful American Petroleum Institute said that there would be "huge political consequences" if the pipeline was blocked.[14] Yet, in another manifestation of a political establishment divided by popular pressure, the pipeline bill was defeated in the Senate by two votes.[15]

The KXL pipeline had become a leading national political issue. Mitt Romney's first TV ad of the presidential election campaign began:

> VOICEOVER: "What would a Romney presidency be like?"
> VIDEO TEXT: "Day 1"
> VOICEOVER: "Day one, President Romney immediately approves the Keystone pipeline, creating thousands of jobs that Obama blocked."[16]

The *New Yorker* observed that KXL had become "the most prominent environmental cause in America."[17] McKibben reflected, "We managed to put something no one knew about at the center of the nation's political agenda."

The KXL campaign brought about a broader transformation in the environmental movement. The Sierra Club, which for 120 years had advocated using only "lawful means," for the first time endorsed civil disobedience.* In February 2013, the Sierra Club, with the unified support of the large environmental groups, NAACP president emeritus Julian Bond, and the Hip Hop Caucus, led nonviolent civil disobedience at the White House, followed by the largest climate rally in US history so far, with an estimated forty thousand participants.[18]

A 2013 article by Katherine Bagley of *Inside Climate News* detailed the transformation wrought by the KXL campaign. In 2009, the "main engine" of climate protection were the biggest green groups, which "spent vast quantities of financial and political capital" lobbying for climate legislation. By 2013, "the main force" was "a messy amalgam of disparate grassroots efforts stretching from Maine to Utah" that has "found common cause" in opposing the KXL pipeline and other tar sands projects. In the language of our heuristic, we might say they had formed a collective subject, able to counteract the action of others, without taking the form of a conventional organization.*

Bagley described how one week in May saw "hundreds of activists march at an Obama fundraiser event" in New York City; two citizens "encase themselves in concrete at a construction site" for the southern leg of the KXL pipeline; citizens of Utah "flood the email inboxes and fax machines of investors for a proposed tar sands mine in Utah with the message 'We will stop you before it starts'"; and hundreds protest the appearance of Canadian prime minister Stephen Harper at the Council on Foreign Relations headquarters in Manhattan.[19]

When President Obama authorized construction of the southern leg of the pipeline, environmental activists and threatened landowners formed a loose resistance movement known as Tar Sands Blockade. An article in *Rolling Stone* detailed how members "locked their necks to excavators in Oklahoma, sealed themselves inside pipe segments in Winona, Texas, and stormed TransCanada's Houston offices." Activists staged a three-month "tree sit-in" in east Texas that forced TransCanada to reroute the pipeline around the blockade.[20]

The anti-KXL movement also began to converge with other on-the-ground direct-action campaigns. A February 2013 "anti-extraction summit" of environmental justice organizations initiated "#FearlessSummer" to organize direct action in "front-line communities" most directly affected by energy extraction and processing. In cooperation, 350.org organized "Summer Heat" to mobilize its constituency to support such actions. Results included more than two hundred arrests at a Chevron oil refinery in Richmond, California; forty-five arrests at a coal-fired power plant outside of Boston; a flotilla of kayaks protesting a natural-gas storage facility on Seneca Lake in New York; and other direct actions in Utah, Texas, and West Virginia.[21]

Opposition to tar sands extraction and the KXL pipeline had started with indigenous people, and it spread far and wide through Indian country. The KXL route crossed hundreds of sacred sites and threatened major sources of drinking water for large reservations. The burgeoning Canadian First Nations movement Idle No More, which was founded to challenge treaty-rights violations, took on KXL as a central issue. Tribal councils from the Lakota to the Nez Perce passed resolutions opposing the pipeline. In January 2013, leaders from many Indian nations journeyed to Pickstown, South Dakota, to draft a document rejecting the KXL and the rest of the tar sands infrastructure. A "Training for Resistance" tour included a "Moccasins on the Ground" gathering on the Pine Ridge reservation in South Dakota, preparing for direct action should the pipeline be approved.[22]

Seeking a preemptive deterrent to pipeline approval, the political action–oriented telephone company CREDO joined with the Rainforest Action Network and The Other 98% to start the "Keystone XL Pledge of Resistance." The campaign was modeled on the 1984 Pledge of Resistance, in which one hundred thousand people promised to commit civil disobedience if the United States invaded Nicaragua; both pledges aimed to deter a political decision by raising its political cost. By May 2014, more than ninety-five thousand people had pledged to risk arrest if the State Department gave the go-ahead to the pipeline.[23] To show the Obama administration that the threat was real, the KXL Pledge of Resistance trained hundreds of local action leaders, helped them develop local action plans in nearly two hundred communities, and organized small "warning-shot" civil disobedience actions in Chicago, Houston, and Boston.[24]

In late April 2014, an improbable but highly photogenic coalition calling itself the "Cowboy Indian Alliance" of farmers, ranchers, and tribal leaders from the pipeline corridor held a five-day "Reject and Protect" encampment in Washington.* A week before they were scheduled to arrive, the Obama administration announced that its decision on the pipeline would again be delayed, probably for many months.

Just before he left office, President Obama rejected the permit application for the KXL pipeline. Donald Trump, however, had campaigned in support of the pipeline, and his administration largely represented the fossil fuel industry, especially its most militant, climate-change-denying segment. To take but one example Trump chose as secretary of state Rex Tillerson, the longtime president of Exxon, which had spent many millions of dollars denying the reality of climate change. One of Trump's first acts after being inaugurated president was to pledge to approve the KXL pipeline. The fossil fuel industry had outflanked the anti-KXL movement by seizing the White House.

The national campaign against the KXL pipeline grew out of the failure to address climate protection through normal legislative and electoral means, exemplified by the apparent impossibility of passing climate legislation or treaties through the US Congress. It represented an effort by the climate protection movement to overcome the gap revealed by the feedback from its efforts.

The KXL campaign transformed the control of new fossil fuel infrastructure from de facto unilateral domination by the fossil fuel industry to a contested realm. It created new coordinations that became the basis for new power and its exercise. It split the political establishment, leading the president of the United States to again and again delay a permit for the pipeline. While ultimately the movement was not powerful enough to keep President Trump from issuing a permit for the pipeline, in the process it transformed the climate and environmental movements and the public.

Why was this rag-tag nonviolent army of KXL resisters able to have such an impact, notwithstanding its lack of conventional power resources and the concentrated wealth and power of the fossil fuel industry and its supporters arrayed against it? What were the sources of its power? What allowed it to divide the political establishment? What made the fossil fuel regime vulnerable despite its wealth and power?

The fossil fuel industry depends upon governments and ultimately the indulgence of society for its existence, its control of resources, and the permits that allow it to operate, destroying local environments and the earth's climate. The growing awareness of its role in climate destruction presents the fossil fuel industry with an existential threat—one that it is well aware of. The underlying vulnerability of the industry is that its business plan is to destroy the planet. Despite industry efforts to deny climate change, hundreds of millions of Americans were aware of the threat to their well-being posed by climate change, and knew that it resulted from the burning of fossil fuels.[25]

The fossil fuel industry's underlying strategy in response was to ensure that restrictions on its freedom to burn fossil fuels were not even considered as serious possibilities. The KXL movement represented the threat—and to a considerable extent the reality—that the danger posed by fossil fuel expansion would be exposed to the public and that the possibility of halting it would be put on the public agenda. Direct action to halt the KXL pipeline turned restrictions on fossil fuel infrastructure from a theoretical debate to a practical contest.

In the US, in contrast to the rest of the world, the political parties are polarized on climate change. The overwhelming majority of Democratic Party members and voters are deeply concerned about it and support restrictions on GHG emissions. Environmental organizations and their supporters are also a significant force within the Democratic Party.

In his first presidential campaign in 2008 Barack Obama made climate change a central issue. But after his election he largely stood aloof as a Democratic Congress failed to pass climate legislation. He failed to use presidential power for climate action until well into his second term. He therefore had significant political vulnerability on climate in his own base—something that Bill McKibben was well aware of when he focused the KXL campaign on Obama's presidential power to refuse a permit for a cross-border pipeline. The movement created a situation where Obama's claims to protecting the climate would ring hollow both before history and before his own constituents.

The fossil fuel industry and its supporters were also a powerful force within the Democratic Party. They were major campaign contributors in many states. Democratic elected officials from fossil fuel dependent areas strongly supported fossil fuel infrastructure expansion. Segments of organized labor directly involved with the KXL pipeline and closely enmeshed with the company building it, and with the fossil fuel industry in general, were a powerful force within the Democratic Party; they eventually pressured the AFL-CIO to lobby the Obama administration and the Democratic Party to support the pipeline. Faced with a divided base, Obama repeatedly put off a decision on the pipeline. But ultimately, confronted with escalating and highly visible public actions, he turned down the KXL permit.

Climate change was far from the only issue raised by the KXL pipeline. In fact, it threatened local environments from the tar sands region in Ontario to the entire Great Plains to its terminal in Texas. Local mobilizations focused on local effects were a critical power factor. The Native American mobilization against the pipeline played a crucial role in defining Native rights as a central issue in the pipeline debate. Resistance by ranchers brought in a property rights dimension. Threats to aquifers and the Sand Hills evoked widespread local opposition. In some cases local resisters were able to block construction and even force a change in the pipeline route.

The KXL resistance represented a collective withdrawal of consent to established authority by a variety of forces in a variety of arenas. It represented a collective refusal to obey authority. It revealed that climate destruction depends on the acquiescence of those whose future it is destroying—and that it can be impeded by disobeying the authority claimed by property owners and the states that back them.*

The struggle over the KXL pipeline vividly illustrates what Gandhi called a "matching of forces." Unlike two armies marching head to head, however, the power of those forces was highly asymmetrical. The wealth, power, and hegemony of the fossil fuel industry was challenged by people sitting in trees, chaining themselves to construction machinery, organizing their neighbors, peacefully surrounding the White House, and joining together in unlikely combinations like the Cowboy Indian Alliance.

The KXL struggle also produced a self-transformation of the climate movement. It brought together local mobilizations against local environmental destruction along the pipeline's route, climate activists from 350.org and beyond, environmental justice groups like the Hip Hop Caucus, direct actionists like Tar Sands Blockade, and large environmental organizations like the Sierra Club that had never previously supported civil disobedience. While its participants often remained part of separate organizations and constituencies, barriers to cooperation— among different tribes, Native and non-Native people, direct actionists and more conventional environmentalists, those identifying themselves as "cowboys" and "Indians"—were lowered and crossed by new forms of coordination. The network form of coordination did not require subsuming these groups into a single organization and assuaged fears that cooperation might lead to loss of autonomy and new dominations.*

The movement was transformed because its participants recognized the necessities of the struggle. Plenty of feedback indicated that the climate fight in general needed new forms of action and organization. And the KXL fight in itself required cooperation among forces that had previously been unconnected or even at odds. The power of the movement depended on drawing together diverse power bases that could be coordinated and combined. It exemplified Michael Mann's view of power as coordination.*

Ultimately the effective power of the climate protection movement will depend on the capacity of the people to withdraw their acquiescence and cooperation from the climate-destroying centers of power that are destroying their future. The KXL struggle helped make the possibility of such action known to a wide public, including millions who are deeply concerned about climate change but uncertain of how they can help halt it. It reframed climate change as something that people can address through personal and collective action, not just through individual consumer choice, legislation, or the conventional political process. It provided an exemplary demonstration of the power of the people, laying the basis for people to assimilate the idea and practice of direct action and civil disobedience.

One indicator of the impact of the KXL struggle: as it grew, scores of other fossil fuel pipeline projects met opposition, protest, and direct action. In the year following President Obama's rejection of the KXL pipeline in November 2015, at least twenty-eight other proposed fossil fuel infrastructure projects in the US were halted as a result of unfavorable economic conditions, environmental concerns, and local resistance.[26] Many of these had been targets of direct-action campaigns.*

The KXL struggle brought echoes from American crises past. The initial initiative by Bill McKibben and his associates grew out of a study of the civil rights movement—in effect an assimilation of past struggles and an accommodation of their patterns to the necessities of the climate movement.* Rev. Lennox Yearwood of the Hip Hop Caucus compared the KXL struggle to the role of Birmingham as the "epitome" of the civil rights movement. The KXL became "the Birmingham for the environmental movement." Defeating the pipeline "will have a ripple effect on the other parts of the country and the world" comparable to the successes of the civil rights movement in Birmingham.[27] If Obama approves the KXL pipeline, said Michael Brune, referring to the fate of Lyndon Johnson, it will be "the Vietnam of his presidency."[28]

If the KXL pipeline ultimately goes into operation it will be a painful defeat for the climate protection movement, but it will also be a stunning example of winning by losing. The campaign against the KXL has educated millions of people about climate change, drawn diverse elements of the climate protection movement into shared goals and coordinated action, and introduced forms of action that provide the movement with new possibilities of power. The climate protection movement emerged from the KXL fight far different and far stronger than it was before.

Nonetheless, the KXL struggle revealed some of the weaknesses of the climate protection movement. The extent of its reach to the public was limited: its largest demonstration, for example, had only forty thousand participants, and only a few thousand people engaged in civil disobedience. As its leaders were well aware, in the end climate change could not be halted one pipeline at a time. The KXL struggle was ultimately unable to overcome the power of the state, property rights, markets, and the fossil fuel industry. These evident gaps laid the groundwork for the future development of the movement.*

CHAPTER 37

The Ecological Shot Heard Round the World

The common-preservation heuristic is not just about interpreting the past; its main point is to improve the future. Over the course of thirty years I used the heuristic to develop a strategy for climate protection that I came to call a "global nonviolent constitutional insurgency." It was in effect an ongoing thought experiment, a series of operations on representations. But it drew on and tried to affect real experiments and real-world developments.[*]

The next three chapters recount the development of that strategy.[1] My strategic approach developed along with the evolution of the climate movement in which I was a participant. I present the strategy through an account of its development. It is a personal account; I am not trying to represent the strategic thinking of the climate-protection movement as a whole, just the development of my own. But it uses historical methods, testing my account against evidence. The evidence includes my own memory of my own experience—a valid source of evidence, but also one that can easily be tainted by self-delusion. The main evidence I use is my writing from the time. I try to show through retrospective reconstruction how my developing strategy was shaped by and embodied the common preservation heuristic.

I first learned about the possibility of climate destruction in the early 1970s, when social ecologist Murray Bookchin wrote, "The burning of fossil fuels (coal and oil) add 600 million tons of carbon dioxide to the air annually." This growing blanket of carbon dioxide, by intercepting heat radiated from the earth, will lead to "more destructive storm patterns and eventually to melting of the polar ice caps, rising sea levels, and the inundation of vast land areas."[2]

I was no stranger to threats of doom. I was born in the aftermath of Hiroshima and my childhood and youth had no closed season from the threat of nuclear holocaust. I did not believe in the benevolence of progress or doubt that my species was capable of self-annihilation. I had responded by being a peace activist participating in the ban-the-bomb movement. When I discovered global warming, I assimilated it to the already-familiar pattern of potential species suicide. Global ecological threats, and specifically global warming, seemed to me to warrant a response similar to the one that was appropriate for nuclear omnicide: a global movement for human survival.*

Frankly, I had no idea what to do with this understanding. All I could think of was to make somewhat feeble attempts to alert people to this looming but rarely recognized problem. In *Common Sense for Hard Times*, for example, Tim Costello and I quoted Barry Commoner's 1971 book *The Closing Circle*: the present course of environmental degradation represents "a challenge to essential ecological systems" that, if continued, "will destroy the capability of the environment to support a reasonably civilized human society."[3]

By the late 1980s climate scientists were confident that the burning of fossil fuels was warming the earth's atmosphere and thereby altering the climate. They shared this information with governments and the public; articles about global warming increased tenfold in US newspapers between 1987 and 1988. Polls conducted in 1988 found that most Americans said the greenhouse effect was very serious or extremely serious and that they worried a fair amount or a great deal about global warming. Less than a fifth said they were not at all worried or had no opinion.

One exceptionally hot day in the summer of 1988 I had a conversation that crystallized what I had been thinking in a hazy way: global warming might be the kind of emerging shared problem from which a new social movement—a new common preservation—might emerge. I sat down and wrote an op-ed that was published in the *Chicago Tribune* called "The Opening Shot of the Second Ecological Revolution."[4]

I opened with the story of my milkman telling me, "I talk with old-timers who can't remember anything like it in sixty, seventy years. It's probably this 'greenhouse effect.'" Put in terms of the common preservation heuristic, my milkman and his neighbors were receiving feedback from the environment that violated his expectations. He also had been hearing about a new climate pattern—the greenhouse effect. He accommodated his existing expectations to incorporate this idea and thereby correct the gap between his expectations and the feedback he was receiving from his experience.*

"If you ask me," he continued, "it's a warning. All the poisons we're putting into the air and the water—if we don't get our act together, we're going to make the earth a place that people can't live on." He saw global warming not simply as a fact but also as a problem. And he extended that problem beyond global warming to include a wider set of ecological impacts. Poisons put in the air and water created a gap between the conditions necessary for human life on earth and the ways people were changing it. And solving that problem required that we "get our act together"—take some kind of collective action.*

When I started talking about the weather, I certainly wasn't expecting a response about the need to take action on global warming. I noted in the op-ed that, "as a historian, I'm always on the lookout for subtle signs that indicate deep changes in social outlook." When the conversation "shifted from local weather to the global biosphere," I felt I was witnessing a fundamental paradigm shift. I called it "the opening shot of the second ecological revolution."

What my milkman's statement represented was the transformation of a representation, a reflective abstraction in which he reinterpreted the simple fact of an unusually hot day as a sign of an existential environmental threat—and of the need for people to change their actions substantially to forestall it. I presented this anecdote to suggest the possibility that my milkman's reframing might be part of a wider social paradigm shift. And I used it as a pattern of such reframing that readers could assimilate into their own thinking and use to accommodate their current representations to interpret the new reality.*

I then used the "ecological revolution" of the 1970s, through which most readers would have lived, as a pattern to adopt and adapt for interpreting the significance of global warming and climate change. That first ecological revolution was based on a new awareness of the interconnectedness of the microenvironment: you cannot poison the bugs without also killing the birds. Ecological thinking was a reflective abstraction that transformed people's understanding of the boundaries and relations among individual organisms and species: each came to be perceived not as an entirely separate entity but as part of an ecosystem whose boundaries connected it as well as separated it from the rest of its environment. It was an instance of what I have called an "ecological shift."*

I modified the familiar idea of local ecological connectedness to suggest the possibility of global ecological connectedness. The greenhouse effect resulting from burning too much fuel worldwide causes droughts in many parts of the world and the heat wave my milkman saw as a warning.

I suggested that we were entering a "second ecological revolution" in which people would recognize the links of the macroenvironment: "Cutting rain forests in Costa Rica or burning coal in Gdansk may contribute to crop failures in Iowa and tree death in the Black Forest." I mentioned several recent ecological catastrophes, from Chernobyl, to acid rain, to a chemical spill on the Rhine, that "cut across national boundaries as surely as DDT cuts across species boundaries."

Both ecological revolutions were about, among other things, transforming boundaries. To recognize the food chain that connected the DDT sprayed on bugs with the poisoning of songbirds was to recognize that the boundaries among individual organisms and species were only relative, semipermeable membranes through which some though not all things could pass. To recognize the global spread of the radiation from Chernobyl or the greenhouse effect resulting from burning too much fossil fuel worldwide was to acknowledge that the boundaries of countries and continents might stop goods and people at the border but were powerless to halt the dissemination of radiation or the effects of greenhouse gases.*

I used the first ecological revolution not only as a pattern for paradigm shift, but also for social movement formation. It had "spawned a popular movement involving millions of people." This movement represented new forms of coordination that cut across established geographical boundaries, reaching everywhere, "even the Soviet bloc and the Third World."

I then identified damage to the global environment as a problem that "threatens the basic conditions on which life depends and poses a clear and present danger." It was a gap between the interest in continuing human life and the conditions people were creating. This problem required a new solution—"a global response."

I suggested as a pattern for such a solution the recent Montreal Protocol, an international agreement to protect the ozone layer by limiting the use of chlorofluorocarbons. It could be modified to design a "binding international agreement to protect the atmosphere" by limiting the production of greenhouse gases. (I was not yet aware of the limitations of the Montreal Protocol as a model for climate protection.)

For some reason, however, governments and politicians were not "racing to meet this looming threat." There was a gap between the feedback that was being received and the accommodation of existing patterns that was necessary to provide for human survival and well-being.

Why was the problem not being solved? The answer lay with the differentiation of power. The measures needed to protect the global ecosphere would "reduce the power of the world's most powerful institutions." National governments would need to accept international controls; corporations forego opportunities to make money at the expense of the environment; military establishments abandon programs that threaten the air and water.

Overcoming those obstacles required countering domination by creating new forms of coordination that cross national and other boundaries. I again drew on the pattern of the first ecological revolution, which "began as a popular movement" and "imposed its own agenda on governments and economies." It brought about "an array of environmental legislation" in dozens of countries. The second ecological revolution would have to act globally, with "international petition drives, worldwide demonstrations and boycotts, and direct action campaigns against polluting countries and corporations."*

In trying to understand the challenge presented by global warming and develop a way to respond to it I drew on many aspects of my heuristic. I identified a gap or problem and indicated a plausible direction for a solution. The basic idea was to create new coordinations in order to solve the problems of the global environment by countering the power of the corporations and governments that were causing them—in cybernetic terms, to construct a collective "steersman" that could move the world system in a different direction. Doing so involved borrowing from and adapting the experience of other movements.*

My prophesy seemed plausible, but as we have seen in the previous chapters of part 3, it would be a quarter of a century before the kind of movement I had envisioned would emerge. I, like others who advocated a global mass movement for climate protection, had two problems. I had little idea of how to bring it about. And I had little idea of how it could exercise power against the forces in the world order that were driving us toward climate destruction. My enlightenment would have to await the emergence of 350.org and the battle over the Keystone XL pipeline.

From 1988 to 2009 I did not write about strategy for climate protection; I assumed that some sort of official climate protection policy was going forward and that I could best help by focusing on one appropriate niche—trying to overcome organized labor's resistance to climate protection policies. I worked first with Global Labor Strategies and then with the Labor Network for Sustainability to do so.

I also worked on a book called *Green@Work* based on the assumption that climate protection policies would have a big impact on jobs and the workplace. In a 2008 draft I wrote confidently, "Global negotiations for a successor to the Kyoto protocol began this year at Bali" and "will culminate at Copenhagen at the end of 2009." The decisions made would have "a significant impact on future patterns of the global economy." And in the US, "National legislation on global warming appears almost inevitable after the 2008 election." The Copenhagen summit and US climate legislation both tanked. I abandoned *Green@Work* and began searching for an alternative climate protection strategy.

CHAPTER 38

The Public Trust and the Constitutional Right to a Stable Climate

In April 2009, US climate czar Carol Browner admitted there would be no US climate protection legislation before the December Copenhagen climate summit and that she didn't know if that conference could agree to binding cuts in GHG emissions. Official climate protection had begun its slow-motion tumble into collapse. There seemed little that climate protection advocates could do about it; they were now face-to-face with the problems of state power and popular powerlessness. Many of them began to seek strategies that went beyond the limits of lobbying and the constitutional "rules of the game."

In response to Browner's admission, I drafted a statement for the Labor Network for Sustainability warning that "the earth is being imperiled by a failure of its political systems" and that the strategy of lobbying governments to fix global warming would not work. Existing institutions, specifically states and markets, have decisively proven themselves unable to halt the plunge toward destruction of the biosphere. National and world political systems are as dysfunctional for survival today as feudal principalities were for protecting their people in the face of capitalism and the modern nation-state.*

States, I continued, are not legitimate if they allow their terrain or their institutions to be used to destroy the global environment.* They have no right to govern. They are climate outlaws whose authority it is not only our right but our obligation to challenge. Property rights are not legitimate if property is used to destroy the global environment. Corporations that emit greenhouse gases have no right to their property. They too are climate outlaws whose ownership it is not only our right but our obligation to challenge.

A climate protection movement, I argued, must be conceived, not as governments agreeing to climate protection measures, but as people imposing rules on states, markets, and other institutions.[1] We can begin to impose these rules locally by direct action wherever we are; we can support each other's actions around the globe; and we can support the right of all the world's people to monitor and halt climate destroying emissions.* The legitimation for policy and action must be global necessity, not just national or other limited interest.*

I said that the movement must impose climate protection rules by direct action. I pointed to recent direct-action blockades of coal facilities as a beginning of this process. It would be necessary to boycott and sanction governments, corporations, and other institutions that threaten the survival of the planet.*

I concluded, "We need to make true for climate protection what President Dwight D. Eisenhower said about peace: 'I think that people want peace so much that one of these days governments had better get out of their way and let them have it.' Tell governments and corporations that they will be regarded as nothing but outlaws if they continue to destroy the earth's environment."[2]

As we have seen in chapter 34, the climate movement did in fact make the leap to direct action and civil disobedience. The justification for such action was generally an individual moral responsibility which actors asserted had a higher claim on their consciences than their duty to obey the law and the state. They did not question the authority of the state to determine the law.

My calling the powers and principalities of the earth outlaws did not do much to undermine their authority. But then, while reviewing a book called *Green Governance*, I stumbled across an idea that was entirely new to me: destroying the earth's climate violated an ancient and widespread legal principle known in the US as the public trust doctrine.[3] I immediately caught on fire with this idea. Here was the legal basis for declaring the governments and corporations that permitted or conducted climate destruction climate outlaws whose authority it is not only our right but our duty to challenge. That discovery has shaped my approach to climate protection strategy ever since.

In a series of suits and petitions initiated in 2011 on behalf of young people, the Atmospheric Trust Litigation Project brought legal actions in all fifty US states and in federal court demanding that these governments fulfill their public trust obligation to protect the atmosphere as a common property. Sixteen-year-old Alec Loorz, founder of Kids vs. Global Warming and lead plaintiff in the federal lawsuit, said, "The government has a legal responsibility to protect the future for our children. So we are demanding that they recognize the atmosphere as a commons that needs to be preserved, and commit to a plan to reduce emissions to a safe level."

The "Climate Kids" suits sought declaratory judgment applying the public trust doctrine to the earth's atmosphere. They ask courts to issue injunctions ordering federal and state governments to reduce carbon emissions to fulfill their duty to protect the climate. Similar suits were initiated for countries around the world.

It was obvious to me that US courts were unlikely to halt fossil fuel emissions on the basis of the public trust doctrine any time soon. But for that very reason the public trust principle could be a powerful justification for direct action to protect the climate. I wrote in the margin of *Green Governance* opposite its presentation of the atmospheric public trust, "But courts won't, so people must."

As soon as I was able to educate myself on the legal and historical background of the public trust doctrine I wrote an article called "Civil Disobedience as Law Enforcement."[4] I noted that two years earlier I had been arrested at the White House in the early Keystone XL sit-ins, but that since then my perspective on such actions had changed. I had come to believe that the US government and other governments around the world are violating their own most fundamental responsibilities to their own people when they allow fossil fuel producers and users to devastate the earth's atmosphere with greenhouse gases. Governments will no doubt continue to treat protesters who block pipelines, coal mines, and power plants as criminals, but "such governments come into court with dirty hands, stained by their dereliction of the duty to protect the common inheritance of their own people."

The public trust doctrine has roots and analogues in ancient societies from Europe to East Asia to Africa, and from Islamic to Native American cultures. It was codified in the *Institutes of Justinian*, issued by the Roman Emperor in 535 AD. The Justinian Code defined the concept of *res communes* (common things): "By the law of nature these things are common to mankind—the air, running water, the sea and consequently the shores of the sea." The right of fishing in the sea from the shore "belongs to all men." The Justinian Code distinguished such *res communes* from *res publicae*, things which belong to the state.

Based on the Justinian Code's protection of *res communes*, governments have long served as trustees for rights held in common. In American law this role is defined by the public trust doctrine, under which the state serves as trustee on behalf of the present and future generations of its citizens. Even if the state holds title to a given resource, the public is the "beneficial owner." As trustee, the state has a fiduciary duty to the owner—a legal duty to act solely in the owner's interest. This principle is accepted today in both common law and civil law systems in countries ranging from South Africa to the Philippines and from the United States to India.

When a trust asset crosses the boundaries of sovereign governments, all sovereigns with jurisdiction over the natural territory of the asset have legitimate property claims to the resource. Thus, all nations on earth are "cotenant trustees" of the global atmosphere. As cotenants they have an undivided right to possess the common property. But they also have a duty not to allow it to be destroyed.*

In addition, international law recognizes regions that lie outside of the political reach of any one nation-state—specifically, the high seas, the atmosphere, Antarctica and outer space—as "global commons" governed by the principle that they are "the common heritage of humankind." But there has been no effective vehicle for asserting our right not to have our common heritage destroyed.

The governmental trustee of the public trust has an active duty of vigilance to prevent decay or "waste"—permanent damage to the asset. If the asset is wasted in the interest of one generation of beneficiaries over future generations, it is in effect an act of generational theft. In short, governments have a fiduciary duty to protect the earth's climate.

As compelling as the logic of the obligation of governments to protect the public trust may be, it was easy to imagine that many American courts would refuse to force governments to meet their obligations. In a brief to dismiss the Kansas suit, lawyers called the claim "a child's wish for a better world," which is not something a court can do much about. "No order issued by the District Court of Shawnee County can hold back global warming, any more than King Canute could order the tide to recede."[5]

Virtually all governments on earth—and their legal systems—are deeply corrupted by the very forces that profit from destroying the global commons. These governments exercise illegitimate power without regard to their obligations to those they claim to represent, let alone to the future generations for whom they are mere trustees.*

Protecting the global commons, I concluded, is not just a matter for governments. The failure of governments to protect the global commons was already turning the climate protection movement to mass civil disobedience, as witnessed by the campaigns against the Keystone XL pipeline, mountaintop-removal coal mining, and coal-fired power plants. Looked at from the perspective of the public trust, however, these actions were not disobedience to law. Indeed, they embodied the effort of people around the world to act on their right and responsibility to protect the global commons. They showed people acting in an emergency situation on an evident necessity. They represented people stepping in to provide law enforcement where corrupt and illegitimate governments failed to meet their responsibility to do so.

"Civil Disobedience as Law Enforcement" pointed out that legal rationales have played a critical role in many movements. They strengthen participants by making clear that they are not promoting personal opinions by criminal means but rather performing a public duty. And they strengthen a movement's appeal to the broader society by presenting its action not as wanton law-breaking but as an effort to rectify governments and institutions that are themselves in violation of the law.* It cited the civil rights movement using the US Constitution's guarantee of equal rights; war resisters using international law forbidding war crimes; and Poland's Solidarity union's appealing to international human and labor rights laws ratified by their own government.*

I argued that the legal obligation of governments to protect the public trust could play a role similar to governments' obligation to protect human rights and eschew war crimes. Those who perpetrate global warming, and those who allow them to do so, should not be able to claim that the law is on their side. Those who blockade coal-fired power plants or sit down at the White House to protest the Keystone XL pipeline can—and should—insist that they are simply exercising their right and responsibility to protect the atmospheric commons they own along with all of present and future humankind.*

Future climate protesters could proudly proclaim that they are actually climate protectors, upholding the law, not violating it. Nobody should expect American judges to start acquitting protesters on public trust grounds any time soon. But juries that try climate protesters should keep in mind that they have the right and the responsibility to acquit those they believe have violated no just law.*

On October 5, 2014, I got a message from Mary Christina Wood putting me in touch with a climate activist named Alec Johnson (a.k.a. Climate Hawk). Johnson ran into an article about the atmospheric public trust and followed up by reading Mary Christina Wood's book *Nature's Trust*.[6] He had thereupon locked himself to a Keystone XL construction excavator in Tushka, Oklahoma, and announced he would argue in court that his action was necessary in order to protect the atmospheric public trust.[7] Johnson was the first defendant anywhere to make a defense based on the constitutional duty of government to protect the climate under the public trust doctrine.

In a statement he prepared for the jury, Johnson argued that his blockade of Keystone XL pipeline construction was necessary because the pipeline threatens our atmospheric public trust, and state and national governments were failing to protect us against that threat. He proclaimed on the basis of the public trust principle, "I wasn't breaking the law that day—I was enforcing it." The judge refused to let Johnson present a necessity defense, but he was allowed to explain his motivation to the jury. Although Johnson could have been sentenced to up to two years in the Atoka County jail, the jury, which under Oklahoma law determined his punishment, sentenced him to a fine of just over $1,000 and no jail time.[8]

Meanwhile, the Climate Kids' cases crawled through the courts. More than five years after the initial suits, federal Judge Ann Aiken of the federal district court in Oregon issued a decision that the federal case could go forward. Judge Aiken endorsed the Climate Kids' argument that the government has a duty under the public trust principle to protect the climate. She quoted a judicial opinion that the right of future generations to a "balanced and healthful ecology" is so basic that it "need not even be written in the Constitution" for it is "assumed to exist from the inception of humankind."[9]

But her decision went far beyond the public trust doctrine to find a constitutional right to climate protection. "I have no doubt that the right to a climate system capable of sustaining human life is fundamental to a free and ordered society." A stable climate system is quite literally the foundation of society, "without which there would be neither civilization nor progress."[10]

Consequently, if "governmental action is affirmatively and substantially damaging the climate system in a way that will cause human deaths, shorten human lifespans, result in widespread damage to property, threaten human food sources, and dramatically alter the planet's ecosystem," then the youth have a claim for protection of their life and liberty under the Fifth Amendment. "To hold otherwise would be to say that the Constitution affords no protection against a government's knowing decision to poison the air its citizens breathe or the water its citizens drink."*

With ludicrous legal justification, the Trump administration applied for a writ of mandamus to prevent the case from going forward. In March 2018—more than a year later—Trump's appeal was rejected, and the federal magistrate judge set a new trial date for October 29, 2018, in federal district court in Eugene, Oregon. Further delays followed. If and when Judge Aiken finally gets to rule on the case, the government will almost certain engage in lengthy appeals to prevent it from ever becoming enforceable law.

But meanwhile, the public trust doctrine was increasingly used to justify civil disobedience by protesters who blocked oil trains, shut off pipeline valves, and otherwise interfered with fossil fuels. In 2018 thirteen protesters who had blocked pipeline construction in West Roxbury, Massachusetts, were given permission to present a necessity defense that included the constitutional right to a stable environment and the public trust; the prosecutor thereupon dropped criminal charges and the judge acquitted them of the remaining infraction charges. It was the first time that defendants were acquitted by a US judge based on climate necessity.[11]

States often claim, or at least act in practice, on the principle that the duty to obey them is absolute and unlimited. As Charles Lindblom puts it, their authority is based on the claim that those subject to it have made an open-ended commitment to obey. Authority is generalized prior consent of the governed to future commands.*

Generalized prior consent makes it easy for legitimate authority to pass over into extended authority, a.k.a. domination. Such domination is rooted in the paradox that people consent to obey authority on the basis of reciprocal commitments of the rulers. However, the rulers do not necessarily keep their end of the bargain.*

Nearly all modern states are in their own theory, if not in fact, bound by constitutions—written or unwritten fundamental rules limiting their action. The duty to obey is premised on their own obedience to those rules. If they violate them, it follows that they abandon their claim to obedience. Of course, they may still try to impose obedience by force or intimidation, maintaining that they have the right to make the rules of the game. But that is no reason—short of a belief in the divine right of those claiming authority—that someone subject to their false claims should acknowledge a duty to obey them.

The fundamental problem that blocks the elimination of GHGs is resistance from the world order. While that resistance has various sources, they are all legitimated by the purported authority of governments. That makes it possible for climate destruction to continue and for governments to apply the law against those who try to stop it. But this really is "extended authority" being used for a purpose nobody has or would ever agree to voluntarily—destruction of the climate on which life and society depend. And if the government is violating its own most fundamental constitutional premises on which its claims to authority are based, then people are justified—as John Locke argued long ago—in rejecting its authority. The practical expression of such rejection is to disobey the state's laws and commands.

Using the public trust doctrine and the right to a stable climate to delegitimize governments is a kind of political jiu-jitsu, in which each government exertion of illegitimate authority only further undermines the legitimacy of its authority.

The public trust and constitutional right to a stable climate started as legal claims that were made in court, intended to allow the government to correct itself. They provided legal principles—a transformation of mental representations—but no vehicle for people to act. But these constitutional arguments held a potential to become a means for group formation and collective action.

CHAPTER 39

A Global Nonviolent Constitutional Insurgency

The common preservation heuristic is designed to nurture collective action in the common interest. How can it help us use the public trust principle, the constitutional right to a stable climate, and similar legal principles to strengthen the struggle for climate protection?

These principles define those claiming authority to be illegitimate usurpers so long as they persistently fail to fulfill their duty to protect the climate. The history of social movements shows that such delegitimation can play an important role in making change.

For the civil rights movement, the US Constitution's guarantee of equal rights meant that sit-inners and freedom riders were not criminals but rather upholders of constitutional law—even if southern sheriffs threw them in jail. For the opponents of apartheid, white supremacy was a violation of internationally guaranteed human rights. For war resisters from Vietnam to Iraq, national and international law forbidding war crimes defined their disobedience not as interference with legal, democratic governments, but rather as a legal obligation of citizens. For the activists of Solidarity, the nonviolent revolution that overthrew Communism in Poland was not criminal sedition, but an effort to implement the international human and labor rights law ratified by their own government. As Jonathan Schell put it in the introduction to Adam Michnik's *Letters from Prison*, these agreements meant that the actions of Michnik and his associates were perfectly legal, "while the means used by the police and judiciary apparatus in Poland" were "in flagrant violation of international agreements."[1]

These examples may seem paradoxical. On the one hand, the protesters appear to be resisting constituted law and the officials charged with implementing it. On the other, they are claiming to act on the basis of law, in fact to be implementing the law themselves against the actions of lawless states. How could such a paradoxical claim serve as the basis for a mass movement?

As I pondered this paradox, I was reminded of the concept of a "constitutional insurgency" developed by law professor and historian James Gray Pope.[2] Pope defined a constitutional insurgency as a social movement that rejects current constitutional doctrine, but that "rather than repudiating the Constitution altogether, draws on it for inspiration and justification." Such an insurgency "unabashedly confronts official legal institutions with an outsider perspective that is either absent from or marginalized in official constitutional discourse." On the basis of its own interpretation of the constitution, such an insurgency "goes outside the formally recognized channels of representative politics to exercise direct popular power, for example through extralegal assemblies, mass protests, strikes, and boycotts." It may hold such actions legal, even though the established courts condemn and punish them.

Pope gave as an example the American labor movement's long insistence that the right to strike was protected by the Thirteenth Amendment, which forbids any form of "involuntary servitude." Injunctions to prevent strikes were therefore unconstitutional. While courts disregarded this claim, the "normally staid" American Federation of Labor maintained that a worker confronted with an unconstitutional injunction had an imperative duty to "refuse obedience and to take whatever consequences may ensue." The radical Industrial Workers of the World told its members to "disobey and treat with contempt all judicial injunctions."

Such insurgencies do not fit neatly into either the idea of a revolutionary overthrow of the government or of reforms conducted within the limits of legally permissible action as courts currently interpret them. In practice, social movements have long beaten a middle pathway between the constitutional discontinuity of revolution on the one hand and reform that fails to challenge the legitimacy of current legal structures on the other. The concept of constitutional insurgency explains how they can do so. It became a central element of the strategy I was developing for climate protection.

The idea of a constitutional insurgency also fits well with nonviolent direct action. Such action is typically extraconstitutional yet not aimed per se at overthrowing the government. Indeed, when Gandhi said during the Indian civil disobedience campaign that "sedition has become my religion," he might as well have said that he had become a constitutional insurgent, fighting for rights that English law enshrined but that its practice was denying to India. (As some conservative historians are wont to point out, the American Revolution also began as a struggle for "the rights of Englishmen.")

A Strategy for Survival

My book *Climate Insurgency: A Strategy for Survival* proposed a global nonviolent constitutional insurgency.

The strategy was largely an elaboration of the development of the global climate movement to that time and a "thought experiment" about its possible future course. The global climate movement had laid the groundwork for countering the underlying obstacles to climate protection. It had constructed a flexible network form of organization that could facilitate rapid coordination and mass mobilization on a global scale and had drawn tens of millions of people into grassroots self-organization. It had established its independence of any nation-state and of any corporate interest. The movement had constructed a common interpretive frame and a common objective: the reduction of atmospheric carbon to a climate-safe level, currently estimated at 350 ppm or less. It had related that frame to issues of social justice and had projected it to hundreds of millions of people. It had moved beyond the limits of lobbying to mass civil disobedience. The global climate movement had become one of the power actors of the world order, able to challenge states, corporations, and other central institutions.

But to realize its objectives, the climate protection movement needed to apply the capacities it had created to overcoming the obstacles to climate protection presented by the world order. It had to limit the blind pursuit of self-interest and self-aggrandizement by states and corporations and nurture means for formulating and pursuing the global common interest in protecting the climate. It needed to overcome the GHG-promoting hegemony imposed by the great powers, above all by the United States. It required a strategy for political, economic, and social transformation that would protect the climate while protecting people's livelihoods and well-being.

I proposed a global nonviolent constitutional insurgency as a thought experiment, a reflective abstraction designed to test what might fill the climate gap. This strategy doesn't require transforming the world order into some kind of global utopia, but it does mean changing it enough to allow effective climate protection.

Why an insurgency? Insurgencies are social movements, but movements of a special type: they reject current rulers' claims to legitimate authority. Insurgencies often develop from movements that initially make no such challenge to established authority, but eventually conclude that it is necessary to realize their objectives.* Their aim may be to overthrow the existing government, but it may instead be to change it or simply to protect people against it. To effectively protect the earth's climate and the future of our species, the climate protection movement may well have to become such an insurgency.*

Why a nonviolent insurgency? The term "insurgency" is generally associated with an armed rebellion against an established government, one that rejects and resists the authority of the state. Whatever its means, however, the hallmark of an insurgency is to deny that established state authority is legitimate and to assert that its own actions are.[3]

A nonviolent insurgency, like an armed insurgency, does not accept the limits on its action imposed by the powers that be. Unlike an armed insurgency, it eschews violence and instead exercises power by mobilizing people for various forms of nonviolent mass action.

The powers that are responsible for climate change could not rule for a day without the acquiescence of those whose lives and future they are destroying. They are only able to continue their destructive course because others enable or acquiesce in it. It is the activity of people—going to work, paying taxes, buying products, obeying government officials, staying off private property—that continually recreates the power of the powerful. A nonviolent climate insurgency can be powerful if it withdraws that cooperation.*

Why a constitutional insurgency? It is often pointed out that electoral politics, lobbying, "pressure group" activity, and similar forms of constitutionally "legitimate" political action accept the established "rules of the game" and operate within their limits. Even if the rules are rigged, participants must accept the outcome of any given round and resign themselves to simply trying again.*

Civil disobedience, while generally recognizing the legitimacy of established law, refuses to obey some part of it. Civil disobedience is moral protest, but it does not in itself challenge the legal validity of the government or other institutions against which it is directed. Rather, it asserts that the obligation to oppose their immoral actions—whether discriminating against a class of people or conducting an immoral war or destroying the climate—is more binding on individuals than the normal duty to obey the law.

A constitutional insurgency goes a step further. It declares a set of laws and policies themselves illegal and sets out to establish law through nonviolent self-help. It is not formally a revolutionary movement because it does not challenge the legitimacy of the constitution; rather, it claims that current officials are in violation of the very laws that they themselves claim justify their authority. Such insurgents view those whom they are disobeying as merely persons claiming to embody legitimate authority, but who are themselves violating the law under color of law—on the false pretense of legal authority. For a constitutional insurgency, "civil disobedience" is actually obedience to law, even a form of law enforcement.[4]

Social movements that disobey established authorities often draw strength from the claim that their actions are not only moral, but that they also represent an effort to enforce fundamental legal and constitutional principles that the authorities themselves are in fact flouting. Such legal justifications demonstrate that those who disobey established authority may not be engaging in crime but rather performing a legal duty. Moreover, they strengthen a movement's appeal to the public by presenting its action not as disregard of the law, but as an effort to rehabilitate governments and institutions that have gone rogue—that themselves are in violation of the law.

Why a global insurgency? The destruction of the climate by GHGs is produced in specific locations; it affects specific locations in every part of the globe; it can only be corrected through global solutions implemented in specific locations. The world order that perpetuates climate destruction is global, but it is produced and reproduced in specific locations around the world. The whole must be changed in order to change the parts; changing the parts is necessary to change the whole.[*]

A global insurgency is less an attempt to overthrow one or another government as an effort to transform the world order.[*] That may seem like an implausible objective, but in some ways transforming the world order is easier than transforming the social and political order of individual nations. World orders are notoriously disorderly and fluid; their structure is maintained primarily by the mutual jostling of independent power centers. Where is the division of the world between two Cold War rivals or the global Keynesian economic regulation of fifty years ago? Moreover, unlike national governments operating under constitutions with officials chosen by elections, the world order has no claim whatsoever to legitimacy. No electorate has ever consented to superpower rivalry or global neoliberalism—or destruction of the earth's climate. It is against this illegitimate but mutable world order that a climate protection insurgency is ultimately aimed.

Global insurgency is also a vehicle for undermining the illegitimate authority of states. Under the public trust doctrine, all people have rights that states, whether their own or others, can't violate. This is the point of public trust "cotrusteeship." Similarly, the right to a stable climate is a human right; while it is guaranteed by the US Constitution, it is also a right of all persons that all governments have a duty to protect. All human beings have valid claims against all states that are destroying a stable climate.

Trial Run: Break Free from Fossil Fuels

How could such a strategy be tested? In May 2016, globally coordinated days of action called "Break Free from Fossil Fuels" provided a chance to assess core elements of a global nonviolent constitutional insurgency.

Near the close of the 2015 Paris climate summit, organizations from around the world announced escalated global actions in May 2016. Building on the burgeoning on-the-ground resistance to new fossil fuel infrastructure, Break Free from Fossil Fuels would use direct action and civil disobedience to "accelerate a global energy transformation" away from fossil fuels. Such civil disobedience would show the fossil fuel industry that it will "no longer benefit from the consent of the people."[5]

The call to Break Free from Fossil Fuels envisioned "tens of thousands of people around the world rising up" to take back control of their own destiny; "sitting down" to "block the business of government and industry that threaten our future"; and conducting "peaceful defense of our right to clean energy." Such a "rising up" amounts to a global nonviolent insurgency—a withdrawal of consent from those who claim the right to rule—manifested in a selective refusal to accept and obey their authority.[6]

The campaign spread to six continents. In Wales, protesters shut down the UK's largest open-pit coal mine for over twelve hours with no arrests. In the Philippines, ten thousand people marched and rallied demanding the cancellation of a six-hundred-megawatt coal power plant project. In New Zealand, protesters blockaded and shut down the Christchurch, Dunedin, and Wellington branches of the ANZ bank, which had $13.5 billion invested in fossil fuels. In Indonesia, banner drops brought a coal terminal to a standstill for hours. In Germany, four thousand people shut down a large lignite coal mine for more than two days. In Australia, two thousand people shut down the world's largest coal port with a kayak flotilla and a railroad blockade. Similar protests occurred in Brazil, Nigeria, Indonesia, South Africa, Ecuador, Canada, Turkey, and other countries around the world. In the US there were major actions near Seattle; Washington, DC; Chicago; Los Angeles; Albany; and Lakewood, Colorado. Organizers called Break Free "the largest ever global civil disobedience against fossil fuels."[7]

But it was not only in its global reach that Break Free prefigured a global climate insurgency. It also applied what organizers called a "new paradigm" to stake out the claim that the world's people have a right and a duty to protect the climate—and that no government can legitimately stop them. The US 350.org organizers of Break Free from Fossil Fuels issued this "Public Trust Proclamation":

We Are Here to Defend the Climate, the Constitution, and the Public Trust

We are here to help our community, our country, and the world Break Free From Fossil Fuels.

While we may risk arrest, we commit no crime.

Today the fossil fuel industry and the governments that do its bidding are laying waste to the earth's atmosphere, the common property of humanity.

We are upholding fundamental principles embodied in the laws and constitutions of countries around the world.

We are upholding the unalienable rights to life and liberty.

We are implementing the public trust doctrine, which requires that vital natural resources on which human well-being depend must be cared for by our governments for the benefit of all present and future generations.

Governments have no right to authorize the destruction of the public trust.

Governments have no right to wreck the rights to life and liberty for future generations.

We are here to enforce the law on governments and corporations that are committing the greatest crime in human history.

Those who take nonviolent direct action—blockade coal-fired power plants or sit down at the White House to protest fossil fuel pipelines—are exercising their fundamental constitutional rights to life and liberty and their responsibility to protect the atmospheric commons they own along with all of present and future humankind.

We proclaim: The people of the world have a right, indeed a duty, to protect the public trust we own in common—the earth's climate.

When we take nonviolent direct action we are law-enforcers carrying out our duty to protect the earth's climate from illegal, dangerous crimes.[8]

Break Free from Fossil Fuels may be the harbinger of a global non-violent climate insurgency—its nonviolent "shot heard around the world." It was globally coordinated, with common principles, strategy, planning, and messaging. It utilized nonviolent direct action not only as an individual moral witness, but also to express and mobilize the power of the people on which all government ultimately depends. It presented climate protection as a legal right and duty, necessary to defend the Constitution and the earth's essential resources on which we and our posterity depend. It represented an insurgency because it denied the right of the existing powers and principalities—be they corporate or governmental—to use the authority of law to justify their destruction of the earth's climate.

In *Against Doom: A Climate Insurgency Manual* I laid out some further steps that a climate insurgency might take, drawing on but extending patterns of climate action that were already underway. Several cities around the US had passed ordinances forbidding fracking in defiance of higher governmental authorities that claimed the right to authorize it; I suggested that such governmental civil disobedience might become an additional aspect of the climate insurgency. Various climate campaigns had organized symbolic tribunals to put governments and polluters on trial for their crimes; I suggested that such tribunals might begin to legitimate disobedience to governmental law and even issue orders authorizing the people to halt climate-destroying activities. Such insurgent action could in effect establish a dual power.

Surely there is no guarantee that a global nonviolent constitutional insurgency—or any other strategy—will halt our race toward doom. Even actions like Break Free from Fossil Fuels will not reverse GHG emissions—unless and until they become a continuous uprising joined not just by thousands but by millions of people around the world. But such a strategy offers at least the possibility of overcoming the forces that are currently ensuring our climate doom.

CHAPTER 40

A Climate Action Plan for Common Preservation

Climate scientists have identified a gap between present and expected GHG emissions in the atmosphere and the level of GHGs necessary to maintain a stable climate. They have calculated the reduction in GHG emissions necessary to establish climate stability. Achieving that reduction will require the formation and implementation of a Climate Action Plan that will realize the targets and timetables proposed by climate scientists. That requires the elimination of almost all fossil fuel burning in developed countries within decades. The Paris agreement endorsed at least as stringent GHG reductions.[1]

Suppose a compelling force—whether court order, political decision, popular demand, international pressure, or climate insurgency—had the power to force countries to fulfill their constitutional duty to establish a stable climate. What policies and practices would be needed to realize that result? How could they be implemented? What obstacles would they face?

While that is a problem to be worked out by many hands over a whole historical epoch, I have tried in a series of articles and books to provide some tentative answers.[2] While these proposals were laid out before the emergence of the Green New Deal into public prominence in 2019, it includes most of the features that have subsequently become key elements of the Green New Deal, as well as others that will need to be incorporated for it to succeed.[3] This chapter presents some of the ways that the common preservation heuristic has contributed to them.

The transition to a climate-safe economy is less a technical than an organization problem. It requires coordinating the activity of millions of people to realize a common purpose. At present there is no means for such coordination and there are many means for particular actors to prevent it.

To reach a climate-safe economy a country will need a vehicle for setting goals. It will need means to plan, coordinate, and implement the entire process. It will require ways to halt the building of new fossil fuel infrastructure and rapidly phase out the burning of fossil fuels. It will have to mobilize the financial, material, technical, and human resources necessary to build a new, climate-safe energy infrastructure and a highly energy efficient economy. It will need to ensure compliance. It must develop ways to correct errors in its course. It will have to maintain popular support. And it will need to ensure that its actions are coordinated with those of the rest of the world.

Unfortunately, both our national and our world order militate against these necessities. They provide no vehicle for setting goals or planning, coordinating, or implementing such a process. Resources are primarily allocated by markets, which can't by themselves coordinate to realize any social purpose beyond profit maximization. They have no effective means for shutting down climate-destroying activities. Most resources are controlled by property owners who have other intentions than climate protection—generally, making a profit. Governments are largely controlled by property owners and particularly by fossil fuel companies. The world order provides little means for international cooperation to utilize global resources for the social purpose of halting climate destruction.

The predominant approaches to climate protection provide little potential for overcoming these world-order obstacles.

First, individuals have been encouraged to reduce their "carbon footprint"; Al Gore's movie *An Inconvenient Truth* ended with a list of things people could do to fight global warming like turning off the lights when they leave a room. The effect of this approach was to blame ordinary consumers for climate change while letting oil companies, electric utilities, and other producers of GHGs off the hook. It led naturally to the question, if we want to halt global warming, must we freeze to death in the dark?*

Second, society could "put a price on carbon." The problem of climate change was defined as the unlimited right of polluters to release GHGs without charge, even though that had costs for other people and the environment. So, under familiar economic principles, the polluters should be required to pay for the costs they imposed on others, for example through a tax or through requiring them to purchase permits to pollute. Elaborate cap-and-trade schemes were included in climate legislation and international agreements, but there was little evidence that these market-based schemes would actually reduce GHG emissions significantly. So far they have proved more effective as a playground for speculators than a means to reduce GHG emissions.

Third, some environmental justice advocates have called for decentralized, community-based energy systems as the solution to GHG emissions. I am personally sympathetic to such approaches, but I have never found plans for how they would actually be implemented in a way that would eliminate fossil fuel burning in the necessary time frame without catastrophic economic consequences. While they may be desirable, they simply do not solve the problem.

Finally, if overall economic activity were reduced, presumably fossil fuel use and GHG emissions would shrink in tandem. Advocates of such "de-growth" sometimes argue that it is the necessary condition for climate protection. No doubt it would be beneficial to "de-grow" many human activities, from war production to casino gambling to adding sugar to water and producing mass obesity. But there is a problem with de-growth as a strategy for climate protection. To bring global GHG emissions down by, say, 80 percent would require halting the production of 80 percent of food, clothing, housing, and every other thing that people need. Starving to death in the dark, indeed! Fortunately, there are better alternatives.[4]

This chapter presents a common preservation climate action plan. Its purpose is not to argue this is the best possible plan, but rather to show how our heuristic can be used to explore solutions to concrete problems like climate change.

This plan was developed in the context of my work on labor and climate change. For that reason, it often emphasizes the roles and problems of US workers. Like any such plan it will require frequent updating.[*]

A Thought Experiment

What changes in society would a climate insurgency need to make to realize its goals? This chapter is a thought experiment in using the common preservation heuristic to answer that question.

In some ways, halting climate destruction is simple. If all those who are adversely affected by GHG emissions simply blocked the facilities that produce and use fossil fuels, or if those who work in such facilities simply refused to perform the operations that produce or use them, GHG emissions would cease.* But because fossil fuels are deeply enmeshed in a complex world order with many dependencies that militate against such an action, halting climate destruction requires a much more complex strategy.*

Eliminating the production of GHGs will cause some unintended consequences that will need to be overcome. It will eliminate most currently available energy, which will need to be replaced with a new energy system. It will lead to job loss for many fossil fuel–producing and –using workers and potentially to economic devastation of their communities. Forestalling such devastation will require a just transition that provides for the livelihoods of affected workers and communities.* The transition also holds the potential for broad economic disruption that could aggravate the economic problems we already face.* That possibility must be forestalled by macroeconomic policies that ensure prosperity. In short, a strategy for overcoming climate destruction must both eliminate the burning of fossil fuels and provide solutions to the problems that their elimination may cause.*

The common preservation climate action plan includes five key elements:

The first is a transition to an economy that does not release GHGs.* That requires a rapid phaseout of fossil fuels and the labor that produces and uses them. It also requires their replacement by fossil-free energy and energy efficiency.*

The second element is to design climate-protection strategies that create a broad-based social interest in climate protection.* This means protecting the well-being of communities that may be threatened by climate-protection measures. It means guaranteeing economic security and good jobs for all who want them. And it means ensuring that climate protection strategies reduce inequality and injustice so that those who have been marginalized and discriminated against in the past are not excluded from the short-term benefits of climate-protection measures.*

Because ordinary people have been largely excluded from power in the economy and the political system, their ability to combat climate destruction and implement alternatives has been limited. So a third element of the program is to empower ordinary people to protect the earth's climate.* This requires the climate insurgency to develop and impose climate action plans that represent ordinary people's short- and long-term climate interests in every sphere of society from the community to the workplace, from corporations to industries, and in public policy at every level.

Global warming has rightly been called history's greatest market failure. Correcting it cannot be left to the market. Thus, a fourth element of the program is to expand the power of public policy to protect the climate in ways that are in accord with ordinary people's interests. This requires government institutions specifically designed to implement the transition to climate protection. It will need bold economic planning, industrial policies, and public investment to guide and facilitate the process.* It will need full-employment macroeconomic policies that prevent unemployment, assure prosperity, and encourage full use of economic resources during the transition.* And it will need public mobilization and redirection of human and material resources that are required for the transition.*

Finally, global warming requires global cooperation. Governments must work together to create a global framework that supports climate-friendly jobs and development—what has been called a "Global Green New Deal." Workers must cooperate globally to pressure their own and all other governments and corporations to make the transition to climate safety.* A global climate protection investment fund is necessary on a scale that mobilizes all underutilized human and material resources worldwide.* Rather than fighting each other for climate-protecting jobs, workers and communities in different countries need to support national policies and international agreements that encourage countries to cooperate in sharing green technologies and expanding production for climate protection.* Legally binding international agreements must phase out and ban the use of fossil fuels worldwide.*

There is precedent for such a rapid national and international economic transformation in the response to the threat of World War II. As Nazi armies spread devastation across Europe in 1940, United Automobile Workers Union president Walter Reuther proposed a startling plan to retool the Depression-ravaged auto industry to build five hundred warplanes a year. The auto magnates scoffed, but soon a massive mobilization put tens of millions of unemployed and underemployed workers to work producing what the war effort required, while shutting down wasteful and unnecessary production that would impede it. Many countries participated in the mobilization and the products were shared among many more. While there are many differences, climate protection is an emergency that can call forth a comparable effort today.[5]*

Overcoming climate destruction is only one small part of creating a healthy and sustainable life for all. But it can be a critical starting point.* The impact of climate change is universally devastating, creating an urgent global common interest. Climate protection can be the leading edge of a broader shift to common preservation.

Transition to 100 Percent Fossil-Free Energy

Burning fossil fuel is currently disrupting the earth's climate system and if continued will eliminate the conditions that have been essential for human civilization.* Fossil fuel energy, however, is an intrinsic feature of the modern world order, on which nearly all aspects of modern life depend. It is also essential for most of the jobs on which workers depend.

American society has accepted and implicitly advocated the continuation of fossil fuel burning, perhaps modestly reduced by cautious climate policies presumed not to interfere with jobs and economic growth.* A program to end climate destruction and save humanity starts, in contrast, from the commitment to rapidly reduce and ultimately eliminate the burning of fossil fuels—while protecting against possible adverse consequences of doing so.*

Rapidly Eliminate Fossil Fuels

Climate scientists have identified the GHG reductions necessary for the survival of human civilization.* The IPCC famously called for a minimum reduction of 80 percent by 2050 in order to keep global warming below a 2°C increase—a goal agreed to in the Paris climate agreement. Past and present delay further increases the rate at which emissions must be reduced—updated targets are closer to 100 percent by 2030. Global carbon emissions will need to be near zero by around 2050.[6]

Climate scientist James Hansen has identified any level of atmospheric GHGs over 350 ppm as incompatible with human life as we have known it. According to Hansen, to reach 350 ppm by the end of the century, starting from 2012 as a baseline, will require a global reduction of 6 percent per year in fossil fuel emissions, combined with the extraction of one hundred gigatons of carbon dioxide from the atmosphere.[7] The fair share of GHG reduction will be substantially higher for wealthy countries like the United States that have contributed large amounts of GHGs in the past.*

Most climate action plans are not designed to reach such scientific targets. They may list various desirable (and often politically expedient) policies or short-term goals but put off the heavy lifting to the future. Even the US federal climate action plan laid out under President Obama did not claim to lay out a pathway to reducing GHG emissions by 80 percent by 2050.*

A common preservation climate action plan for a fossil-free economy should include frequent interim targets that require steady year-on-year reductions rather than postponing more difficult reductions to the future.[8]* It should provide for a phased development that takes advantage of early opportunities but also lays the groundwork for later programs. And it should provide for course correction along the way. This plan is based on a phaseout of fossil fuel energy rapid enough to meet scientific goals, with a comparably rapid expansion of fossil-free energy to compensate for the loss.

Rapidly Expand Energy Efficiency and Fossil-Free Energy

Simply halting the burning of fossil fuels would lead to immediate national and global catastrophe. The dependence of modern civilization on fossil fuel energy means that the proverbial "freezing to death in the dark" would be the immediate fate of millions or perhaps billions of people.* The fossil fuel industry takes advantage of this basic dependence, as well as its own immense wealth and power, to discourage the implementation of alternative energy sources.* Government climate action plans so far do not lay out a program for a transition to a fossil-free energy system.[9] Markets have significantly failed to invest adequately in energy efficiency and renewable energy, even when it would have been profitable to do so.[10]*

Studies show that replacement of fossil fuel energy by renewable energy and energy efficiency is technically feasible and suggest various pathways to achieve it.[11] This transition can be accomplished through commercially available technologies; moreover rapid expansion of research and markets will likely lead to rapid improvement in technology along the way. The transition can be based on renewable energy technologies that cut the GHGs released by production combined with energy efficiency measures that reduce the amount of energy needed.* It will not require nuclear energy, large-scale modifications of earth systems through geo-engineering, or carbon capture and storage, each of which is likely to be far slower, more costly, and more environmentally dangerous than rapid conversion to renewable energies and energy efficiency. There will be only a small need for natural gas as a transitional fuel.*

The most important areas for transition are electricity, transportation, and buildings. Fossil fuels burned to produce electricity, the largest single emitter of GHGs, can be replaced by wind, solar, and hydro energy sources, smart grids, new energy storage technologies, and increased efficiency. Petroleum-based private transportation can be replaced with cars, trucks, trains, and public transit powered by renewable electricity. Freight transportation can be converted to rail transport and electric vehicles. Virtually all buildings can be made much more efficient through insulation, weatherization, cogeneration, and solar and geo-thermal heating, cooling, and hot water. Many other strategies, ranging from industrial redesign to "smart-growth" integration of urban and transportation planning, and from expanding forests to reducing fossil fuel use and applying carbon-sequestering techniques in farming, will also contribute.* Every workplace, industry, and community will have a role in building a climate-safe economy.

Numerous studies have detailed how this transition can be made. The Labor Network for Sustainability's report, "The Clean Energy Future: Protecting the Climate, Creating Jobs, and Saving Money," for example, shows that the United States can reduce greenhouse gas emissions by 80 percent by 2050 while adding half a million jobs per year and saving Americans billions of dollars on their electrical, heating, and transportation costs.[12]

Ensure That Climate Protection Benefits Workers

Everyone shares a common interest in climate protection. Many workers will find jobs helping protect the climate.* If climate policy produces enough jobs to reduce unemployment, it will benefit nearly all workers. But if fossil fuel use is eliminated, specific groups of workers who extract, process, transport, and use fossil fuels are likely to lose their jobs.* If eliminating fossil fuels leads to unemployment and economic disruption, all workers are likely to suffer.* If established patterns of unequal access to good jobs remain unchanged, workers who are subject to discrimination and exclusion will receive little benefit from climate protection measures.* If the new climate-safe economy replaces good jobs with poor ones, workers who get those jobs will receive little benefit and the conditions of other workers will be subject to downward pressures as well. A common preservation program for climate protection will integrate common needs and the needs of specific groups of workers into a unifying strategy that realizes them all.*

World War II home-front mobilization provides one model, though an imperfect one, for transforming the labor market to meet the needs of climate transition.* The government recruited workers previously outside the workforce, led the training effort, steered the location of employers and workers, and created labor rights and standards that led to the greatest gains in wages, job security, and union representation in American history.* The number of Americans employed outside the military rose by 7.7 million between 1939 and 1944, even while millions more left the civilian labor force for the military. Government boards redirected workers to military production, sometimes by threatening to draft them otherwise.* Women entered the industrial workforce on an unprecedented scale and government provided training for millions of workers.* The National War Labor Board set wages and required employers to bargain collectively with their employees' unions.* Government built housing and provided health care and childcare for war workers.[13] War labor policies were often biased toward business and were frequently challenged by organized labor and wildcat strikes,[14] but there is little question that overall they provided a historic improvement in the power and living standards of American workers.*

A common preservation climate action plan requires changes at least on the scale of World War II economic mobilization, but rather different specific policies. These policies are in line with traditional working-class objectives such as full employment, high minimum standards for wages and working conditions, a skilled and educated workforce, protection for those who lose their jobs, and provision for those who, for whatever reasons, should not be in the workforce.*

Protect Those Who May Be Threatened by Climate Policies

Workers and their communities largely depend for their livelihoods on jobs that produce and use fossil fuel energy. While climate protection will produce far more jobs than it eliminates, it may also threaten the jobs of some workers in fossil fuel producing and using industries. It is unjust that any worker should suffer through no fault of their own because of a policy that is necessary to protect society. A common preservation climate program must create alternative jobs or livelihoods or be responsible for mass unemployment—and a resulting rebellion against climate protection.*

Adequate climate action plans must provide a just transition for workers and communities that may otherwise be negatively affected. This must include requirements that employers retrain and find jobs for those affected, give them priority for new jobs, provide economic benefits that allow not only a decent livelihood but a start on a new life, ensure decent retirement benefits for those who choose it, and invest in local communities to provide them a future beyond fossil fuels.[15]*

While programs such as the Trade Adjustment Assistance (TAA) have often been inadequate at best, there are examples of transition programs that work. From 1994 to 2004, for instance, the US Department of Energy conducted a Worker and Community Transition Program that provided grants and other assistance for communities affected by shutdown of nuclear facilities. A nuclear test site in Nevada, for example, was repurposed to demonstrate concentrated solar power technologies.*

Alternative jobs can be provided not only in clean energy but also in other work the public needs; they should be provided not only where existing jobs are lost but also where potential fossil fuel jobs are not created because of climate protection policies. For example, a Labor Network for Sustainability study, "The Keystone Pipeline Debate: An Alternative Job Creation Strategy," laid out how more jobs could be created for pipeline workers by renewing water and other pipeline infrastructure than by building the Keystone XL pipeline for tar sands oil.[16]*

Guarantee Economic Security and Jobs for All Who Want Them

Climate protection will create millions of new jobs. It will also require the recruitment, training, and deployment of tens of thousands of workers. A common preservation climate action plan should be designed to provide the maximum number of good, secure, permanent jobs with education, training, and advancement.*

Studies such as the Labor Network for Sustainability's "The Clean Energy Future" show that renewable energy and energy efficiency can potentially produce substantially more jobs than fossil fuels. They could contribute to job growth in manufacturing, construction, operations, and maintenance. Nonetheless, climate protection is unlikely in itself to fully eliminate unemployment.*

To counter the insecurity of working-class life in general and the specific fear that climate protection may lead to job loss, climate protection policies need to incorporate the principle of a job for everyone who wants one.* The frontline of establishing full employment can be the expansion of jobs that support climate protection. Keynesian macro-economic full-employment policies are necessary both to ensure jobs for all who want them, and to mobilize the productive capacity needed to build a climate-safe society.* Where other policies have not led to full employment, government should serve as the employer of last resort for all who want to work, putting them to work on climate protection and other socially needed activities.[17] Such a program should be combined with a "Nordic-style" welfare system that provides income support for the unemployed close to that of employed workers, combined with job training, regional economic development, and other strong support for reemployment.[18]*

Use Climate Transition to Remedy Inequality and Injustice

The power of those affected by climate destruction is weakened because working people and society are divided by inequalities and division along race, ethnic, gender, and other lines. Therefore challenging such unjust divisions is not only right in itself; it is necessary for developing the power to overcome climate destruction.*

Most climate action plans take for granted existing injustices and inequalities. Climate protection can serve as a means to counter inequality and social injustice, but it will require deliberate policies to do so. A common preservation climate action plan can serve as a vehicle to move toward a more just and equal society.*

Full employment and good, stable jobs that protect the climate provide part of the basis for this transition. Yet specific policies are needed to provide a jobs pipeline for those individuals and groups who have been denied equal access to good jobs. And climate action plans need to be designed to remedy the concentration of pollution in marginalized and low-income communities, the lack of transportation, education, health, and other facilities in poor neighborhoods, and the many other results of past discrimination.*

Not only are jobs and unemployment distributed very unevenly among different groups and localities, so are job skills and experience. Climate-protection jobs require a wide range of skills, from the most highly technical to just having the ability to show up for the job and follow instructions. While this makes it possible to provide jobs for a wide range of workers, it also has the danger of providing only low-quality dead-end jobs for those who are already most economically deprived.*

Worker recruitment needs to include strong racial, gender, age, and locational affirmative action to counter our current employment inequalities. Climate protection needs to make use of workers' existing skills while at the same time developing new ones that reduce these inequalities. Programs need to provide job ladders within and across employers lest those who currently face only dead-end jobs continue to face only dead-end jobs in the post–fossil fuel economy.*

Ensure Quality of Climate Protection Jobs

Climate protection will inevitably provide jobs. But can it provide good jobs?

For several decades, the tendency of the US economy has been toward insecure, contingent work, often with low wages and few health insurance, pension, or other benefits. "Green jobs" can similarly provide low wages, health and safety hazards, and gross violation of labor rights. Climate protection will therefore require deliberate policies to raise wages and increase job security, especially for those at the lower end of the labor market, to counter that tendency.*

A common preservation climate action plan should ensure sustained, orderly development of the work sectors where climate protection jobs are concentrated.[19] This requires planning for technical and physical development and for financing. It needs to support socially responsible, high-wage "high-road" employers, prevailing wage provisions like those required by the Davis-Bacon Act, and project labor agreements negotiated between unions and employers to ensure that climate-protection jobs elevate rather than depress wages and working conditions.[20]*

The deterioration in quality of jobs is directly related to the reduction in the size and bargaining power of labor unions. Reinforcing the rights of workers to express themselves freely, organize, bargain collectively, and engage in concerted action on the job should be an explicit part of public policy for the climate-protection sector, as it was for war industries during mobilization for World War II. Workers should be the ones to decide whether or not they want union representation; employers in the climate sector should be required to sign and abide by neutrality agreements.*

Protect the Climate from Below

Climate protection requires the devolution of power both upward and downward. The downward devolution means that ordinary people will move into spheres of decision-making from which they have largely been excluded.[21]* One way to accomplish this is through alliances of workers and communities intervening in the decisions of the institutions that directly affect them.[22]* Alliances are often facilitated when boundaries are weak, for example when workers and community members are the same people in different roles.*

Promote Community-Worker Climate Action Plans

The US federal government, many cities and states, and many corporations, universities, and other institutions have climate action plans, some of them in place for decades. But, so far, they rarely lay out a pathway to a fossil fuel–free energy system. Often targets are inadequate; they don't include policies that will actually meet those targets; they don't provide good or steady jobs; they perpetuate prevailing patterns of inequality and injustice; and they function as window dressing rather than the actual basis of public policy.*

A community-worker climate action program must instead seek effective means to rapidly reduce and ultimately eliminate GHG emissions. Some policies that could be incorporated into such plans are outlined throughout this chapter.

Many climate action plans are not really intended to be implemented—as revealed by their lack of concrete programs to implement goals, the infrequency of serious efforts to implement them, and the massive resistance that arises when serious efforts are made to implement them.* Climate-protection policies are regularly overridden by other official policies and concerns, such as fiscal needs, energy policies, and transportation objectives. They are also overridden by the ability of private interests to disregard them—or to shape public policy in their own interest.* Rather than window dressing, community-worker climate action plans must become a bedrock of public policy, around which other policies are shaped to achieve the many objectives that society pursues for its members' well-being.

Empower Labor and Communities Locally

Today a large swath of community-based, local, and regional programs are already engaged in promoting the transition to a climate-safe economy and society. Even in a government-led transition, they can on their own initiative implement community-based renewable energy such as rooftop solar collectors, energy-use-reduction measures such as residential weatherization, financial mobilization through community investment funds, and new patterns of consumption such as shared bicycles. Perhaps most importantly, they can provide both popular participation in the transition to climate protection and a means to hold the institutions of transition accountable.*

Climate-protection programs can counter inequalities in local economies.* They can require contractors to hire from the local community.[23]* They can also use climate protection policies to encourage broad-based local ownership through locally owned small businesses, cooperatives, and public enterprises.* Such enterprises can provide needed jobs and services while helping stabilize vulnerable community economies, protecting them from the unpredictable fluctuations of uncontrollable outside forces.*

Empower Workers and Communities in the Workplace

Workers and workplaces do not exist as a separate sphere; they are embedded in communities and more broadly in the institutions of civil society.* Workers are organized in central labor councils based in cities, regions, and states. They can help form broad coalitions to enforce climate protection in communities, with leadership and support from civil society institutions such as schools and religious congregations.

Through these coalitions, workers and allies can establish climate action plans at the community level and ensure that they are adequate to achieve scientific targets and friendly to worker and allied constituencies. They can pressure local governments and institutions to shape such plans in ways that counter inequality and provide pathways to justice and employment for marginalized and discriminated-against groups. Where there is resistance to the necessary reduction in fossil fuel emissions and the infrastructure that supports it, the climate insurgency can if necessary engage in direct action and civil disobedience designed to mobilize public action to force compliance.*

Many workplaces already have their own climate action plans. Where they do not, workers and communities can demand that they be established. Where that demand is resisted, workers and communities can draft their own climate action plans, demand negotiations over them, and start implementing them on their own where they can.*

Workers are the eyes and ears of their communities, the country, and humanity inside the workplace. Workers and communities have a right to know about the GHG pollution produced in their workplaces and the materials they use and produce, the right to monitor implementation of climate action plans, and the right to blow the whistle on environmental abuses. Where workers are not accorded these rights, they have an obligation to protect the public through whistleblowing and direct action, for example through "green bans" that authorize workers to refuse climate-destroying labor.*

Ultimately, public policy should mandate climate action plans in every workplace with a role for workers and communities in designing and implementing them.* It should authorize workers to serve as an independent check on what is really going on inside their workplace.*

Such a role requires workers and communities to act on behalf of society as a whole, rather than exclusively for the narrow interests of particular groups—indeed, this is the justification for providing them such authority.* It challenges "management's right to manage"—a doctrine currently asserted by the courts and generally accepted by unions.* It inserts workers and communities into the planning process that determines the purposes and methods of production and investment.* It thereby challenges the bundle of property rights as currently defined.*

Empower Workers and Communities in Corporations

The strategic decisions affecting GHG emissions are generally made not in the local workplace but at the level of the corporation.* Most large corporations already have some kind of climate action plan for the corporation as a whole—and those that don't can be pushed to establish them. Currently, such plans vary from serious efforts to reduce emissions to fig-leaf programs whose purpose is not climate protection but public relations. Workers and communities can demand that corporate climate action plans achieve science-based targets. They can demand that workers be protected from adverse side effects of corporate climate action, for example through contract clauses that ensure that climate policy will not be used as an excuse to lay off workers or increase their workload. They can demand the right to monitor implementation of workplace climate action plans and to blow the whistle on environmental abuses.*

At the same time, workers and communities can participate constructively in employer climate protection efforts. They can negotiate over climate action plans and their implementation. In many instances, this will require new negotiating structures that involve community groups and the many different unions that typically represent workers in any corporation, as well as the large proportion of workers who lack union representation.* In the case of international corporations, some form of "international framework agreement" may be the appropriate vehicle for negotiations.[24] Workers can promote new climate protection goods and services or even present an alternative vision for their company's future.*

As with workplace initiatives, such actions challenge "management's right to manage." They can provide a starting point for participating in company planning more generally. They can also help initiate new systems of corporate governance, accountability, and reporting that are necessary to represent the interests of a wider range of stakeholders and to require corporations to act in line with environmental, economic, and social sustainability.[25]*

Empower Workers and Communities in Industries

A fossil-free economy will require transformation not just of individual workplaces and companies, nor just of the economy as a whole, but of specific industries and economic sectors.* Industry-wide planning is necessary to capture synergies and economies of scale, establish level playing fields, and ensure that different parts of an emerging climate protection system work together—large-scale, long-term necessities that cannot be provided by the market.* Here, public climate policies, industry-wide collective bargaining, and cooperation among businesses in the same industry need to go hand in hand.

A prime example of such cooperation was the reconstruction of the US auto industry under President Obama's economic recovery plan. Auto corporations, the UAW, and the federal government agreed to a large long-term increase in energy efficiency to cut carbon emissions. This involved cooperative planning for retooling the industry, large-scale federal support for developing new technology, and substantial public investment in modernizing the industry on a lower-carbon basis. The result was a steady decrease in carbon pollution, an increase of jobs for auto workers, and an end to the crisis that threatened to nearly eliminate auto production in the United States.

Electricity provides another case where industry-wide coordination is necessary for successful GHG emission reduction. Energy production and distribution is an integrated system tied together by power lines and other infrastructure into the electric grid. Moving to entirely renewable energy requires a far more sophisticated and decentralized energy system that can integrate everything from rooftop solar installations to massive wind farms. It therefore requires long-term planning and investment; the public sector must provide these if the private sector is unable or unwilling to do so. Unions can be leaders in bringing together the players for such a transformation if they are willing to put the universally shared need to protect the climate front and center in the design of the new energy system.

Transportation similarly requires integrated transformation that includes massive expansion of public transit; reorganization of freight transportation to reduce emissions; conversion to electric, fuel cell, and other low-emissions vehicles; and practical access to walking and biking routes. This requires not just switching from one kind of vehicle to another, but restructuring of metropolitan areas, great expansion of renewable energy, and redesign of freight systems.* The Teamsters union has taken a great leap forward here, advocating for a new intermodal transportation system and trying to draw the other public and private sector players into cooperation around it.*

Finance is a principal means by which resources are allocated to future uses. Financialization has meant that a huge and growing proportion of wealth is invested not to produce needed goods and services, but rather to pursue speculative gains based purely on the fluctuations of markets, especially financial markets themselves.* Downsizing the financial sector and returning it to the role of servant rather than master of the real economy is necessary to provide the resources for climate protection and other social needs and to stop magnifying the economic gyrations driven by a highly speculative economy. This can be achieved by such means as financial reregulation, the imposition of a "Robin Hood" tax on financial transactions, and expansion of public purpose finance.*

Similar programs are necessary for agriculture, forestry, manufacturing, waste management, and many other industries.[26]

Power from Below in the Political Arena

Individual citizens, community groups, and parties and other political organizations all participate in a variety of ways in the political arena. To illustrate how the climate protection movement can affect the political arena, we will take the example of organized labor.*

Organized labor is represented in the political process in the federal government, every state, and every large county and municipality. It participates in political parties, elections, and lobbying. While it rarely has power to govern on its own, it exercises influence over public policy by participating in coalitions and by exercising a leadership role.*

Organized labor and the broader working-class movement can use that power to help write party platforms and select and support candidates who back the worker climate protection agenda. It can lobby legislators and the executive branch to establish or improve—and implement—climate action plans. It can mobilize the public for legislation that implements climate protection. It can participate in lawsuits to force implementation of climate protection policies on public trust, human rights, and other grounds.*

Government employees can play a special role. They have access to information that they can make public either in their official role or as whistleblowers. Those involved in climate protection-related activities and policies are uniquely qualified to speak out to the public—as the union representing US Environmental Protection Agency employees did so powerfully against the Bush administration's gag orders on EPA scientists. They are in a position to develop and present plans for more effective climate protection policies. They can influence elected government officials. And through their collective bargaining with their employers, they can promote worker climate protection policies—and create an avenue for their enforcement.*

Despite these channels for worker influence, the unfortunate reality is that the dominant power over government is currently exercised by corporations and the wealthiest 1 percent. So effective climate protection requires more than just action within the established limits of institutionalized power. It must include a process of democratization that makes it possible for all people to participate on a level political playing field in which the common interests of the majority can determine public policy.* And it must include a climate insurgency that asserts the illegitimacy of existing governments as long as they are complicit in the destruction of the climate on which people and planet depend.*

Protect the Climate from Above

Replacing fossil fuel energy with climate-safe energy requires enormous changes in the economy and society. Effective measures have been blocked by the power of the fossil fuel industry; the inhibitions produced by neoliberal ideology and policy; the weakness and corruption of democratic institutions; and the imperatives of a market that, if it is regulated at all, is regulated in the interest of the fossil fuel industry.* Where they are unable to block climate protection entirely, the fossil fuel industry and its allies have advocated dubious programs such as cap-and-trade and carbon offsets that, with modest exceptions, have failed to reduce GHG emissions.*

There are three main approaches to GHG reduction. The first, which has dominated climate legislation and treaty negotiation, consists of "putting a price on carbon emissions" to discourage GHGs through taxation, fees, cap-and-trade systems with markets for emission quotas, or similar means. The second, which is widely discussed and frequently implemented on a small scale, consists of local, often community-based initiatives designed to produce renewable energy and reduce energy consumption on a decentralized basis. The third, perhaps less often delineated by proponents than excoriated by opponents, consists of a government-led approach based on economic planning, public investment, resource mobilization, and direct government intervention in economic decisions.* Rapid reduction of GHG emissions will undoubtedly require all three.*

Establish Government Agencies to Implement the Transition

Mobilization for climate protection is an emergency that, like mobilization for World War II, requires powerful governmental agencies dedicated to the purpose that can plan and implement the transition to a climate-safe economy. This will require transcending the shibboleths of neoliberalism.*

Such institutions will need to establish financial incentives and disincentives; raise capital; implement labor force strategies; organize funding for infrastructure such as railways and transmission lines; fund research and development; set and monitor energy efficiency standards for buildings, appliances, and equipment; train and retrain workers and professionals; and set industrial location policies.* Further, they will need to coordinate the multifaceted activities of federal agencies, state and municipal governments, corporations, and civil society groups.*

Such coordination, as during World War II, will require a central governmental authority.* Yet because of the extended period of transition, measures are necessary to prevent such an authority from pursuing its own aggrandizement or that of other social forces.* We don't need another body like the Pentagon or the National Security Agency provided with vast powers and resources but no genuine accountability.

One proposed solution is to create two independent agencies.[27] The first, following the general model of the War Production Board, would have overall responsibility for GHG reduction. Such a climate mobilization authority would conduct technical requirement studies, set and enforce production goals, institute efficient contracting procedures, cut through inertia and bureaucratic red tape, and serve as the coordinating agency for all transition activities. The second agency, independent of the executive branch and above the climate mobilization authority, would report to Congress and the public. It would define GHG reduction targets and timetables, lay out a national climate action plan, ensure transparency in the climate mobilization authority, identify problems and failures, and initiate course corrections.*

Use Economic Planning, Industrial Policy, and Macroeconomics to Guide the Transition

The British government's *Stern Review* in 2006 called climate change the "greatest market failure in history."* While market mechanisms should be used where they have proven effective, public authority, planning, and investment are necessary where they haven't. A common preservation climate action program will rely on public planning and investment to provide a planned, orderly, sustainable transition to a climate-safe economy.*

If America's economic mobilization for World War II had been left to the market, it is doubtful that Detroit's auto production would have been shut down to allow more production of airplanes or that a company like Hamilton Propellers would have increased its output to sixty times over prewar levels. While markets were not eliminated during the war, war production required that public authorities take responsibility for critical decisions previously left to the market.* If today's climate emergency is to be effectively met, where the market cannot or will not do the job, government and citizens must similarly step in to ensure that the job gets done.*

Climate protection requires the capacity to make long-range plans that affect many aspects of life. Governing climate protection is in some ways similar to governing the nation's transportation system. It requires making decisions, such as whether to build highways or railways, that will shape the life of the country for decades to come. It requires the technical capacity to design and engineer such complex systems. It requires taking into account a wide range of economic, environmental, and social factors—and maximizing beneficial side effects while minimizing undesirable ones.*

Government will have to map out what is needed to realize climate action plans, lay out the sequence of economic development, find sources of funding, identify and eliminate bottlenecks, help develop public or private enterprises that will do what is needed, keep the production pipeline full to provide stable demand and employment, and step in to meet needs that the private economy is not addressing. Some of this can be done by expanding the role of existing agencies; some may require new, nonmarket institutions such as public purpose nonprofit developers and financial institutions, part of whose mission is to provide stable jobs for local workers and communities.

Planning will be necessary to ensure that climate protection produces not just a flurry of economic activity, but rather a stable growing sector that provides steady jobs and advancement for hundreds of thousands of workers. It must involve planning for the transition to climate protection as a whole, not just be a collection of separate programs. For example, expansion of energy efficiency and fossil fuel–free energy are interdependent and must go hand in hand, with planned sequencing of the entire transition. Similarly, expansion of manufacturing for climate protection will need to be coordinated with the installation of the products.

The Obama administration's Clean Power Plan, despite its inadequacies and ambiguities, required states and corporations to make defined GHG emission reductions on a legally enforceable schedule. While it gave them great flexibility in how to do so, it did not allow them to evade targets by falsely claiming that ineffectual incentives would realize them. It required them to plan, invest, and disinvest to meet a compulsory emission reduction schedule. Auto companies were led to cooperate with the Obama administration's plan for emission reduction as part of the reconstruction of the auto industry because their survival depended on the plan's massive public investment in the auto industry.* Where necessary, such compulsory planning and implementation should be included in all climate action plans.

While neoliberalism has condemned Keynesian macroeconomic policies designed to provide full employment, the abandonment of such regulation of the economy as a whole led to the deepest economic crisis since the Great Depression and an ongoing aftermath of income polarization and impoverishment. In such a context, rapid transition to climate safety carries the risk of broad economic disruption. That possibility must be forestalled by macroeconomic policies that ensure full employment.* Such policies, implemented in the context of the transition to climate protection, will reduce the fear that climate protection may threaten prosperity, and give ordinary people a greater stake in the transition.

Acquire the Resources for Climate Transition

The principal elements of a new, climate-safe economy are energy efficiency, reduction in energy use, and low-GHG renewable energy. All of these are cost-efficient—in the long run, they will be cheaper and provide more benefits than the fossil fuels they replace. The Labor Network for Sustainability report, "The Clean Energy Future," shows a pathway for meeting climate protection goals that will simultaneously create more jobs and save money, and reduce the cost of electricity, heating, and transportation by $78 billion compared to current projections from now through 2050. In the long run, climate protection pays for itself.

Climate protection will inevitably have some start-up costs, however, so investments have to be made in order to realize its benefits. The payback period is far shorter than many other investments, providing a high rate of return on investment. Nonetheless, markets have failed to make adequate investment in renewable energy and increased energy efficiency, even where it would have been profitable to do so.[28] If the market won't pay for climate protection, how can it be paid for?

Public borrowing through bond sales can provide substantial and inexpensive funds due to the ability of the Federal Reserve to buy public infrastructure bonds at low rates. Public purpose banks, credit unions, and investment and loan funds can provide more decentralized financial resources, especially for smaller-scale and community-based projects. If need be, the Federal Reserve can simply buy infrastructure bonds, just as it did with Treasury securities in 1940 to finance the war effort.*

A tax on fossil fuel extraction or GHG emissions or a "cap-and-dividend" program can provide market incentives that complement more direct climate protection measures. Progressive taxation, particularly on carbon-wasting luxury goods such as private jets, can counteract any negative effects on income equality. Such devices as energy pricing incentives, user fees, and on-bill financing (which allows energy consumers to pay for energy-saving investments out of the resulting savings on their energy bills) can also play a role.*

Thousands of individuals and institutions have joined the fossil fuel "divest-invest" movement, modeled on the highly successful movement to disinvest from apartheid South Africa. Religious organizations, unions, municipalities, foundations, and many other institutions are withdrawing their investments from fossil fuel companies; pledges to divest are now in the trillions of dollars. But strategies to invest the freed-up money in climate protection have only just begun. Federal and state governments should take the lead by divesting from all fossil fuel investments and creating revolving funds for the transition to a climate-safe economy. They should then lead a campaign for all individuals, institutions, and businesses to divest from fossil fuels and invest the proceeds in the revolving funds.*

Municipal governments and institutions such as universities, museums, churches, and schools are important economic actors. They should make reducing their GHG emissions their first investment prior-ity. They can invest in fossil fuel reduction programs in their neighbor-hoods and communities and use the resulting savings for their insti-tutional and community climate protection initiatives. They can serve as "anchor institutions" for the transformation of their surrounding communities, using their purchasing power to support and encourage local economic development.

Another potential source for funding the transition to climate safety could be legal damages and fines collected from corporations for envi-ronmentally harmful practices. Governments may take legal action to recover "natural resource damages"—as seen in the settlements for the 1989 Exxon Valdez and 2010 BP oil spills, for example. The Comprehensive Environmental Response, Compensation, and Liability Act (CERCLA) enacted in 1980, known as the "Superfund" law, provides broad federal authority to clean up hazardous substance releases and authorizes the US Environmental Protection Agency to compel the parties responsible to pay for the cleanup—even if the releases happened long before the legislation was passed. Comparable legislation could hold major fossil fuel producers and emitters responsible for their colossal damage to the earth's climate—and the colossal cost of remediating it.[29]*

Protect the Climate and Promote Jobs Globally

Overcoming climate destruction is a global task.* It requires eliminating GHG emissions and providing secure livelihoods for all. This ultimately requires binding international agreements that outlaw GHG emissions and provide the international basis for a just global economy.* Climate protection need not wait for such agreements, however. International cooperation can start on an ad hoc basis long before it is institutional-ized in international agreements.*And international agreements will be far more effective in the context of established local and national climate protection measures.

Global climate protection can serve as the starting point for chal-lenging other disastrous consequences of neoliberalism and unregu-lated globalization.* It can promote an alternative pattern for the global economy. It can replace ever-growing inequality and the downward leveling of labor and environmental conditions with a new economic pattern that protects the earth's climate while creating jobs and improv-ing livelihoods for workers and the poor.[30]* It can replace trade wars over climate-protecting goods and services with cooperative, mutually managed trade with the purpose of rapidly increased production of GHG-reducing goods and services and new jobs.*

Develop a "Global Green New Deal"

A solution to both the climate and jobs problems requires that the world abandon neoliberalism and adopt a new strategy that puts the world's human resources to work meeting the world's urgent need for economic transformation that radically reduces GHG emissions. A decade before the emergence of the Green New Deal as a popular national program, such a global regime was widely advocated as a "Global Green New Deal."[31]*

In the depths of the Great Depression, US President Franklin D. Roosevelt launched the New Deal—a set of government programs to provide employment and social security, reform tax policies and business practices, and stimulate the economy, as well as establish environmental programs such as reforestation and soil conservation. It included the building of homes, hospitals, school, roads, dams, and electrical grids. The New Deal put millions of people to work and created a new policy framework for American democracy.

In response to the Great Recession and the climate crisis, unions from around the world, represented by the International Trade Union Confederation, partnered with the United Nations Environment Programme to promote a Global Green New Deal as a solution to both crises.[32]* UN Secretary-General Ban Ki-moon said the financial crisis required massive global stimulus, and called for "an investment that fights climate change, creates millions of green jobs and spurs green growth."* What the world needs, in short, is a "Global Green New Deal."

The imagery of the New Deal evoked opposition to laissez-faire capitalism and a call for government leadership and investment.* For a brief period, many countries in fact launched initiatives that resembled a Green New Deal. Meanwhile, the International Monetary Fund (IMF) called for trillions of dollars of deficit spending, and governments around the world did in fact provide trillions of dollars of budgetary economic stimulus, although much of it went for bailouts to banks and financial institutions rather than job creation or climate protection.

Once the most acute phase of the financial crisis was over, however, global economic policy rapidly shifted to extreme austerity and, in the aftermath of the Copenhagen summit fiasco, largely abandoned climate protection programs. The result was a decade of mass unemployment, burgeoning inequality, unending debt crises, and ever-mounting GHG emissions.

The idea of a Global Green New Deal expresses the interests of people worldwide for full employment through climate protection. It represents a program that can unify climate protection and antiausterity forces in all countries and provide an alternative to the failures of neoliberalism.[*]

Establish a Global Fund to Mobilize Underutilized Resources for Climate Protection

According to the International Labor Organization (ILO), 192 million workers were unemployed worldwide in 2018.[33] Trillions of dollars of unspent cash sits in the accounts of large enterprises.[*] A common preservation climate action plan should include a global trust fund designed to mobilize global human, financial, and material resources for job-creating climate protection.[34]

How large should such a fund be? At least large enough to mobilize all unused and underused human and material resources that can help the transition to a climate-safe world. A study sponsored by the World Economic Forum evaluated how much global investment is needed for "clean-energy infrastructure, sustainable and low-carbon transport, energy efficiency in buildings and industry, and for forestry" to limit the global average temperature increase to 2°C above preindustrial levels.[35] It found that at least $0.7 trillion needs to be invested annually beyond current levels. Therefore, between 1 and 2 percent per year of global GDP needs to be invested effectively in climate protection worldwide.[*]

Where can the money come from? As with funding for national programs, global funding can come from taxing, borrowing, recovery of damages, and mobilizing unused resources through global fiscal policies. Taxes should include a tax on carbon emissions and a "Robin Hood" tax on financial transactions. Global fiscal policy should include the use of IMF Special Drawing Rights or other forms of "paper gold."[36*] Such a fund can be the starting point for global macroeconomic policies designed to counter inadequate and fluctuating global economic demand and the "race to the bottom" of unregulated global competition.[*]

Mutually Manage Trade in Climate-Protecting Goods and Services

Globalization and neoliberal trade regimes have pitted workers and communities around the world against each other in a fight for climate-protecting jobs. For example, China is allocating massive public resources to developing a "green energy economy." Chinese export of "green" products, while reducing costs for solar and wind installation industries in the US, is outcompeting American solar and wind manufacturers. In response, US labor and others have advocated punishing China under WTO rules—for making climate protection more affordable!*

A climate protection movement cannot support a policy that pits workers against workers and discourages the growth of climate-protecting industries and jobs. It should oppose both escalating trade wars and the free trade utopia of neoliberalism. Instead, it should advocate a strategy of mutually managed trade that encourages all countries to develop their climate protection industries and technologies as rapidly as possible, while sharing the benefits in a way that protects workers in both developing and developed countries—not to mention the planet as a whole.* Far from discouraging government subsidies for climate protection jobs, public policy should encourage all countries to compete to see who can provide them the most effective subsidies.*

Unions should cooperate globally to propose their own rules for trade in climate-protecting goods and services that will provide an alternative to both free trade and protectionism.* The purpose of such agreements is to create jobs for all by accelerating production of climate-protecting goods and services. Such agreements could also promote technology sharing, to help reduce the cost and expand the market for climate-protecting goods and services. Such agreements could revise, override, or carve out an exception to WTO rules for climate-protecting trade.* Cooperation could start on a bilateral basis—for example, between the US and China—but should expand into a global regime for promoting the climate protection economy.* Such agreements could be the beginning of an alternative to WTO-style profit-driven globalization.*

Legally Ban Fossil Fuels Worldwide

Humanity will not be safe until binding, enforceable global agreements require the rapid reduction of GHG emissions to zero.* Global climate negotiations have failed to reach such an agreement. Such an agreement most likely will be achieved when it embodies changes that already have been fought for, won public support, and been at least partially realized at the local and national levels. The struggle to eliminate fossil fuels locally and nationally can lay the basis for doing so globally.*

The abolition of slavery—perhaps the greatest struggle for labor and human rights of all time—took more than a century. It was conducted simultaneously by an international abolitionist movement, local and national movements within each country, and the victims of slavery themselves. Abolition was pursued by both legal and extraconstitutional means. Slavery was abolished country by country and empire by empire. It was ultimately outlawed globally (though not fully eliminated) in 1948 by Article 4 of the UN's Universal Declaration of Human Rights.*

The abolition of climate destruction is a task of a similar magnitude—and similarly one that is difficult though not impossible. But it must be accomplished in less than half the time.*

Conclusion to Part 3

The common preservation heuristic was developed to help understand social problems and construct solutions to them. It uses a historical and developmental method to interpret the past and evaluate its implications for future action. It is used in part 3 to provide a plausible strategy for correcting climate change through common preservation.

The heuristic starts by identifying a problem or gap and the conditions that a solution to it would have to meet. "Climate Protection as Common Preservation" uses the heuristic to identify the problem of climate change and to make a preliminary plan or outline of how common preservation might go about solving it. The heuristic suggests patterns that have solved similar problems and might be applied to this one. In the case of climate change, we can learn from other problems where common interests were ultimately realized by common preservation.

If a problem has not yielded a solution, it is likely to be because there are obstacles to solving it. Identifying these obstacles is an important step in solving the problem. "The World Order of Climate Destruction" uses the heuristic to identify the basic social patterns that have prevented an effective response to climate change. These include such features of our world order as nation-states, property relations, markets, and fossil fuels. It uses the heuristic to show how each of these, and the world order they form, has impeded efforts to prevent human self-destruction through destruction of the climate.

To understand why the solving of problems has failed, it is necessary to construct a historical account of efforts to solve them and the process of their failure. "Official Climate Protection from Rio to Paris" uses the heuristic to construct a historical narrative that explains the successes and failures of climate protection efforts.

The emergence of new common preservations requires a process of self-organization. In the case of the climate movement, this took place most dramatically with the "self-assembly" of the global climate action network 350.org. "Development of the Climate Movement: Self-Organization" uses the heuristic to give an account of the construction of this new social movement.

A movement may emerge, but to contribute to common preservation it must develop effective ways to act. In so doing, it also changes itself. "Development of the Climate Movement: Countering Power" uses the heuristic to probe the self-transformation of the climate movement through its shift from lobbying and legislation to direct action and civil disobedience.

The construction of a strategy for solving a social problem is also a historical and developmental process. "The Ecological Shot Heard Round the World" initiates an account of my personal effort to use the heuristic to develop a more adequate strategy for climate protection. It provides the backstory of the proposal for a climate insurgency.

The world order that blocks solutions to climate change is supported by the general acceptance of existing governments as legitimate authority—an acceptance based on their claim to the consent of their people. But in fact those governments and the nation-state system they compose threaten the very existence of the people they claim to represent, something to which those people would never knowingly and freely consent. This creates a gap between governments' claim to authority and the constitutional principles they maintain justify it. "The Public Trust and the Constitutional Right to a Stable Climate" describes the identification of this gap, and the challenges to climate destruction have been brought in the courts and in the streets based on constitutional rights and dereliction of government duties.

Over the past quarter century I have used the common preservation heuristic to develop a climate protection strategy based on a global climate movement that refuses to accept the legitimacy of the states that are aiding and abetting the destruction of the earth's climate. "A Global Nonviolent Constitutional Insurgency" describes the development of this idea and some of the ways the heuristic was used to construct it. That illustrates more generally how to use the heuristic to construct strategies for social change.

A strategy for common preservation must draw people together to form a collective entity capable of acting. But it must also identify the changes in society that are necessary to solve its problems and realize its goals. "A Common Preservation Program for Climate Protection" exemplifies how to use the heuristic to develop a program for such a transformation.

Conclusion: The Future of Common Preservation

I told you that to tell you this:

We know that our species is engaged in an escalating mutual destruction whose limits are unknown. We know that we are powerfully driven by the instinct for self-preservation. We know that today self-preservation can only be realized through common preservation. We know from history that human beings are capable of developing new forms of common preservation. We know, however, that people are also capable of pursuing self-aggrandizement rather than common preservation even though it means their own mutual destruction.

This book is my attempt to throw a tiny weight on the balance between common preservation and mutual destruction. It tries to show that shifts to common preservation are possible; that they actually happen; and that human individuals and groups can encourage them. It provides a heuristic to help us do so in concrete situations—such as the process of mutual destruction in which we are now enmeshed.

There is no trial-and-error learning without error. But the error we are now making is irreversible and threatens to put an end to all learning, at least by humans. We need to take the feedback from our mutual destruction as a signal to halt our current course and construct a new one. I hope this book will help us figure out how to do so.

Today the veneer of a rational world order has been stripped off, leaving little but a chaotic war of all against all. The most plausible path I can see to restoring some kind of rationality for humanity is unification around the common interest in limiting climate change and other mutual destruction. We need to form a collective subject for common preservation—a Common Preservation Movement.

Today competing power centers struggle to increase their own power vis-à-vis each other and those they dominate. The result is mutual destruction that threatens our well-being and even survival. But as living beings and even more as human beings we have the capability to change the patterns that guide our actions. Indeed, human and other living beings have always had to change in order to survive.

The common threat we face creates a common interest. Individuals and groups can now provide a secure future for ourselves and our descendants only by providing a secure future for each other—and for our species as a whole.

As the record of past extinctions of species and of human groups shows, successful adaptation is not inevitable. Whether we transform our ways of acting in order to preserve our future life does not depend on anyone but ourselves.

You and I are engaging with others in our own mutual destruction. Even if we want, we can't as individuals stop doing so. That requires new patterns of common preservation.

We can respond to our self-inflicted doom with denial or despair. Or we can try common preservation.

New patterns of common preservation are necessary, but are they possible? The answer is, people create them every day and have done so throughout human history. And what happens is possible.

If we human beings were mechanical products of our genes or our environment, such a transformation would hardly be possible. But we are actors, counter-actors, adaptors, transformers, creators, problem solvers, self-correctors—in short, equilibrators. We apply our patterns to reshape the world; we also reshape our patterns so as to better reshape the world.

In the face of what seem like overwhelming forces and a cruel fate it is easy to despair. But we are not helpless. We are acted on by our world, but we can also act on it.

We may seem to be in the hands of blind forces that are hurtling us toward destruction. But we don't have to act blindly without regard to the consequences of our action. For we are not blind. We have the capacity to observe the consequences of our action, to evaluate them, and to modify the way we act in the future. Call it learning or call it a feedback loop, it means that we are not forced to keep being the same broken record. We can equilibrate and reequilibrate our action.

Nor are we restricted to learning by trial and error. We can represent our world and ourselves in our minds and conduct thought experiments on those representations. And through language we can share our knowledge and our thinking, make common plans and decisions, and guide our action jointly. We can think about things in new ways. We can equilibrate our thinking.

Our current life strategies are leading to our mutual destruction. But we can recognize the danger and we can equilibrate our strategies. If our way of making things is producing devastating climate change, we can modify the way we make things. If our way of governing ourselves threatens to unleash nuclear holocaust, we can change the way we govern ourselves. Our strategies are, after all, nothing but what we make them.

It's true that we are divided into many often-conflicting groups separated by boundaries that impede our ability to cooperate in our common interests. But we are not—either as individuals or as groups—closed systems. "No man is an island, entire unto himself." We survive only through our relations with the world and with each other. Our groups are not entirely sealed off from each other, but mingle and intersect and overlap. People are continually equilibrating the relations among their groups to bring their relations closer to their needs. We can modify our groups and construct new ones that allow us to connect and cooperate to forestall our mutual destruction and realize our common preservation.

We all have goals that at times are stumbling blocks to common preservation. They can often discourage us from pursuing common interests and make us believe that others will never join in doing so. To work together we don't have to entirely abandon our individual and particular goals. But we do have to recognize that none of them can now be realized unless we subordinate them to the goal of common preservation. We have to reequilibrate our goals, rearrange their priorities, and reconsider what is really most important to us.

We see individuals and groups pursuing their own ends without coordination and often in conflict. We see the results of their lack of coordination in unintended side effects like global warming and interaction effects like military arms races and economic races to the bottom. But we have the capacity to overcome this disorder by equilibrating our coordination. We can mutually assimilate each other's patterns and mutually accommodate them to each other to achieve our common ends.

We face powerful people and institutions some of which, some of the time, will refuse to do what is necessary for our common survival. But their domination depends on the cooperation and acquiescence of those who obey their authority. If enough of us choose to, we have the means to overcome their power by ending our obedience.

As individuals we cannot overcome either disorder or domination. That is why solving our problems requires a process of mutually developing new common preservations.

Our new common preservations can liberate us from disorders and dominations. But they can also sow the seeds of new disorders and dominations. To forestall that possibility, we must ensure that the new patterns of common preservation we construct provide for ongoing reequilibration to nurture coordination and limit the concentration of power. To do so we can make use of network forms of coordination through which we mutually share information, planning, and the guidance of action to realize our goals without giving up our own capacity to act.

The task we have to accomplish is unprecedented. But the means we need to accomplish it are proven and at hand. We need to address each other as equilibrators: as people who, through our mutual interaction, have the capacity to create new patterns of common preservation that can halt our course toward mutual destruction. We need to use our capacity for equilibration to identify how our strategies are going wrong, propose corrections to each other, test them out, evaluate the results, and test again.

The poet William Blake instructed us to water the Tree of Life, which can penetrate the "stone walls of separation" with a "mingling of soft fibres of tender affection."[1] In his vision of Jerusalem, a community transcending the inhumanity of his day, he prophesied,

> Mutual shall build Jerusalem
> Both heart in heart and hand in hand.[2]

A transformation from mutual destruction to common preservation is possible, for we equilibrators have the capacity to transform our own patterns. But that transformation is anything but inevitable. It depends on what we people, we equilibrators, choose to do. To paraphrase Dr. Martin Luther King Jr., we can live together as brothers and sisters or we can perish together as fools.

Commentaries for Part 3

CHAPTER 32 Climate Protection as Common Preservation

* **It uses the common preservation heuristic . . .** Feedback from failure is often the starting point for new solutions ("Identifying Problems," 130).

* **The scientific confirmation of human-caused global warming** . . . A common preservation heuristic inquiry normally starts from a problem or gap ("Identifying Problems," 130).

* **The consequences could be predicted . . .** A feedback loop may be incomplete or broken, failing to bring the information to the location where the action is controlled ("Identifying Problems," 130.).

* **The human failure to halt climate change . . .** Problems can result from unintended side and interaction effects ("Countering Disorder," 179).

* **It results from an inability . . .** Inability to close a gap is often the result of a failure of coordination ("Transforming Coordination," 163).

* **This paradox is a form of alienation . . .** Unintended consequences represent a form of alienation in which actions achieve something other than the ends intended by the actor ("Transforming Coordination," 163).

* **As we saw in chapter 28 . . .** Even in a system with some self-correcting elements particular counteractions may fail ("Solving Problems," 135.).

* **The solution to climate catastrophe . . .** A gap can be overcome by combining actors that together can counteract the gap in a way that they could not do independently ("Solving Problems," 135).

* **Producing that change . . .** Changing relations among people is tantamount to transforming humanity. The boundaries among economic, social, and political life are only relative, with many connections across them; therefore, making changes in one may require making complementary changes in others. ("Transforming Boundaries," 156.)

* **Under such conditions . . .** Failure of existing strategies and recognition that problems are shared and could be better addressed by collective action form the core elements of the pattern of shift to common preservation ("Conclusion to Part 2," 201).

* **As a result, millions of people around the world . . .** The emergence of new common preservations can be an uneven process of which there are harbingers ("Solving Problems," 135).

* **Despite the indicators of apocalyptic climate change . . .** The gap between the expectation of a stable climate and the reality of climate change is increasingly recognized but the action taken to correct it is inadequate or even counterproductive ("Transforming Means," 144).

* **Call it self-annihilation . . .** Established patterns—structural barriers—prevent cooperation for common survival and reinforce actions producing self- and mutual destruction ("Transforming Coordination," 163).

* **Part 3 interprets climate destruction . . .** Our interpretation of climate protection uses both concrete historical examples of past actions and patterns from our heuristic that compile features of multiple past actions ("The Tools," 118).

* **It is a story of compensation . . .** New capabilities develop through compensation for error ("Equilibration: The Secret of Development," 81).

CHAPTER 33 The World Order of Climate Destruction

* **This chapter uses the common preservation heuristic . . .** The world order includes systems features that remain stable over time coexisting with features of disorder. To understand it requires disentangling these elements ("Countering Disorder Combined with Domination," 189). We use historical methods to construct an account of the development of the world order ("What Is History?" 29, and "Transforming Representation," 151).

* **The elements of the world order . . .** These patterns are neither nested nor part of a unitary system; rather, their boundaries overlap ("Transforming Boundaries," 156).
* **They have engaged in a mock effort . . .** Strategies can include deception of other actors ("Transforming Representation," 151).
* **States and their leaders . . .** Actors' intentions and strategies need to be interpreted in the context of the various systems in which they are operating ("The Tools," 118).
* **While the nation-state system can seem . . .** This account of the development of nation-states illustrates de-reifying a concept to portray it as a process rather than a thing ("Adventures of the Dialectic," 45).
* **It was a prime example . . .** "The Abolition of Society," 69.
* **The budding capitalists . . .** New coalitions can transform systems ("The Power of the Powerless," 73).
* **It is sometimes known . . .** An increase in domination at a national level was accompanied by an increase of disorder at a global level ("Countering Disorder Combined with Domination," 189).
* **The shift from feudal to national organization . . .** Different elements of the world order, such as political and economic systems, are "open systems" dependent on interchange with their environment ("Open Systems," 64).
* **In the "age of democratic revolutions" . . .** Domination can be transformed by alliances of lower elements in a hierarchical system ("The Power of the Powerless," 73).
* **Nonetheless, states generally continued . . .** The combination of innovation and continuity in the emergence of the democratic state illustrates the reciprocity of continuity and change ("Assimilation and Accommodation: The Secret of Equilibration," 88).
* **Nations were conceived as a people . . .** The reconceptualization of the relation between individuals and nations illustrates the transformation of representations ("Transforming Representation," 151).
* **The purpose of these movements . . .** "Transforming Differentiation," 170.
* **Many states used their political authority . . .** Authority can be extended beyond the purpose of its original grant ("Transforming Coordination," 163).

* **To varying degrees economic coordination . . .** "Transforming Coordination," 163.

* **The product of the nation-state system . . .** These nations engage in both conflict and cooperation ("The Power of the Powerless," 73).

* **The lack of vehicles . . .** National boundaries block decentering and coordination ("Transforming Boundaries," 156).

* **The rights to access a piece of property . . .** Each element of the property rights bundle represents a differentiation ("Transforming Differentiation," 170).

* **Even the most privatized "fee simple" property ownership . . .** The boundaries of property ownership are relative and complex ("Transforming Boundaries," 156).

* **The state, conversely . . .** Dependence can lay the basis for inequality of power ("Transforming Power," 174).

* **Human life depends on the resources . . .** Human beings and humanity as a whole are open systems, dependent on their interchange with their environment ("Open Systems," 64).

* **The illusion of property rights . . .** Changes in social forms and in their representation in thought went hand in hand ("Transforming Representation," 151).

* **Conversely, community rights to glean . . .** Change in relations among classes, like other transformations, need not be symmetrical ("The Power of the Powerless," 73).

* **Property rights change . . .** Property rights may appear to be fixed phenomena but they can be "de-reified" into processes ("Adventures of the Dialectic," 45).

* **Property law evolved . . .** The separation of ownership and management represented a new differentiation ("Transforming Differentiation," 170).

* **Business firms evolved . . .** Coordination of entities and lowering of their boundaries merged them into new, larger entities. This generally needed to be followed by further internal and external reorganization. ("Transforming Boundaries," 156, and "Transforming Coordination," 163.)

* **In the 1930s . . .** Expanded labor rights facilitated workers' collective action that partially transformed their powerlessness ("Transforming Power," 174).

* **By the mid-twentieth century . . .** Through the concentration and centralization of capital domination grew more concentrated ("Countering Domination," 185).

* **Property rights also allow them . . .** Differentiated power over resources provides unequal power over their use ("Transforming Differentiation," 170).

* **In practice, however . . .** The use of the power of law to authorize and protect climate destruction is a form of extended authority ("Transforming Power," 174).

* **Markets are where fossil fuels . . .** Markets provide post-facto coordination in the absence of proactive command and network organization ("Transforming Coordination," 163).

* **Their vulnerability to crisis . . .** Markets represent a form of disorder that is unable to realize collective human purposes without nonmarket regulation and which is prone to crisis through various types of gaps that produce market failures ("Countering Disorder," 179).

* **As this feudal economic organization atrophied . . .** The replacement of guilds and serfdom by the market illustrates the transformation of coordination from one form to another ("Transforming Coordination," 163).

* **Market control of production . . .** The gap between individual and collective interest is known in mainstream economics as the "isolation problem"; in Marxian economics it appears as the "fetishism of commodities." It is a form of alienation in which action produces something other than intended. ("Countering Disorder," 179.)

* **The emerging system of markets . . .** Systems may coexist and produce synergisms and systems effects, yet be nonunitary, overlapping, and poorly coordinated with each other ("Transforming Boundaries," 156).

* **By the twentieth century . . .** Domination and disorder may coexist not only within systems but also as a result of interaction among overlapping systems like states and markets ("Countering Disorder Combined with Domination," 189).

* **From the 1930s through the 1960s . . .** Countercyclical policies designed to reduce unemployment of labor and resources represent strategies to counteract gaps ("Solving Problems," 135).

*   **Corporations radically expanded . . .** This process of "economic globalization" represented a transformation though not an abolition of national boundaries and national economic institutions and a relative strengthening of international financial institutions designed to regulate the global economy ("Transforming Boundaries," 156).

*   **The result was a global "race to the bottom" . . .** A race to the bottom represents an uncontrolled self-amplifying feedback process (sometimes referred to as "positive feedback") and one type of market failure ("Feedback," 58, and "Countering Disorder," 179).

*   **At the end of the eighteenth century . . .** The wood shortage was a gap compensated by an accommodation of existing practices by substituting coal for wood ("Solving Problems," 135).

*   **The expansion of fossil fuel use . . .** The increase in productivity and the transformations of technology were unanticipated and unintended secondary effects of the increasing use of fossil fuels ("Countering Disorder," 179).

*   **Conversely, wars were fought . . .** In a world order structured by domination and disorder an apparently beneficial development like increased energy resources could ironically become the cause of mutual human destruction ("Countering Disorder Combined with Domination," 189).

*   **The colossal wealth and power . . .** The progressive concentration of fossil fuel wealth represents a transformation of differentiation ("Transforming Differentiation," 170).

*   **It created immense concentrated wealth and power . . .** The rise of fossil fuels represents a transformation of power and domination ("Transforming Power," 174).

*   **The institutions representing public interests . . .** The rise of globalization and neoliberalism was a transformation of power and domination ("Countering Domination," 185).

*   **The immense wealth and power of the fossil fuel industry . . .** The growth of dependence on fossil fuels and the concentrated wealth of the fossil fuel industry transformed the pattern of domination ("Transforming Power," 174).

CHAPTER 34 Official Climate Protection from Rio to Paris

*   **Nonetheless, climate protection advocates . . .** The example of CFC regulation was assimilated but inadequately accommodated ("Solving Problems," 135).

*   **It was a process led by a collection . . .** What appeared to be climate protection through common preservation was actually the perpetuation of disorder, indeed, of the war of all against all ("Countering Disorder," 179).

*   **In 1988, before UN climate negotiations even began . . .** The campaign against effective GHG reduction measures represents anticipatory counteraction, sometimes known as "feed forward" ("Forestalling New Disorder and Domination," 195).

*   **That dependence also gave the industry hegemony . . .** The utilization of dependence can be parlayed into power ("Transforming Power," 174).

*   **According to physicist and historian Spencer Weart . . .** The retardation of one entity's climate protection action by the drag of another's is a system effect ("Open Systems," 64).

*   **The Kyoto solution . . .** This strategy presupposed the assumption that markets operate in the real world the way they do in economists' models. However, the reality of markets is ubiquitous market failure, in which common interests are not realized due to the reality of disorder. ("Countering Disorder," 179.)

*   **Meanwhile, the patterns of disorder and domination . . .** "Countering Disorder Combined with Domination," 189.

*   **But their efforts had an unintended consequence . . .** "Countering Disorder," 179.

*   **While it never succeeded in banning the bomb . . .** The overcoming of national boundaries by the development of a peace movement advocating common preservation made it possible to impose common human interests on disordered, conflicting power centers ("Countering Disorder Combined with Domination," 189).

CHAPTER 35 Development of the Climate Movement: Self-Organization

*   **At first it was closely intertwined . . .** "Transforming Differentiation," 170.

* **Although the movement originally concentrated on education** . . . Differentiation within the climate protection effort was followed by polarization and conflict ("Expropriating Marx," 41).
* **As climate protection from above** . . . The development of social movements requires an interactive rather than a direct causal explanation ("Solving Problems," 135).
* **While its primary organizational expression** . . . New entities can emerge from existing ones via differentiation and the development of boundaries; separate entities can merge or dissolve into others ("Transforming Boundaries," 156).
* **As national governments equivocated** . . . Entities at lower levels of a system may take initiatives at variance from the rules and policies of higher levels that supposedly control them. They may do so individually or collectively. ("Transforming Power," 174.)
* **Yet most people remained passive victims** . . . Absence of coordination and representations of the possibility of effective collective action meant that people appeared and felt powerless ("Transforming Representation," 151).
* **It was a textbook example** . . . "Equilibration and Social Movements," 99.
* **In 2006 McKibben and the Sunday Night group** . . . The Vermont climate activists assimilated forms of action that were well established and widely familiar at that time ("Solving Problems," 135).
* **The Middlebury team developed** . . . "The Tools," 118.
* **And to shift the debate** . . . The internal effect of turning isolated individuals concerned about climate into a movement was seen as going hand in hand with the intended external impact on Congress ("Solving Problems," 135).
* **There were "sororities and retirement communities . . ."** People in interstitial locations linked up around a set of common concerns and objectives to form a source of coordinated power that could attempt to impose a new configuration on central institutions ("The Abolition of Society," 69).
* **The Middlebury team** . . . Development can occur by taking an existing pattern and extending it ("Solving Problems," 135).
* **350.org redefined the problem** . . . Replacement of national targets rooted in national economic objectives by a common human objective illustrates an "ecological shift" in which what was

seen as separate elements are re-represented as part of a whole or system ("Transforming Representation," 151).

* **Subsequently, 350.org would carry its "decentralized networking"** . . . "Transforming Coordination," 163.
* **Despite such developments** . . . Feedback indicated that current action was failing to solve the climate problem, but did not clearly indicate an alternative means that would close the gap ("Identifying Problems," 130).

CHAPTER 36 Development of the Climate Movement: Countering Power

* **Indeed, "if the tar sands are thrown into the mix . . ."** The reinterpretation of feedback from the pipeline project transformed the representation of its implications to reveal a catastrophic gap between the building of the pipeline and the conditions necessary for human life ("Identifying Problems," 130).
* **The class had read Taylor Branch's** . . . Activists assimilated the lessons of the civil rights movement and accommodated them to meet the needs of the climate movement ("Solving Problems," 135).
* **The sit-ins constituted an exemplary action** . . . Action was observed and assimilated by others, for whom it pointed to gaps between their own action and their new representation of possibilities and necessities ("Transforming Representation," 151).
* **And they led many people** . . . Lower levels of a system may transgress the limits established by higher levels, especially if they collaborate in doing so ("Transforming Power," 174).
* **The Sierra Club** . . . The KXL struggle led to a transformation of means ("Transforming Means," 144).
* **In the language of our heuristic** . . . "Equilibration and Common Preservation," 104.
* **In late April 2014** . . . A lowering of boundaries among these sometimes antagonistic groups resulted from and helped make possible their formation into a collective subject ("Transforming Boundaries," 156).
* **It revealed that climate destruction** . . . "Transforming Power," 174.
* **The network form of coordination** . . . "Transforming Coordination," 163, and "Countering Domination," 185.

* **It exemplified Michael Mann's view** . . . "The Abolition of Society," 69.
* **Many of these had been targets** . . . When social movements and forms of action seem to "spread by contagion," it is often a result of observing and representing the action of others and then imitating those actions ("Transforming Representation," 151).
* **The initial initiative by Bill McKibben** . . . "Solving Problems," 135.
* **These evident gaps** . . . Development creates new gaps which then require new equilibrations ("Identifying Problems," 130).

CHAPTER 37 The Ecological Shot Heard Round the World
* **But it drew on and tried to affect** . . . "The Tools," 118.
* **Global ecological threats** . . . "Solving Problems," 135.
* **He accommodated his existing expectations** . . . "Solving Problems," 135.
* **And solving that problem required** . . . "Identifying Problems," 130.
* **And I used it as a pattern of such reframing** . . . "Solving Problems," 135.
* **It was an instance** . . . "Transforming Representation," 151.
* **To recognize the global spread of the radiation** . . . "Transforming Boundaries," 156.
* **The second ecological revolution** . . . Jeremy Brecher, "The Opening Shot of the Second Ecological Revolution."
* **Doing so involved borrowing from** . . . "Solving Problems," 135.

CHAPTER 38 The Public Trust and the Constitutional Right to a Stable Climate
* **National and world political systems** . . . Feedback from previous efforts showed that the system traits of domination and disorder excluded means for correcting its drive toward self-destruction through climate change ("Countering Disorder Combined with Domination," 189).
* **States, I continued, are not legitimate** . . . Authority is based on prior agreement to obey future rules and commands—in short, to obey the law. Such consent is legitimated by explicit or implicit mutual promises. Authority becomes illegitimate where those promises are violated. Law becomes a unilateral exercise of power rather than a product of consent. ("Countering Domination," 185.)

* **We can begin to impose these rules locally . . .** This strategy proposed a pattern of development in which limited initial actions could be progressively transformed to a larger scale. It fitted Michael Mann's idea of interstitial development, linking, and imposing a new configuration on the whole ("The Abolition of Society," 69).

* **The legitimation for policy and action . . .** These alternative bases for legitimacy produce a matching of forces between alternative worldviews, paradigms, or virtual representations ("Transforming Representation," 151).

* **It would be necessary to boycott and sanction . . .** These forms of action drew on the experience of many past social movements with how the power of the apparently powerless can be asserted by means of coordination and utilization of dependence ("The Power of the Powerless," 73).

* **As cotenants they have an undivided right . . .** The public trust principle cuts across national boundaries and directly challenges the principle of absolute national sovereignty ("Transforming Boundaries," 156).

* **These governments exercise illegitimate power . . .** "Transforming Power," 174.

* **And they strengthen a movement's appeal . . .** Such a strategy utilizes widely accepted principles, such as government based on the consent of the governed, making it unnecessary to introduce and develop entirely novel ones. This underlies the strategy of "constitutional insurgency" presented in the next chapter. It supports a developmental rather than an entirely revolutionary process of change—one that presupposes the interdependence of transformation and continuity. ("Assimilation and Accommodation: The Secret of Equilibration," 88.) Such constitutionalism can also help forestall movements like the climate insurgency from themselves becoming agents of domination and disorder. ("Forestalling New Disorder and Domination," 195.)

* **It cited the civil rights movement . . .** I referenced these examples to provide familiar patterns that activists could modify by using the public trust doctrine as a basis for civil disobedience to protect the climate. ("Solving Problems," 135.)

* **Those who blockade coal-fired power plants . . .** The atmospheric public trust principle transformed the representation of

noncooperation and obstruction from criminal acts to enforcement of law ("Transforming Representation," 151).

* **But juries that try climate protesters . . .** Action can expose gaps that require transformation of existing patterns. Such actions can initiate a developmental process that becomes the basis for further actions on a wider scale. ("Transforming Means," 144.)

* **"To hold otherwise would be to say . . ."** Aiken's statement embodied the view that the authority of government is based on its obligations to the people ("Countering Domination," 185).

* **Authority is generalized prior consent . . .** "Transforming Power," 174.

* **However, the rulers do not necessarily keep their end . . .** "Countering Domination," 185.

CHAPTER 39 A Global Nonviolent Constitutional Insurgency

* **Insurgencies often develop from movements . . .** The proposed transition to a climate insurgency is an example of a pattern of development, in E.P. Thompson's phrase a "historical concept" ("What Is History?," 29).

* **To effectively protect the earth's climate . . .** The proposal to reject current rulers' claim to legitimate authority illustrates the transformation of an observed historical pattern into a strategic plan of action. The historical pattern is first assimilated and then modified to fit the strategic problem at hand. ("The Tools," 118.)

* **A nonviolent climate insurgency . . .** Withdrawal of cooperation can work because of the dependence of the higher level of a system on the cooperation of lower levels ("Transforming Power," 174).

* **Even if the rules are rigged . . .** The insurgency strategy illustrates the transformation of an observed historical pattern into a strategic plan of action. The historical pattern is first assimilated and then modified to fit the strategic problem at hand. ("Solving Problems," 135.)

* **The whole must be changed . . .** "Countering Disorder Combined with Domination," 189.

* **A global insurgency . . .** Transforming the world order entails reequilibrating the relations of parts and whole, in particular transforming the entities and boundaries of the nation-state system. It

also entails, in Michael Mann's terms, an outflanking of nation-state power. ("Transforming Boundaries," 156.)

CHAPTER 40 A Climate Action Plan for Common Preservation

* **It led naturally to the question . . .** In a system of mental representation that defines people as isolated rather than social individuals it appears logical to treat individual consumer decisions as the primary means for individuals to affect society ("Transforming Representation," 151).

* **Like any such plan . . .** Identifying limitations of a proposed solution can serve as a basis for correcting them ("Solving Problems," 135).

* **If all those who are adversely affected . . .** The potential ability of the people to halt fossil fuel emissions illustrates the power of the powerless ("The Power of the Powerless," 73).

* **But because fossil fuels are deeply enmeshed . . .** Strategies adapt means and ends to overcome or compensate for a gap ("Solving Problems," 135).

* **Forestalling such devastation . . .** Such a just transition provides an example of forestalling disorder by means of anticipatory compensation ("Forestalling New Disorder and Domination," 195).

* **The transition also holds the potential . . .** Potential disorder is always possible in an economic system that lacks the means to utilize human and material resources to realize human purposes other than capital accumulation. ("Countering Disorder," 179).

* **In short, a strategy for overcoming climate destruction . . .** Successful transformation must include means for forestalling new domination and disorder ("Forestalling New Disorder and Domination," 195).

* **The first is a transition . . .** Eliminating fossil fuel burning is the primary means for compensating for or closing the gap that is causing global warming ("Transforming Means," 144).

* **It also requires their replacement . . .** Substituting for lost fossil fuel energy exemplifies compensation for side effects and interaction effects ("Transforming Coordination," 163).

* **The second element . . .** Anticipating problems and taking measures to counteract them in advance is a means of forestalling

disorder and negative side effects ("Forestalling New Disorder and Domination," 195).

* **And it means ensuring that climate protection strategies . . .** Such compensatory measures can be regarded as "side payments" that create commitment to a program by those who might not necessarily support it ("Transforming Ends," 147).

* **So a third element of the program . . .** Climate protection from below is an example of transforming power ("Transforming Power," 174, and "The Power of the Powerless," 73).

* **It will need bold economic planning . . .** Proactive planning will partially transform a disorderly market as a means of coordination to reach common goals ("Transforming Coordination," 163).

* **It will need full-employment macroeconomic policies . . .** "Keynesian" macroeconomic policies represent a compensation for the disorder of the market ("Countering Disorder," 179).

* **And it will need public mobilization . . .** A redirection of resources to climate protection represents a transformation of power ("Transforming Power," 174).

* **Workers must cooperate globally . . .** Such global transition represents a transformation of coordination and a limiting of power centers ("Transforming Coordination," 163; "Transforming Power," 174).

* **A global climate protection investment fund . . .** A global climate fund is a way of transforming global economic disorder by means of public policy compensations ("Countering Disorder," 179).

* **Rather than fighting each other . . .** The change from competition to cooperation requires decentering and a program to reconstruct particular interests into common interests ("Transforming Representation," 151; "Transforming Ends," 147).

* **Legally binding international agreements . . .** Such international agreements forestall future disorder and domination by imposing new, binding patterns ("Forestalling New Disorder and Domination," 195).

* **While there are many differences . . .** My use and modification of WWII mobilization shows the adoption and adaptation of a pattern by assimilating and accommodating it. As Polya would put it, "Here is a problem similar to yours that has been solved in the past." ("The Tools," 118.)

* **Overcoming climate destruction** . . . Viewing climate protection as a step toward broader goals is a developmental approach ("The Tools," 118).

* **Burning fossil fuel** . . . Identifying the problem ("Identifying Problems," 130).

* **American society has accepted** . . . Continuing or expanding the burning of fossil fuels is the current equilibrium or steady-state of the world order—a.k.a. "business as usual" ("Open Systems," 64).

* **A program to end climate destruction** . . . Such a program closes the gap while preventing or compensating for negative side effects of doing so ("Solving Problems," 135).

* **Climate scientists have identified** . . . Defining the gap that needs to be closed can start to define the solution: what is necessary to close the gap ("Identifying Problems," 130).

* **The fair share of GHG reduction** . . . Differentiation may require compensation. More wealth and/or greater emissions may require more GHG reduction. ("Transforming Differentiation," 170.)

* **Even the US federal climate action plan** . . . An actor can purport to pursue an end knowing that their action will not reach it ("Solving Problems," 135).

* **A common preservation climate action plan** . . . Interim targets exemplify a cybernetic trajectory with built-in course correction ("Feedback," 58).

* **The dependence of modern civilization on fossil fuel energy** . . . Effective action includes anticipating and forestalling or compensating for potential negative side effects ("Countering Disorder," 179).

* **The fossil fuel industry takes advantage** . . . The fossil fuel industry uses its unequal power to counteract challenges to its preferred policies ("Transforming Power," 174).

* **Markets have significantly failed to invest adequately** . . . Such underinvestment is a market failure—a failure to coordination needs and capabilities ("Transforming Coordination," 163).

* **The transition can be based** . . . Reduction in energy use compensates for reduction in fossil fuel energy produced ("Solving Problems," 135).

* **There will be only a small need . . .** Comparisons of virtual representations of alternative courses of action represent thought experiments ("Transforming Representation," 151).

* **Many other strategies . . .** Plans can be made more specific and concrete by differentiating the elements of the necessary transformation ("Transforming Means," 144).

* **Many workers will find jobs . . .** The growth of climate-protecting jobs illustrates positive side effects or synergisms ("Countering Disorder," 179).

* **But if fossil fuel use is eliminated . . .** Loss of jobs due to climate policies illustrates negative side effects or synergisms ("Countering Disorder," 179).

* **If eliminating fossil fuels leads to unemployment . . .** Interaction effects result in rebounding impacts on the whole economy ("Countering Disorder," 179).

* **If established patterns of unequal access . . .** Differentiation can lead to inequality and injustice ("Transforming Differentiation," 170).

* **A common preservation program . . .** This relationship between part and whole is the basis for Gramsci's concept of a "historic bloc" that integrates the goals of distinct constituencies into a common program of broader social changes that realizes them all ("Transforming Ends," 147).

* **World War II home-front mobilization . . .** World War II mobilization serves as a pattern that we then accommodate to apply to climate protection ("Solving Problems," 135).

* **The government recruited workers . . .** Government policy transformed the role of workers as a differentiated group and the spatial location of labor and production ("Transforming Differentiation," 170).

* **Government boards redirected workers . . .** Government boards transformed coordination from primarily market to partially command forms ("Transforming Coordination," 163).

* **Women entered the industrial workforce . . .** Mobilization transformed gender boundaries and the boundaries between employed and unemployed ("Transforming Differentiation," 170).

* **The National War Labor Board . . .** The War Labor Board transformed the disorder of the labor market with coordinated wage

setting and other policies. These could of course themselves be poorly coordinated or unjust. ("Countering Disorder," 179.)

* **War labor policies were often biased . . .** These changes, especially the establishment of unions and collective bargaining, but also the regulation of the labor market, transformed power relations between workers and employers ("Transforming Power," 174).

* **These policies are in line . . .** For workers, climate policies could be a means of achieving existing goals by new means ("Transforming Means," 144).

* **A common preservation climate program . . .** Alternative jobs and livelihoods are in effect side payments to compensate for side effects, including rebellion against such side effects ("Countering Disorder," 179).

* **This must include requirements . . .** Just transition provisions are means to compensate for unintended side effects ("Countering Disorder," 179). They are also means of reducing domination by limiting employers' freedom to exploit workers ("Countering Domination," 185).

* **A nuclear test site in Nevada . . .** Pollin, Garrett-Peltier, and Heintz, *Green Growth*, 310; applying past transition programs to climate illustrates selecting a pattern and accommodating it ("Solving Problems," 135).

* **For example, the Labor Network for Sustainability study . . .** This jobs plan constitutes a thought experiment to construct possible alternative courses ("Transforming Representation," 151).

* **A common preservation climate action plan . . .** Producing good quality jobs through climate policy is utilizing beneficial side effects ("Countering Disorder," 179).

* **Nonetheless, climate protection is unlikely . . .** The correction provided by climate jobs would help, but be inadequate, to fill the gap ("Solving Problems," 135).

* **To counter the insecurity . . .** A jobs guarantee counters a potential threat ("Countering Disorder," 179).

* **The frontline of establishing full employment . . .** Macroeconomic policy is a means for countering the disorder of the market ("Countering Disorder," 179).

* **Such a program should be combined . . .** Public policies can correct the market. Replacing market with public decision-making

represents a shift in the boundary between public and private spheres. ("Countering Disorder," 179; "Transforming Boundaries," 156.)

* **Therefore challenging such unjust divisions . . .** Challenging inequality can be a way of transforming both differentiation and power ("Transforming Differentiation," 170; "Transforming Power," 174).

* **A common preservation climate action plan . . .** A side effect of climate policy can be to reduce inequality ("Transforming Differentiation," 170).

* **And climate action plans need to be designed . . .** Reducing discrimination constitutes compensating for differentiation ("Transforming Differentiation," 170).

* **While this makes it possible . . .** Compensations can be inadequate to eliminate deviations from the goal ("Solving Problems," 135).

* **Programs need to provide job ladders . . .** Job ladders across skills, occupations, and employers represents the transformation of differentiations and boundaries ("Transforming Differentiation," 170).

* **Climate protection will therefore require . . .** Labor market policies can counteract interaction effects in a disorderly system characterized by labor market competition and the resulting race to the bottom ("Countering Disorder," 179).

* **It needs to support socially responsible . . .** Labor standards regulations are means for countering disorder and transforming employer/employee power relations ("Countering Disorder," 179; "Transforming Power," 174).

* **Workers should be the ones to decide . . .** Union representation is a means for correcting lack of coordination among workers in the workplace and labor market and for countering domination and differentiation of power ("Transforming Coordination," 163; "Countering Disorder Combined with Domination," 189).

* **The downward devolution . . .** Empowering workers and communities to protect the climate illustrates transforming boundaries and thereby transforming power relations ("Transforming Boundaries," 156).

* **One way to accomplish this . . .** Coalitions from below are a common mechanism of change in systems ("Transforming Power," 174).

* **Alliances are often facilitated . . .** Overlap among different roles can facilitate decentering ("Transforming Boundaries," 156).
* **Often targets are inadequate . . .** Sometimes a proposed correction is inadequate ("Solving Problems," 135).
* **Many climate action plans are not really intended . . .** Policy proposals may reflect concealed or false-flag ends ("Transforming Ends," 147).
* **They are also overridden . . .** Official climate policies often reflect unequal power and domination ("Countering Domination," 185).
* **Perhaps most importantly . . .** Climate protection from below can be a means of countering domination and forestalling new domination ("Countering Domination," 185).
* **Climate-protection programs can counter inequalities . . .** Climate programs can counteract differentiations ("Transforming Differentiation," 170).
* **They can require contractors . . .** Changed power relations can be embodied in rules ("Transforming Power," 174).
* **They can also use climate protection policies . . .** Differentiation can be transformed by redistribution of wealth and power ("Transforming Differentiation," 170).
* **Such enterprises can provide . . .** Change in ownership can help transform disorder. So can new boundaries. ("Countering Disorder," 179.)
* **Workers and workplaces do not exist . . .** The boundaries of communities and workplaces are relative and overlapping ("Transforming Boundaries," 156).
* **Where there is resistance . . .** Direct action utilizes dependence on the cooperation and acquiescence of the people ("Transforming Power," 174).
* **Where that demand is resisted . . .** Entities can initiate actions in pursuit of their goals; these can impact other entities ("Solving Problems," 135).
* **Where workers are not accorded these rights . . .** These direct actions are forms of correction. They transform existing boundaries and power relations. ("Transforming Boundaries," 156; "Transforming Power," 174.)
* **Ultimately, public policy should mandate . . .** Worker responsibility illustrates regulation in civil society ("Countering Disorder," 179).

* **It should authorize workers . . .** Worker counterpower illustrates Norbert Weiner's idea of cybernetic counteracting from below as a means of democratic control ("Feedback," 58).

* **Such a role requires workers and communities . . .** Worker responsibility to society as a whole represents a form of decentering, in which workers reconstruct their roles to represent social rather than exclusively special interests ("Countering Disorder," 179).

* **It challenges "management's right to manage" . . .** An expanded worker role transforms differentiation ("Transforming Differentiation," 170).

* **It inserts workers and communities . . .** An expanded worker role transforms coordination ("Transforming Coordination," 163).

* **It thereby challenges . . .** An expanded worker role transforms power ("Transforming Power," 174).

* **The strategic decisions affecting GHG emissions . . .** An inquiry needs to identify actors capable of counteracting—in this case, corporations ("Identifying Problems," 130).

* **They can demand the right . . .** Evaluation of feedback and countering deviations from goal can be ongoing ("Countering Disorder," 179).

* **In many instances . . .** New relations among different unions and groups of workers transform coordination ("Transforming Coordination," 163).

* **Workers can promote new climate protection goods and services . . .** Worker proposals for production and products constitute thought experiments on virtual representations ("Transforming Representation," 151).

* **They can also help initiate . . .** Worker interventions are means of transforming boundaries, power, and domination ("Countering Domination," 185).

* **A fossil-free economy . . .** A multilevel system may require transformation at multiple, possibly overlapping, levels ("Transforming Boundaries," 156).

* **Industry-wide planning is necessary . . .** Industry-wide planning entails transforming coordination ("Transforming Coordination," 163).

* **This requires not just switching . . .** Metropolitan restructuring represents a transformation of coordination ("Transforming Coordination," 163).

* **The Teamsters union . . .** Intermodal transportation illustrates the transformation of boundaries ("Transforming Boundaries," 156).

* **Financialization has meant . . .** Market failure is a failure of coordination. The disorder of the market means actors are not led to achieve social purposes or even narrow purposes of economic growth. ("Countering Disorder," 179.)

* **This can be achieved by such means as . . .** Policies like a Robin Hood tax would reduce financial disorder ("Countering Disorder," 179).

* **To illustrate how the climate protection movement . . .** Power can be projected across boundaries from one realm to another ("Transforming Boundaries," 156).

* **While it rarely has power . . .** Currently exercised capabilities of an entity provide a starting point for thought experiments about possible expanded capabilities that might be realized through further development ("Transforming Representation," 151).

* **It can participate in lawsuits . . .** The institutionalized power of unions can be utilized for new purposes ("Transforming Ends," 147).

* **And through their collective bargaining . . .** Power may be transformed by realigning the accountability of institutions and the individuals within them ("Transforming Power," 174).

* **It must include a process of democratization . . .** Democratization represents transforming domination ("Countering Domination," 185).

* **And it must include a climate insurgency . . .** For self-preservation through common preservation, actors must disobey authority that is being used for mutual destruction ("Countering Domination," 185).

* **Effective measures have been blocked . . .** Domination and disorder present obstacles to problem-solving ("Countering Disorder Combined with Domination," 189).

* **Where they are unable to block . . .** Actors can pursue objectives through false flag operations and other deceptions intended to lead other actors to construct false representations ("Transforming Representation," 151).

* **The third . . .** These strategies correspond to the three forms of coordination: market, network, and command ("Transforming Coordination," 163).

* **Rapid reduction of GHG emissions . . .** Climate protection requires transforming coordination ("Transforming Coordination," 163).

* **This will require transcending . . .** Transforming representations may be necessary for effective action ("Transforming Representation," 151).

* **Such institutions will need to establish . . .** Public control of decision-making constitutes a transformation of power ("Transforming Power," 174).

* **Further, they will need . . .** Integrated regulation of diverse functions and entities constitutes a transformation of coordination ("Transforming Coordination," 163).

* **Such coordination, as during World War II . . .** A degree of centralized control may be necessary to counter disorder ("Countering Disorder," 179).

* **Yet because of the extended period of transition . . .** A means is necessary to forestall new domination ("Forestalling New Disorder and Domination," 195).

* **It would define GHG reduction targets . . .** Periodic reevaluation institutionalizes correction based on feedback ("Forestalling New Disorder and Domination," 195).

* **The British government's *Stern Review* . . .** Market failure represents the failure of feedback systems in a disorderly environment ("Transforming Coordination," 163).

* **A common preservation climate action program . . .** Planning will transform coordination ("Transforming Coordination," 163).

* **While markets were not eliminated during the war . . .** Planning transformed coordination ("Transforming Coordination," 163).

* **If today's climate emergency . . .** Complementing the market with planning embodies a transformation of power ("Transforming Power," 174).

* **It requires taking into account . . .** Planning requires mental representation of the world and experimental operations on it ("Transforming Representation," 151).

* **Auto companies were led to cooperate . . .** Utilization of dependence transformed power and led to new forms of cooperation ("Transforming Power," 174; "Transforming Coordination," 163).

* **That possibility must be forestalled . . .** Countercyclical macroeconomic policy is a means to forestall new disorder ("Forestalling New Disorder and Domination," 195).

* **If need be, the Federal Reserve . . .** Public financing transfers resources across boundaries ("Transforming Boundaries," 156).

* **Such devices as energy pricing incentives . . .** Tax and other transfer programs transform coordination by transforming the market ("Transforming Coordination," 163).

* **They should then lead a campaign . . .** Divestment transfers resources across boundaries to new entities. It transforms control of wealth. ("Transforming Power," 174.)

* **Comparable legislation could hold . . .** Liability for costs of climate change would counteract the disorder maintained by the right of property owners to burn fossil fuels ("Countering Disorder," 179).

* **Overcoming climate destruction . . .** Global action means transforming national boundaries that impede climate protection ("Transforming Boundaries," 156).

* **This ultimately requires . . .** International agreements aim to forestall future disorder and domination ("Forestalling New Disorder and Domination," 195).

* **International cooperation can start . . .** Using informal cooperation as a building block for formal agreements is a developmental approach ("Solving Problems," 135).

* **Global climate protection can serve . . .** Solutions can be generalized to apply to problems beyond the initial one they addressed ("Solving Problems," 135).

* **It can replace ever-growing inequality . . .** Transition to a climate-safe society can provide a representation of the world that people can assimilate for other purposes ("Transforming Representation," 151).

* **It can replace trade wars . . .** By forcing states to cooperate social movements can counter disorder through recoordination based on the formation and realization of collective purposes ("Transforming Coordination," 163).

* **A decade before the emergence . . .** Transforming representations can lead to new coordinations that transform power and disorder ("Transforming Representation," 151).

* **In response to the Great Recession . . .** Advocates of a Global Green New Deal selected a historical pattern and modified it ("Solving Problems," 135).

* **UN Secretary-General Ban Ki-moon . . .** Such a stimulus constituted a compensation for the demand deficit of the disorderly global economy manifested in the Great Recession ("Countering Disorder," 179).

* **The imagery of the New Deal . . .** The green new deal paradigm transformed the representation of the world and the norms for evaluating it ("Transforming Representation," 151).

* **It represents a program . . .** Formation of alliances from below can be a means of systems change ("Transforming Power," 174).

* **Trillions of dollars . . .** Unemployment and surplus capital represent a gap demonstrating disorder and failure of coordination ("Transforming Coordination," 163).

* **Therefore, between 1 and 2 percent . . .** One to two percent of global GDP would compensate for the gap identified by climate scientists between the current GHG trajectory and the need to reduce GHG emissions ("Identifying Problems," 130).

* **Taxes should include a tax . . .** Funding of climate protection is a compensation for the gap between present and needed GHG reductions ("Solving Problems," 135).

* **Such a fund can be . . .** A climate fund can serve as the starting point for the development of global Keynesian macroeconomic policy as a means to transform the disorder of the global economy ("Countering Disorder," 179).

* **In response, US labor . . .** Competitive downward spirals are a feature of market failure and other system disorders ("Countering Disorder," 179).

* **Instead, it should advocate . . .** Disorder can be overcome by cooperation ("Countering Disorder," 179).

* **Far from discouraging government subsidies . . .** Under some circumstances regulated markets can provide a socially beneficial "race to the top" ("Transforming Coordination," 163).

* **Unions should cooperate globally** . . . Systems can be transformed by linking those at the bottom across boundaries ("Transforming Power," 174).
* **Such agreements could revise** . . . Domination can be transformed by changing rules ("Countering Domination," 185).
* **Cooperation could start on a bilateral basis** . . . Partial measures can develop into universal ones ("Transforming Ends," 147).
* **Such agreements could be the beginning** . . . A global regime for producing climate protection would transform disorder ("Countering Disorder," 179).
* **Humanity will not be safe** . . . Binding, enforceable agreements forestall future disorder and domination ("Forestalling New Disorder and Domination," 195).
* **The struggle to eliminate fossil fuels** . . . This developmental strategy moves from local to global and from informal to institutionalized change ("Solving Problems," 135).
* **It was ultimately outlawed globally** . . . The abolition of slavery was developmental, culminating in a universal law ("Countering Domination," 185).
* **But it must be accomplished** . . . Determining the necessary magnitude and speed of change is often part of defining the conditions for a solution to a problem ("Identifying Problems," 130).

Notes

FOREWORD

1   Jessica Glenza, Alan Evans, Hannah Ellis-Petersen, and Naaman Zhou, "Climate Strikes Held around the World—As It Happened," *Guardian*, March 15, 2019, https://www.theguardian.com/environment/live/2019/mar/15/climate-strikes-2019-live-latest-climate-change-global-warming.

INTRODUCTION

1   "Meat Sales Drop 80% in Places as the Boycott Begins," *New York Times*, April 3, 1973, http://www.nytimes.com/1973/04/03/archives/meat-sales-drop-80-in-places-as-the-boycott-begins-middleincome.html?_r=0.

2   Deirdre Carmody, "Consumers Scoff at Ceiling and Step Up Boycott Plans," *New York Times*, March 31, 1973, http://www.nytimes.com/1973/03/31/archives/consumers-scoffat-ceiling-and-step-up-boycott-plans-politicians.html

3   "Gallup Poll Finds One Third Will Eat Less Meat," *New York Times*, May 17, 1973.

4   "350.org's Call to Action," *CNN*, October 29, 2009.

5   Lindley Darden, "Strategies for Discovering Mechanisms," *Philosophy of Science* S69 (2002): S354–65.

6   Jeremy Brecher, *Save the Humans? Common Preservation in Action*, 2nd ed. (Oakland: PM Press, 2020).

CHAPTER 1

1   Marina Sitrin, email message to author, September 11, 2011.

2   Jeremy Brecher, "We Are the 99%," in *Strike!* 50th anniversary ed. (Oakland: PM Press, 2020), 372–87. See also Writers for the 99%, *Occupying Wall Street: The Inside Story of an Action that Changed America* (New York: OR Books, 2011); Brecher, "A Night in the Park: Occupy Wall Street Observed," *First of the Month*, http://www.firstofthemonth.org/archives/2011/10/public_happines.html; Brecher, "The People Out of Doors: Change You Can Believe In," *The Nation*, October 21, 2011; Brecher, "The 99 Percent Organize Themselves," *The Nation*, November 4, 2011; Brecher, "Occupy Climate Change," *The Nation*, March 14, 2012; Brecher, "Occupy Mayday: Not Your Usual General Strike," *Common Dreams*, March 26, 2012; Brecher, "Occupy and the 99% Opposition," *The Nation*, July 9, 2012; Brecher, "The Power of the Powerless," *Tidal* no. 3 (September 2012).

3   The "booty" from those raids displayed in this book is not meant to represent a full portrait of the thinkers involved. Nor is the use of some ideas from a thinker intended to imply agreement with their other ideas.

4   Robert Jervis, *System Effects: Complexity in Political and Social Life* (Princeton, NJ: Princeton University Press, 1997).

CHAPTER 2

1   Howard Fast, *Freedom Road* (New York: Duell, Sloan & Pearce, 1944).

2   W.E.B. Du Bois, *Black Reconstruction in America* (New York: Harcourt, Brace and Co., 1935).

3   Du Bois, *Black Reconstruction*, 57.

4   Du Bois, 67.

5   Du Bois, 57.

6   Du Bois, 725–26.

7   Jeremy Brecher, *Strike!* (San Francisco: Straight Arrow Books, 1972), 314ff.

8   George F. Addes and R.J. Thomas, "Introduction," in Henry Krause, *The Many and the Few* (Los Angeles: Plantin Press, 1947).

9   Jeremy Brecher, *Strike!* (San Francisco: Straight Arrow Books, 1972), 314.

10   Amy Bass, *Those About Him Remained Silent: The Battle over W.E.B. Du Bois* (Minneapolis: University of Minnesota Press, 2009).

11   Jubilee School, *The Future of Our History*, video about the student project on W.E.B. Du Bois, YouTube, January 5, 2015, https://www.youtube.com/watch?v=oKJ2MdlryYI.

CHAPTER 3

1   Ernest G. Schachtel, *Metamorphosis: On the Development of Affect, Perception, Attention, and Memory* (New York: Basic Books, 1959).

2   "Man" was used as a generic term for "human," even by many feminist writers, until the early 1970s. See, for example, Kate Millett, *Sexual Politics* (Garden City, NY: Doubleday, 1970).

3   Schachtel, *Metamorphosis*, v. Dorothy Lee also directed me to Taoism, telling me to read Alan Watts's *Nature, Man, and Woman*, which led me on to volume 2 of Joseph Needham's *Science and Civilization in China*, and this no doubt helped make me receptive to systems theory's emphasis on interrelatedness. Needham was an embryologist before becoming a historian of Chinese science, and he stressed the parallels between ancient Chinese philosophies and modern scientific theories of embryonic development.

4   Schachtel, *Metamorphosis*, 3.

5   Schachtel, 13.

6   Amartya Sen, *Development as Freedom* (New York: Oxford University Press, 1999).

7   Schachtel, *Metamorphosis*, vi.

8   Schachtel, 5.

9   Schachtel, 9.

10   Schachtel, 7.

11   Schachtel, 5. In my copy I have notes from an early reading headed "Schachtel vs. Freud." Notations include: "Organism active—reaches out for relation to world." "Affect accompanies action, is not a substitute." "Focus on modes of relatedness of person to environment and their transformation."

12 Schachtel, *Metamorphosis*, 9.

13 Schachtel, 15.

14 *America and the New Era*, 21. http://archive.lib.msu.edu/DMC/AmRad/americanewera.pdf.

15 Jeremy Brecher, "Forty Years with Tim," *Global Labor Strategies*, http://laborstrategies.blogs.com/global_labor_strategies/2009/12/forty-years-with-tim.html.

16 Jeremy Brecher and Tim Costello, *Common Sense for Hard Times* (Boston: South End Press, 1979), 203–7. http://www.jeremybrecher.org/downloadable-books/commonsense.pdf.

17 Jeremy Brecher, "What Can 99-Percenters Learn from the History of Social Movements?" (lecture, Occupy New School and CUNY Committee on Globalization and Social Change, New York, NY, November 22, 2011).

18 The sequence of development for Occupy Wall Street is presented in detail in Jeremy Brecher, *Strike!*, 50th anniversary ed. (Oakland: PM Press, 2020), chapter 10, 341–87.

CHAPTER 4

1 E.H. Carr, *What Is History?* (Cambridge: Cambridge University Press, 1961), 33. Carr's approach has been subject to extensive criticism. See for example, Geoffrey Elton, *The Practice of History* (Hoboken, NJ: Wiley-Blackwell, 1991).

2 E.P. Thompson, *The Poverty of Theory* (London: Merlin, 1978), 235.

3 Thompson, *Poverty of Theory*, 235–36.

4 Thompson, 237.

5 Thompson, 231.

6 Thompson, 231. Historical logic probably falls into the category G. Polya calls "plausible reasoning" based on "heuristic syllogisms" in contrast to "demonstrative reasoning" based on "demonstrative syllogisms." G. Polya, *How to Solve It*, 188. See "How to Solve It" below.

7 Rosa Luxemburg, "The Mass Strike, the Political Party and the Trade Unions," in *Rosa Luxemburg Speaks* (New York: Pathfinder Press, 1970), 182.

8 Thompson defines "process" somewhat obscurely as "a total logic of changes of sets of interrelated activities." *Poverty of Theory*, 263.

9 Thompson, *Poverty of Theory*, 237. Thompson quotes Sartre: "History is not order. It is disorder: a rational disorder. At the very moment when it maintains order, i.e. structure, history is already on the way to undoing it." *Poverty of Theory*, 230.

10 Thompson, *Poverty of Theory*, 237. Thompson frequently counterposed historical "logic" or "tendency," or "pressure" as well as "expectation," to "law." See, e.g., 230. See also E.H. Carr, *What Is History*, 72. Carr points out that today natural scientists, similarly, do not generally view their work as producing "laws" in the sense understood by seventeenth and eighteenth century scientists. Another way to approach this distinction is to say that history lies between disciplines like sociology and philosophy in which general truths predominate and individual cases are little more than instances of a wider truth and the collection and presentation of facts about the past without a meaningful relationship to how the facts were produced and what their implications might be—what is sometimes disparaged as "antiquarianism." History must navigate the quasi-regular world in between.

11 Thompson, *Poverty* of *Theory*, 231.

12 *Poverty of Theory*, 232. Elsewhere he states that history affords "evidence of necessary causes" but never of "sufficient causes" (230).

13 Carr, *What Is History?*, 32. Thompson rightly emphasizes that the historian's tests are not against isolated "facts" but rather against "the evidence." *Poverty of Theory*, 320.

14 Jeremy Brecher, *History from Below: How to Uncover and Tell the Story of Your Community, Association, or Union* (West Cornwall, CT: Stone Soup Books, 2018), 13. http://www.jeremybrecher.org/books/historyfrombelow/#page/1/mode/1up

15 Carr, *What Is History?*, 136.

16 *What Is History?*, 140. Such views were part of the self-conception of the historical discipline almost from its inception. The ancient Greek historian Polybius wrote of the "special province" of the "science of history" that it included "to learn why it was that a particular policy or arrangement failed or succeeded. For a bare statement of an occurrence is interesting, to be sure, but not instructive; but when it is supplemented by a statement of cause, the study of history becomes fruitful. For it is by applying analogies to our own circumstances that we get the means and basis for calculating the future; and from learning from the past when to act with caution, and when with greater boldness, in the present." (Polybius, *Historia* XII, 25e, quoted in Savoie Lottinville, *The Rhetoric of History* [Norman: University of Oklahoma Press, 1976], 46.)

17 This book also represents such a "rational reconstruction," drawing selectively on my experiences and emphasizing what I believe to be relevant to the problem it addresses.

18 Carr, *What Is History?*, 143. Knowledge like Thompson's expectations that "do not impose a rule" but that do "hasten and facilitate the interrogation of the evidence" is useful for action because it advises actors what to expect while leaving open the possibility that their actions may themselves affect the outcome.

19 Brecher, *Strike!* (Boston: South End Press, 1977), 319. "Afterword: A Challenge to Historians" from which this discussion is drawn has been omitted in later editions.

20 "The Widening Horizon." Carr explicitly defends the concept of progress as a necessary justification for the sacrifices imposed on the living generation for the sake of generations yet unborn (*What Is History?*, 158). This has been interpreted as an apology for Soviet Communism, which Carr is often accused of defending. It seems to me that making the future better than it would otherwise be is an equally adequate, and more defensible, justification for sacrifice than an argument that human life is ever improving.

21 Brecher, *Strike!* (1977), 319.

CHAPTER 5

1 Gary Roth, *Marxism in a Lost Century: A Biography of Paul Mattick* (Leiden: Brill, 2014). See also my review of *Anti-Bolshevik Communism* in *Our Generation*, 15, no. 3 (Fall 1982). Mattick was unusual among postwar American Marxists in trying to apply Marx's economic analysis in *Capital* to contemporary capitalism. This led him to much greater skepticism than most about the extent to which Keynesian policies could permanently ameliorate, let alone overcome,

the contradictions Marx diagnosed as inherent in capitalism. See *Marx and Keynes: The Limits of the Mixed Economy* (Boston: Porter Sargent, 1969).

2   In connection with this course I also read a wide swath of secondary Marx interpretation, such as Karl Korsch's *Karl Marx* (New York: John Wiley & Sons, 1938) and I.I. Rubin's *Essays on Marx's Theory of Value* (Detroit: Black and Red, 1972).

3   Friedrich Engels, "Preface," in Karl Marx, *The Communist Manifesto* (Chicago: Henry Regnery Company, Gateway Edition, 1954), 7. Read carefully, Engels's statement may be equivocal on whether socialist revolution is inevitable, but surely the great majority of readers both of the *Manifesto* and other works of Marx and Engels have taken them to say that it is, and reasonably so based on their texts. There are also contrary Marxist texts, of course, such as Rosa Luxemburg's statement that bourgeois society faced the alternatives of "transition to socialism or regression into barbarism." (Rosa Luxemburg, *The Crisis in German Social Democracy*, also known as *The Junius Pamphlet* [Zurich: 1915], https://www.marxists.org/archive/luxemburg/1915/junius/)

4   E.P. Thompson wrote that Marxist concepts, to be judged superior to others, must "stand up better to the test of historical logic," although it is not certain that he always followed this rule himself (*The Poverty of Theory*, [London: Merlin, 1978], 236).

5   This analysis derived in part from Barrington Moore, *Social Origins of Dictatorship and Democracy: Lord and Peasant in the Making of the Modern World* (Boston: Beacon Press, 1993). Something similar happened after Mao with the Chinese Communist Party's introduction of many aspects of capitalism.

6   Engels wrote in his preface to the *Manifesto* that its "fundamental proposition" is "destined to do for history what Darwin's theory has done for biology."

7   This can also be a problem today with "postmodern" theories that sometimes go beyond a critique of determinism to a general dissolution of historical connectedness.

8   It was one of the less attractive tendencies of Marxist tradition to substitute irony and sarcasm for explicit discussion of values, ethics, and morality. The avoidance of explicit discussion of values is characteristic of social groups who assume their own moral superiority, making explicit statements unnecessary. Marxism ironically parallels the cult of "Western values" in this respect. Both eliminate the need for value dialogue with those who disagree or come from different value traditions. As John Brown Childs indicates, this generates a politics grounded in the expectation that others will or should convert to one's own obviously superior position. See John Brown Childs, *Transcommunality: From the Politics of Conversion to the Ethics of Respect* (Philadelphia: Temple University Press, 2003). See also the discussion below on Piaget's ideas about decentering and coordination of values.

9   Karl Marx, *The Eighteenth Brumaire of Louis Bonaparte* (1852).

10 Marx and Engels, "Theses on Feuerbach," in *The German Ideology* (Moscow: Progress Publishers, 1964), 647.

CHAPTER 6

1   Karl Marx, *Capital*, vol. 1 (Moscow: Progress Publishers, 1965), 356.

2   Marx, *Capital*, vol. 1, 356.

CHAPTER 7

1   Søren Kierkegaard, *Fear and Trembling and The Sickness unto Death* (Garden City, NY: Doubleday Anchor, 1954), 170–72.

2   Jeremy Brecher and Tim Costello, *Common Sense for Hard Times* (Boston: South End Press, 1979), 5–6.

3   Marx drew on, but also radically revised, the version of the dialectic he found in Hegel. As David Harvey puts it, Hegel's dialectic was, or at least has frequently been interpreted as, "just a matter of thesis, antithesis, and synthesis." This gave rise to a rather simplistic teleology like "class struggle under capitalism necessarily gives rise to a classless socialism." (David Harvey, *Justice, Nature & the Geography of Difference* [Oxford: Blackwell, 1996], 57.)

Some interpreters, like Harvey, basing themselves on Marx's intellectual practice rather than on his and Engels's explicit formulations, argue that Marx's dialectic is less a necessary logical structure than "a flow of argument and practices" (57). At the opposite pole is Friedrich Engels, who argued that "the dialectical laws are really laws of development of nature, and therefore are valid also for theoretical natural science" (*Dialectics of Nature*, "II. Dialectics"). While I find Harvey's view more congenial, Engels's is certainly closer to what "dialectics" has meant to most Marxists historically. For a useful summary of the Marxian dialectic seen as "a flow or argument and practices," see Harvey 48ff. and references given there.

4   Engels's *Dialectics of Nature* is a principal source for later interpreters, but different schools have debated endlessly whether Marx's views were really the same as those presented by Engels.

5   Bertell Ollman, *Dance of the Dialectic: Steps in Marx's Method* (Urbana-Champaign: University of Illinois Press, 2003), 13.

6   E.H. Carr's discussion of progress in history represents a confluence of "Whig" and Marxist ideas of progress. In the 1970s, portrayals of history as a sequence of radically different worldviews so little connected that they are incomprehensible to each other became widespread.

7   The priority of production is sometimes justified by the argument that the means of human existence must be produced for human life to proceed. But one might as well argue that human biological reproduction is prior to production because people must be born before they can produce. The priority of production is at other times defended as empirically validated by historical research. But as we saw in "Re:Marx" above, the empirical historical case for Marx's "fundamental proposition" is pretty unconvincing even for the paradigm case of the transition from feudalism to capitalism.

8   Ollman, *Dance*, 13. Buckminster Fuller echoed this approach in his witty statement, "I seem to be a verb." Ollman stresses the roots of Marx's approach in the philosophy of "internal relations."

9   Quoted in Ollman, *Dance*, 4. To see the kind of problem this way of speaking can generate, consider, for example, Engels's statement that "Even simple mechanical change of place can only come about through a body at one and the same moment of time being both in one place and in another place, being in one and the same place and also not in it" (Friedrich Engels, *Anti-Duhring* (New York: International Publishers, 1939), part 1, chapter 12). See also M. Mark

Mussachia, "On Contradiction in Dialectical Materialism," *Science & Society* 41, no. 3 (Fall 1977): 257–80.

10   Ollman, *Dance*, 4.

11   Manning Marable regularly uses the term "racialization" and "racialized minorities" to remind readers that "race" is not a trait of individuals but the product of a social process.

12   Such tendencies are obviously not unique to Marxism. In fact, they arise to some degree from the very nature of paradigms. But countering them requires applying, rather than rejecting, forms of testing against evidence that are in principle open to all.

13   Ollman, *Dance*, 74.

14   The ever-changing meaning of words and concepts makes it difficult to test for internal consistency as well as for fit to evidence.

15   Engels, *Dialectics of Nature*, "II. Dialectics."

CHAPTER 8

1   Rosa Luxemburg, "The Politics of Mass Strikes and Unions," *Gesammelte Werke* vol. 2 (Berlin: Dietz, 1981), 465.

2   Jeremy Brecher, *Strike!*, 50th anniversary ed. (Oakland: PM Press, 2020), 323.

3   Brecher, 324,

4   Robert B. Westbrook, *John Dewey and American Democracy* (Ithaca: Cornell University Press, 1991) provides a useful guide to Dewey's thought and the social dimension of American pragmatism. While Marcus Raskin, one of my mentors at the Institute for Policy Studies, considered himself a follower of Dewey, I, like most others of my generation, never really studied him. No doubt I absorbed some of Dewey's ideas from reading and commenting on Marcus Raskin's *Being and Doing* (New York: Random House, 1971) in manuscript.

5   Westbrook, *John Dewey and American Democracy*, xiv.

6   John Dewey, "The Ethics of Democracy" (1888), in *The Early Works, 1882–1898* (Carbondale: Southern Illinois University Press, 1967), ed. Jo Ann Boydston, 1–248.

7   Harry K. Wells, *Pragmatism: Philosophy of Imperialism* (New York: International, 1954), 132. For the roots of this view, see the discussion of Randolph Bourne's criticism of Dewey's support for World War I in Westbrook, *John Dewey and American* Democracy, 195ff.

8   John Dewey, "Contributions to A Cyclopedia of Education" (1911), in *Middle Works* (Carbondale: Southern Illinois University Press, 1976), ed. Jo Ann Boydston. Like Schachtel, Dewey and others in the pragmatic tradition regarded humans as inherently active.

9   Quoted in Westbrook, *John Dewey and American Democracy*, 128.

10   Westbrook, 130.

11   Jeremy Brecher, "Intellectuals and Class Consciousness," *Root & Branch* 4.

12   Marxists have differed greatly on the relation between Marx's ideas and pragmatism. Marx's "Theses on Feuerbach,"—with their statement that "The question whether objective truth can be attributed to human thinking is not a question of theory but a practical question. Man must prove the truth ... of his thinking in practice"—sure sounds like Dewey-style pragmatism to me. The affinity between Marxism and Dewey's pragmatism was pointed out by

Sidney Hook in *Toward an Understanding of Karl Marx* (New York: John Day, 1933). Hook's conception of workers' democracy through democratic workers' councils found expression in the 1934 platform of the short-lived American Workers Party, led by A.J. Muste, which I read as I was preparing *Strike!* For Hook and Dewey, see Westbrook, *John Dewey and American Democracy*, 463ff. For Dewey's critique of the unscientific character of Marxism, see Westbrook, 469ff, especially his revealing debate with Leon Trotsky.

The workers' council tradition moved between an approach similar to Hook's and one that emphasized the "scientific" character of Marxism and specifically the objectivity of its analysis of capitalist economics and its prediction of inevitable collapse. *Toward an Understanding of Karl Marx* was criticized by Paul Mattick in a short book called *The Inevitability of Communism* for failing to recognize the scientific character of Marx's theory of capitalism and its crisis. But Anton Pannekoek was critical of the kind of determinism expressed by Mattick. See Serge Bricianer, *Pannekoek and the Workers' Councils* (St. Louis: Telos Press, 1978), 233ff.

Jean-Paul Sartre seems to have come to a view similar to pragmatism. In *Search for a Method* he wrote that "the foundation of anthropology is man himself, not as the object of practical Knowledge, but as a practical organism producing Knowledge as a moment of its *praxis*" (New York: Vintage, 1968), 179.

13   Brecher, *Strike!* (Boston: South End Press, 1977), 316. The Marxist theorist Paul Mattick made a surprisingly parallel "Darwinian" argument: Even once-revolutionary labor organizations, in order to succeed in the era of capitalist prosperity, had to abandon their revolutionary character in order to escape repression and compete effectively with nonrevolutionary ones. Paul Mattick, "Spontaneity and Organization," in *Anti-Bolshevik Communism* (London: Merlin Press, 1978), 117ff.

14   Of course, strikes and other forms of conflict themselves can serve as vehicles for reintegrating discordant social elements back into the status quo. The use of strikes as largely empty rituals of social protest, followed by a return to normal life, illustrates this point. For a large auto strike as an example, see William Serrin, *The Company and the Union* (New York: Knopf, 1973). For a more theoretical sociological view, see Louis Coser, *The Functions of Social Conflict* (Glencoe, Illinois: Free Press, 1956).

15   V.I. Lenin, *Collected Works*, vol. 5 (Moscow: Progress Publishers), 375.

16   Lenin, *Collected Works*, vol. 5, 383–84.

17   Rosa Luxemburg, "Organizational Question of Social Democracy" (also published elsewhere as "Leninism vs. Marxism"), in *Rosa Luxemburg Speaks* (New York: Pathfinder Press, 1970), 130. The focus in *Strike!* on action as the privileged source of learning and development was perhaps overdone. As the great American labor historian David Montgomery wrote in a critique of *Strike!*, "Mutualism is manifested in values, loyalties, and thoughts, as well as in actions." He made sure to add, "This is not to say that intellectual confrontation with hegemonic bourgeois ideas *is* the revolution either, much less that socialist consciousness must be brought to workers from without their ranks." David Montgomery, "Spontaneity and Organization: Some Comments," *Radical America* 7, no. 6 (November–December 1973).

18   I also wrote a critique of *History and Class Consciousness* by the Marxist theo-rist Georg Lukács, who argued that the working class was unable to achieve a true conception of its position in society by itself because of the fragmenta-tion of modern capitalist society. He used this alleged incapacity to bolster Lenin's view that socialist class consciousness "would be implanted in the workers 'from outside.'" (Georg Lukács, *History and Class Consciousness: Studies in Marxist Dialectics* [Cambridge, MA: MIT Press, 1971]. Cited in Jeremy Brecher, "Intellectuals and Class Consciousness," *Root & Branch* 4.) I argued in response that class formation was not just a matter of "intellectual persuasion," but rather "a response to the problems people faced and the means of action needed to address them." The class struggle constitutes "a series of social experiments" through which the working class clarifies for itself the actual structure of society and the real nature of the problems it faces. At first, individual workers try to solve their problems individually and. fail; they soon come to see that they must cooperate with those they work with to win anything. These groups in turn see that they must support one another or be defeated one by one. It gradually becomes clear that "workers are powerless when they are isolated," but that "the more closely they cooperate, the stronger they become." (Brecher, "Intellectuals and Class Consciousness," *Root & Branch* 4.)

19   "Symposium on *Strike!*," *Radical America* 7, no. 6 (November–December 1973).

CHAPTER 9

1   I remember seeing Norbert Wiener's book *The Human Use of Human Beings* around the house in my youth and not being able to make head or tail of it. But I was no doubt indirectly influenced by cybernetics via Kenneth Boulding and others I was reading in the *Journal of Conflict Resolution*. I learned many of the basic cybernetic concepts from John Bowlby, *Attachment and Loss* (New York: Basic Books, 1969), which used them to explain children's attachment behav-ior. Only when I picked up Gregory Bateson's *Steps to an Ecology of Mind* (New York: Ballantine, 1972) did I begin to appreciate the significance of cybernetics. Bateson played an important role both in drawing out the deeper implications of cybernetics and in popularizing it. (I much later learned that my mentor Dorothy Lee had participated in one of the early Macy conferences on cyber-netics organized by Weiner and Bateson.)

2   My friend the late Joe Eyer and his collaborator Peter Sterling have pointed out that physiological systems do not in fact aim for a single homeostatic target, but rather vary their targets over a very wide range of possible targets depend-ing on the functional needs of the moment. They coined the term "allostasis" to characterize such variable goals of feedback systems. See Peter Sterling, "Principles of allostasis: optimum design, predictive regulation, pathophysiol-ogy, and rational therapeutics" in J. Schulkin, *Allostasis, Homeostasis, and the Costs of Adaptation* (Cambridge: Cambridge University Press, 2004). Of course, behind such targets may lie meta-targets, such as individual or species survival or well-being, that ultimately regulate temporary targets and therefore the goals of action. See Peter Sterling, "Point of View: Predictive Regulation and Human Design," *eLIFE*, June 29, 2018, https://elifesciences.org/articles/36133

3   Technically, this is a description of "negative feedback" which reduces deviation from a goal. Cyberneticians also describe "positive" or "deviation-amplifying" feedback, feed-forward, and various other kinds of information circuits.

4   For the historical background to Wiener's work, see Flo Conway and Jim Siegelman, *Dark Hero of the Information Age* (New York: Basic Books, 2005), and David Noble, *Forces of Production: A Social History of Industrial Automation* (New York: Knopf, 1984), p. 48ff.

5   For further discussion of causal vs. cybernetic explanation, see Gregory Bateson, "Cybernetic Explanation," in *Steps to an Ecology of Mind*, especially 399.

6   Aleksandr Bogdanov, a Russian Marxist whose "Tektology" is often viewed as a precursor to cybernetics, used the metaphor of cooperation in a workshop in preference to more biological patterns like organisms and their environments for his "general science of organization," which he dubbed "Tektology" (*Essays in Tektology: The General Science of Organization*, second English edition [Seaside, CA: Intersystems, 1984]). (Original works published 1919–1921.) Michael Chapman suggests that Bogdanov's approach might allow further development of Piaget's theory by "going beyond the analogy between subject-object relations and organism-environment interaction toward a model that explicitly includes equilibration in intersubjective interaction" (Michael Chapman, "Equilibration and the Dialectics of Organization," in *Piaget's Theory: Prospects and Possibilities*, ed. Harry Beilin and Peter Pufall [Hillsdale, NJ: Lawrence Erlbaum, 1992].)

7   Noble, *Forces of Production*, 71.

8   Noble, 73–4.

9   Noble, 74.

10   Noble, 73–76.

11   Noble, 74, 76.

12   Flo Conway and Jim Siegelman, *Dark Hero of the Information Age*, 332. See the final chapters of Conway and Siegelman for an explanation of the decline of cybernetics as a unified program, including personal and family factors, institutional conflicts, and the redirection of national security funding to rival research efforts.

CHAPTER 10

1   Bertalanffy's ideas and their historical development are presented in Ludwig von Bertalanffy, *General Systems Theory: Foundations, Development, Applications* (New York: George Braziller, 1968). For the early historical background of such systems approaches in biology, see Evelyn Fox Keller, "Organisms, Machines, and Thunderstorms: A History of Self-Organization, Part One," *Historical Studies in the Natural Sciences* 38, no. 1 (2008), http://dx.doi.org/10.1525/hsns.2008.38.1.45. For their subsequent development under the general rubric of complexity theory see Evelyn Fox Keller, "Organisms, Machines, and Thunderstorms: A History of Self-Organization, Part Two. Complexity, Emergence, and Stable Attractors," *Historical Studies in the Natural Sciences* 39, no. 1 (2009), http://dx.doi.org/10.1525/hsns.2009.39.1.1.

2   Stephen Jay Gould, "Utopia (Limited)," *New York Review of Books*, March 3, 1983, 23. Gould could have added ecosystems and the biosphere as a whole to the sequence.

3   Gould, "Utopia," 25. For a survey of more recent developments in biology along the lines of Gould's approach see James Shapiro, *Evolution: A View from the Twenty-First Century* (Upper Saddle River, NJ: FT Science Press, 2011).

4   Robert B. Westbrook, *John Dewey and American Democracy* (Ithaca: Cornell University Press, 1991), 127, footnote 15.

5   See "The Abolition of Society" below, particularly the discussion of Michael Mann.

6   Bertalanffy, *General Systems Theory*, 52–53. Perhaps in reaction to the social manipulation facilitated by "systems analysis," both Norbert Wiener and Bertalanffy emphasized the role of individuals per se in contradistinction to society. But the same argument could apply to collective as well as individual actors.

7   Robert Jervis, *System Effects: Complexity in Political and Social Life* (Princeton, NJ: Princeton University Press, 1997.)

8   Brass Workers History Project, *Brass Valley: The Story of Working People's Lives and Struggles in an American Industrial Region* (Philadelphia: Temple University Press, 1982), https://archive.org/details/brassvalleystoryoobrec_o.

CHAPTER 11

1   Buckley, *Modern Systems Research for the Behavioral Scientist* (Chicago: Aldine, 1969), 490. For a later attempt to apply systems theory to society, see Niklas Luhmann, *Social Systems* (Stanford: Stanford University Press, 1995). For a critical review, see Takis Fotopoulos, "Systems Theory and Complexity: A Potential Tool for Radical Analysis or the Emerging Social Paradigm for the Internationalized Market Economy?" *Democracy & Nature* 6, no. 3 (November 2000), 421–46.

2   I won't try here to summarize all of Mann's conceptually rich approach, only those aspects that I use as part of my own. In particular I leave to the side his attempt to classify power networks in terms of *ideological, economic, military,* and *political* power. It is difficult to see the validity of such categories independent of a particular purpose. For Mann's project of a history of power they play a useful role, but early on he concedes that "real institutionalized networks of interaction do not have a simple one-to-one relationship to the ideal-typical sources of social power." They are "functionally promiscuous" (17). For purposes of social change, recognizing their promiscuity is crucial. For as Mann later acknowledges, "Actual social movements normally mix up elements of most, if not all, power sources in more general power configurations" (Michael Mann, *The Sources of Social Power,* vol. I: *A History of Power from the Beginning to A.D. 1760* (Cambridge: Cambridge University Press, 1986), 523.

3   Mann, *The Sources of Social Power,* 2.

4   Mann, 2. However, he in fact adopts a definition of a society as "a network of social interaction at the boundaries of which is a certain level of interaction cleavage between it and its environment. A society is a unit with boundaries, and it contains interaction that is relatively dense and stable; that is, it is internally patterned when compared to interaction that crosses its boundaries." (13) This would surely correspond to some definitions of an open system.

5   *The Sources of Social Power,* 6, citing Parsons. I generally prefer to speak in terms of "coordination" rather than "cooperation" because "cooperation" may carry

the connotation that a coordination is voluntary and mutually beneficial. Such terms as "coerced cooperation" and "exploitative cooperation" sound paradoxical, but unfortunately they reflect real phenomena.

6   This is similar to the distinction made in the introduction to *Strike!* between the power of "some people to tell others what to do" and the power of "people directing their own action cooperatively toward common purposes." *Strike!* (2020), 4–5.

7   *The Sources of Social Power*, 6. Whether "inherent tendency" implies "inevitability," and how such a tendency may be countered, are critical questions for democracy.

8   See Charles E. Lindblom, *Politics and Markets: The World's Political-Economic Systems* (New York: Basic Books, 1977) for the concept of "extended authority."

9   Mann, *The Sources of Social Power*, 6–7.

10   Mann, 7.

11   Mann states explicitly that his is "a developmental, though not an evolutionary or a teleological, history" (*The Sources of Social Power*, 31).

12   Mann, 522.

13   Mann, 21. Mann uses "ideology" in the sociological, not the Marxian, sense.

14   Jeremy Brecher, Tim Costello, and Brendan Smith, *Globalization from Below* (Cambridge, MA: South End Press, 2002), 25.

CHAPTER 12

1   William Blake, "The Song of Los," in *The Poems of William Blake*, ed. W. H. Stevenson (London: Longman, 1971), 246.

2   Jeremy Brecher, *Strike!*, 50th anniversary ed. (Oakland: PM Press, 2020), 2. See also Jeremy Brecher and Tim Costello, *Common Sense for Hard Times* (Boston: South End Press, 1979), 3–4.

3   Brecher and Costello, *Common Sense for Hard Times*, 57. See note 27 on 240 for a literal translation of Brecht's poem by Martin Esslin.

4   Gandhi has also received considerable criticism for his policies towards Muslims and toward those then known as "untouchables" and now as Dalits.

5   Mohandas K. Gandhi, *Indian Opinion*, November 11, 1905.

6   Quoted in Gene Sharp, *Waging Nonviolent Struggle*, vol. 1 (Boston: Porter Sargent, 2005), 84.

7   Quoted in Sharp, *Waging Nonviolent Struggle*, vol. 1, 84.

8   Quoted in Sharp, vol. 1, 84.

9   Quoted in Sharp, vol. 1, 41–42.

10   Quoted in Sharp, vol. 1, 85.

11   Sharp, vol. 1, 85.

12   Sharp, vol. 1, 8–9.

13   Karl Marx, "The Working Day," sec. 7, "The Struggle for the Normal Working Day," in *Capital*, vol. 1 (Moscow: Progress Publishers, 1965).

14   Sharp, *Waging Nonviolent Struggle*, 35.

15   In systems terms, the process of change from below requires a system whose subsystems can form goals that are autonomous from the wholes of which they are part, and can form coalitions around goals that are not the same as the current goals of the whole and those subsystems that are currently dominant within it. This can be easier in systems of overlapping networks like those

portrayed by Michael Mann than in nested systems where each subsystem is totally enclosed within its metasystem.

16 Jervis, *System Effects*.

17 Sharp, *Waging Nonviolent Struggle*, vol. 1, 47.

18 Jeremy Brecher, "The Vietnam Moratorium," *Liberation Magazine*, May 1969, http://www.hippy.com/modules.php?name=News&file=article&sid=118

19 Jeremy Brecher, Tim Costello, and Brendan Smith, *Globalization from Below* (Cambridge, MA: South End Press, 2002), 21.

20 Jeremy Brecher, *Against Doom: A Climate Insurgency Manual* (Oakland: PM Press, 2017), 22.

21 Brecher, *Against Doom*, 24. See part 3 below.

CHAPTER 13

1 Scattered through Ernest Schachtel's book *Metamorphosis* were references to Piaget. Even though it was at least a decade before I discovered Piaget's own writings, this early exposure to the idea of development no doubt helped make me receptive to his ideas when I encountered them directly. So did Schachtel's emphasis on the active character of human beings and the alternation between open receptiveness to the unique features of an object and the effort to fit it into already known patterns—perhaps for me an *Anlage* for Piaget's central concepts of accommodation and assimilation. I have benefited greatly from the opportunity to discuss Piaget with Eleanor Duckworth, author of the wonderful exploration of the implications of Piaget's ideas for education *"The Having of Wonderful Ideas" and Other Essays on Teaching and Learning* (New York: Teachers College Press, 1996), who worked with Piaget for more than two decades.

2 Piaget developed his initial ideas decades before the emergence of cybernetics, but he increasingly reconfigured them in cybernetic terms. "I see a tight relationship between my models and cybernetic models.... I did not use cybernetic terminology when I began talking of [equilibration], but nonetheless since the beginning I have insisted that it was ... a self-regulation. And of course today cybernetics is precisely that, the study of self-regulating models. This self-regulating kernel is at the very heart of all of the development of intelligence" (Richard I. Evans, *Jean Piaget: The Man and His Ideas* [New York: Dutton, 1973], 45–46). This set of interviews and documents provides some of Piaget's most accessible formulations. For a perceptive account of how Piaget's systems theory compares with and differs from others, see Michael Chapman, "Equilibration and the Dialectics of Organization," in *Piaget's Theory: Prospects and Possibilities*, ed. Harry Beilin and Peter Pufall (Hillsdale, NJ: Lawrence Erlbaum, 1992), 46ff.

3 In my first attempt to explain Piaget's ideas, I noted that in trying to write historical accounts of social movements I had come up against the problem of "how is it possible to conceive of human groups, organizations, and societies which both maintain themselves over considerable periods of time, *and* are subject to radical transformation?" Jeremy Brecher, "History, Society, and Genetic Structuralism" (unpublished manuscript, 1970s).

4 Terrance Brown and Kishore Julian Thampy, "About the Translation," in Jean Piaget, *The Equilibration of Cognitive Structures: The Central Problem of*

Intellectual Development (Chicago: University of Chicago Press, 1985), xv. This book was also previously translated with the title *The Development of Thought* (New York: Viking, 1977). I have used both translations.

5   I was always struck by the fact that Piaget published *The Equilibration of Cognitive Structures* when he was nearly eighty as a reworking of a book he had written long before because "since the models of equilibration developed there have proved inadequate, the whole problem must be reexamined" (xvii). I found it inspiring that such self-correction was central not only to Piaget's theory but also to his practice.

6   As we have seen with Marx, this is a common problem in understanding, and writing about, theories that involve "internal relations" among their elements.

7   Michael Chapman, "Equilibration and the Dialectics of Organization," in Beilin and Pufall, *Piaget's Theory*, 40.

8   Piaget, *The Equilibration of Cognitive Structures*, xvii. He sometimes called his general approach "constructivism."

9   Piaget from time to time touched on such social dimensions himself. Regarding the application of the same abstract aspects of theory to individual and social phenomena, Piaget wrote, "There exist common mechanisms which are found in all domains of the human sciences. And the rules, values and signs which we take in this text to be essential social facts presuppose exactly such operational, regulatory and semiotic mechanisms" (preface to *Sociological Studies*, 25).

10   See Greg Downey, "Balance between Cultures: Equilibrium Training," http://neuroanthropology.net/2008/11/30/balance-between-cultures-equilibrium-training/.

11   In one of his last works, Piaget notes the possibility of synthesis of his genetic structuralism with "the functionalism found in the work of J. Dewey." In the functionalist perspective, "all mental activity, in particular cognitive activity, proceeds from a tendency to satisfy needs. Needs themselves consist of momentary disequilibria, and their satisfaction consists of reequilibrations." Needs are manifested in terms of "interests." Interest is "a relationship between the subject's needs and the object's characteristics. Something becomes "interesting" to the degree that it answers some need, a form of compensation." Interest also "frees the subject's energies and incites action in the direction of the object." It is thus a "positive feedback regulation." *The Equilibration of Cognitive Structures*, 68.

12   Some of Piaget's specific results have been disconfirmed or superseded by subsequent research, a normal process in a scientific field. His views have also been criticized for various forms of cultural bias. Left-wing critics have sometimes portrayed his approach as representing the values and practices of Western industrial capitalism and its technological reason. See, for example, Herbert Marcuse, *One-Dimensional Man* (Boston: Beacon, 1964) and Susan Buck-Morss, "Socio-economic Bias in Piaget's Theory and Its Implications for Cross-Culture Studies," *Human Development* 18 (1975): 35–49. Noam Chomsky famously challenged Piaget's view of equilibration in the development of language. (See Jean Piaget, *Language and Learning: The Debate Between Jean Piaget and Noam Chomsky* [London: Routledge & Kegan Paul, 1980].) While many of these criticisms have some validity, I don't think they invalidate the more abstract dimensions of Piagetian ideas that I use in my heuristic. My use of

those abstract dimensions does not imply an endorsement of all of Piaget's own efforts to apply his theories to social phenomena.

13 *Strike!* was completed before I started studying Piaget seriously, but I had gleaned many similar ideas from Schachtel, Dewey, Marx, Ilse Mattick, and Paul Mattick Jr.

CHAPTER 14

1 Piaget expresses common pragmatist themes, such as the role of problems, the centrality of action, and a loop between theory and practice. As a youth, long before he started studying cognitive development in children, Piaget wrote a "Sketch of a Neo-Pragmatism" which he stated in an autobiographical article "presented an idea which has since remained central for me": that "action in itself admits of logic" and that, therefore, "logic steps from a sort of spontaneous organization of acts." ("Jean Piaget, an Autobiography" in Richard I. Evans, *Jean Piaget: The Man and His Ideas* [New York: Dutton, 1973], 113.)

2 Jean Piaget, *The Child and Reality* (Harmondsworth: Penguin, 1975), 70.

3 To clarify levels of the analysis: There is a holistic relation between an actor and its environment as a whole. Within that there are patterns or schemes that relate to particular objects in the environment.

4 Note that this account includes the kind of negative "cybernetic explanation" discussed in chapter 9 above, in which an event is explained by showing how the other things that might possibly have occurred couldn't or didn't.

5 I wrote an account of the 1973 meat boycott in *Common Sense for Hard Times* as I was engrossed in studying and trying to understand Piaget. Even though the account does not explicitly reference his ideas, they are not hard to detect in the way I told the story. Here I make their role explicit.

CHAPTER 15

1 This interaction may be restricted to a part of the entity: a particular pattern or scheme. It may also be restricted to a particular object in the environment. Development may also occur through interaction among patterns within an entity.

2 These general features of a pattern are more or less equivalent to the norms or goals or steady-states or boundary conditions of a system.

3 Jean Piaget, *The Equilibration of Cognitive Structures: The Central Problem of Intellectual Development* (Chicago: University of Chicago Press, 1985), 10.

4 Jean Piaget, *The Development of Thought* (New York: Viking, 1977), 7.

5 Piaget, *The Development of Thought*, 26.

6 Piaget also calls the change that eliminates a gap a new coordination. The idea of coordination is familiar from the physical development of children: Clumsy and awkward movements become precise and graceful through the improved coordination developed through practice. As Piaget puts it, the result of improving equilibration is "a system of coordinated movements functioning for a result or an intention." Thus equilibration is a practice of closing gaps by acts of coordination. The steersman's rudder coordinates the desired course of the boat with its current momentum. Piaget also describes equilibration as a form of regulation or control. The equilibration cycle as a whole regulates or controls the particular patterns that it maintains or modifies.

7   Piaget, *The Child and Reality*, 40.

8   Piaget treats reflective abstraction as a special case of the regulation of regulations. What is happening at a lower level is assimilated and reconstructed at a higher level. The recent development of new technologies for studying the functioning of the brain make it likely that arguments about human consciousness will develop in radically new ways in the foreseeable future, possibly rendering a great deal of past speculation obsolete.

9   Piaget, *The Equilibration of Cognitive Structures,* 3. Stephen Jay Gould's idea of "punctuated equilibrium" in paleontology presents a similar pattern. For a discussion of the distinction between Piaget's "open" and other "closed" systems theories, see Michael Chapman, "Equilibration and the Dialectics of Organization," in Beilin and Pufall, *Piaget's Theory*, 47–48.

10   Jean Piaget, *Structuralism* (New York, Harper Torchbook, 1971), 140.

CHAPTER 16

1   The interpretation of Occupy Wall Street in this chapter is further spelled out in chapter 10 of the 2015 and 2020 updated editions of *Strike!*.

2   The interpretation of the climate protection movement in this chapter is based on part 1 of *Climate Insurgency: A Strategy for Survival* (London: Routledge, 2016).

3   See parts 1 and 2 of Jeremy Brecher and Tim Costello, *Common Sense for Hard Times* (Boston: South End Press, 1979); "The Unknown Labor Dimension of the Vietnam War Era Revolt," in Jeremy Brecher, *Strike!* (2020), 235–56.

4   For proposals for the climate direct-action movement, see Jeremy Brecher, *Against Doom: A Climate Action Manual* (Oakland: PM Press, 2017).

CHAPTER 17

1   Piaget's translators generally use the term "egocentricity" or "egocentrism." However, in English this connotes and sometimes even denotes a person who is vain, selfish, and narcissistic—meanings Piaget's use of the term does not intend. I have substituted "autocentric" and "autocentricity" throughout this text.

2   See chapter 10, "Open Systems," 68.

3   For Piaget, these same principles govern individual and collective subjects. He criticized an "atomistic" conception of society that starts from individuals regarded as unconnected to society. But he also rejected views that would give groups or societies a reality separate from that of the interactions that make them up. He criticized Durkheim's view that society is "the origin of logical thought and of truth itself" which "imposes these on the minds of individuals by means of intellectual and moral 'constraint.'" Jean Piaget, *Biology and Knowledge* (Chicago: University of Chicago Press, 1971), 98. See also Jean Piaget, *Structuralism* (New York: Harper Torchbook, 1971), 76ff, and "Explanation in Sociology."

      Piaget's perspective on society fits with Gandhi's approach to power. Society and those who govern it are not some separate thing over and above the people who make society up. Rather, society is composed of people's everyday action. Power is not the inherent possession of the powerful, but rather depends on the cooperation of others. And because society is not a unitary thing, that cooperation can be withdrawn.

4   *Biology and Knowledge*, 98. See also *Structuralism*, 76ff. His rather obscure statement was that the relationship between individuals and the social group comprises "a relational totality in which individual operations and cooperation form one inseparable whole in such a way that the laws of the general coordination of actions are, in their functional nucleus, common to inter- and intra-individual actions and operations."

5   Piaget in Evans, *Jean Piaget, the Man and His Ideas*, 19–20. Some attempts to apply systems theory to society try, on the contrary, to abolish the subject. In the forward to Niklas Luhmann, *Social Systems* (Stanford: Stanford University Press, 1995), Eva Knodt wrote, "Systems theory turns away from the knowing subject to a reality that consists solely of self-referential systems and their 'empirically' observable operations" (quoted in Takis Fotopoulos, "Systems Theory and Complexity," in *Democracy and Nature*, xvii, www.democracynature. org/dn/vol6/takis_complexity.htm)

6   While Piaget focuses on the cognitive aspect of the formation of collective subjects, it also involves emotions, culture, values, and other less purely cognitive aspects of life. This theme is developed by such thinkers as E.P. Thompson and Raymond Williams.

7   Decentering can be aided by the capacity for reflective abstraction. Representations of possible situations, proposed actions, and anticipated results—i.e. "thought experiments"—can be communicated among different individuals and groups while remaining reversible. So can proposed alternatives and final agreement on a joint course of action. This capacity for shared thought experiments makes uncoerced but purposeful collective decision making possible.

8   *Structuralism*, 139. Piaget says this formulation applies "on the plane of knowledge (as, perhaps, on that of moral and aesthetic values)."

     This process is surprisingly close to Sartre's concept of "de-serialization." See for example "From Seriality to Group," in Wilfrid Desan, *The Marxism of Jean-Paul Sartre* (Garden City, NY: Doubleday Anchor, 1966. (Sartre puts this process in the context of interests as well as cognitive viewpoints.) While Piaget was quite hostile to Sartre's early existentialism (see *Insights and Illusions of Philosophy* throughout), he later defended the "constructivism" of the *Critique of Dialectical Reason*, and observed that Sartre's remaining "subjectivist difficulties" are "the remains of his earlier existentialist phase" (*Structuralism*, 121). There is also an affinity between Piaget's distinction between an "external universality" and "a process of coordinating and setting in reciprocal relations" on the one hand and Sartre's distinction between "totality" and "totalization" on the other.

9   Michael Chapman makes a similar distinction in "Equilibration and the Dialectics of Organization," in *Piaget's Theory: Prospects and Possibilities*, ed. Harry Beilin and Peter Pufall (Hillsdale, NJ: Lawrence Erlbaum, 1992), 49ff. Another distinction between individual and collective subjects is that collective subjects, unlike living individual subjects, can dissolve into their constituent parts and cease to exist as subjects while the living individuals who composed them live on.

10 Jeremy Brecher, Tim Costello, and Brendan Smith, *Globalization from Below* (Cambridge, MA: South End Press, 2002), 10, 15.

11 *Structuralism*, 119.

12 Piaget's concept of ideal equilibrium, and his research on the "moral development of the child," have sometimes been used to assert an objective value hierarchy in which the stages of individual development define an ethical or moral standard. Whether or not there is any validity to this idea, and whether Piaget himself adopts it, it has proven extremely susceptible to autocentric and ethnocentric interpretations. It would be exceptional to find expositors of such views who do not believe their own society, and people like themselves, are somewhere near the pinnacle of the hierarchy.

13 Richard Isador Evans, *Jean Piaget, the Man and His Ideas* (Boston: E.P. Dutton, 1973), 125.

14 Ideal equilibrium represents a "regulative ideal" which provides regulation or guidance even though it may be impossible to fully realize. For social movements, it implies that they are not faced with an either/or choice between internal authoritarianism or chaos. For society it suggests there is not an either/or choice between state command and other forms of domination or unregulated markets and other forms of disorder. The process of decentering described by Piaget provides the basis for a very different form of social relations in which individuals voluntarily share knowledge and coordinate their action to achieve common goals. Networks and other forms of free coordination provide an alternative toward which social organization can develop.

CHAPTER 18

1 G. Polya, *How to Solve It: A New Aspect of Mathematical Method*, 2nd ed. (Princeton, NJ: Princeton University Press, 1971), 2.

2 Rainer Maria Rilke, *Letters to a Young Poet* (Boston, W. W. Norton, 1993)

3 Polya, *How to Solve It*, 172.

4 Polya, 4.

5 Polya, 12, 198.

6 Polya, 73.

7 Polya, 4.

8 Polya, 2–3.

9 Polya, 10.

10 Polya, 40.

11 Polya, 10.

12 Polya, 149–52

13 Polya, 13.

14 Polya, 61. Indeed, Polya notes that scientific knowledge is based on experiments and measurements combined with mathematical reasoning, and asserts that even mathematical knowledge rests on "a broad experimental basis" that is "broadened by each problem whose result is successfully tested (61).

15 Polya, *How to Solve It*, 188.

16 Polya, 188.

17 Jeremy Brecher, *History from Below: How to Uncover and Tell the Story of Your Community, Association, or Union* (West Cornwall, CT: Stone Soup Books, 2018), 13.

18   Polya, *How to Solve It*, 2.

19   Polya, 157.

20   Polya, 157–58.

21   Polya, 133.

22   Jeremy Brecher, *Strike!*, quoting Ruth McKenney, *Industrial Valley* (New York: Harcourt, Brace, 1939).

23   "Historical Analysis of How Labor Changes on Key Issues," Labor Network for Sustainability, http://www.labor4sustainability.org/wp-content/uploads/2014/11/pdf_11042014.pdf.

24   Polya points out that there are often multiple routes to a solution. Checking a solution is essentially a question of resolving the problem by a different route. (Polya, *How to Solve It*, 15.)

25   Polya, 14–15.

26   The method of inquiry of the "scientist" or "scholar" is only a refinement and extension of the "common sense" method of inquiry of the actor. It is a transposition to a metalevel of what those it studies do. In general the patterns used in the heuristic are transposable among various different levels and domains. Part 2 is in effect a "reconstruction at a higher level" of the materials in part 1, constructed through their mutual assimilation and accommodation.

27   Such complementary of conceptual elements is reminiscent of Piaget, who used many different concepts to look at intellectual development. As Flavell put it, the choice of any one unifier is almost arbitrary. Because the model is holistic, each part is interrelated. Indeed, many of the concepts attack the same problem from different points of view: egocentrism, equilibrium, structure, centering, decentering, states and transformation, transduction, etc. According to Flavell, Piaget considered the various concepts "as multiple expressions of a single cognitive orientation rather than as a string of unconnected attributes" J.H. Flavell, *The Developmental Psychology of Jean Piaget* (Princeton, NJ: D. Van Nostrand, 1963), 161. Quoted in Shawn W. Rosenberg, Dana Ward, and Stephen Chilton, *Political Reasoning and Cognition: A Piagetian View* (Durham, Duke University Press, 1988), 48.

CHAPTER 19

1   Equilibration itself doesn't require a pressing problem. Anyone who watches children at play can frequently see the emergence of new equilibrations, individual and collective. But collective shifts in the strategies by which people live their lives are unlikely without a compelling problem.

2   See "Learning by Doing" in part 1. For a social application see also Mac Brockway (Tim Costello), "Keep on Truckin'," *Root & Branch* 2, https://libcom.org/library/keep-truckin.

3   E.P. Thompson, *The Poverty of Theory* (London: Merlin, 1978), 363.

4   A central theme of Herbert Marcuse's was the need to judge societies and social practices against their own potential. A society that provided less freedom than its own capacities made possible, for example, practiced "surplus repression." Herbert Marcuse, *One-Dimensional Man* (Boston: Beacon, 1964).

5   See Brecher, *Save the Humans? Common Preservation in Action*, 2nd ed. (Oakland: PM Press, 2020), part 4, 140–80.

6   See Jeremy Brecher, "Uniting for Peace," *ZNet*, April 2, 2003, and Jeremy Brecher, "Uniting for Peace," *Global Policy Forum*, March 20, 2003, https://www. globalpolicy.org/component/content/article/167/35375.html.

7   See Global Labor Strategies, "Beyond China's New Labor Contract Law," http:// laborstrategies.blogs.com/global_labor_strategies/china/page/2/.

8   See Brecher, *Save the Humans?*, part 5, 196–99, for discussion of a "human preservation movement."

CHAPTER 20

1   See Talcott Parsons, *The Social System* (London: Routledge & Kegan Paul, 1970).

2   Gregory Bateson, *Steps to an Ecology of Mind* (New York: Ballantine, 1972), 399.

3   The conceptualization of a goal does not necessarily correspond perfectly to the closing of a gap. Therefore a problem may be solved, a gap closed, and equilibrium established without the goal as the actor conceived it being realized. Successful adaptation can occur without the actor having a valid knowledge of how it occurred; often we just "feel our way" to a solution and regard it as a resolution when the problem doesn't give us any more trouble.

4   Gregory Bateson points out that patterning is equivalent to the concept of redundancy in communications theory. "The message material is said to contain 'redundancy' if, when the message is received with some items missing, the receiver is able to guess at the missing items with better than random success" ("Redundancy and Coding," in *Steps to an Ecology of Mind*, 413–14).

5   See Frans de Waal, *Chimpanzee Politics* (Baltimore: Johns Hopkins, 1983) for a fascinating glimpse of the intermediate balance of instinct and invention observable in the self and common preservation strategies of one of our closest relatives.

6   Nonlinear dynamic systems theories deal with such radical change using such concepts as bifurcation, phase transitions, and strange attractors to explain such discontinuous change. See for example J.A. Scott Kelso, *Dynamic Patterns: The Self-Organization of Brains and Behavior* (Cambridge, MA: MIT Press, 1995.) Evelyn Fox Keller indicates the limitations of nonlinear dynamic systems theories for understanding living beings: "The critical properties of function, agency, and purpose continue to mark organisms . . . apart from all the emergent phenomena of nonlinear dynamical systems" ("Self-Organization, Self-Assembly, and the Inherent Activity of Matter" [Hans Rausing Lecture, Uppsala University, 2009], p. 19, https://selforganizationbiology2011.files.wordpress.com/2011/04/ efk09.pdf).

7   Matthew Arnold, "Stanzas from the Grande Chartreuse" (1855), https://www. poetryfoundation.org/poems/43605/stanzas-from-the-grande-chartreuse.

CHAPTER 21

1   This passage draws on Jeremy Brecher and Tim Costello, *Common Sense for Hard Times* (Boston: South End Press, 1979), 4–5. Our concept of strategy was influenced by Alfred Chandler, *Strategy and Structure: Chapters in the History of the American Industrial Enterprise* (Cambridge, MA: MIT Press, 1962).

2   Jeremy Brecher, *Strike!* (San Francisco: Straight Arrow Books, 1972), 316.

3   Such gaps might also arise for other reasons, for example because people had developed new aspirations or because new possibilities had emerged, or

because established patterns came into conflict with each other. See next chapter, "Transforming Ends."

4   "Chapter Eight: Labor in the New World Economy," in Jeremy Brecher and Tim Costello, *Global Village or Global Pillage* (Cambridge, MA: South End Press, 1998).

5   Brecher, *Save the Humans?*, part 5, "Human Preservation," 182–218.

CHAPTER 22

1   Jean Piaget addresses this question in terms of the "coordination of values." Man "believes in a multiplicity of values, orders them hierarchically and thus gives meaning to his existence by decisions that constantly go beyond the limits of his actual knowledge." Jean Piaget, *Insights and Illusions of Philosophy* (New York: World, 1971), 209, 211. For Piaget's interpretation of some of the factors affecting the coordination of values, see "Explanation in Sociology," *Sociological Studies*, 43.

2   See John Bowlby, *Attachment and Loss*, vol. 1: *Attachment* (New York: Basic Books, 1969) and Peter Marris, *Loss and Change* (London: Routledge & Kegan Paul, 1986).

3   Jeremy Brecher, "Doctor Wall Street: How the U.S. Health-Care System Got So Sick" *Z Magazine*, June 2008.

4   Leon Trotsky, *History of the Russian Revolution* (Pathfinder, 1980).

5   Those who pursue insane goals, such as global destruction for its own sake, or who are willing to disregard the consequences of actions as merely the pettifogging of the "reality-based community," may not be persuaded by such arguments. But people with highly diverse and even conflicting values and worldviews can share a recognition that their various goals can now only be achieved through common preservation.

CHAPTER 23

1   See also Jean Piaget, *Sociological Studies* (London: Routledge, 1995) on the nature of tacit operations vs. propositional operations in social relations.

2   The processes by which such tacit or unconscious knowledge and action is constructed are complex and often difficult to observe often difficult to observe. Recent research indicates that they involve both regulation by gene expression and regulation that can best be understood as trans-individual. See Ernest L. Rossi, *The Psychobiology of Gene Expression* (New York: Norton, 2002). They may also involve forms of "distributed processing" or "neural nets" that as a functioning whole may represent phenomena through their propensity to respond, but that don't map any particular object or event to any particular representing element.

3   Malcolm Gladwell, *Blink: The Power of Thinking without Thinking* (New York: Little, Brown and Company, 2005).

4   Jeremy Brecher, *Banded Together: Economic Democratization in the Brass Valley* (Urbana: University of Illinois Press, 2011).

5   Jeremy Brecher, *Strike!* (2020), 37.

CHAPTER 24

1   "For a Better Future: The 1933 New Haven Garment Strike," New England Historical Society, http://www.newenglandhistoricalsociety.com/new-england-historical-society-history-brief-7-3-2013/.

2   Bishop Joseph Butler, preface to *Fifteen Sermons Preached at the Rolls Chapel* (1729).

3   See E.P. Thompson's detailed study of this uncompleted process in *The Making of the English Working Class* (New York: Vintage Books, 1963).

4   Boundaries are patterns maintained by actions. Boundaries are also a case of differentiation. Boundaries whose permeability varies are selective compensations—i.e. equilibrations.

5   The formation of social groups—a.k.a. collective or concerted or interindividual subjects or actors-in-common—is addressed further in "Transforming Coordination" below.

6   Mann, vol. 1, 1.

7   Mann, vol. 1, 13.

8   For a sophisticated interpretation of historical boundary change see Saskia Sassen, *Territory, Authority, Rights: From Medieval to Global Assemblages* (Princeton, NJ: Princeton University Press, 2006).

9   Jeremy Brecher and Tim Costello, *Global Village or Global Pillage* (Cambridge, MA: South End Press, 1998).

10   Jeremy Brecher, "Introduction," in *Global Visions: Beyond the New World Order*, eds. Jeremy Brecher, John Brown Childs, and Jill Cutler (Boston: South End Press, 1993), xix.

11   Jeremy Brecher, *Save the Humans?*, part 5, 182–218.

CHAPTER 25

1   Michael Mann, *The Sources of Social Power,* vol. I: *A History of Power from the Beginning to A.D. 1760* (Cambridge: Cambridge University Press, 1986), 6, paraphrasing Talcott Parsons.

2   Clay Shirky, *Here Comes Everybody: The Power of Organizing without Organizations* (New York: Penguin, 2008).

3   See, for example, Walter W. Powell, "Neither Market nor Hierarchy: Network Forms of Organization," *Research in Organizational Behavior* 12 (1990).

4   Charles E. Lindblom, *Politics and Markets: The World's Political-Economic Systems* (New York: Basic Books, 1977).

5   This process is interpreted by Adam Smith as a "hidden hand" and by Marx as "the fetishism of commodities." "Market signals" are often equated to "feedback," but they regulate very differently from the active, intentional compensation described in "Solving Problems" above.

6   The spontaneous evolution of a common language involves an adaptation of each user to cumulative changes whose origins are in most cases unknown to them. Deliberate efforts at linguistic reform, such as the attempts by Noah Webster and the French Academy to inculcate "correct" American or French language usage, represent attempts to replace such unplanned mutual adaptation with command.

CHAPTER 27

1   *Strike!* (Boston: South End Press, 1977), viii. For a related view, see Frances Fox Piven, *Challenging Authority: How Ordinary People Change America* (New York: Rowman & Littlefield, 2006). "Ordinary people exercise power in American politics mainly at those extraordinary moments when they rise up in anger

and hope, defy the rules that ordinarily govern their daily lives, and, by doing so, disrupt the workings on the institutions in which they are enmeshed" (1).

2 Mohandas K. Gandhi, *Indian Opinion*, November 11, 1905.

3 Gene Sharp, "Part One: Power and Struggle," in *The Power of Nonviolent Action* (Boston: Porter Sargent, 1973), 4.

CHAPTER 28

1 Various thinkers have made similar distinctions. Karl Marx observed that capitalism combined anarchy in the market with domination in the workplace. American political scientist Charles Lindblom contrasted market failures and political failures. Jean Piaget distinguished two impediments to "ideal equilibrium": autocentrism or failure to coordinate with the viewpoint of others and social constraint that accepts an imposed external viewpoint.

2 Sartre divided human behavior into praxis and the "practico-inert." Jean-Paul Sartre, *Critique of Dialectical Reason* (London: New Left Books, 1960), 788.

3 Gregory Bateson, "Metalogue: Why Do Things Get in a Muddle?," in Gregory Bateson, *Steps to an Ecology of Mind* (New York: Ballantine, 1972).

4 Carr, *What Is History?* (Cambridge: Cambridge University Press, 1961), 64.

5 In cybernetic theory this phenomenon is known as "deviation-amplifying feedback" or "positive feedback." It was the bête noire of Norbert Wiener. The term "positive feedback" has developed such different connotations in common language that it is now confusing to use it for its original meaning.

6 See, for example, Gregoire Nicolis and Ilya Prigogine, *Exploring Complexity: An Introduction* (New York: W.H. Freeman, 1989).

7 "Introduction to Avant-Guard Swiss Sculptor Jean Tinguely," https://theculturetrip.com/europe/switzerland/articles/the-art-of-destruction-jean-tinguely-and-dadaism/.

8 Mel Duncan, "Making Minnesota Connections," in Jeremy Brecher and Tim Costello, eds., *Building Bridges: The Emerging Grassroots Coalition of Labor and Community* (New York: Monthly Review Press, 1990), 164.

9 See Clay Shirky, *Here Comes Everybody: The Power of Organizing without Organizations* (New York: Penguin, 2008).

CHAPTER 29

1 For a brilliant discussion of the way in which such dependence can be manipulated by those with power, see "Hitler and Roman Foreign Policy" in Simone Weil's essay "The Great Beast," in *Selected Essays 1934–1943* (London: Oxford University Press, 1962), 101ff.

2 Jeremy Brecher, "Terminating the Bush Juggernaut," Institute for Policy Studies, May 1, 2003. https://ips-dc.org/terminating_the_bush_juggernaut/.

CHAPTER 31

1 William Blake, "The Grey Monk," in *The Poems of Blake*, ed. W.H. Stevenson (London: Longman Group, 1971), 584–85.

2 Adam Michnik, *Letters from Prison* (Berkeley: University of California Press, 1985).

3 NAFFE, *Making Networks Work*, http://www.fairjobs.org/sites/default/files/Making+Networks+Work.pdf.

4   For the redesign of jobs, see Jeremy Brecher, "Socialism Is What You Make It," in *Socialist Visions*, ed. Steve Rosskamm Shalom (Boston: South End Press, 1983). For subsidiarity, see Jeremy Brecher, Tim Costello, and Brendan Smith, *Globalization from Below* (Cambridge, MA: South End Press, 2002), 42–43. For property as a "bundle of rights" that can be unbundled and redistributed, see Jeremy Brecher, "A Legal Blueprint for Our Ecological Survival," *On the Commons*, September 20, 2013, http://www.onthecommons.org/magazine/legal-blueprint-our-ecological-survival#sthash.29eXKTpV.dpbs and Jeremy Brecher, *Climate Solidarity: Workers vs. Warming* (Takoma Park, MD: Labor Network for Sustainability, 2017), 9–10, http://www.labor4sustainability.org/wp-content/uploads/2017/06/Climate-Solidarity.pdf.

5   "Eternal vigilance is the price of liberty—power is ever stealing from the many to the few.… The hand entrusted with power becomes … the necessary enemy of the people. Only by continual oversight can the democrat in office be prevented from hardening into a despot: only by unintermitted Agitation can a people be kept sufficiently awake to principle not to let liberty be smothered in material prosperity." Wendell Phillips, *Speeches Before the Massachusetts Anti-Slavery Society* (1853), 13. Similar phrases have been attributed to many others.

CHAPTER 32

1   The notes in the Commentary section (pp. 317–341) relate the descriptions and analyses of climate protection to the patterns laid out in the heuristic. They illustrate how the tools can be used for interpretations of and solutions to problems. Comments include references to the relevant chapters and pages in the book.

2   This reflects a broader process analyzed by J.A. Scott Kelso. "Identifiable Signatures or Fingerprints Can Be Detected in *Advance* of Upcoming Change." J.A. Scott Kelso, *Dynamic Patterns: The Self-Organization of Brain and Behavior* (Cambridge, MA: MIT Press, 1995), 16. Kelso's models frequently involve isolated violations of existing patterns as disequilibrium increases, followed by either a phase change or a return to normal constraints.

3   Jeremy Brecher, *Against Doom: A Climate Insurgency Manual* (Oakland: PM Press, 2017), 17.

4   Jeremy Brecher, *Climate Insurgency: A Strategy for Survival* (London: Routledge, 2016); *Against Doom: A Climate Insurgency Manual*; and *Climate Solidarity: Workers vs. Warming* (Takoma Park, MD: Labor Network for Sustainability, 2017), https://www.labor4sustainability.org/wp-content/uploads/2017/06/Climate-Solidarity.pdf. Reference information for facts and quotations in part 3 can be found in these three books unless otherwise noted.

CHAPTER 33

1   My use of the concept "world order" to characterize the state of human social organization at a given time has been influenced by the work of Richard Falk. See also Jeremy Brecher, "World Government," *Zeta*, June 1988. Among Falk's voluminous writings on the subject, see "The World Order Approach," in Richard Falk, *The Promise of World Order* (Philadelphia: Temple University Press, 1988).

2   For an account similar to the one presented here but with greater emphasis on the role of workers and wage labor, see Jeremy Brecher, *Climate Solidarity:*

Workers vs. Warming, chapter 2. For an account similar to the one presented here but with greater emphasis on the less structural, more immediate barriers to climate protection, see Jeremy Brecher, *Climate Insurgency: A Strategy for Survival*, chapter 5, "Why Climate Protection Has Failed." Despite differences of emphasis, I believe these accounts are compatible. However, if there are discrepancies among them, I would urge, to paraphrase Gandhi, that readers accept the most recent account, unless they prefer another one, in which case they should accept that one. I don't think there is much significant difference in their practical application.

3 John Gerrard Ruggie, "Territoriality and Beyond: Problematizing Modernity in International Relations," *International Organization*, 47, no. 1 (Winter 1993). The historical discussion of the development of the nation-state system in this chapter draws on Jeremy Brecher, "The 'National Question' Reconsidered," *New Politics* (Summer 1987); Quentin Skinner, *The Foundations of Modern Political Thought* (Cambridge: Cambridge University Press, 1978); Michael Mann, *The Sources of Social Power*, vol. 1 (Cambridge: Cambridge University Press, 1986) and vol. 2 (Cambridge: Cambridge University Press, 1993); and Saskia Sassen, *Territory, Authority, Rights* (Princeton, NJ: Princeton University Press, 2006).

4 Economic growth has been an objective of states from the ancient encouragement of agricultural improvement to today's promotion of a rising gross domestic product. See Edmund Burke III, "The Big Story," in Edmund Burke III and Kenneth Pomeranz, *The Environment and World History* (Berkeley: University of California Press, 2009).

5 Benedict Anderson, *Imagined Communities* (London: Verso, 1983).

6 Larry Elliot, "World's Eight Richest People Have Same Wealth as Poorest 50%," *Guardian*, January 15, 2017, https://www.theguardian.com/global-development/2017/jan/16/worlds-eight-richest-people-have-same-wealth-as-poorest-50.

7 See Jeremy Brecher, "A Legal Blueprint for Our Ecological Survival," *On the Commons*, September 20, 2013, http://www.onthecommons.org/magazine/legal-blueprint-our-ecological-survival.

8 For a classic examination see A.A. Berle and Gardner Means, *The Modern Corporation and Private Property* (1932). Recent Supreme Court decisions have expanded rights such as freedom of speech, financing of elections, and liberty of conscience to corporations, which have the effect of reciprocally restricting rights of the people.

9 Bruce Upbin, "The 147 Companies That Control Everything," *Forbes*, October 22, 2011, https://www.forbes.com/sites/bruceupbin/2011/10/22/the-147-companies-that-control-everything/#1a6ef4155105.

10 See Mary Christina Wood, *Nature's Trust* (New York: Cambridge University Press, 2014).

11 Michael Mann, *Sources of Social Power*, vol. 1, 513. See also Saskia Sassen, *Territory, Authority, Rights*.

12 On economic globalization see Jeremy Brecher and Tim Costello, *Global Village or Global Pillage* (Cambridge, MA: South End Press, 1998), and Jeremy Brecher, Tim Costello, and Brendan Smith, *Globalization from Below* (Cambridge, MA: South End Press, 2002). For the relation between globalization and the common preservation heuristic, see "Part 4: Discovering Globalization from Below," in Jeremy Brecher, *Save the Humans?*.

13   Edmund Burke III, "History, Energy, and the Environment," in Burke and Pomeranz, *The Environment and World History*, 45.

14   John R. McNeill, "Global Environmental History in the Age of Fossil Fuels," *Cartografare il presente*, June 23, 2008, http://www.cartografareilpresente.org/article254.html.

15   Craig Collins, "Petroleum Junkies of the World, Unite!," *Truthout*, November 25, 2011.

16   "*Fortune* Global 500," CNN Money, http://moneyi.cnn.com/magazines/fortune/global500/2013/full_list/. Totals calculated in Sean Sweeney, "Unions, Climate Change and the Great Inaction" (Trade Unions for Energy Democracy), http://global-labour.net/wp-content/uploads/2014/08/Unions-and-Climate-Change-and-the-Great-Inaction-June-10.pdf.

17   "Scientific Consensus: Earth's Climate Is Warming," NASA website, http://climate.nasa.gov/scientific-consensus.

CHAPTER 34

1   Elizabeth Kolbert, "The Catastrophist," *New Yorker*, June 29, 2009, https://www.newyorker.com/magazine/2009/06/29/the-catastrophist.

2   Spencer Weart, "International Cooperation," http://www.aip.org/history/climate/internat.htm, accessed September 19, 2014. Extensive information and interpretation on the history of climate science and policy is maintained by physicist and historian Spencer Weart at http://www.aip.org/history/climate/index.htm.

3   "U.N. Climate Change Negotiations," statement by AFL-CIO Executive Council, February 20, 1997.

CHAPTER 35

1   Bill McKibben, *Fight Global Warming Now* (New York: Holt, 2007).

2   McKibben, *Fight Global Warming Now*.

3   For a discussion of the role of social networking in relation to in-the-flesh social action, see Brendan Smith and Jeremy Brecher, "Is Social Networking Useless for Social Change?," *Huffington Post*, October 7, 2010, https://www.huffingtonpost.com/brendan-smith/social-networking-is-malc_b_753274.html.

CHAPTER 36

1   Greenpeace International, *The Greenpeace Chronicles* (Amsterdam: Greenpeace International, 2011), 126, http://www.greenpeace.org/international/Global/international/publications/other/Greenpeace-Chronicles.pdf.

2   Stacy Morford, "NASA's James Hansen, 28 Activists Arrested Protesting Mountaintop Mining," *SolveClimate*, June 23, 2009.

3   An entity like "Native peoples" includes many nesting and overlapping subdivisions, ranging from tribes to differentiated economic interests to differential responses to health impacts ("Transforming Boundaries," 160).

4   For background on early indigenous opposition to Alberta tar sands development see Lori Waller, "We Can No Longer Be Sacrificed," *Briarpatch,* June 9, 2008, https://briarpatchmagazine.com/articles/view/we-can-no-longer-be-sacrificed.

5   Bob Wilson, "Forging the Climate Movement: Environmental Activism and the Keystone XL Pipeline" (Environments and Societies Series, University of California–Davis), November 20, 2013, http://environmentsandsocieties.ucdavis.edu/files/2011/11/Wilson-ES-11.20.2013.pdf.

6   Bill McKibben, "Good News: Tar Sands Action Joined 350.org," http://tarsandsaction.org/2012/01/02/good-news-tar-sands-action-joining-350-org/.

7   Bill McKibben, *Oil and Honey* (New York: Times Books, 2007), 32.

8   McKibben, *Oil and Honey*, 56.

9   Jane Kleeb, "LIUNA Partners with Anti-Union Forces, AFP, ALEC, Koch," *Bold Nebraska*, February 24, 2013, http://boldnebraska.org/liuna-partners-with-anti-union-forces-afp-alec-koch/.

10   Cole Stangler, Rebecca Burns, and Mike Elk, "Frack Till You Drop," *In These Times*, May 23, 2014, http://inthesetimes.com/working/entry/16720/frack_till_you_drop.

11   Jeremy Brecher and the Labor Network for Sustainability, "Stormy Weather: Climate Change and a Divided Labor Movement," *New Labor Forum*, January/February 2013.

12   McKibben, *Oil and Honey*, 45.

13   McKibben, 80.

14   McKibben, 82.

15   McKibben, 87. The House subsequently passed the bill again.

16   McKibben, 128.

17   Ryan Lizza, "The President and the Pipeline," *The New Yorker*, September 16, 2013, https://www.newyorker.com/magazine/2013/09/16/the-president-and-the-pipeline.

18   McKibben, *Oil and Honey*, 251, 253, 255. See also Bob Wilson, "Forging the Climate Movement." 350.org, with its usual lack of turf protection, encouraged the Sierra Club to take the lead.

19   Katherine Bagley, "To Defeat Keystone, Environmental Movement Goes from Beltway to Grassroots," *Inside Climate News*, May 23, 2013.

20   Zoe Carpenter, "Tar Sands Blockade: The Monkey-Wrenchers," *Rolling Stone*, April 11, 2013.

21   Kristin Moe, "#FearlessSummer: How the Battle to Stop Climate Change Got Ferocious," *Yes!*, September 10, 2013. See also Wen Stephenson, "'We Have to Shut It Down,'" *The Nation*, August 5, 2012; Wen Stephenson, "Grassroots Battle against the Big Oil Beast," *The Nation*, October 28, 2013; Steve Early and Suzanne Gordon, "California Refinery Town Hits Chevron with One-Two Punch," *Counterpunch*, August 6, 2013.

22   Crysbel Tejada and Betsy Catlin, "Indigenous Resistance Grows Strong in Keystone XL Battle," *Waging Nonviolence*, May 8, 2013.

23   "Sign the Keystone XL Pledge of Resistance," Credo Action. https://act.credoaction.com/sign/kxl_pledge Accessed May 21, 2014.

24   Ken Butigan, "The Keystone XL Pledge of Resistance Takes Off," *Waging Nonviolence*, June 21, 2013, and Elijah Zarlin, "Here's What's Coming Up with the Keystone XL Pledge of Resistance," *CREDO Action*, August 21, 2013.

25   For further analysis of public opinion see *Against Doom: A Climate Insurgency Manual* (Oakland: PM Press, 2017)., chapters 8 and 9.

26 Zahra Hirji, "It's Not Just Dakota Access. Many Other Fossil Fuel Projects Delayed or Canceled, Too," *Inside Climate News*, December 5, 2016, https://insideclimatenews.org/news/06052016/fossil-fuel-projects-cancellations-keystone-xl-pipeline-oil-coal-natural-gas-climate-change-activists.

27 Bob Wilson, "Forging the Climate Movement" (Environments and Societies Series, University of California–Davis, November 20, 2013), 27, http://environmentsandsocieties.ucdavis.edu/files/2011/11/Wilson-ES-11.20.2013.pdf.

28 Sarah Wheaton, "Keystone XL Pipeline Fight Lifts Environmental Movement," *New York Times*, January 24, 2014.

CHAPTER 37

1 In this chapter I present but do not attempt to justify the climate insurgency strategy. For fuller elaboration, see *Climate Insurgency*, "Part II: A Plausible Strategy for Climate Protection." For arguments supporting its potential effectiveness in eliminating obstacles to climate protection see Chapter 11: Overcoming the Obstacles to Climate Protection.

2 Murray Bookchin, "Ecology and Revolutionary Thought," originally published in 1964 in Bookchin's newsletter *Comment* and reprinted in Murray Bookchin, *Post-Scarcity Anarchism* (Berkeley: Ramparts Press, 1971), 22. Quoted in *Climate Insurgency*, 11.

3 Barry Commoner, *The Closing Circle* (New York: Alfred A. Knopf, 1971) quoted in Jeremy Brecher and Tim Costello, *Common Sense for Hard Times* (Boston: South End Press, 1979), 134.

4 Jeremy Brecher, "The Opening Shot of the Second Ecological Revolution," *Chicago Tribune*, August 16, 1988. http://articles.chicagotribune.com/1988–08–16/news/8801230163_1_greenhouse-effect-poisons-forests.

CHAPTER 38

1 The power of the powerless emerges when coordination among those currently ruled within a system makes it possible for them to exercise counter-dependence against those who rule them ("Transforming Power," 178). Rules can develop from a single act to a tacit pattern to an institution to law widely accepted as binding ("Transforming Coordination," 136).

2 "World Leaders Fiddle While the World Burns: Time for a New Climate Strategy," Statement by the Labor Network for Sustainability, April 29, 2009.

3 Burns H. Weston and David Bollier, *Green Governance: Ecological Survival, Human Rights, and the Law of the Commons* (Cambridge: Cambridge University Press, 2013), 238–42.

4 Jeremy Brecher, "Civil Disobedience as Law Enforcement," *Waging Nonviolence*, August 14, 2013. My education came primarily from Mary Wood's article and book and references therein.

5 Lawrence Hurley, "The Mother behind Kids' Long-shot Legal Crusade," *E&E News*, December 19, 2012. https://www.eenews.net/stories/1059974030.

6 Jeremy Brecher, "Why Getting Arrested to Resist the Keystone XL Is Legally Justified," *Waging Nonviolence*, April 24, 2014, https://wagingnonviolence.org/feature/getting-arrested-resist-keystone-xl-legally-justified/.

7 Jeremy Brecher, "Climate Activist Argues Resistance Is Necessary to Protect the Public Trust," *Common Dreams*, October 18, 2014, https://www.

commondreams.org/views/2014/10/18/climate-activist-argues-resistance-necessary-protect-public-trust.

8   Jeremy Brecher, "A New Wave of Climate Insurgents Defines Itself as Law-Enforcers," *Waging Nonviolence*, February 29, 2016, https://wagingnonviolence.org/feature/break-free-from-fossil-fuels-public-trust-domain/.

9   Kelsey Cascadia Rose Juliana v. United States of America, Opinion and Order, https://static1.squarespace.com/static/571d109b04426270152febe0/t/5824e85e6a49638292ddd1c9/1478813795912/Order+MTD.Aiken.pdf.

10   Kelsey Cascadia Rose Juliana v. United States of America.

11   See Jeremy Brecher, "A Climate Constitution in the Courts and in the Streets," *Common Dreams*, June 6, 2018, https://www.commondreams.org/views/2018/06/06/climate-constitution-courts-and-streets.

CHAPTER 39

1   Jonathan Schell, "Introduction," in Adam Michnik, *Letters from Prison* (Berkeley: University of California Press, 1987). For the role of law in relation to social movements, see Brendan Smith, "Why War Crimes Matter," in Brecher, Cutler, and Smith, *In the Name of Democracy* (New York: Metropolitan Books, 2005).

2   James Gray Pope, "Labor's Constitution of Freedom," *The Yale Law Journal* 106 (1997), http://papers.ssrn.com/sol3/papers.cfm?abstract_id=1622865.

3   The closely related term "civil resistance" is sometimes used to describe a somewhat broader set of movements of which constitutional insurgencies are a subset. *Civil Resistance and Power Politics* by Adam Roberts and Timothy Garton Ash (Oxford: Oxford University Press, 2009) portrays a variety of such movements and observes that they are "civil" in the sense that "they had a civic quality, relating to the interests and hopes of society as a whole"; in some cases "the action involved was not primarily disobedient, but instead involved supporting the norms of a society against usurpers"; and the "generally principled avoidance of the use of violence was not doctrinaire" (4). The distinctive hallmark of insurgencies is that they reject the authority of the state. For a discussion of the distinction between civil disobedience and civil resistance, see Ellen Barfield, "Defending Resistance," *WIN*, Spring 2011, http://www.warresisters.org/content/defending-resistance. "Resistance is understood to include legally challenging the government's behavior, and urging juries and judges to uphold the citizen's right and responsibility to protest government wrongdoing by acquitting accused resisters." While Gandhi is often portrayed as the apostle of "civil disobedience," he wrote, "I found that even 'Civil Disobedience' failed to convey the full meaning of the struggle. I therefore adopted the phrase 'Civil Resistance.'" (P.K. Rao, September 10, 1935.)

4   Jeremy Brecher, "Civil Disobedience as Law Enforcement," *Waging Nonviolence*, August 14, 2013, http://wagingnonviolence.org/feature/civil-disobedience-as-law-enforcement/.

5   "It's Time to Break Free from Fossil Fuels," *350.org*, https://350.org/its-time-to-break-free-from-fossil-fuels/.

6   "It's Time to Break Free from Fossil Fuels."

7   Oliver Milman, "'Break Free' Fossil Fuel Protests Deemed 'Largest Ever' Global Disobedience," *Guardian*, May 16, 2016, https://www.theguardian.com/environment/2016/may/16/break-free-protest-fossil-fuel.

8   "Break Free Proclamation: We Are Here to Defend the Climate, the Constitution, and the Public Trust," in Jeremy Brecher, *Against Doom: A Climate Insurgency Manual* (Oakland, CA: PM Press, 2017), iv.

CHAPTER 40

1   The facts and estimates in this chapter date from the mid-2010s. Obviously they will continue to change, the time available to reduce GHGs will shorten, and the speed required for GHG reduction will accelerate.

2   Jeremy Brecher, Joe Uehlein, and Ron Blackwell, "If Not Now, When? A Labor Movement Plan to Address Climate Change," *New Labor Forum* 23, no. 3 (Fall 2014). http://www.labor4sustainability.org/wp-content/uploads/2014/09/NLF541793_REV1.pdf; Jeremy Brecher, *Climate Insurgency*, chapters 8–9; *Climate Solidarity*, chapter 7.

3   See, for example, Jeremy Brecher, "18 Strategies for the Green New Deal: How to Make the Climate Mobilization Work," Labor Network for Sustainability, 2019, https://www.labor4sustainability.org/wp-content/uploads/2019/02/18Strategies.pdf.

4   For a critique of de-growth with references to the literature advocating it, see Robert Pollin, "De-Growth vs. a Green New Deal," *New Left Review* 112 (July–August 2018), https://newleftreview.org/II/112/robert-pollin-de-growth-vs-a-green-new-deal.

5   Brecher, Uehlein, and Blackwell, "If Not Now, When: A Labor Movement Plan to Address Climate Change," http://www.labor4sustainability.org/wp-content/uploads/2014/09/NLF541793_REV1.pdf.

6   There is no cure for climate change as long as we continue putting GHGs into the air. But once we approach zero emissions, the expansion of forests and other carbon sinks can begin to draw carbon out of the atmosphere and restore climate balance. This is a huge global task which will require the labor of people around the world.

7   James Hansen et al., "The Case for Young People and Nature: The Path to a Healthy, Natural, Prosperous Future," available at http://science.the-environmentalist.org/2011/05/case-for-young-people-and-nature-path_05.html. GHG reduction will have to be accelerated to compensate for delay in starting the process.

8   For an analysis of the "equity curve" required to balance reductions over time see John Humphries, "GHG Emissions Reduction Trajectories," *CT Roundtable on Climate and Jobs*, July 15, 2015, http://www.ct.gov/deep/lib/deep/climatechange/gc3/member_communications/humphries_2015_0717b.pdf.

9   Official climate plans provide insufficient accommodation to what is actually needed ("Solving Problems," 139).

10   See "Why Is This Affordable?" in Labor Network for Sustainability, 350.org, and Synapse Energy Economics, "The Clean Energy Future: Protecting the Climate, Creating Jobs, Saving Money," 2015, http://climatejobs.labor4sustainability.org/national-report/.

11   For a review of such studies, see Laurence L. Delina and Mark Diesendorf, "Is Wartime Mobilization a Suitable Policy Model for Rapid National Climate Mitigation?" *Energy Policy*, July 2013, section 2, http://www.sciencedirect.com/science/article/pii/S0301421513002103. See also Robert Pollin, Heidi Garrett-Peltier, and James Heintz, *Green Growth: A Program for Controlling Climate*

Change and Expanding U.S. Job Opportunities (Washington, DC: Center for American Progress, 2014), http://cdn.americanprogress.org/wp-content/uploads/2014/09/PERI.pdf. See also Labor Network for Sustainability, "The Clean Energy Future."

12   Labor Network for Sustainability, Synapse Energy Economics, and 350.org, "The Clean Energy Future," http://www.labor4sustainability.org/wp-content/uploads/2015/10/cleanenergy_10212015_main.pdf.

13   Jeremy Brecher, "Chapter 8: Making a Country Climate-Safe," in *Climate Insurgency: A Strategy for Survival* (London: Routledge, 2016).

14   Jeremy Brecher, chapter 6, "The War and Post-war Strike Wave," in *Strike! Revised, Expanded, and Updated Edition* (Oakland: PM Press, 2020), 223–33.

15   For a fuller account of just transition policies, see Jeremy Brecher, "A Superfund for Workers: How to Promote a Just Transition and Break Out of the Jobs vs. Environment Trap," *Dollars and Sense*, November/December 2015, http://www.labor4sustainability.org/wp-content/uploads/2015/10/1115brecher.pdf. See also Arjun Makhijani, "Beyond a Band-Aid: A Discussion Paper on Protecting Workers and Communities in the Great Energy Transition," Institute for Energy and Environmental Research and Labor Network for Sustainability, http://labor4sustainability.org/files/pdf_06142016_final.pdf.

16   Kristen Sheeran, Noah Enelow, Jeremy Brecher, Brendan Smith, "The Keystone Pipeline Debate: An Alternative Job Creation Strategy," Economics for Equity and Environment and Labor Network for Sustainability, http://www.labor4sustainability.org/files/__kxl_main3_11052013.pdf.

17   Jeremy Brecher, "Climate Jobs for All: A Key Building Block for the Green New Deal," *Common Dreams*, December 5, 2018. https://www.commondreams.org/views/2018/12/05/climate-jobs-all-key-building-block-green-new-deal. See also Jeremy Brecher and Joe Uehlein, "Twelve Reasons Labor Should Demand a Green New Deal," *In These Times*, December 12, 2018, http://inthesetimes.com/working/entry/21634/labor_green_new_deal_ocasio_cortez_sunrise_movement_unions.

18   For Nordic welfare systems see Jeremy Brecher, "Labor, Sustainability, and Justice," Labor Network for Sustainability, August 17, 2011, http://www.labor4sustainability.org/wp-content/uploads/2011/09/labor-sustainability-and-justice.pdf.

19   While in most instances public policy should aim to provide stable long-term employment, in the case of construction workers who normally work on relatively short-term jobs it should include mechanisms to provide steady employment as workers move from project to project.

20   Good Jobs First, "High Road or Low Road? Job Quality in the New Green Economy," February 3, 2009, recommends among other things that "green jobs" specify wage requirements for subsidies; wage standards and prevailing wage requirements for contractors; and web-based disclosure of company compliance. http://www.goodjobsfirst.org/sites/default/files/docs/pdf/gjfgreenjobsrpt.pdf.

21   Worker, community, and public participation in workplace and corporate decision-making is essential via climate action plan formulation, implementation, and review. This provides a vehicle for incorporating the public interest without requiring continuous state supervision. This approach draws on ideas

on regulation in civil society from Peter Dorman, "The Publicly Controlled Economy: Crisis and Renewal," *Legal Studies Forum* 21, no. 1 (1997).

22 Such alliances have been the focus of much of my writing, including *Building Bridges* and *If All the People Were Banded Together*.

23 "Just Energy Policies: Reducing Pollution and Creating Jobs," NAACP, February 2014, presents such requirements as a vehicle for racial and economic justice. http://action.naacp.org/page/-/Climate/JustEnergyPolicies%20 Compendium%20EXECUTIVE%20SUMMARY%20FINAL%20FEBRUARY%20 2014.pdf.

24 SustainLabour, "Occupational Health and Safety and Environmental Clauses in International Framework Agreements," http://www.sustainlabour.org/ documentos/en335_2010.pdf.

25 See Labor Network for Sustainability, "Labor, Sustainability and Justice: A Review Essay on 'Exiting from the Crisis: A Model for More Equitable and Sustainable Growth.'"

26 For an example of a plan for worker-friendly, industry-wide transition see Jeremy Brecher, "Fixing Bad Chemistry: Workers, Jobs, Toxics and the Future of the Chemical Industry, A Discussion Paper for Chemical Industry Workers and Allies," Labor Network for Sustainability, 2014, http://labor4sustainability.org/ files/pdf_badchemistry.pdf.

27 This approach is based on Laurence L. Delina and Mark Diesendorf, "Is Wartime Mobilization a Suitable Policy Model for Rapid National Climate Mitigation?" *Energy Policy*, July 2013, section 2, http://www.sciencedirect.com/science/article/ pii/S0301421513002103.

28 Private investment in fossil fuel–reducing activities has not been forthcoming even in many cases where such investments would have paid for themselves or even made a profit. A 2007 study by the McKinsey consulting firm found that the US could rapidly cut 28 percent of its greenhouse gases at fairly modest cost and with only small technological innovations. According to study director Jack Stephenson, "These types of savings have been around for 20 years." But according to another research team member, "There is a lot of inertia, and a lot of barriers." To give but one example, if tenants pay for their heating, landlords have no incentive to buy any but the cheapest, least energy efficient furnaces. Matthew L. Wald, "Study Details How U.S. Could Cut 28% of Greenhouse Gases," *New York Times*, November 30, 2007, http://www.nytimes.com/2007/11/30/ business/30green.html.

These findings raise doubts that policies that rely on charges for carbon emissions will in fact promote massive investment in climate protection activities.

29 See Mary Christina Wood, "Recouping Natural Resource Damages," in *Nature's Trust* (New York: Cambridge University Press, 2014), 185ff. For a proposal on recouping natural resource damages at a global level, see Julie-Anne Richards and Keely Boom, *Carbon Majors Funding Loss and Damage* (Berlin: Heinrich Boll Foundation, 2014), http://www.boell.de/sites/default/files/carbon_majors_ funding_loss_and_damage_kommentierbar.pdf.

30 Jeremy Brecher and Tim Costello, "Outsource This? American Workers, the Jobs Deficit, and the Fair Globalization Solution," North American Alliance

for Fair Employment, April 2004, http://web.mit.edu/outsourcing/class5/ OutsourceThis.pdf.

31 Both climate protection and economic cooperation ultimately require demilitarization and policies of global common security.

32 United Nations Environment Program, "Green Jobs: Toward Decent Work in a Sustainable, Low-Carbon World," 2008, http://www.unep.org/PDF/ UNEPGreenjobs_report08.pdf, and International Trade Union Confederation, "Trade Unions and Climate Change," 2009, http://www.ituc-csi.org/IMG/pdf/ climat_EN_Final.pdf. See also Jeremy Brecher, "Green Jobs in a Global Green New Deal," http://www.jeremybrecher.org/green-jobs-in-a-global-green-new-deal/.

33 "ILO: Unemployment and decent work deficits to remain high in 2018," https:// www.ilo.org/global/about-the-ilo/newsroom/news/WCMS_615590/lang--en/ index.htm.

34 For a fuller discussion of a global trust fund, see "A Global Trust Fund for the Global Public Trust," in Brecher, *Climate Insurgency: A Strategy for Survival* (London: Routledge, 2016). For an interesting historical precursor, see Jeremy Brecher, Tim Costello, and Brendan Smith, "Global Labor's Forgotten Plan to Fight the Great Depression," *History News Network*, March 22, 2009, http:// historynewsnetwork.org/article/69169.

35 Brecher, *Climate Insurgency*, 103.

36 See Brecher, *Climate Insurgency*, 104–7, for the use of Special Drawing Rights— "paper gold"—for a global climate protection fund.

CONCLUSION

1 "Jerusalem," quoted in David Erdman, *Blake: Prophet against Empire* (Princeton, NJ: Princeton University Press, 1969), 471.

2 "Jerusalem," plate 27, in Erdman, *Blake*.

Index

"Passim" (literally "scattered") indicates intermittent discussion of a topic over a cluster of pages.

prior consent of the government. *See*
"generalized prior consent"
private property. *See* property
problem identification, 130–34
problem-solving, 119–27 passim, 135–43
progress, 34–35, 46, 52, 94, 256, 341n20
property, 219–22
public trust doctrine, 221–22, 262–69
passim, 274–76
public workers. *See* government
employees

Rainforest Action Network, 243, 249
Reconstruction, 20
"reflective abstraction" (Piaget), 97, 152,
353n8
refusal to obey. *See* disobedience
representation, transformation of,
151–55
resistance to pipeline construction,
163–64, 243–54 passim, 267
resistance to water privatization, 177
Reuther, Walter, 282
right to manage. *See* "management's
right to manage"
right to pollute, 214, 222, 232–33,
279–80
Rilke, Rainer, 120
Rio Summit, 1992. *See* Earth Summit,
Rio de Janeiro, June 1992
Roberts, Adam, 366n3
Romney, Mitt, 247
Russian Revolution of 1917, 140, 150,
195, 196

Sanders, Bernie, 103
Sartre, Jean-Paul, 345n12, 354n8
satyagraha, 74–76, 107
*Save the Humans? Common
Preservation in Action* (Brecher), 112,
146, 155
Schachtel, Ernest: *Metamorphosis*,
23–25, 27, 350n1
Schell, Jonathan, 269
self-destruction and mutual
destruction, 181, 188, 309–11 passim;
climate change as, 208–10, 214–28
passim, 256

self-organization and self-
transformation, 3, 9, 23, 71, 98; in
climate activism, 236–42 passim
Sharp, Gene, 115; *Politics of Nonviolent
Action*, 75, 76–77, 176
shirtwaist workers. *See* garment
workers
Sierra Club, 187, 247, 252
sit-ins, xiii, 79, 177, 186, 248; anti-
pipeline, 4, 164, 245, 263; civil rights
movement, 4, 141, 269
Sitrin, Marina, 14
slavery, 181, 182; abolition, 77, 187, 305;
United States, 25, 77
Smith, Adam, 41, 42, 170
social constraint, 104–11
social differentiation, 41–42
social networks. *See* networks
"Solidarity Forever," 74
The Sources of Social Power (Mann),
69–72 passim, 160
South Africa, xiii, 187, 269, 300
Stamp Act, 26–27
states. *See* nation-states
*The Stern Review on the Economics of
Climate Change* (Butler), 297–-2
Strike! (Brecher), 21, 29–35 passim,
41, 49, 73–74, 87, 148, 154–55, 176;
criticism of, 56; differentiation, 171;
on mass strikes, 31–32, 52–53, 114,
144–45
strikes, 114–15, 176, 186, 193, 345n14;
Akron, Ohio, 97, 123, 167;
Connecticut, 106–7, 156–57;
Thirteenth Amendment and, 270;
twenty-first century, xiii–xiv. *See
also* general strikes; mass strikes;
student strikes
Students for a Democratic Society
(SDS), 316
student strikes, viii, xv
subsidies. *See* government subsidies
Superfund law. *See* Comprehensive
Environmental Response,
Compensation, and Liability Act
(CERCLA)
systems theory, 66–67, 75, 77, 81,
88–90 passim, 158, 175, 354n5

About the Contributors

Jeremy Brecher has participated in movements for nuclear disarmament, civil rights, peace, international labor rights, global economic justice, accountability for war crimes, climate protection, and many others. He is the author of fifteen books on labor and social movements, including the national best seller *Strike!* He has received five regional Emmy awards for his documentary film work. He is currently policy and research director for the Labor Network for Sustainability.

Todd E. Vachon is a union carpenter turned educator and faculty member in the School of Management and Labor Relations at Rutgers University. He currently directs the University's labor education extension program, developing programs for workers, unions, and justice-focused organizations. Todd earned his PhD in sociology from the University of Connecticut, where he helped to organize the GEU-UAW Local 6950 and served as the first local president. His research and writing focus on inequality, labor, climate change, and justice—all topics he cares about deeply. His current project is a book about the American labor-climate movement.

ABOUT PM PRESS

PM Press is an independent, radical publisher of books and media to educate, entertain, and inspire. Founded in 2007 by a small group of people with decades of publishing, media, and organizing experience, PM Press amplifies the voices of radical authors, artists, and activists. Our aim is to deliver bold political ideas and vital stories to all walks of life and arm the dreamers to demand the impossible. We have sold millions of copies of our books, most often one at a time, face to face. We're old enough to know what we're doing and young enough to know what's at stake. Join us to create a better world.

PM Press
PO Box 23912
Oakland, CA 94623
www.pmpress.org

PM Press in Europe
europe@pmpress.org
www.pmpress.org.uk

FRIENDS OF PM PRESS

These are indisputably momentous times—the financial system is melting down globally and the Empire is stumbling. Now more than ever there is a vital need for radical ideas.

In the years since its founding—and on a mere shoestring— PM Press has risen to the formidable challenge of publishing and distributing knowledge and entertainment for the struggles ahead. With over 450 releases to date, we have published an impressive and stimulating array of literature, art, music, politics, and culture. Using every available medium, we've succeeded in connecting those hungry for ideas and information to those putting them into practice.

Friends of PM allows you to directly help impact, amplify, and revitalize the discourse and actions of radical writers, filmmakers, and artists. It provides us with a stable foundation from which we can build upon our early successes and provides a much-needed subsidy for the materials that can't necessarily pay their own way. You can help make that happen—and receive every new title automatically delivered to your door once a month—by joining as a Friend of PM Press. And, we'll throw in a free T-shirt when you sign up.

Here are your options:

- **$30 a month** Get all books and pamphlets plus 50% discount on all webstore purchases

- **$40 a month** Get all PM Press releases (including CDs and DVDs) plus 50% discount on all webstore purchases

- **$100 a month** Superstar—Everything plus PM merchandise, free downloads, and 50% discount on all webstore purchases

For those who can't afford $30 or more a month, we have **Sustainer Rates** at $15, $10, and $5. Sustainers get a free PM Press T-shirt and a 50% discount on all purchases from our website.

Your Visa or Mastercard will be billed once a month, until you tell us to stop. Or until our efforts succeed in bringing the revolution around. Or the financial meltdown of Capital makes plastic redundant. Whichever comes first.

Save the Humans?
Common Preservation in Action

Jeremy Brecher

ISBN: 978-1-62963-798-3
$20.00   272 pages

We the people of the world are creating the conditions for our own self-extermination, whether through the bang of a nuclear holocaust or the whimper of an expiring ecosphere. Today our individual self-preservation depends on common preservation—cooperation to provide for our mutual survival and well-being.

For half a century Jeremy Brecher has been studying and participating in social movements that have created new forms of common preservation. Through entertaining storytelling and personal narrative, *Save the Humans?* provides a unique and revealing interpretation of how social movements arise and how they change the world. Brecher traces a path that leads from the sitdown strikes on the pyramids of ancient Egypt through America's mass strikes and labor revolts to the struggle against economic globalization to today's battles against climate change.

Weaving together personal experience, scholarly research, and historical interpretation, Jeremy Brecher shows how we can construct a "human survival movement" that could "save the humans." He sums up the theme of this book: "I have seen common preservation—and it works." For those seeking an understanding of social movements and an alternative to denial and despair, there is simply no better place to look than *Save the Humans?*

"This is a remarkable book: part personal story, part intellectual history told in the first person by a skilled writer and assiduous historian, part passionate but clearly and logically argued plea for pushing the potential of collective action to preserve the human race. Easy reading and full of useful and unforgettable stories. . . . A medicine against apathy and political despair much needed in the U.S. and the world today."
—Peter Marcuse, author of *Cities for People, Not for Profit: Critical Urban Theory*

"Over the last decades, Jeremy Brecher has known how to detect the critical issues of a period, to sort the many realities of suffering and injustice, and to emerge with a clear, short, powerful description. He does it again in this important book-it is about people: how our system devalues people and what needs to be done."
—Saskia Sassen, author of *Territory, Authority, Rights*

"One of America's most admired activist-scholars shines his light on the path forward, reminding us that social change is both possible and urgent."
—Mike Davis, author of *City of Quartz: Excavating the Future in Los Angeles*

Strike! 50th Anniversary Edition

Jeremy Brecher with a Preface by Sara
Nelson and a Foreword by Kim Kelly

ISBN: 978-1-62963-800-3
$28.95   640 pages

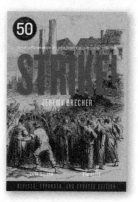

Jeremy Brecher's *Strike!* narrates the dramatic story
of repeated, massive, and sometimes violent revolts
by ordinary working people in America. Involving
nationwide general strikes, the seizure of vast industrial
establishments, nonviolent direct action on a massive
scale, and armed battles with artillery and tanks, this exciting hidden history is told
from the point of view of the rank-and-file workers who lived it. Encompassing the
repeated repression of workers' rebellions by company-sponsored violence, local
police, state militias, and the U.S. Army and National Guard, it reveals a dimension
of American history rarely found in the usual high school or college history course.

Since its original publication in 1972, no book has done as much as *Strike!* to bring
U.S. labor history to a wide audience. Now this fiftieth anniversary edition brings
the story up to date with chapters covering the "mini-revolts of the 21st century,"
including Occupy Wall Street and the Fight for Fifteen. The new edition contains
over a hundred pages of new materials and concludes by examining a wide range
of current struggles, ranging from #BlackLivesMatter, to the great wave of teachers
strikes "for the soul of public education," to the global "Student Strike for Climate,"
that may be harbingers of mass strikes to come.

"*Jeremy Brecher's* Strike! *is a classic of American historical writing. This new edition,
bringing his account up to the present, comes amid rampant inequality and growing
popular resistance. No book could be more timely for those seeking the roots of our
current condition.*"
—Eric Foner, Pulitzer Prize winner and DeWitt Clinton Professor of History at
Columbia University

"*Magnificent—a vivid, muscular labor history, just updated and rereleased by PM Press,
which should be at the side of anyone who wants to understand the deep structure of
force and counterforce in America.*"
—JoAnn Wypijewski, author of *Killing Trayvons: An Anthology of American Violence*

"*An exciting history of American labor. Brings to life the flashpoints of labor history.
Scholarly, genuinely stirring.*"
—*New York Times*